Teaching Politics beyond the Book

Teaching Politics beyond the Book

Film, Texts, and New Media in the Classroom

Edited by
ROBERT W. GLOVER AND DANIEL TAGLIARINA

Companion website: http://teachingpolitics.continuumbooks.com

B L O O M S B U R Y

NEW YORK · LONDON · NEW DELHI · SYDNEY

Bloomsbury Academic

An imprint of Bloomsbury Publishing Plc

175 Fifth Avenue
New York
NY 10010
USA

50 Bedford Square
London
WC1B 3DP
UK

www.bloomsbury.com

First published 2013

© Robert W. Glover and Daniel Tagliarina, 2013

Library of Congress Cataloging-in-Publication Data
Teaching politics beyond the book : film, texts, and new media in
the classroom / edited by Robert W. Glover and Daniel Tagliarina.
p. cm.
Includes bibliographical references and index.
ISBN 978-1-4411-0560-8 (hardcover : alk. paper) – ISBN 978-1-4411-2511-8
(pbk. : alk. paper) 1. Political science–Study and teaching. 2. Teaching–Aids and
devices. 3. Mass media in education. 4. Critical pedagogy. I. Glover,
Robert W. II. Tagliarina, Daniel.
JA86.T42 2013
320.071–dc23
2012021345

ISBN: HB: 978-1-4411-0560-8
PB: 978-1-4411-2511-8
ePub: 978-1-4411-9911-9
ePDF: 978-1-4411-7978-4

Typeset by Newgen Imaging Systems Pvt Ltd, Chennai, India
Printed and bound in the United States of America

CONTENTS

ABOUT THE CONTRIBUTORS

Editors

Robert W. Glover is the CLAS-Honors Preceptor of Political Science, a joint appointment in the Honors College and the Department of Political Science at the University of Maine. His research focuses generally on democratic theory, political engagement, and the politics of immigration. His primary research interests are democratic theory, human rights, immigration politics, and political science teaching and learning. His recent research has been featured in *Political Studies, Philosophy & Social Criticism, PS: Political Science and Politics,* and *The Journal of Political Science Education.*

Daniel Tagliarina is a PhD candidate at the University of Connecticut. His research investigates constitutive effects between American conservatives' rhetoric and social understandings of rights, focusing on religion and sexual orientation. His dissertation is entitled "The Countersubversive Culture Crusade: The New Christian Rights, Rights Mobilization, and Public Schools." He teaches classes about public law and political theory.

Authors

Robert M. Bosco is an Assistant Professor of International Studies at Centre College. Bosco's areas of expertise include international relations theory, international security, and early modern political thought. His research focuses on religion and international politics. Robert was a 2009–10 Research Fellow in Religion and International Affairs at Harvard University's Belfer Center for Science and International Affairs. His work has appeared in the *International Political Science Review,* the *Journal of International Relations and Development,* and the *International Studies Encyclopedia.* Bosco received his BA in philosophy from Wheaton College in Massachusetts, his MA in international politics from the School of International Service at American University, and his PhD in political science from the University of Connecticut.

Joan L. Conners is Associate Professor of Communication Studies at Randolph-Macon College in Virginia. She teaches classes in American campaigns and elections, communication law and ethics, and gender and communication. Her research involves media coverage of US Senate campaigns, and the use of media by candidates. Conners is co-author of *Perspectives of Political Communication: A Case Approach* (Allyn & Bacon, 2008) with Lauren Bell and Ted Sheckels. Her past political cartoon research has involved analyses of portrayals of Barack Obama and Hillary Clinton in the 2008 Democratic Primaries, a comparison of portrayals of George W. Bush and John Kerry from the 2004 Presidential Election, as well as representations of Congress, and US cartoon portrayals of Saddam Hussein, and has appeared in election issues of *American Behavioral Scientist*, as well as the *Harvard International Journal of Press/Politics*. She regularly incorporates relevant political cartoons as well as comic strips into her class lectures.

Christopher R. Cook is an Assistant Professor at the University of Pittsburgh at Johnstown. He received his PhD from the University of California, Santa Barbara, in 2004. His previous work on American foreign policy in Africa has appeared in *African Studies Quarterly* and *African and Asian Studies*. He is also serving as an Associate Editor for the Africa Peace and Conflict Network website.

Travis L. Gosa is an Assistant Professor of Social Science at Cornell University. He holds faculty appointments in the graduate fields of Africana Studies and Education, and is affiliated with the Cornell Center for the Study of Inequality. He received his PhD in Sociology from the Johns Hopkins University in 2008, along with a Certificate in Social Inequality. He has been an education policy analyst at both the Maryland State Department of Education and American Institutes for Research in Washington, DC. Prof. Gosa teaches courses on race, education, hip-hop, and the African American family. His research examines the social worlds of Black youth, new racial politics, music, and digital inequality. Gosa's recent essays have been published in *Teacher's College Record, Journal of Popular Music Studies, Popular Music and Society,* and *The Journal of American Culture*. He has a manuscript in progress entitled, "The School of Hard Knocks: A Hip-Hop Theory of Black Schooling and Educational Reform."

Nina Therese Kasniunas is an Assistant Professor of Political Science at Goucher College. She received her PhD from Loyola University Chicago and her current research focuses on interest groups and the legislative process as well as the pedagogy of political science. Recent publications include *Campaign Rules: A 50 State Guide to Campaigns and Elections with*

Dan Shea and chapters in *Moral Controversies in American Politics* (with Margaret Ellis) and *Campaigns on the Cutting Edge* (with Mark Rozell). Current research projects include examining the impact of active learning strategies on civic engagement and the influence of interest groups in congressional committees.

Ari Kohen is the Schlesinger Associate Professor of Political Science and Director of the Forsythe Family Program on Human Rights and Humanitarian Affairs at the University of Nebraska-Lincoln. Kohen's first book, *In Defense of Human Rights: A Non-Religious Grounding in a Pluralistic World*, was published by Routledge in 2007. Recent articles have appeared in *Human Rights Review, Journal of Human Rights, Critical Review of International Social and Political Philosophy, Social Justice Research,* and *Polis*. Kohen was the 2006 Irmgard Coninx Foundation Research Fellow at the Wissenschaftszentrum Berlin für Sozialforschung and, most recently, was recognized with the University of Nebraska's 2011 College Distinguished Teaching Award. Kohen holds a PhD in political science from Duke University.

Michael Kuchinsky is an Associate Professor of Political Science at Gardner-Webb University in North Carolina. He teaches courses in international relations, comparative politics, African and Middle Eastern politics, political economy and development. His research focuses on religion and global politics, the role of civil society in development and peacebuilding, and issues in political science pedagogy. He has a PhD in International Studies from the University of South Carolina (1999). He has worked for several nongovernmental organizations directing and coordinating food security and public policy education programs. He is an ordained clergy person in the Lutheran church.

Jeffrey S. Lantis is a Professor of Political Science/International Relations in the Department of Political Science at the College of Wooster. Lantis teaches courses in the fields of Foreign Policy, Diplomacy, and International Relations. A former President of the Active Learning in International Affairs Section (ALIAS) of the International Studies Association (ISA), Lantis was co-recipient of the 2010 Deborah J. Gerner Innovative Teaching Award in International Studies, the highest teaching award bestowed by the ISA, with Kent Kille and Matthew Krain. He is a member of the Program Committee of the American Political Science Association's Teaching and Learning Conference, and has directed active and teaching workshops for faculty at the University of South Australia, Adelaide, Australia; Moscow State Institute for International Relations, Russia (MGIMO-University); and the Institute for International Relations, University of Brasilia. Lantis also has published numerous works on international security, foreign policy analysis, and active teaching and learning. He is author of four books, including *The Life and Death of International Treaties* (2009), *The Global Classroom: An Essential Guide to Study Abroad (2009), Strategic Dilemmas and the Evolution of German Foreign Policy Since Unification* (2002), and co-editor for *Foreign Policy in Comparative Perspective: Domestic and International Influences on State Behavior* (forthcoming, 2011). In addition, he has published articles on simulations and experiential learning in *International Negotiation, International Studies Perspectives,* and *PS: Political Science & Politics.*

Simon Lightfoot is Senior Lecturer in European Politics and POLIS Director of Teaching and Learning at Leeds University in the United Kingdom. He has an interest in learning and teaching issues and has just completed a C-SAP funded project looking at the use of podcasting in politics (with Dr. Jason Ralph and Dr. Naomi Head). In 2009 he won the Political Studies Association's Bernard Crick Prize for Outstanding Teaching and was awarded a developmental University Teaching Fellowship.

Jill D. Miller is currently completing her PhD in Political Science at Georgia State University and holds a Juris Doctor from Seton Hall University School of Law. Previously, she was an instructor of Political Science at Macon State College in Macon, Georgia. She teaches on issues related to American Government, Constitutional Law, International Law, International Relations, and Comparative Politics. Her research interests include international law and state compliance, international organizations, foreign policy, and political science education. Jill practiced law in the fields of international humanitarian law, immigration, contracts, taxation, conflicts, antitrust, and European Union law.

William J. Miller is an Assistant Professor of Public Administration at Flagler College after receiving his PhD in Urban Studies and Public Affairs from the University of Akron in 2010. His research focuses on public opinion in both domestic and international contexts, political science education, and campaigns and elections. His work has appeared in *Journal of Political Science Education, Journal of Common Market Studies, Journal of Political Marketing*, and *Studies in Conflict & Terrorism.* Book chapters have been included in Stephen Craig and David Hill's *The Electoral Challenge* (CQ Press) and John Ishiyama and Marijke Breuning's *21st Century Political Science* (Sage). He is currently completing three book projects: *Stuck in the Middle to Lose: Tea Party Effects on 2010 U.S. Senate Elections* (Lexington Books, forthcoming 2011), *State and Local Government and Politics: Where Government Takes Action* (National Social Science Press, forthcoming 2011), and *The Election's Mine—I Draw the Lines: The Political Battle over Redistricting at the State Level* (Lexington Books, forthcoming 2012).

Chapman Rackaway is an Associate Professor of Political Science at Fort Hays State University. Rackaway earned his PhD in at the University of Missouri in 2002. Rackaway's primary research interests are political communication and electoral campaign strategies. A regular editorial board member and contributor to American Democracy Project monographs, Rackaway has also published in the *Journal of Politics, PS: Political Science and Politics, Social Science Computer Review,* and *Journal of Political Science Education.* Rackaway has published chapters in numerous edited volumes as well, on topics ranging from state legislative campaigns, to popular culture reflections on politics, to news framing during campaigns. With William Lyons and John Scheb, he is the author of the fifth edition of American Government: Politics and Political Culture, an American Government textbook published by Kendall-Hunt. Rackaway is also the author of Communicating Politics, a forthcoming electronic multimedia textbook through Soomo Publishing

Shyam K. Sriram is an Instructor of Political Science at Georgia Perimeter College and an Adjunct Professor of Political Science at Morehouse College. He received his BA in Political Science from Purdue University, his MA in Political Science from Georgia State University and is currently a doctoral student in the Department of Criminal Justice at Georgia State. A Chicago native, by way of India, Sriram is also a former DJ and Assistant Program Director at WRAS-Atlanta, 88.5 FM. He is deeply fascinated by the relationship between music and politics and is always focused on developing new techniques for conveying his passion for politics to his students. When not teaching or studying, Sriram spends his time hiking, traveling, writing, or exploring Atlanta with Shahbana, his gorgeous bride. You can read his blog, "American Muslim," at ashadu.blogspot.com.

Patrick F. Vining is a student majoring in Political Science and Economics at Southeast Missouri State University. He is currently president of the campus Student Government and is highly involved with his fraternity, Lambda Chi Alpha.

Jeremy D. Walling is an Associate Professor of Political Science at Southeast Missouri State University. He received his PhD in 2005 from the University of Kansas and his MPA from Missouri State University in 1998. He studies state politics and intergovernmental relations, American national institutions, and public administration ethics and accountability. His work has appeared in *The Constitutionalism of American States, The Handbook of Administrative Ethics,* and *Public Personnel Management,* the last two with H. George Frederickson. He is currently working on *The Election's Mine—I Draw the Lines: Redistricting in the American States* with William J. Miller.

Steven Williamson is a PhD Candidate in Political Science at the University of Connecticut. He holds an MA in Political Science from the University of Rhode Island and currently resides in Providence, Rhode Island. His research deals with issues of inclusion and marginalization in the political process with a particular focus on Latin America. He teaches comparative politics and has used Zombie Apocalypse as the foundation of a semester-long, in-class exercise.

Kent Worcester is a Professor of Political Science at Marymount Manhattan College, where he teaches courses on modern and contemporary war, democratic theory, modern political thought, Plato's *Republic*, and comics and graphic novels. He is the author or co-editor of six books, including *C.L.R. James: A Political Biography* (1996) and, most recently, *Arguing Comics: Literary Masters on a Popular Medium* (2004) and *A Comics Studies Reader* (2009), both of which he co-edited with Jeet Heer.

Dannagal G. Young is an Assistant Professor of Communication at the University of Delaware where she studies the content, audience, and effects of political humor. Her research on media effects and the cognitive implications political humor has appeared in numerous books and journals, including *Media Psychology*, *Political Communication*, *Popular Communication International Journal of Press/Politics*, *Journal of Broadcasting and Electronic Media*, and *Mass Media and Society*. In 2011, she launched *Breaking Boundaries*, a website and symposium dedicated to the interdisciplinary study of entertainment and politics, funded by the University of Delaware's Center for Political Communication. Danna is also an improvisational comedian, performing regularly with the improv comedy troupe, ComedySportz Philadelphia, since 1999.

PREFACE

Over a century ago, the preeminent French sociologist Emile Durkheim wrote of "social facts." Much of our daily life, he argued, adheres to a complex and socially determined set of expected behaviors. When going about our business, adhering to these social expectations, we fool ourselves into thinking we are acting completely autonomously. Step outside of those expected patterns of behaviors and we quickly realize what a dense, socially constructed world we inhabit.[1]

This edited volume is a collective effort to think through the "social facts" of teaching politics to students today. Many of the themes of political life remain remarkably resilient—justice, democracy, conflict, protest, and community. Yet educators also reside in an era that is unique and novel. New technological platforms exist to share information with our students, and for our students to interact with one another. Innovations in classroom technology have made the incorporation of visual, audio, and interactive media into our curricula nearly effortless. Online bookstores have democratized access to media, such that the availability of a text is practically no longer a consideration in crafting curricula. In many senses, while core themes of political life remain the same, the opportunities available to us as we teach our students about such topics are more diversified than they have ever been.

As a result of this heavily mediatized and information-driven age, student expectations regarding information flow and educational process are changing as well. The present generation of students has grown up in an era characterized by easy access to information and experiential forms of knowledge acquisition. The "social facts" of their learning environment have changed and as educators, we must be prepared to adapt. This edited volume is the beginning of a conversation about how we might meet the changing expectations of our students, and fully harness the pedagogical power of both old and new "nontraditional texts" within the classroom.

We would like to thank the individuals who shared in the inception and creation of this innovative volume. We humbly thank the authors contained within. For their pioneering perspectives, for their hard work, and willingness to share their ideas with others, we are eternally grateful. We also thank our generous and adept editor Marie-Claire Antoine at Continuum/Bloomsbury. Her expertise, guidance, and support were immeasurable and we are deeply grateful. Lastly, we thank those close to us who showed endless patience and support as we worked on the many stages of putting the volume together.

Robert Glover would like to thank his tremendously supportive friends, colleagues, and family (most especially his wonderful mother, Margaret and his two amazing sisters Carrie and Dianna). Daniel Tagliarina would like to thank his fantastic family, friends, and colleagues, but most of all, his eminently supportive wife and partner, Corinne, and their joyful son, Alex. Last but not least, we are immensely thankful for our talented, creative, and thoughtful students. The rewards of working with such inquisitive young people at the formative years of their political socialization are incalculable. They are an endless source of professional and personal motivation for us and we are humbly indebted to them.

Robert W. Glover　　Daniel Tagliarina
University of Maine　*University of Connecticut*

Note

1　Emile Durkheim, "What is Social Fact?" in *The Rules of Sociological Method,* ed. Steven Lukes (New York: The Free Press, 1982 [1895]): 50–9.

INTRODUCTION

"Like Captured Fireflies . . ."

Robert W. Glover

*She aroused us to shouting, bookwaving discussions . . .
our speculation ranged the world. She breathed curiosity
into us so that we brought in facts or truths shielded in our
hands like captured fireflies.*

JOHN STEINBECK[1]

Those of us who have devoted our lives to education have likely all had one teacher (or several) who possessed a unique ability to inspire us. It is these individuals who drove us to dive into challenging texts with gusto, whose discussions and lectures left us rapt, and whose questions and provocations animate our thoughts even today. In the quote above, John Steinbeck recounts one such figure to his son, who is asking him why school is necessary if it is such drudgery. Steinbeck concedes that schooling can often be a tiresome chore, but argues that a single dedicated educator can make it all worthwhile. He goes so far as to suggest that even in his late adulthood, he remains the "unsigned manuscript" of this inspirational teacher, a figure who possesses "deathless power."[2]

To those outside of education, or those poor unfortunate wretches never lucky enough to have a teacher who truly inspired them, perhaps Steinbeck's words sound like tired cliché. Yet those of us socialized to truly value education understand that these claims can be more than empty words. These ideas serve as the cornerstones of our institutions and the lifeblood of our professional lives. The precious, fragile moments in which we spark students' interests and begin to foster a lifelong passion for learning are equal parts beautiful and fragile. Such instances truly are, as Steinbeck says, like "captured fireflies"—stunning, yet momentary.[3] Intoxicating, yet fleeting.

However, while education's inspirational capacity may have an element of timelessness, teaching is nevertheless a dynamic, ever-changing endeavor. The context of education is one of flux: the material changes, the technology by which we share and transmit information evolves, the institutions within which education occurs incrementally adapt, and both educators and students are always within a dynamic state of personal growth and change.

What is striking then is the resistance to *pedagogical* and *curricular* change which we sometimes encounter within institutions of higher education. The universities we inhabit are fundamentally different than they were even 10 or 20 years ago, and differ radically from their institutional origins. Yet we often cling tenaciously to older models of teaching, standard and static approaches to higher education. We may dismiss those whose methods differ from ours, who employ innovative new texts and teaching styles, or engage in experiential and active learning. Though higher education is often cast as the wellspring of society's most innovative thinkers and problem-solvers, it can, in its approach to teaching and learning, be remarkably insular and closed-minded.

This edited volume is an effort to break out of these parochial tendencies as we teach core political concepts, processes, and events. As educators teaching within this field, we employ a variety of "texts" in the classroom for the purposes of exposing students to narratives of injustice, political struggle, power and domination, and democratic contestation. Textbooks and lecture certainly constitute one such text. Yet what is noteworthy in human history is the tremendous power of literature, film, and other forms of narrative to elevate our understanding of a political injustice, of human suffering and humiliation, while igniting the desire to alleviate such societal shortcomings. The educational intent of such mediums is, almost by definition, more implicit than more traditional materials. Yet their power to move the "reader" is often more profound. Furthermore, as technological media proliferate, we potentially gain still more mechanisms through which to teach our students about contemporary political realities.

Literature, film, music, and other new forms of media present tremendous opportunities for teaching students about politics. Yet the concrete ways that we might utilize such "texts" within our classrooms remain under-researched in scholarship on teaching and learning. How might we structure our engagement with "nontraditional texts" in ways that maximize their potential to spur critical thinking and intellectual growth among our students? What challenges and obstacles accompany such pedagogical methods? These questions have yet to be dealt with in a systematic way, and in the absence of such systematic treatment, educators looking to embrace new media must deploy such strategies using a painstaking process of trial and error.

While a systematic guide for the curious educator is missing, a growing number of scholars have devoted their research to curricular innovation regarding the use of alternative "texts" in the classroom. Most prominently, with regard to teaching politics, this literature has focused upon the use of film within the classroom. This is a disciplinary interest which has now been extended to television, as the quality and depth of contemporary television dramas has been expanding in recent years. Shows such as *The Sopranos, The Wire,* and *Mad Men* follow a novelistic structure, employ multilayered and multidimensional narratives, and take up profound political themes via a variety of engaging plotlines. At the same time, shows such as *The Daily Show* or *The Colbert Report* provide biting social commentary and humorous insights into contemporary political life.[4] Educators interested in expanding curricula have turned to these shows not only to engage students with media more familiar to them, but because the shows themselves constitute an untapped avenue into political commentary and analysis. To ignore them would neglect an important resource for our teaching.

While the majority of such pedagogical efforts have been focused upon film and television, this is hardly the only terrain that the scholarly literature on teaching and learning has traversed. These initial forays have now been extended to an array of other mediums in political science and related social scientific disciplines: literature and memoir,[5] art and political cartoons,[6] popular music,[7] and simulations and active learning technologies.[8]

However, in general we feel that more detailed and systematic examination of *how* to utilize such texts in the classroom is lacking. First, articles and discussions of teaching often tend to be concise discussions of a particular text or method, in the context of a particular course. This can preclude theoretically informed justifications of why strategies were adopted, and often require a rather superficial treatment of initial learning objectives, and whether these objectives were met in the classroom. Even in the most respected academic journals within political science, discussion of teaching sometimes takes on a somewhat journalistic tone. Little discussion is given to the theories driving one's curricular decisions, detailed discussion of learning outcomes, or the challenges that accompany such strategies.

Second, much of the existing research remains bound within the disciplinary subfields of political science (international relations, political theory, American politics, and so on). There has yet to be a systematic effort to integrate discussion across subfields into a single volume, to treat the study of politics as a cohesive whole, unified across a set of core themes. As a result, despite a nascent literature on this dimension of pedagogy, it remains the case that educators looking beyond traditional modes of teaching politics must often resort to trial-and-error or ad hoc consultation with like-minded colleagues.

As the section introductions and chapters on the following pages demonstrate, our volume has broad accessibility across the various disciplines and subfields that study political phenomena. The topics of these chapters run the gamut from judicial decision-making to urban politics, from political philosophy to American political campaigns, from interstate conflict to political economy, African politics, and beyond. The authors in this volume discuss a variety of innovative "texts" utilized in conjunction with these diverse topics: film, television, literary fiction, theatre, music, social networks, cartoons, and graphic novels.

Our hope is that this volume can provide guidance to those seeking to teach politics while utilizing innovative texts and pedagogical models. The educators here present honest portraits of the potential for such heterodox teaching methods, yet they are equally honest about the limitations and shortcomings of their efforts. These authors devote significant attention to the *challenges* that accompany our efforts to "teach politics beyond the book." The chapters provide testimony as to the transformative potential of curricular innovation. Furthermore, while challenges accompany any effort at pedagogical transformation, the educational outcomes discussed suggest these risks are well worth it. The "deathless power" which Steinbeck so eloquently described is not only a "perk" of our professional lives. Like all forms of power, it constitutes a personal responsibility. The thoughtful insights contained here potentially offer us a means to harness this power, enriching the educational experience and deepening the political knowledge of our students.

Notes

1 John Steinbeck, "Like Captured Fireflies," *California Teachers Association Journal* 51 (1955): 7–9.
2 Ibid.
3 Ibid.
4 Staci L. Beavers, "The West Wing as a Pedagogical Tool," *PS: Political Science and Politics* 35 (2002): 213–16; Staci L. Beavers, "Getting Political Science in on the Joke: Using *The Daily Show* and Other Comedy to Teach Politics," *PS: Political Science and Politics* 44 (2011): 415–19; Jody C. Baumgartner and Jonathan C. Morris, "Jon Stewart Comes to Class: The Learning Effects of *America (The Book)* in Introduction to American Government Courses," *The Journal of Political Science Education* 4 (2008): 169–86.
5 Terri L. Deibel, "Teaching Foreign Policy with Memoirs," *International Studies Perspectives* 3 (2002): 128–38; John Horton and Andrea T. Baumeister,

Literature and the Political Imagination (London: Routledge, 1996); Darcy Wudel, "Shakespeare's *Coriolanus* in the Political Science Classroom," *PS: Political Science & Politics* 35 (2002): 217–22; Kimberly Cowell-Meyers, "Teaching Politics Using Antigone," *PS: Political Science & Politics* 39 (2006): 347–49; Christine Pappas, " 'You Hafta Push': Using Sapphire's Novel to Teach Introduction to American Government," *The Journal of Political Science Education* 3 (2007): 39–50; Paul Sheeran, *Literature and International Relations (*Aldershot: Ashgate, 2007); Andrea Ciliotta-Rubery, "A Crisis of Legitimacy: Shakespeare's *Richard II* and the Problems of Modern Executive Leadership," *The Journal of Political Science Education* 4 (2008): 131–48.

6   Girma Negash, "Art Invoked: A Mode of Understanding and Shaping the Political," *International Political Science Review* 25 (2004): 185–201; Joan Conners, "Barack versus Hillary: Race, Gender, and Political Cartoon Imagery of the 2008 Presidential Primaries," *American Behavioral Scientist* 54 (2010): 298–312.

7   John Street, *Rebel Rock: The Politics of Popular Music* (Malden, MA: Blackwell, 1986); John Street, *Politics and Popular Culture* (Philadelphia, PA: Temple University Press, 2007); John Street, "Breaking the Silence: The Role of Music and Musicians in Political Participation," *Critical Review of International Social and Political Philosophy* 10(3): 321–37; John Street, Seth Hague, and Heather Savigny, "Playing to the Crowd: The Role of Music and Musicians in Political Participation," *British Journal of Politics and International Relations* 10 (2008): 269–85; Catherine Beighey and N. Prabha Unnitham, "Political Rap: The Music of Oppositional Resistance," *Sociological Focus* 39 (2006): 133–43; Halvard Leira, "Anarchy in the IR!" *International Studies Perspectives* 8 (2007): vi–vii; Joseph A. Kortaba and Phillip Vannini, *Understanding Society through Popular Music* (Boca Raton, FL: Taylor & Francis, 2009): J. Christopher Soper, "Rock and Roll Will Never Die: Using Music to Engage Students in the Study of Political Science," *PS: Political Science & Politics* 43 (2010): 363–7.

8   Jeffrey S. Lantis, Lynn M. Kuzma, and John Boehrer, eds, *The New International Studies Classroom: Active Teaching, Active Learning* (Boulder, CO: Lynne Reiner, 2000); William James Stover, "Teaching and Learning Empathy: An Interactive, Online Diplomatic Simulation of Middle East Conflict," *Journal of Political Science Education* 1 (2005): 207–19; Alma G. Blount, "Critical Reflection for Public Life: How Reflective Practice Helps Students Become Politically Engaged," *Journal of Political Science Education* 2 (2006): 271–83; Sarah M. Wheeler, "Role-Playing Games and Simulations for International Issues Courses," *Journal of Political Science Education* 2 (2006): 331–47; Sharon Werning Rivera and Janet Thomas Simons, "Engaging Students through Extended Simulations," *Journal of Political Science Education* 4 (2008): 298–316; Jeffrey S. Lantis, Kent J. Kille, and Matthew Krain, "Active Learning across Borders: Lessons from an Interactive Workshop in Brazil," *International Studies Perspectives* 9 (2008): 411–29; Dana Michael Harsell, "Wikis in the Classroom: Faculty and Student Perspectives," *Journal of Political Science Education* 6 (2010): 310–14; Jeffrey S. Lantis, Matthew Krain, and Kent J. Kille, "The State of Active Teaching and Learning

Literature," in *The International Studies Compendium Project, Volume X*, ed. R. A. Denemark (Malden, MA: Wiley Blackwell, 2010): 6574–92; Michael Baranowski and Kimberly Weir, "Power and Politics in the Classroom: The Effect of Student Roles in Simulations," *Journal of Political Science Education* 6 (2010): 217–26; Daniel J. Coffey, William J. Miller, and Derek Feuerstein, "Classroom as Reality: Demonstrating Campaign Effects through Live Simulation," *Journal of Political Science Education* 7 (2011): 14–33.

PART ONE

Literary texts

Introduction

Perhaps the most common form of "nontraditional" text in the classroom, literary texts are an increasing presence on course syllabi. Consequently, literature is an ideal place for this volume to begin. Although now commonplace, it is imperative that we, as educators, think about how we integrate literature into the classroom and toward what pedagogical end. Though we frequently encounter literature in contemporary courses the question of which literary texts to use, how, when, and why is worthy of further scrutiny. Literature should not be chosen simply as a means to "break up the routine." Rather, educators must pay careful attention to the ways in which literary texts help them better achieve stated learning objectives. The chapters in this section provide useful information regarding how and why to select literary texts for integration in the college classroom, as well as discussing the educational benefits of doing so. These discussions can serve as a springboard for educators to design their own classes utilizing literary media. All three chapters contain examples from the authors' experiences using literature and then address synergies between these texts and common politically themed courses, which should be foremost in our minds as we think about innovative course design.

Literature, through its narrative structure and ability to communicate diverse viewpoints, can produce beneficial cognitive dissonance within students, enabling deeper reflection, and hopefully retention, of course material. Literature is inherently an expressive medium, with the added benefit of being able to portray worlds that do not exist, as well as experiences that are radically different than what the students in the classroom may have personally felt. By placing students *within* the events being studied, literature, properly used, has the power to force students to examine questions of political agency. Situating students within the unfamiliar or the completely fictional creates a disjuncture between the student and what exists, creating room for critical evaluation of characters' actions and the stories' systemic structures. Furthermore, literature's immediacy potentially helps students examine their own complicity and responsibility in shaping ongoing political practice. These qualities of literature potentially produce a greater resonance than standard academic textbooks. A personalized narrative of events may simply be more powerful and engaging than the treatments offered in even the best standard-format textbooks. Literary texts should be considered based on their potential for increasing engagement with the political content of any course.

Along these lines, the chapters in this section explore ways to contextualize ongoing political events and perennial political questions through literary texts, but also how to use literature as a means of challenging the "conventional wisdom" of political life. In the first chapter, Bosco offers a thoughtful discussion of how the Bible can be read as political literature. Many students will likely have read the Bible as a religious, scriptural text. Yet the experience of reading the Bible "politically" challenges students to develop their critical faculties, as they must examine the text with new analytical lenses. Literary texts, even when already familiar to the students, can make new ideas accessible and encourage critical thinking on diverse topics such as obligation, political economy, violence, power, and liberation.

In his chapter, Kuchinsky focuses on another benefit of using literary texts: contextualizing the unfamiliar. He discusses the use of non-Western literature when studying comparative politics, as this literature can ground the academic discussion of politics in places unfamiliar to the students utilizing the empathic aid of literature. Kuchinsky also offers pedagogical justifications for using literature in a variety of ways to have the literature dovetail with the main themes and goals of a class focusing on events and regions unfamiliar to most of the students within the classroom.

Finally, Glover and Tagliarina offer yet another approach to literary texts within the classroom. They argue that starting with literary texts can, given the right political topic, help to motivate students to critically evaluate contemporary political reality better than merely covering the "facts" of said political topics. They feel that this is particularly the case in times of crisis, where the urgency and volatility embedded within the "facts" of a situation may push us in nonreflective, noncritical directions. Literature in this sense offers us a means to access the thoughtful and reflective realm of critical thinking, even when the prevailing societal winds provide neither. While the chapter focuses specifically on utopian socialist literature as a means to understand contemporary economic challenges, the pedagogical lessons are easily applied to other political areas.

All three chapters consider using nontraditional literary texts to further explore the themes central to an array of political themes. As the authors of the chapters argue, literary texts are frequently natural companions to lessons and themes already in courses focusing on politics and political concepts. Integrating literary texts frequently does not mean a substantive redesign of courses. Rather, the authors suggest that thought be given to how literary texts can introduce, illustrate, or challenge topics and ideas already present in courses. As with the media covered in subsequent sections, it is not our aim to advocate the addition of any or all forms of nontraditional media, but rather to expand the discussion of what media *could* be integrated to further class goals and deepen the students' learning experiences. In the pedagogical discussions in each chapter of this section, the authors provide useful guidance with regard to how this might be done utilizing the literary medium.

CHAPTER ONE

The Bible as a pedagogical resource in the college classroom

Robert M. Bosco

To some students, the Bible represents the word of God. For others, the Bible is a myth with little contemporary relevance unless one is already a religious person. Whether they are atheists or believers, for many students—and perhaps many educators, too—the meaning of the Bible is already closed. What could be the use, then, of bringing the Bible into the college classroom? I suggest that the preformed assumptions that students bring to the Bible are not liabilities but pedagogical assets. The key to a successful and rewarding experience with the Bible in the college classroom, at least in my own discipline of political science, lies precisely in turning this interpretive closure to one's advantage.

The most effective way to do this pedagogically is to read the Bible as a political document. By this I mean exploring with an open mind the potential political meanings, messages, and implications of the Bible stories. The purpose is to create within the student a cognitive disequilibrium between the unexpected and the familiar. As the editors of this volume remind us, cognitive disequilibrium—unsettling those questions or interpretations that students take to be settled—lies at the heart of critical pedagogy.[1] Reading the Bible politically thus teaches students two important lessons: that politics lurks in unexpected places, and that revisiting long-held assumptions is itself a political skill worth cultivating.

In introductory courses in political theory, the context in which I have most often taught the Bible, I trace the theme of breaking away from established modes of thinking from Socrates/Plato (*Crito* and *Republic*), through the Bible, on to Machiavelli (*The Prince*), and finally to Marx and Lenin. During this journey students study the struggle between old and new ways of thinking as they read of the tension between Socrates and his fellow Athenians, Adam and Eve and the serpent, Moses and the Israelites, the Hebrew prophets and the ancient kings, Jesus, his followers, and the Jewish and Roman leadership, the Prince and his subjects, and finally the Marxist intellectual and the reluctant proletariat. The Bible provides much more than an unorthodox interlude between the classics; it anchors the introductory political theory course by providing students with an object lesson in the struggle to bring citizen-subjects to new conceptions of justice. Settled ways of thinking also include inherited systems of ethics and morality, which only heightens the pedagogical possibilities when the Bible is read alongside Plato's critique of the city-state gods, Marx's criticisms of bourgeois morality, or the Prince's strategic approach to prevailing Judeo-Christian common sense.

In this essay, I trace only a few of the ways in which the Bible may be used in the college classroom, with a focus on political science. I have selected for review episodes from Genesis, Exodus, the Book of Kings, the Prophetic books, and the stories of Jesus in the New Testament. I begin with the creation story in the book of Genesis, unfolding the theme of imagining political worlds different from our own from discussions of political obligation and the ideal polity. I then explore the relationship between liberation and violence in the book of Exodus, the nature and function of political power in some selections from Kings, and the concept of collective guilt in the prophetic books. I end with a brief discussion of my experience teaching the Biblical stories about Jesus in the political science classroom.

Reading the Bible politically is most effective in small, discussion-based classes in political theory, especially at the introductory level. It is important that students have ample opportunity to grapple aloud with the potential political implications of the Bible, for the results can be transformative. In addition, discussion based-classes place far more pressure on the instructor than lecture-based courses, as the quality of the conversation depends in large part on the quality and timing of the educator's guiding questions. At the end of each subsection in this essay, I therefore provide a brief list of some discussion questions that have worked particularly well in class. Although these sample questions are intended for use in an introduction to political theory classroom, the themes of the Bible can also travel to other subfields within political science. With this in mind, I have also included at the end of each subsection some remarks on how the Bible is relevant to the study of international politics.

Genesis and Exodus

They could find no flaw
In all of Eden: this was the first omen.[2]

Students begin their encounter with the Bible as a political document with the creation story of Genesis. In classroom discussion, I encourage students to explore the potential political meanings of the creation story as widely and fully as they can. It often takes some time for this conversation to truly hit its stride. Students may be hesitant at first; after all, as noted above, for many students the story of Genesis is a myth, irrelevant unless one is already religious. In my experience however, pressing students on exactly why the story of Genesis is "irrelevant" for politics very often results in vigorous and imaginative classroom discussion.

In Genesis, students read of how the Hebrew God creates two trees in the Garden of Eden, one to give life and the other the power to know right from wrong.[3] Adam and Eve are forbidden to eat the fruit of the tree of knowledge, for if they do so they will die.[4] A serpent then arrives with a message: contrary to what God has told Adam and Eve, knowledge of right and wrong has nothing at all to do with death, but God's hubris. God is afraid of what will happen, the serpent argues, if his creation should come to know everything that he knows. Thus tempted, Adam and Eve eat from the tree of knowledge and are then condemned to exile from Eden.

Is this creation story political? I find it useful to begin class discussion about the potential political meanings of the Genesis story with questions about authority and obedience. Beneath Adam and Eve's primordial act of disobedience lie a number of questions about why human beings disobey authority and when, if ever, we have a right to. Students soon wonder whether human beings disobey political authority out of a sense of pride. It is worth taking the time to explore together precisely what pride is in a political context, that is, whether it refers to a feeling of invincibility, an overcompensation for weakness, a desire to remake the world in one's image, or a desire for glory. Having read Plato's *Republic* prior to the Bible, students are prepared to compare and contrast the pride of Adam and Eve with the Platonic position regarding the balance of qualities within the soul. For Plato, justice in the polity cannot come into being without the successful cultivation of self-discipline and obedience (or temperance) within the individual soul. For those students who find the Platonic conception of justice appealing, Adam and Eve may personify the *imbalances* of the unjust soul, when appetitive desire rejects the principle of temperance and refuses to submit to higher authority.

The disobedience of Adam and Eve raises wider questions about the nature of political and social change. Perhaps self-love or envy can help to explain movements for social and political change and the desire to remake society in a revolutionary image. Furthermore, if it is true that pride is what in large part animates public acts of disobedience, this suggests that we are wrong to expect any lasting stability in our public affairs, and are condemned instead to a world of constant social and political upheaval. Following this line of interpretation, it pays to be skeptical of large-scale blueprints for revolutionary change. Like the serpent in the garden, revolutionary leaders play on our pride, our need for self-recognition, and our self-love; they can only lead the polity to instability and ruin. Genesis is a story of origin that is also a warning: it is better to obey the powers that be, lest we disturb the delicate balance of a rightly ordered polity. Such an interpretation of Eden implies that projects that trumpet the final arrival of justice through sweeping social, political, or economic change express a utopian impulse that human beings can fundamentally remake their world.

As the broader political implications of Genesis become clear, some students will begin to take issue with this interpretation of the story. They may come to see that the true utopian vision lies not outside of Eden but that the Garden itself represents a utopia for the powerful in which all obey orders, right and wrong is decided by the few, and dissenters are deservedly exiled or punished. For these students, the exile from Eden represents human beings' first, primordial act of breaking free from this utopia of the powerful.

The first act of disobedience thus raises the question whether Adam and Eve are better off inside or outside of Eden. I often channel the in-class discussion about political obligation into a conversation about the nature of the ideal polity. This provides another through-line of engagement with Plato (the ideal polity) through to the stories of Jesus (the Kingdom in the "here and now") to Machiavelli (the impossibility of the ideally just polity) and finally to Marx. To anticipate Marx for example, one might steer the conversation about Genesis by asking students to consider our contemporary utopias. From our everyday lived experience in a capitalist political economy, one might ask whether other ways of organizing the world such as socialism, religionism, or ecologism represent our contemporary utopian promises. There is also capitalism itself. Not many of us today can truly imagine what may lie beyond or outside of global capitalism. Perhaps it is better to stay inside our system and not challenge it at all. It is after all a system that promises precisely what Eden promised: total freedom if one accepts the parameters, no wants unsatisfied, no needs unfulfilled. Capitalism also holds out an Edenic vision of human domination over nature without shame, without guilt, and has recently appropriated to itself the very notion of the human being as caretaker of nature. Perhaps calls for "corporate social responsibility," with which many students will be familiar, are symptomatic of this attitude. From this perspective, life is surely better within a capitalist form of political economy, for no other available system better empowers human beings to exercise their freedom of choice.

There is of course another interpretation. Other students prefer to turn the formula of Eden inside out: it is capitalism itself that represents the false utopian promise. Free market capitalism does indeed promise guilt-free dominion over nature, but this promise is founded on an illusion. Free market capitalism holds out the modern myth—our modern Eden—that human beings can exercise their freedom through consumption and the satisfaction of needs and desires without social, economic, or environmental consequences. While capitalism promises effective human control over nature without damage, guilt, or shame, it is in fact the expansion of global capitalism that depends on the destruction of nature. The complete human freedom that capitalism promises is also a myth: we cannot escape the bombardment of lifestyle marketing (e.g. "Chase What Matters"; "Live Richly.") Rather, consumption convinces us that we have needs and desires that we do not in fact have, creates inequality and injustice, and deteriorates our relationships with each other and our natural environment. On this, alternative reading, what is utopian does not lie outside of capitalism, but capitalism *itself* is the utopia. The utopian promise exists inside of the world we are living in now, but it is a false Eden.

Students quickly realize that Genesis is not simply a story of how the universe came about. Classroom exploration of the potential political meanings of Genesis raises fundamental questions of political obligation and the ideal forms of social, political, and economic life. The story of Genesis reflects the theme of breaking free from established worlds and encourages students to imagine alternatives to the established order. This is an important skill to cultivate in our time, as it has become increasingly difficult to imagine such alternatives. We are told for instance that liberal democratic capitalism has triumphed over its ideological competitors.[5] In the words of Slavoj Žižek, perhaps "we are all Fukuyama-ists now."[6] The difficulty of imagining outsides and alternatives to what exists today is precisely the theme that will carry students from Plato, through the Bible, to Machiavelli, and beyond.

Exodus: Violence and liberation

The book of Exodus is precisely about how difficult it is to break away from the comfortable and the familiar. Yet the story of the liberation of the ancient Israelite community is not simply a linear tale of emancipation from slavery to arrival in a promised land. It is not a story of Moses' triumph. Rather, it is a story of Moses' problems as he attempts to move a stubborn people who, like us, cling to familiar notions of justice. Exodus illustrates well the problem of how difficult it is for a society to change its conception of justice, and raises the possibility that a good deal of violence and coercion may be necessary to achieve this. These themes are evident from the very beginning of the Exodus story. Early on for example, Moses encounters an Egyptian mistreating a Hebrew slave. He intervenes, killing the Egyptian and hiding his body in the sand.[7] Following this, Moses witnesses two Hebrews fighting among themselves. When he attempts to intervene and point out that each belongs to "the same people" they reject him: "who put you in charge of us and made you our judge?"[8]

Students often perceive two points in their first encounter with Moses. First, that Moses seems to have been born with what Aristotle would call a "sense of justice." Moses' sense of justice involves a righteous indignation against slavery and oppression, but it is not a nonviolent sense of justice. Moses kills the Egyptian oppressor, presaging the use of violence on a mass scale to achieve Israelite liberation later. Second, from the very beginning, it seems that Moses has a serious legitimacy problem. In another instance of foreshadowing, early Hebrews, while they chafe under a brutal system of slavery that divides them among themselves, do not seem so willing to accept a revolutionary leader who will lead them to freedom. Though fully cognizant of their enslavement, the Hebrews nonetheless cling to what is familiar, a theme that runs from the early encounter with Moses to the construction of the golden calf, and beyond. From the very beginning it seems, liberation is not easy to achieve, but rather involves a great deal of violence and coercion.

The relationship between violence and liberation deepens as students read about the apocalyptic suffering and catastrophe visited upon the Egyptians. After a number of plagues including famine, physical torture of boils and wounds, crop destruction, and total darkness, God promises a "final punishment" for Egypt.[9] The entire nation's first-born sons and animals are killed.[10] In the lead-up to their liberation, Israelites are also urged to take with them all of Egypt's gold and riches.[11] Violence is not only at the center of Moses' sense of justice, but also plays a prominent role in the liberation of the Israelites generally. As Exodus unfolds, God, acting through Moses, turns violence and coercion on the Israelites themselves. Later, God will command the early Israelite kings to visit utter destruction on other peoples (such as the Amalekites) who lived in the Promised Land before the Israelites arrived.

The Exodus story thus raises the question of how much violence and destruction must be done for freedom to be achieved and for a new conception of justice to come into being. There is always an element of revenge in violence, and students must ponder whether the violence done to the Egyptians by God through Moses was an act of liberation, justice, revenge, or some combination of all of these. Perceptive students will point out that the series of horrible plagues and other misfortunes visited upon Egypt served a dual purpose: to help secure Israelite liberation and establish Moses' legitimacy as a revolutionary leader in the eyes of the Israelites themselves. Revolutionary violence, it seems, is both an act of revenge and a legitimating spectacle.

Discussion questions: Genesis and Exodus

The following represents a selection of discussion questions that have worked well in guiding class conversation about Genesis and Exodus. They are meant to guide discussion in the context of an introductory course in political theory. In addition, some ideas on potential application to international politics follow.

Genesis:

- Is Yahweh, the God of Genesis, like a Platonic Philosopher-King?

- Why do we disobey political authority? Do we ever have a right to? Should we be punished for doing so?

- What impulses or emotions lie behind movements for social or political change?

- When and why do we become unhappy or dissatisfied with our social or political condition? In such circumstances, what is the "right" thing to do?

- Are there political visions that we consider "utopian" today? What are they? Why do we consider them beyond our reach?

- Is there a sense in which pre-exile Eden represents how our political life *ought* to be? What features of life before the Fall seem attractive, and why?

Exodus:

- Why did Moses have such legitimacy problems?

- Is Moses a Platonic Philosopher-King?

- Why was it so hard for Moses to change the Israelites' established ways of thinking?

- Is knowledge of justice alone enough to craft a just polity?

- Why do liberation movements involve so much violence?

- Why do liberated peoples become so conservative?

- Does violence have a place in politics? What is it?

- To what extent was Egyptian society responsible for the slavery of the Israelites? Did Egypt deserve the punishment it received?

- Upon leaving Egypt, God encourages the Israelites to take Egypt's riches with them. What conception of justice does this reflect? What do liberated peoples deserve? At what point has justice been done?

- How much of justice is revenge or retribution?

Genesis, Exodus, and international politics

It is possible to use Genesis and Exodus as springboards for discussion about international politics. Genesis raises at least two important themes in this regard. The first is the extent to which human nature can explain the actions of nations. Logical connections that flow from this theme range from the Christian Realism of Reinhold Niebhur to the classical Realism of Hans Morgenthau. Second, the book of Genesis raises a number of ethical questions about global capitalism and its relationship to the environment. The Genesis story portrays a divinely sanctioned order in which human beings have dominion over nature. It is worth exploring with students whether this foundation myth is in any sense true, and to what extent it is desirable. What responsibilities do we have to the natural environment, if any? Do we have a right to any of the earth's riches? If so, where does this right come from?

The book of Exodus draws our attention to narratives of liberation and violence in global politics. Violence in the name of liberation from tyranny purportedly underpins recent US interventions in the Middle East, for example. Some students have loved ones involved in this effort or are active duty themselves. The idea that a nation must sacrifice its own to help others achieve freedom connects directly with the Mosaic narrative of violence in service of national liberation: is violence justified in such cases? The question of whether violence has a legitimate place in global politics comes to us directly from the pages of Exodus.

Violence is also used in Exodus as a legitimating spectacle and as pure revenge. Examples abound in our present time. What is the meaning and purpose of the US campaign of "shock and awe" in the invasion of Iraq following the events of 9/11? Was there an element of revenge in the US invasion of Iraq? Why was it so important for both the US and Iraq that Saddam Hussein be tried—and killed—in Iraq by Iraqis? Exodus thus raises for students the question of exactly how much justice involves violence, retribution, and revenge.

The books of Kings and the Hebrew prophets

Your nation is a ship with its rigging loose,
Its mast shaky,
Its sail not spread.[12]

Through the narrative of Exodus, students are introduced to the fundamental contradictions of freedom. What are we to make of a journey from bondage into liberation that is founded on violence? How can a journey to freedom involve such coercion? The interconnected themes of justice, violence, and liberation become more apparent in the books of Samuel,[13] the Books of Kings,[14] and the prophetic books (Isaiah, Job, Jeremiah, Amos, Micah). To begin, it is in the book of Samuel that the Israelite search for liberation reaches a puzzling phase. For it is in this book that the Israelites, having just achieved liberation from an oppressive political system, immediately demand to be ruled by a king.

The book of Samuel records historical events that took place about 1050–950 BCE. In the passages from this book that I assign (1 Sam. 8, and 15–17), the Israelites come to Samuel and insist on a king to rule them and lead them in battle so they may be "like all the other nations." Samuel, unsure how to answer, asks God for advice. Human beings always set up false idols, God argues, and false idols always disappoint. This time it will be no different. Nonetheless, God concedes: give the Israelites what they want. This concession comes with a warning, however, as Samuel returns to the Israelites with a litany of the tragedies that will befall them if they are ruled by a king.[15] Kingship will bring class stratification, severe inequality of wealth, and forced labor. Kings will take all that society values and give nothing back. Interestingly, the situation begins to resemble life under the Egyptians. Yet the Israelites ignore God's warnings and press their demands. Samuel gives in, and Saul is made king.

Why would the people of Israel choose to ignore the catalogue of injustices presented to them and opt for a political system that seems to resemble the very one from which they have just escaped? The Israelite experience with kingship suggests that following periods of upheaval and disorientation, subjects desire a return to the status quo as soon as possible. Perhaps we look to political power for certainty, and achieving this security requires a good amount of selective ignorance about the injustice around us and collective amnesia about the past. The ancient Israelite demand to be ruled by a king shortly after liberation illustrates this fundamentally conservative, counter-revolutionary impulse quite well.

The message from the Bible here is again, grim. The story of Israelite kingship suggests that entrusting our security and stability to political power is no guarantee of either. Indeed, from Saul, to David, to Solomon, the Bible traces the gradual disintegration and decay of Israelite society. Class inequality, social and economic injustice, mass theft, war, corruption, and greed: all of this represents the natural life cycle of the political powers that we entrust with our security. Political power is ultimately unstable and can always be counted on to bring injustice into being. As students move through the stories of ancient Israelite kings[16] they gradually come to see the shape of the larger narrative: Samuel's prophecies about kingship are in fact fulfilled to the letter. Israel is too far gone, and the cycle of liberation from oppressive rule and back again is completed.

Hebrew prophets such as Isaiah, Amos, Jeremiah, Ezekiel, and Micah thundered passionately against the tragic self-destruction of their own society, which they deeply loved. The prophets spoke of the selfishness and corruption of political leaders, the widespread social, legal, and economic injustices, the overconsumption and overindulgence, the wild parties, false pieties, bribes and pay-offs. Interpreting such overconfidence and moral oblivion as national weakness, the prophets exhort their nation to break from its all-to-comfortable ways and change its conception of justice. If it does not, Israel will experience widespread war, destruction, and perpetual insecurity. Interestingly however, the prophets never hold rulers alone responsible for the widespread malaise. Rather, all are held responsible for the nation's complacency and disintegration. Indeed, for the Hebrew prophets, collective guilt and collective responsibility are very real phenomena.

Does collective guilt make sense to us today? For some students, the very concept of collective guilt is morally repulsive for what it suggests: that the innocent people of a nation bear responsibility for injustice and thus deserve the misfortune visited upon them. I remind students however that we often apply the concept of collective guilt quite easily to other societies. How many times for example do we hold "Arab" or "Muslim" or "Islamic" society or culture collectively responsible for the production of radical extremism? Perhaps all of us are collectively responsible when our polity decays into injustice, or when the environment on which we depend can no longer bear us. The point is not so much that human beings deserve social and economic hard times, but rather, that all of us bear some responsibility for when these conditions emerge. The Hebrew prophets thus raise the question of the extent to which the concept of collective guilt still retains moral force for us today.

What is more, according to the Old Testament prophets, all of us are responsible for changing our society's conception of justice. Violent retribution, rampant social and economic inequality, neglect of the elderly, the orphan, the poor, the marginalized—none of this seemed to faze ancient Israelite society. Neglect of the poor and less fortunate was made even worse by the society's pretensions to piety and righteousness: "you wonder why the Lord pays no attention when you go without eating and act humble . . . on those same days you give up eating, you think only of yourselves and abuse your workers."[17] Repulsed by such hypocrisy, Isaiah, like Amos, Jeremiah, Ezekiel, and others, reminds the nations of the earth that they are less than nothing, straws in a storm, "dust on the balance scales."[18]

The Hebrew prophets strive to bring a new conception of justice to the Israelites. Anticipating Marx, the prophets reveal structural injustice and recommend in its place social and economic equality and care for the less fortunate, the vulnerable, and the poor. Furthermore, not unlike Socrates, the prophets proclaim the message that each individual has a role to play in bringing justice to the polity. According to the prophets this can be done in a number of ways: by unmasking hypocrisy, speaking out against mistreatment of the laborer, pointing out corruption, and curtailing arbitrary violence. Should the nation shrink from this responsibility, it will face collective punishment. Indeed, the nation of Judah, the southern kingdom, would in fact experience such brutal collective punishment at the hands of the Assyrians.

Discussion questions from Kings and prophetic books

Kings

- Why were the Israelites warned about kings? What were the warnings, and why did the Israelites not heed them?

- What do the stories in the Book of Kings tell us about our ability to achieve a truly just polity?

- According to Plato, what did the Philosopher-King "know"? Did Saul, David, or Solomon know the same?

- How do rulers become corrupted, and whose fault is it when they do?

- What can people do in the face of corrupt leadership?

- How much do we owe our government? Absolute obedience? Or should our obedience be conditional?

Prophets

- According to Plato, what did the Philosopher-King "know"? Did the Hebrew prophets know the same?

- According to Ezekiel, Isaiah, Amos, and Micah, what makes a nation "great"? Why do nations decline?

- Do we believe today in the concept of collective guilt? For example, how much are we responsible for the economic and ecological tragedies that befall us? What about the tragedies that befall others?

- To what extent are everyday people responsible for the injustices they experience?

- How can the problem of collective responsibility be rectified politically? How does a society go about cleansing itself from collective guilt?

- Do the Hebrew prophets have any other potential political messages for us today? If so, what might they be?

Kings, prophets, and international politics

Both the book of Kings and the prophetic books contain important questions for global politics. The book of Kings for example highlights the contradictory nature of the desire for self-determination. On the one hand a desire for nationhood, for recognition, security, and perhaps glory, may lie behind the Israelite demand for a king. Yet the Israelite desire for self-determination tears the young society apart and according to the prophets, leads to widespread corruption and injustice. Clearly, Israel gained no more security after becoming a nation than it had before. The book of Kings thus provides educators with ample opportunity to raise the issue of how both movements for self-determination and newly independent states are to apportion authority, handle their external affairs, and develop their sense of justice.

Perennial themes of global politics are also evident in the prophetic books. For example, Isaiah, Jeremiah, Ezekiel, Amos and Micah each pose the question, what makes a nation great? Is it the presence of justice, military prowess, obedience to a higher power, a morally upright population, the responsible use of violence, or something else? Second, what causes nations to decay? Is it the increased corruption of its leaders, invasion by a foreign power, the reluctance of the population to take its destiny into its own hands, or the insufficient redress of past wrongs?

Educators may also wish to focus on the theme of collective guilt, just as relevant to global politics as to domestic politics. Regarding our own nation, to what extent does our "way of life" or our foreign policy bear some responsibility for the phenomenon of violent terrorism in the world? Regarding others, can the citizens of other nations be considered collectively guilty for the actions of their rulers, justifying economic sanctions? Are states that "harbor terrorists" as guilty as terrorists themselves? At the center of international ethics lies the issue of how to apportion guilt and responsibility in global politics, and who is to do so.

Finally, one may also use the prophetic books to raise the question of hypocrisy in global affairs. The prophets, after all, railed against false piety. They were revolted by disingenuous displays of concern and the use of moral pretense as a cover for self-interest. Educators of global politics will be familiar with how this theme leads directly to the ethical questions surrounding humanitarian intervention. Such conversations about guilt, blame, responsibility, and hypocrisy are difficult but worth having with our students. The books of the Hebrew prophets provide an unexpected and refreshing way to raise these topics and questions in the global politics classroom.

The Biblical stories of Jesus

Christ on the cross had to be interpreted anew . . . *not to defend oneself*
. . . that had been the lesson.

NIETZSCHE[19]

The Biblical stories of Jesus introduce students to the political implications of forgiveness, nonviolence, and love of the enemy. In addition, the persecution and death of Jesus introduces a complicated political problem: precisely what is it about the message of nonviolence, forgiveness, and love of enemy that is so threatening to established political power? And what precisely *is* the political meaning of the Jesus stories?

Students respond in various ways to this question. For some students, Jesus' message is one of obedience to the political powers that be. Students often cite the example of the "coin of Caesar" story to support this claim. For others, Jesus represents a form of rebelliousness and resistance that is principled and nonviolent. Finally, some students have even suggested that according to the Jesus stories, we are to adopt an attitude of indifference to political power, neither seeking it for ourselves nor working for it on behalf of others.

Most often, students come to see Jesus as an ambiguous political figure, a man whose message bears multiple, even contradictory, interpretations. Throughout all of this, the riddle still remains as to why nonviolence, love of enemy, and "turning the other cheek" are so threatening to political power. Jesus was clearly not the leader of a mass movement; neither did he ever claim to be "king of the Jews" or for that matter the ruler of anyone at all. In his desert encounter with Satan, Jesus declines political power outright. In the Garden of Gethsemane, when a follower draws his sword against the Roman captors, Jesus pushes the sword away. In Matthew, we read of how Jesus tells his followers "not to worry about your life, about having something to eat, drink, or wear."[20] And while certain statements may have implied it, Jesus never came out once and counseled disobedience to the Roman governors. Nonetheless, Jesus maintained that he did not come to bring peace, but the sword.[21] What might Jesus have meant by this? What type of conflict might he be referring to?

Jesus' apparent quietism and passive acceptance of fate at the hands of political authority may have led to his own torture and earthly death. Taken out of a religious context, the life and death of Jesus seem to suggest that when taken to the extreme, forgiveness, nonviolence, and "turning the other cheek" lead not to security but to self-destruction. As Machiavelli will point out in *The Prince*, any virtue taken too far will soon turn into its opposite in the form of a vice, resulting in the self-destruction of the ruler and a weakening of the polity.

The figure of Jesus must be seen in the context of what students read before and will read after. Like Socrates, Plato's Philosopher-King, Moses, the Hebrew prophets, and Machiavelli's Prince, Jesus sets out to change a society's conception of justice. Later in the course students will revisit the figure of Jesus (and all of the other Bible readings) when they encounter both Machiavelli and Marx. There is a natural bridge between the stories of Jesus and Machiavelli's Prince, for in his own efforts to change taken-for-granted conceptions of justice the Prince rejects precisely Jesus' New Testament morality in favor of an Old Testament one. In the case of Marx, students will consider whether the Marxist vision of economic communism and structural justice share something in common with the vision of Jesus and the community of his followers. Indeed, student conversations about the political implications of the stories of Jesus in the Bible thus do not end when the Bible readings have finished.

Discussion questions: The New Testament

- What was Jesus' attitude toward political authority? Do you find this attitude admirable, disturbing, exciting, subversive, or what?

- Who found Jesus threatening, and why?

- Who obeyed Jesus, and why?

- Is Jesus similar to or different than Socrates? Do the two represent complimentary or contrasting messages about politics?

- Who are our enemies, and can or should we ever love or forgive them?

- Can or should we ever forgive political authorities? When?

- Nietzsche thought that the message of Jesus was one of moral weakness. What do you think Nietzsche meant? Do you agree?

- Considering the assigned selections from Matthew, Mark, Luke, and John, are there different versions of the trial and execution of Jesus? What are they? Might there be political reasons for the different versions of Jesus' life?

- Reread Acts 5.29: "We don't obey people. We obey God." Should religious people ever (dis)obey political authority? When, and why? How would Jesus have answered this question?

- Compare Acts 5.29 with Romans 13. What does each passage suggest about the nature and function of political power? With which do you agree? Why?

The New Testament and international politics

The stories of Jesus in the New Testament raise a number of questions that bear immediately on the study of global politics. For example, do apology and forgiveness have any place in relations between and among states? Should nations apologize for past acts of genocide, ethnic cleansing, or civilian death? States struggle with whether to apologize for past atrocities and the implicit admission of guilt that formal apologies contain. Apologies and forgiveness can help heal past wounds, as in South Africa, but in the form of amnesty agreements forgiveness may undermine the application of justice, as in Afghanistan or Algeria. On the other hand, as the story of Jesus' crucifixion suggests, forgiveness and humility may also carry a heavy price, the ultimate sacrifice being security and survival. Nonetheless, communities continue to demand reparations and apologies from states for past events, even though it is unclear how much security or justice should be sacrificed for the value of forgiveness. The Biblical stories of Jesus also raise the matter of loving one's enemy. What might love of enemy mean in the context of global politics? Might it mean obeying the laws of war (*jus in bello*), making war more humane, or something more radical such as outlawing war altogether? In such cases the tension between Old and New Testament conceptions of justice are directly relevant to international affairs. The Biblical stories of Jesus provide an ideal starting point from which to introduce the moral and ethical questions of international politics.

Conclusion

We do indeed live and teach in "hard times." It is increasingly difficult to imagine an outside to global capitalism, even though the market demonstrates over and over its affinity with both man-made and natural disasters.[22] In our time we have experienced financial crisis and natural and man-made disasters in New Orleans, Turkey, Haiti, and Japan. Students come to realize that the Bible is the story of human beings' psychological struggle with these same issues: catastrophe and disaster, responsibility, shame, and guilt. The Biblical drama is not simply a drama between unbelieving human beings and a God who demands obedience. It is rather the psychic and emotional drama between peoples and their natural, social, and political worlds.

The people of ancient Israel are much like us: they stubbornly cling to the familiar truths they have always known, and involve themselves in contradictions of which they are only dimly aware. Indeed, taken as a whole, the Bible expresses at least one central paradox that, when one thinks about it, is quite cruel. Human societies are collectively responsible for the tragedies that befall them, but justice can never be done on the earth. Earthly justice—social and political justice—is unstable and will tilt toward injustice in very short order. Reading the Bible politically challenges students to think for themselves about what or who is the source of this injustice. Perhaps one way out is to tackle injustice at its source: human pride. But can political affairs ever be immune from human pride? The Biblical stories of Jesus seem to suggest that perhaps human pride can be broken with humility, a love and compassion that is universal and extends to all. But this way is difficult: it is the path of suffering, imprisonment, exile, and death. The stories of Jesus highlight the enormous sacrifice involved in working to bring collective responsibility to light.

By the end of a reading of the Bible in a political theory class, nonreligious students are often surprised to learn that the Bible is precisely about human beings' struggle with injustice and inequity on the earth, and what this means for both individual and collective action. Many religious students are confounded: the stories do not seem to mean what they thought they meant. The political significance of Jesus is particularly ambiguous. Received interpretations about what the Bible is "supposed" to mean, it seems, offer little guidance about what is to be done in the political realm. The reconstruction of meaning must begin all over again, but this time, on one's own terms. Reading the Bible politically is thus a powerful critical pedagogical tool; for in the case of the Bible, the medium is the lesson.

Postscript: Paper topics

The goal of using the Bible in the political science classroom is to help students learn the politically valuable skill of questioning their own settled assumptions. Developing this skill requires a combination of discipline and imagination. To assess this skill I assign a series of paper topics (normally take-home essays) that employ a comparison-contrast approach. This approach requires students to compare and contrast how various figures or texts will deal with a given question or theme. The purpose of the comparison-contrast approach is to force students to use their imaginations in order to explore the main themes of political theory. If students perform well on these transhistorical and intertextual exercises, it suggests that they are beginning to learn how to think beyond the settled and the familiar.

In these assignments, I ask students to choose three texts, figures, or sources and compare and contrast them on a given question or theme. The specific questions vary and can be made more precise in various ways, but past essay topics have generally included:

- What might a "just" polity look like? (Plato, Moses, Jesus, Machiavelli, Marx.)

- To what extent can human characteristics be molded or manipulated by political leaders? (Plato, Genesis, Machiavelli, Jesus.)

- What place does violence have in politics? Who is justified in wielding violence? Is it possible to use violence justly? To what end? (Moses, Machiavelli, the Hebrew prophets, Jesus, Marx.)

- What is human pride and what role does it play in politics? (Plato, Genesis, Machiavelli, Jesus.)

- What makes a nation great? (Plato, Machiavelli, Hebrew Prophets, Jesus.)

- What is hypocrisy? Is it a political virtue or a political vice? (Plato's Philosopher-King, the Hebrew prophets, Machiavelli, and Jesus.)

- What is freedom? (Genesis, Marx, Machiavelli, Jesus.)

It is also possible to take a more explicitly transhistorical approach to the comparison and contrast exercise. Such assignments have included:

- How would Plato and Machiavelli (or Marx and Machiavelli) interpret the political significance of Jesus' crucifixion and death?

- How would Plato and Machiavelli interpret Jesus' temptations in the desert?

- How would Machiavelli and Marx interpret Jesus' Sermon on the Mount?

- How would Plato and Machiavelli interpret the political significance of Genesis?

- Consider 1 Corinthians 2.8: "The rulers of this world don't know anything about wisdom."

How would Plato/Machiavelli/Marx/the Hebrew prophets respond to this statement? Would they agree or disagree?

- What do rulers need to know in order to govern effectively? What personal qualities or characteristics must they have? Compare and contrast Jesus, Plato, Machiavelli, and the Hebrew prophets on this question.

● Consider Romans 13: "You should obey the rulers because you know it is the right thing to do, not just because of God's anger." How would Plato/Machiavelli/Marx/the Hebrew prophets respond to this statement? Would they agree or disagree?

Notes

1 See Glover and Tagliarina's chapter in this volume.
2 Donald Justice, "The Wall," *New and Selected Poems* (New York: Alfred A. Knopf, 2003): 34.
3 Genesis 2.9. This and all Biblical references taken from: The American Bible Society, *The Holy Bible, Contemporary English Version* (New York, NY: The American Bible Society, 1995).
4 Genesis 2.17.
5 Francis Fukuyama, *The End of History and the Last Man* (New York, NY: Free Press, 2006).
6 Robert Sinnerbrink, "Goodbye Lenin? Žižek on Neo-Liberal Ideology and Post-Marxist Politics," *International Journal of Žižek Studies* 4 (2010): 7.
7 Exodus 2.12.
8 Exodus 2.14.
9 Exodus 7.3–4.
10 Exodus 11; also 12.29–30.
11 Exodus 3.21–22; also 12.36.
12 Isaiah 33.23.
13 1 Samuel 15–17.
14 1 Kings 2–6, 8–9.
15 1 Samuel 8.
16 1 Samuel 15–17, 1 Kings 2–6, 8–9.
17 Isaiah 58.3.
18 Isaiah 40.
19 Friedrich Nietzsche, *The Will to Power* (New York: Vintage, 1967): 103.
20 Matthews 6.25.
21 Matthews 10.34.
22 Naomi Klein, *Shock Doctrine: The Rise of Disaster Capitalism* (New York: Picador, 2007).

CHAPTER TWO

Literature from the Global-South: Underutilized resources for the (international) politics classroom

Michael Kuchinsky

Quid ergo Athenis et Hierosolymis—What has Athens to do with Jerusalem?

The above quotation by the theologian, Tertullian, from his *On Prescription against Heretics* is often interpreted to mean that concerns of reason and revelation served two different purposes; that the truths of philosophy (reason) and theology (revelation) were separated. When conversations occur about pedagogy and the political science classroom, the possible uses for teaching political science from literature, and more specifically those literatures from the Global-South, are often also left out. What does fiction have to add to our political theories, and what value do these literatures have for the international politics classroom?

Not wishing to settle the above question by Tertullian, the following pages argue in favor of using lesser known literatures from the world's developing and underdeveloped regions (the Global-South) when teaching politics. Five different classroom strategies will be explored. These strategic comments will be followed by a case example where the figurative Athens and Jerusalem share a common boundary of discourse for an entire semester—the interdisciplinary classroom where political science and literature are used to discuss a common focus. The chapter closes with some comments about assessment and getting started. But first, why is it necessary to make a special comment about "literatures of the Global-South?"[1]

Almost any review of the resource catalogues used by political science and international relations teachers for their classes leads to an obvious conclusion. The majority of materials to choose from, and certainly the choices among commonly used political science textbooks, are written by political scholars from North America and Europe even when the subjects may be comparative regional studies. Though available scholarly works by non-Western or Global-South political scientists have increased in the post-Cold War years, teachers must still search and make intentional choices to move away from more familiar resources. It can take greater effort to find scholarly material from non-Western authors.

The resource decision gets complicated for the educator who wishes to use fiction to augment her/his teaching, and perhaps even more so when the question is asked, "what about literature from the regions that are the subject of my international politics class?" Though we recognize that in an increasingly globalized world using authors from the Global-South may encourage greater understanding from these regions, we may not be familiar enough with them to make those choices.

Thus, the challenge in the title—using underutilized materials—potentially requires three steps down unfamiliar pathways. There is (1) the choice to look for and include scholars who are writing from the Global-South, followed by (2) the choice to use fiction to augment or replace other materials, and there might be (3) the choice to find literatures and authors that are entirely unfamiliar to us. If it can be such a chore, why would anyone choose to "go that route?"

A small but growing literature on the importance of connecting literature in the teaching of political subjects divides between "why" questions and "how to" ones. These authors ask "why is literature relevant for the study of international politics, or in what way do literary portraits of political life become important for international politics?" Other questions follow, such as "how can one incorporate these methods for the purpose of teaching and learning?"

General answers about the importance of using literature to teach international affairs focus on the students and their learning experience. The authors cited below for their "how to" and "with what" materials incorporate literature to improve student learning. Using literature may liven up teaching, personalize abstract materials, promote interdisciplinary learning, highlight subjects that might be forgotten, invite competing viewpoints for consideration, or stimulate alternative visions for future political communities. A more specific comment on the importance of fiction for political science includes its role in sparking critical thinking and student intellectual creativity, so that students may agilely move between past and present political realities when doing comparative analysis.[2]

The ubiquitous effects of globalization in today's world might be another answer to the "why" question. The world is getting more complex and so are the trends, numbers of agents, challenges, and influences on international politics. Therefore, to understand these trends requires paying attention to more voices who are attempting to clarify today's political processes. Literary voices/stories push the discourse toward levels of meaning and understanding, adding to the pursuits of political description, analysis, and prescription. The use of literature would then "measure an understanding of previous prevailing and future social and political relations" due to their ability "to reveal complex patterns that permeate a range of historical and contemporary settings," and thereby "help decipher international relations."[3] In other words, literature can provide comparative value in distinctive ways across time and space, even exposing the motivations of those who had the power of political action in our globalized world.

More of the "fiction with politics" literature aims to provide guidance to the user by pragmatically discussing concerns over what literature to use. Almost any literature might be fair game. For some it has been the works of Shakespeare,[4] for others portions of classical Greek drama,[5] or works of poetry from different cultures and regions,[6] or classics of modern literature,[7] followed by more popular pieces of fiction[8] including science fiction. The beauty of using shorter pieces such as poetry is their use as a quick entry point for both affective and cognitive learning about a political context or issue, while short stories provide advantages over whole novels when class opportunities are limited.[9] Plays offer an immediate opening to alternative teaching pedagogies (dramatic readings), as well as significant connections between agents and events brought on by the cohesion of a developing narrative.

Advocates for using literature in political science classrooms do so for various pedagogical reasons. Literature can be motivational for student learning, framing, and mobilizing questions for students on the importance of civic engagement and citizenship.[10] Literary characters may personalize more abstract concepts and theories of politics and political behavior, opening up discussions on politically important and relevant ideas for the student.[11] Literature may provide a wider appreciation of the political importance of history and historical thinking revealing political nuances broader than dualistic categories of "right and wrong" or "good and bad."[12] Fiction may motivate the introductory student to move from apathy regarding civic and political life to a more participatory perspective.[13]

It should be apparent that within fiction, the teacher can find almost any political theme to augment political discourse in the classroom. One could easily construct a seminar (probably already done) on the nature of politics according to "Bill Shakespeare," or by just using literature as the sole textual sources! Paul Sheeran's book, *Literature and International Relations: Stories in the Art of Diplomacy*, defends this effort, linking literary resources to traditional political subjects such as war and conflict, the state and its powers, or issues of leadership, while all along cautioning against the too easy recourse of choosing familiar authors and books to avoid literature from non-Western sources.[14]

After the choice to use literature (in general or from the Global-South) has been made, what follows are the considerations of when and how to use them for teaching political realities and concepts. The chapter turns next to a review of five pedagogical uses of global literary resources for the classroom.

What can I do with these literary materials in my classroom?

There is a pragmatic consideration when choosing to use fiction to teach political science. It should do something for the instruction of the class. The following questions might aid the instructor in determining the classroom purpose of the literary resource:

1   When should a piece of fictional literature be used? Why then?
2   What primary learning purpose will be achieved by using literature?
3   How do materials from the Global-South augment these considerations?
4   What assessment strategy should be used to evaluate the outcomes?

The questions are not unique to the use of non-Western authors and literary sources. Questions like these would be used in any deliberation about teaching strategies and media, and an answer to number three was discussed above when considering the complexity of today's political world. Five strategies are worth considering.

The teacher-scholar may wish to use literature as a class introduction to open a theme that will be useful throughout the course. He or she may wish to use literature as a type of summation reinforcing previous learnings. Literature can open up a creative process highlighting a theme less often covered. A piece of literature might highlight an important aspect of a people's experience, a central focus on their political understanding or identity. Fiction might also be useful as a form of consciousness-raising to initiate a counterintuitive response or lesson. The latter two purposes might be used to underscore an important political concept or intensify a student's experience with a significant but less known political personality, moment, or issue. These purposes may overlap with one another.

The use of literature from the Global-South can build upon these five purposes for teaching politics with literature in the classroom, especially for the international politics class. Educators would expect most students to be less familiar with authors of the Global-South adding to the learnings of purposes three, four, and five. Secondly these authors come from the non-Western context possibly addressing the West or Global-North from a critical or even adversarial position. Thus, using literature from the Global-South, in addition to the above general thoughts about using literature in the classroom, moves the instructor to consider how these less-familiar literatures:

a. initiate class discussion on topics important for the class and through the Other's (Global-South's) eyes;

b. summarize class discussions through the "Other's" eyes;

c. highlight an important aspect of a people's experience central to their historical and political understanding or identity; or

d. underscore a political concept or intensify the understanding of an important political person or moment through the non-Western setting; and

e. offer an alternative voice to commonly held positions and information.

Choosing Global-South literature is likely to provide alternative information, target affective as well as cognitive responses, question or critique norms and interpretations, or raise consciousness and be experienced counterintuitively from more traditional perceptions. Coming from the Global-South, the literary resource may challenge, or critique long-held or never-considered understandings and assumptions.

The author has used literature from the developing world for all of these purposes—as an introduction, for summation, to develop understanding of political communities, to intensify knowledge, or to introduce an alternative voice. Literature has been used for purposes of providing information and content, to analyze differing political realities, and to challenge with an alternative, consciousness-raising, or counterintuitive perception or assumption. Some examples of how literature from the Global-South can be used in the politics classroom follow in the next section.

Examples for using Global-South literature

Obviously, the catalogue of relevant literatures that arise from the Global-South for the political science classroom is broad and includes all lands, nation-states, and peoples. This in itself can be a problem. It may be the "how to get started" problem. The classroom examples in this section incorporate the above outlined purposes of literature—to introduce significant classroom themes, to summarize large amounts of information, to highlight an aspect of the course, or to provide alternative perspectives and analysis.

Using appropriate fiction at the beginning of a course introduces concepts, themes, and narrative histories likely to be used and reused over time. The strategy embraces one of the benefits of fiction. Every reader can engage the literary text and develop their "class voice" even when they are still less familiar with the class's content. Critical awareness and comparative analysis skills get used even when general content or historical context are unfamiliar.

Though it is an older book, South Africa/Botswana author Bessie Head's *When Rain Clouds Gather* offered many introductory concepts at the beginning of my international development classes. Its description of competing economic visions and development plans—from the neocolonialist to household-level collectivities—provided several days of free-ranging discussion while eliciting concepts about development theory and practice. The book's primary characters might be shallow or even stereotypical—an older woman providing maternal memory to the village's problems; a reformist ex-patriot with ideas straight out of a development textbook; a disgruntled subruler using ethnic strife to increase his local power; and a British administrative retainer struggling to identify his position in an independent regime. However Head's story moved students to discuss benefits of agricultural cooperatives, food security, gender roles in the household economy, colonial elites and development, social capacity, and a laundry list of topics current to the average international/economic development class. Students spoke about development before they were familiar with the theories and history of development.

The above depicts some benefits for using fiction to introduce a subject. A course's conceptual vocabulary is practiced while opening up perceptual differences about development between the Global-South and Global-North. Although the initial learning curve may be high, students referred back to chapters from the text when the class turned more formally to discussions of gender analysis and development, or food security and cash cropping. Students also encountered choices brought on by development decisions that are beyond their experience. Head describes the choice of an adolescent boy who must go away to stay in the bush with the cattle, ultimately leading to tragic consequences. The story stirred conversations about risk, poverty, and household choices not always apparent in more abstract writing.

Literature may be useful not only for the purposes of introduction, but for summation of all or part of a course's material. By coming at the end of a course section, fiction ties together previous conversations and conceptual discussions with a memorable narrative. Using the literatures from the Global-South can add an alternative summary that enhances the reality of regional and cultural differences or global complexity.

The study of China through Mao-Zedong, his revolution and ideology, was a significant component of a two semester-long program called the International Scholars Program[15] that aimed at understanding significant changes of the twentieth century. Two pieces of fiction were used while teaching the China section with one of these acting as a summation to clarify the encompassing power of Maoist ideology. This was Lois Wheeler Snow's collection of plays from the Cultural Revolution period of China entitled, *China on Stage*. The plays, such as "The Red Lantern," brought into focus previous class discussions about Mao's Long March, the twentieth-century relationship between China and Japan, Mao's rhetoric of a permanent revolution, and how other states that also experienced colonialism could be attracted to China's revolutionary success. Because Madame Mao was so instrumental in the onset of China's Cultural Revolution and the revived use of drama to strengthen revolutionary sentiment, reading the plays linked well with the course's other fictional text, Anchee Min's *Becoming Madame Mao*.

Here again, the use of fiction provided benefits to the class by binding together course themes and histories. Using plays from China's Cultural Revolution wove together the origins and history of the Chinese Revolution, its ideals and ideologies, with representative and leading personalities, and its present significance. By using dramatic reading and taking on character roles, class members not only encountered the intellectual qualities of the texts, but the emotional (and rhetorical) ones as well.

For many years, my practice has been to include at least one piece of fiction in regional politics courses. I do this for one of the three latter reasons identified above—to highlight regional history from a less-heard perspective, to expand on an essential concept or individual, or to provide an alternative voice less featured in resources for a more general and introductory class. Since these books originate in the histories and personalities of the studied region, they also provide a less abstracted voice of regional authenticity. The following examples for the use of literature from the Global-South come from regional politics classes for the Middle East and Sub-Saharan Africa.

The modern history of the Palestinian people is a central narrative of Middle Eastern politics and history. The chronic qualities of the conflict(s) and the numerous efforts at resolving it (them) fall alongside other long-lasting cleavages that destabilize the region, such as Iraqi and Iranian relationships, ethnic hopes for self-determination (the Kurds among others), the competition between Iran and the Saudis, or the triangle between Morocco, Algeria, and the Western Sahara. In the case of a Middle East politics class, what is there not to like in a story that brings together basic human aspirations for home with homelessness, security with the vulnerability of refugees, terror given and received, economic and political diaspora, conflicting human rights claims, and competing visions for a national identity and destiny. The rising and falling aspirations of the Palestinian people mirror much of the drama, comedy, tragedy, even fairy tale narratives that might have been told around Middle Eastern evening fires.

The book *Days of Dust* by Halim Barakat was first published in Arabic in 1969 just 2 years after the events that anchor the story, and since then published in English. Its plot moves from just days before the 1967 attack on Israel by its neighbors and concludes with the aftermath of Israeli victory through the responses by the defeated Palestinian characters. Barakat invents characters representing idealistic, professional, and ideological differences among Palestinians to diversify our understanding of "the Palestinians." The hopes and despairs of the characters are woven together with their activities during the conflict. Like a diary, the characters recount daily choices while reflecting upon the region's conflicts. Lines near the end of the book elicit its (and the region's) many tensions—"the tragedy was not that they had lost the war but that they had lost it without heroism."[16]

Barakat's book could represent all three latter uses of literature from the Global-South for a political science class. It conveys the importance and disillusionment of the national pursuit by Palestinians in a personalized, often conflicted, and multidimensional manner. It singles out a piece of history and lionizes it to the level of communal narrative. It suggests the importance of competing (if not mutually exclusive) narratives for the same events by the peoples most dearly impacted by them. It can lead into many related themes about nationalism, relationships among Arabs (and Arab institutions) with the Palestinians, and of course, Palestinians everywhere with Israel.

A common theme in African politics is the intervention by external powers into the internal affairs of African states and the difficulty of state-building. African history holds many examples of this whether coming during the colonial period, the time of national self-determination, the Cold War period's proxy wars, or in Africa's present-day struggles for economic independence and democracy.

J. P. Clark's Nigerian-based play, *All for Oil*, sounds initially as if the subject is about Africa's current political economy and energy, especially the challenges found in West Africa. In one sense, it is. Oil is an important part of the play. It takes place in Nigeria among competing ethnic interests. But the time frame is all wrong (or all right depending on your point of view). Clark's book is not set in the present, but during the height of British colonial oversight at the beginning of the twentieth century. Britain's Governor-General, Lord Frederick Lugard, is a character though in absentia. All of a sudden, today's questions about oil dependency and energy wealth, ethnic conflicts, and relations among the world's superpowers, have a strategic timeline straddling the twentieth century. Political theories such as structuralism and liberal capitalist development clash while national interests compete across the boundaries of time in Clark's Nigeria. Readers of *All for Oil* are given alternative renderings of one of Africa's enigmas—how can one be so resource wealthy, and yet so impoverished and underdeveloped? Clark, I believe, purposively bends history and forces the reader to imagine Africa's current political landscape from more than one historical period or explanation. The usefulness of Clark, and perhaps any use of alternative voices, is more about calling into question the answers that have become known, comfortable, and presumed correct.

Up until now, the suggestion has been that literature from the Global-South can be strategically used in the political science class for several targeted purposes. Can it do more? Can it partially anchor or provide materials for an entire course? Paul Sheeran's book about literary connections to many subjects within international relations, discussed previously, affirms that possibility. What follows is a more developed case of an interdisciplinary and team-taught course that studied twentieth-century revolutions. Political/economic theories about revolutions and historical case studies, combined with fiction from the revolutionary contexts in this hybrid but holistic example of the use of literature in political science.

The political science/literature interdisciplinary classroom

Literature, with an emphasis on literature originating from the Global-South, has been described so far as a valuable resource that can supplement or complement the teaching of political science and the telling of political narrative. When used throughout a course, such as in the case described below, literature can become an essential dialogue partner *with* and sometimes *in* the political narrative. All of the above purposes of the use of literature can be present.

We have an "honors program" and a Global Studies major at my university which require students to take seminars as part of their degree program. The seminars can be innovative times for faculty (as well as the students) and facilitate new course development. The seminars opened the opportunity for a multidisciplinary course design with interdisciplinary learning, melding political and literary materials around cases of revolutionary change during the twentieth century. Multidisciplinary refers to the use of theories and content from different disciplines to explore a course's common theme. In this course on modern revolutions, the materials used included political theories about revolutions, historical materials, and pieces of literature from the revolutionary contexts, usually the Global-South. Interdisciplinary learning seeks to fuse materials and ideas from distinct disciplines in a more complicated discourse of narratives that can compete, correlate, or conflict with each other for the purpose of new insights. Both of these aims were part of the Revolutions seminar as political and literary theory mixed together with contextual information and literary examples from the Global-South. An abbreviated syllabus of the course has been included as an appendix to the chapter.

The concept of "narrative" is useful for such a course. It is a methodological concept that straddles political and literary theory. It is a story, or sometimes the meta-story from which other stories emanate or collide.[17] Narrative is a dynamic and evolving text incorporating empirical and normative information. It is the grist for textual analysis and a valued contribution to both the humanities and the social sciences.

The seminar followed a three-point path. The first was to provide the student with some theoretical foundations from the humanities and social sciences. Theoretical writings about political revolutions were set alongside methodological material on historical and literary narrative analysis. Here was also the time to discuss differences between revolutionary processes and reformist ones, whether violence was necessary, and distinctions between powers of coercion and persuasion.

The second part of the course focused on the revolutions. Using cases from Africa, Asia, Europe, Latin America, and the Middle East was meant to convey the ubiquity of revolutionary change. They also provided comparative value for exploring the differences and commonalities of each context, and how a theory might explain more in one context than another.

In a sense, this was an elaborate case-study approach to learning. Information about the revolutionary context was provided. Historical documents and pertinent economic indicators gave students some "hard" data for the settings. Students read case chapters from a type of revolutions textbook, and online resources would be used (writings of Chairman Mao, the life of Sandino, etc.) to add on layers of content to the case. Discussions from the previously studied theories blended with the layers of political and historical sources.

Literature from the revolutionary setting (usually the Global-South)— sometimes a drama, a novel, or a memoir—was then added to the case methodology. The class discussed the piece apart from its political relevance to squeeze out literary interpretations and value the literature in its own right. Then came time to combine the many layers of information—how did they correlate, conflict, challenge, and support one another? Finally, as the case studies moved from location to location, comparisons could be made to develop a more complex and fuller understanding of revolutions, who participated in them and why they occurred.

The third part of the class, the students' research projects and student/faculty consultations, began early in the course. The student selected a revolutionary case, moved through a prescribed research and writing process, and developed a case that mirrored the approach taken in class. The students wove together political theory, historical narrative, and a literary voice into a new and individual piece of research. The results were stunning and provided a collegial environment for students and faculty alike. Most of the projects would later be presented at a student research conference hosted by the honors program.

Some thoughts on assessment

Allusions have been made to different means of evaluation in this chapter. The following will not be systematic, but anecdotal. There are many publications on developing and using assessment grids and strategies.

Instructors can identify various concepts that they believe are essential within a literary reading and how they relate to wider materials in the course. As a measure of the depth of a student's discussion or the breadth of their participation, a discourse grid using these concepts can be created and then shared with students.

Using literature opens the door for different forms of critical book reviews. These can be traditional reviews that ask students to debate an author's themes, characters, flaws, and style, or more targeted ones that ask the student to consider what knowledge or questions about the region, course subject, or theory are raised by using literature from the Global-South. The latter type of book review coincides with the uses for literature described above, especially if the book was chosen to highlight an alternative voice or point of view.

The "Revolutions" course described a research process common to many upper division courses. The interaction between faculty and student deepens as the student develops a project thesis, literature review, initial draft, and final project and presentation. The process blended materials in the student's literature review just as the course blended interdisciplinary content and methodologies. The student's project determined how well the course's use of multidisciplinary and interdisciplinary knowledge encouraged a more holistic discourse about revolutions.

Testing procedures can incorporate nontraditional literatures to evaluate how well the student integrates abstract theoretical material with content analysis. Though not a piece of fiction, but certainly a nontraditional resource, Dan Koeppel's book *Banana* was a supplemental text in an international political economy (IPE) class. Following class discussions, the text was used in a summary-like manner to conclude a section on IPE theory and structures. Students were asked to write an essay analyzing how various IPE theories, and financial, trade, knowledge, and security structures could be identified in *Banana*. The task became a dialogue on how well the students could use the course's conceptual material to analyze a richly detailed and focused alternative text, one that was written for the general public.

How can I get started?

It can be time consuming to search for politically useful literature from the Global-South. Where does one start? How does one become knowledgeable about all the world's regional authors? The short answer is one cannot. If we specialized in one region of comparative politics, we are less familiar with others. Many books referred to in this chapter come from my research interests of the Middle East and Sub-Saharan Africa. They are representative and should lead to the idea that other literary resources can be found fitting to our courses, regional emphases, and projects.

Some commercial publishers offer specialty catalogues to highlight non-Western authors. The Lynne Rienner Publishing Company and Penguin Group have catalogues devoted to global literature and hard-to-find authors. The aforementioned *Days of Dust* was a featured selection. The Heinemann Publishing Company provides its *African Writers Series*, and a parallel *Asian Writers Series*. Bessie Head's *When Rain Clouds Gather* is one of many books in the series. Lesser known African authors may be found through the African Books Collective (ABC). J. P. Clark's *All for Oil* was one of them. Few of the ABC books ever make it into publishing houses for larger markets. Lynne Rienner also offers an older edited volume entitled *African Novels in the Classroom*. In it are book descriptions that may offer an easier route to usable fiction resources for politics and global studies classes.

Several regional studies textbooks include chapters on literature and how authors' works relate to area trends and challenges. In these textbooks, literature has agency in a region's evolving political context and history. Some textbooks on Africa, Pacific Asia, the Caribbean, Latin America, or the Middle East, provide bibliographies of regional authors and their works.[18] Some general political science textbooks also emphasize using literature, films, or pop-culture to teach politics, such as Van Belle and Mash's *A Novel Approach to Politics*.

Online resources abound. There are sample syllabi with literary references available on the internet. Web-based references of short stories, novels, poems and poets, memoirs, and essays from the Global-South in the public domain can be found through internet research.

Political science professional associations are also resources for the teacher interested in using literature in the classroom. The American Political Science Association (APSA) supports the research section, Politics and Literature, with online links to further journal and research resources. An APSA journal, *PS: Political Science and Politics,* is devoted to political science pedagogy and articles on teaching with literature regularly appear. Likewise, an International Studies Association section is "Active Learning in International Affairs (ALIAS)," which supports teaching international studies through many methodologies.

If once upon a time it was unclear what Athenian reason and the revelation of Jerusalem had to say to each other that need not be the case between literature and political science. Literature can be used variously in the politics classroom. Our increasingly interdependent and globalizing world requires including voices that are less often heard. As representative voices, the authors and literature from the Global-South become valuable partners in our teaching.

Appendix: Abridged sample syllabus

Honors Seminar, 395/396 A—Revolution(s)

Fall 2009, Gardner-Webb University

Course rationale

The nature of change in global societies can be static or dynamic, evolving or cataclysmic, bound up by internal forces or aided by external interventions. One of the most interesting forms of change is revolution. Revolutions involve dramatic changes of political, economic, or social-cultural forces and institutions through varying degrees of conflict. As Chairman Mao once said, "it is not a leisurely activity." Revolutions have occurred on all continents. Their origins have been particularly diverse across the last century providing lessons for future states, communities, social groups, and perhaps, even global orders. This course combines insights from contextual literatures and from political and economic theory to better understand this form of social change . . . one intimately connected to our nation's heritage.

What is the connection between politics and literature? As Edward Said argued in *Culture and Imperialism*, literature can reflect the policies of the nation-state and the political attitudes of citizens—elites and to a lesser degree masses. Literature can also critique the nation or other political group, or offer personal interpretations of revolutions and other political activities. We will read novels, nonfiction, and a play, and analyze their narrative methods for presenting revolutions. We will struggle with questions like "what is the role of the writer and literature in society," and "how can literature written after the fact have political influence?"

Style of instruction: This course will be a team taught seminar. Each case will be developed both through the historic/political/economic analysis depicted within the theoretical material on revolution, change, and mass movements; and each case will devote time to the literary context of the authors and their content. The instructors will use electronic resources and online learning to help stimulate dialogue on the subjects of revolution and change.

Course objectives

1 To understand the relationship between cultural products such as literature and the impact of historical/social/political context on them, and to study literature as a form of response to/interaction with the colonial/postcolonial experience.

2 To gain a deeper understanding and appreciation of both political science and literary studies, how they relate to discursive practices, and issues and debates within the field.

3 To gain an overview of the historical and social context of different types of revolution in various societies.

4 To enter into dialogue with the critical work of this field.

5 To practice and strengthen oral presentation skills in preparation for the students' senior capstone project.

Plagiarism and the honor code

When it comes to thinking about plagiarism, don't do it. Plagiarism is just plain wrong. Cheating on examinations will not be tolerated. When it comes to the honor code, honor it. Provide all resource citations. This course will comply with all of the rules and regulations bound within the school honor code. Infractions will not be tolerated and swift action will be taken against any violations. Should a student be caught cheating or plagiarizing, she/he will receive an F for the course.

Using someone else's words or ideas without giving credit is plagiarism. "Someone else" includes work by people you know, material posted or sold online, and material printed in books or periodicals, either print or electronic. Resubmitting work you have done for another class without receiving prior permission from your professor will be considered academic dishonesty and will receive the same penalty.

Books and readings will be based upon theory and cases. They will include political works and representative samples of literature from the locations, times, or in retrospective.

1 James Defronzo—*Revolutions and Revolutionary Movements*, 3rd edition.

2 On library reserve:

   a. "War and Revolution" and *"The Meaning of Revolution"*— Hanna Arendt

    b. "Introduction and Summary of *The Anatomy of Revolution*"—Crane Brinton

    c. "Explaining Social Revolution" from *States and Social Revolution*—Theda Skocpol

    d. "Theories of Revolution," and "The Future of Revolution in the Countryside" from *Caught in the Crossfire* by T. David Mason.

3 Literature related to individual case contexts include:

— Gao Xingjian. *One Man's Bible* (China)

— Giaconda Belli. *The Country under my Skin* (Nicaragua).

— Manoucher Parvin. *Cry for my Revolution* (Iran).

— Alez La Guma, *In the Fog of the Seasons' End* (South Africa)

— Tom Stoppard, *Rock and Roll* (Czechoslovakia)

— Selected secondary source essays on the literary works/theories of literature and revolution.

Other resources: The instructors reserve the right to consider films and other visual materials when appropriate, including live performances.

The project: The student will choose a revolution of the twentieth century to investigate on their own. This case will not be part of the case studies used in class. The student's project will use the interdisciplinary approach modeled in class. The paper should be approximately 20 pages in length using standard margins and fonts, typically Times New Roman.

Project components: At various intervals during the semester, you will have assignments due, as indicated on the syllabus that will show your progress in working on your project. These assignments will include the following: (1) an one-page statement of your chosen case study: which revolution and which literary text you have chosen and any preliminary thoughts you have on them; (2) an annotated bibliography of sources you are using to research your case study and literary text; (3) a Project Conference that you will have with each professor to discuss your progress with your project and to work on any questions/problems, etc. you may be experiencing; (4) a Rough Draft that you will submit to each professor; (5) a Presentation to the class where you will present your project; and (5) the Final Draft.

Examinations: The mid-term examination will cover literary, economic, and political theory materials related to revolution as well as the case studies and literature covered up to that point. The final will be cumulative in scope providing the student time to compare and contrast lessons across revolutionary experiences and literatures.

Notes

1 There have been many terms used to describe the developing world. The term, Global-South, has some current acceptance among peoples of the world who remain in positions of less economic and physical well-being, while including subcommunities in highly developed countries that may share common realities with them.

2 Cheryl Laz, "Science Fiction and Introductory Sociology: The *Handmaid* in the Classroom," *Teaching Sociology* 24 (1996): 54–63.

3 Paul Sheeran. *Literature and International Relations* (Burlington, VT: Ashgate Publishing Company, 2007): 5.

4 Darcy Wudel, "Shakespeare's *Coriolanus* in the Political Science Classroom," *PS: Political Science & Politics* 35 (2002): 217–22.

5 Kimberly Cowell-Meyers, "Teaching Politics using *Antigone*," *PS: Political Science & Politics* 39 (2006): 347–9.

6 Martha K. Goodman, "Using Middle Eastern Literature and Allusions in Class," *VCCA Journal* 7 (1992): 14–25.

7 Anthony F. Lang and James M. Lang, "Between Theory and History: *The Remains of the Day* in the International Relations Classroom," *PS: Political Science & Politics* 31(1998): 209–15.

8 April Morgan, "*The Poisonwood Bible:* An Antidote for what Ails International Relations?" *International Political Science Review* 27 (2006): 379–403.

9 The *Longman Anthology of World Literature* edited by David Damrosch and published by Pearson Longman is a handy anthology of poetry from the Global-South. A collection of essays covering many political, historical, and philosophical concerns from the regions of the Global-South would be *The Post-Colonial Studies Reader,* edited by Bill Ashcroft, Gareth Griffiths, and Helen Tiffin, and published by Routledge Publishing. Two collections of wonderful short stories, especially for grappling with the growing reality and necessity of hybridity on account of globalizing trends include Jhumpa Lahiri's *Interpreter of Maladies* and Salman Rushdie's *East, West.*

10 Charles C. Turner, "The Motivating Text: Assigning Hanna Arendt's *Eichmann in Jerusalem,*" *PS: Political Science & Politics* 28 (2005): 67–9.

11 Wudel, "Shakespeare's *Coriolanus*," 217.

12 Lang and Lang, "Between Theory and History," 214.

13 Cowell-Myers, "Teaching Politics Using *Antigone*," 347.

14 Another effort at linking fiction with many aspects of political science, but in the form of a textbook, is Douglas Van Belle and Kenneth Mash's *A Novel Approach to Politics,* and published by the Congressional Quarterly Press.

15 The program was offered at Goucher College in Maryland. The author taught in the program.

16 Halim Barakat, *Days of Dust* (Boulder, CO: Lynne Rienner Publishers, Inc., 1997): 179.

17 A current transatlantic discourse uses narrative to describe and better understand influences on policy and policy-makers, and questions over change and continuity that occur when national or global narratives no longer "fit."

Some of those engaged in the dialogue about narratives and international relations include Alister Miskimmon, Monroe E. Price, and Laura Roselle.

18 The Lynne Reinner publishing company offers a series of general textbooks that highlight regional authors and literatures. These include: April and Donald Gordon's *Understanding Contemporary Africa*; Jillian Schwedler and Deborah Gerner's *Understanding the Contemporary Middle East*; Richard Hillman and Thomas D'Agostino's *Understanding Contemporary Latin America* and *Understanding the Contemporary Caribbean*; and Katherine Kaup's *Understanding Contemporary Asia-Pacific*.

CHAPTER THREE

Critical pedagogy in hard times: Utopian socialist literature as a means for rethinking capitalism within the classroom

Robert W. Glover and Daniel Tagliarina

Introduction: The onset of "hard times" and the need for critical pedagogy

In mid-2007, Americans received their first whiff of the economic "hard times" to come through a series of developments in subprime mortgage markets.[1] As we now know, this boom in subprime lending would have serious consequences for the United States and global economies. In order to deflect the risk associated with such loans, banks and lenders bundled the subprime products into mortgage-backed securities sold to banks abroad. These complex financial products exposed the entire global financial system to the risk of the subprime system, often masked behind anemic and poorly regulated credit rating systems. As delinquencies and defaults accelerated in the mid-2000s, investors and financial institutions felt the effects. By 2008, the scale of the secondary effects stemming from the subprime housing sector was clear: devastating losses for investors, sharp declines in home values, coupled with stagnation and contraction within the stock market. These macro-level economic developments filtered down to the population in the form of a precarious financial existence and increased suffering, hardship, and uncertainty. By one estimate, US household wealth shrunk by roughly 10 trillion dollars in 2008.[2] The "great recession," the most significant economic crisis in the United States since its namesake roughly 80 years ago, was upon us.

As with any crisis, there are immediate lessons we might draw. Subprime lending is, at best, a mixed blessing. Many individuals gained access to home ownership and the equity that accompanies it. Yet the way which lending proceeded, as well as the general recklessness of lenders *and* borrowers, had distressing implications. The contagion with which the subprime crisis spread to other economic sectors and to other areas of the globe reminded us of the risks of global economic interdependence. Yet the economic crisis has produced a broader, less immediate political imperative as well. Things need to change. We cannot reduce the problems we encounter to a temporary "blip on the radar screen," awaiting market correction. "Change," that by now dubious signpost of contemporary American politics is the suggestion offered from every economic school and every corner of the ideological spectrum. All agree that contemporary capitalism needs fundamental restructuring and that this unique cluster of institutions, actors, and attitudes may not be the vehicle to carry our economic aspirations much further into the twenty-first century.

Yet the economic crisis produces a more profound set of questions than immediate policy responses, questions crucially tied to teaching and learning. Packed within these calls for change are a series of ethical questions regarding the character of contemporary capitalism itself that we must contemplate as a society, both now and in future generations. Behind suggestions for regulation and government subsidy lay a penetrating set of questions regarding the proper role of the state in economic regulation. Recommendations regarding caps on executive compensation stimulate deeper debates regarding the ethical metrics operative when remunerating managerial skill or economic risk. These challenges foster active reflection upon the ways in which we reconcile corporate hierarchy with our democratic sensibilities, or deal with the increasing fluidity between economic and political power. One might likewise consider whether our attitudes toward consumption, economic gratification, debt, and the risks borne by consumers are sustainable or desirable.

The challenges our society faces are not simply questions of which technocratic "fixes" will get our economy "back on track." Rather, our present situation requires an assessment of moral responsibility, and a critical, penetrating reflection upon the ethical imperatives we have inscribed upon our economic lives. In turn, our pedagogical orientation must be reflective, rather than strictly focused upon pragmatic solutions. With these considerations in mind, we will make a somewhat counterintuitive argument about the ways educators can help students understand times of economic crisis. We argue that the starting point should not be the immediate facts, details, and suggested policy responses or, at least, not strictly this. Such proposals emerge from the existing capitalist order, and may be too institutionally embedded to force imaginative reflection capable of creating a less volatile alternative. Furthermore, the uncertainty of the contemporary crisis potentially provokes alarmist modes of thinking, knee-jerk reactions which shut down sustained, critical reflection. Instead, we suggest that we harness this unique chance to unsettle our students' preconceived ideas about contemporary capitalism and foster a more expansive exploration of possible alternatives.

In so doing, we rely upon insights from a strain of psychology known as "cognitive constructivism." Its recent research has documented the prevalence of "automatic thinking" or "mindlessness" within human cognition.[3] Such analysis suggests that apparently thoughtful and engaged action may actually be repetition of long-settled, prior ideas. Our responses may be so routine and automatized that active reflection actually becomes unnecessary. Those operating in this fashion are engaged in an automated process, not consciousness-raising intellectual activity. Accessing new knowledge and fostering a critical sense of oneself and others, requires educators to expose students to ideas, settings, and perspectives that actively destabilize and de-center their prior understandings.[4] Swiss developmental psychologist Jean Piaget, whose body of work informs this research, refers to such situations as "disequilibria," the states of disjuncture which "force the subject to go beyond his current state and strike out in new directions."[5]

Here, we argue that the contemporary economic crisis offers such a moment of disjuncture. This specific moment of rupture can enrich our students' grasp of the normative and ethical elements packed within our form of contemporary economic organization.[6] Thus, in addition to "instructing" students with regard to the complex "facts" of the crisis, we suggest a more diffuse approach involving the use of utopian socialist literature. We argue that utopian socialist literature, likely alien to most American college students, enables the critical distance necessary to analyze capitalism as "outsiders," rather than within the volatility of the existing capitalist system. In particular, we focus on the utopian socialist literature of Edward Bellamy, and engage in qualitative analysis of our in-classroom use of the novel *Looking Backward* at various stages within the crisis to foster critical analysis. We close by discussing the value of disequilibria in teaching economic crisis and the responsibilities, which economic "hard times" thrust upon political science educators.

Piaget, cognitive constructivism, and the educational potential of "hard times"

Cognitive constructivism, as initially formulated by Swiss psychologist Jean Piaget, is one attempt to explain the ways in which human beings acquire and structure knowledge. Piaget's thinking is complex and underwent many shifts throughout his long career. The core assumption of the constructivist approach is that "individuals are actively involved throughout their life in constructing personal meaning from their experiences."[7] Cognitive constructivism is rooted in the idea that we, ". . . actively restructure knowledge in highly individual ways, basing fluid intellectual configurations on existing knowledge, formal instructional experiences, and a host of other influences that mediate understanding."[8]

From this perspective, a variety of interpersonal and contextual features shape our thinking as we confront new information, as well as how we respond in an educational context.[9] These manifest themselves in cognitive **"equilibrations,"** attempts to apply previously held knowledge as well as to amend our understanding of concepts in the face of more robust knowledge. We begin from a point of **"disequilibrium,"** cognitive disjunctures which "force the subject to go beyond his current state and strike out in new directions."[10] Such moments entail the abandonment of obsolete ideas in favor of newer understandings (**"accommodation"**). Yet we remain attached to preconceived frameworks, which assist us in understanding our world (**"assimilation"**).[11] Piaget refers to the mental and physical response structures created through this process as **"schemata."** These structures enable comprehension of the deluge of information that we encounter in our daily lives.[12] Yet they form within a deeply individualized social and contextual environment, which explains personal variations in cognitive development.

Piaget's model of cognitive development yields insights crucial to pedagogical practice. First, our minds naturally order our experiences, and we actively seek to dispel "cognitive dissonance" through strategies of assimilation or accommodation. The human mind cannot comfortably hold incommensurable ideas simultaneously. Inherent cognitive characteristics will eventually compel us to accept one idea at the expense of others. In this sense, "equilibrations" are an essential part of both cognitive development and intellectual maturity, helping us to dispense with prior, incomplete understandings. As Windschitl notes, the core pedagogical point we draw from Piaget's model is that the "teacher's task is to help students move from their inaccurate ideas toward conceptions more in consonance with what has been validated by disciplinary communities."[13] Harmony, balance, and equilibrium are essential in our pursuit of knowledge.[14]

Yet this model also suggests that pure dismissal of elements which breach one's existing schemata can cripple cognitive development, producing inability to accommodate or assimilate new experiences. Piaget argues that "conflict" and "perturbation" are vital to cognitive development.[15] Aspects that problematize our existing schemata are intrinsically important, even if they do not displace prior modes of action and thought. Piaget asserts, "even if [disequilibrium] only stabilizes that action, enrichment has nevertheless occurred . . . perturbing elements, and compensatory accommodation to them, engender new knowledge."[16] Thus, we must continually engage intellectual elements that destabilize our prior-held ideas and actions. Conflict is the intellectual pathway to more advanced forms of knowledge and thought.

Researchers within educational psychology have developed Piaget's ideas concerning knowledge acquisition and the dichotomy between "automatic thinking," relying upon past schemata with little-to-no accommodation or assimilation, and "mindfulness," a more cognitively rich form of thinking that amends previously held equilibria.[17] Many educational psychologists have explored "sociocognitive conflict" to identify "productive elements in social interaction that lead as a causal mechanism to cognitive developing."[18] Again drawing implications for teaching, Windschitl notes that Piagetian ideas have fostered ". . . teaching strategies which involve challenge to, or development of, the initial ideas of the learners and ways of making new ideas accessible to them" as well as "the provision of opportunities to utilize new ideas in a range of contexts."[19]

To this end, Piaget's work has also been marshaled to support diversity in higher education.[20] Gurin argues that racially and ethnically diverse settings have a much higher probability of exposing students to the settings that Piaget and others support as essential for engaged thinking and acquiring knowledge.[21] Building upon the work of Diane Ruble, Gurin claims that "uncertainty, instability, and possible anxiety" lead to *attitudinal* difference, which negates stultifying traditions that reward regurgitating previously held ideas.[22] These situations provide

> novelty and unfamiliarity due to the transition to a new intellectual environment, opportunities to identify discrepancies between students with distinct pre-college social experiences, [and] diversity as a source of multiple and different perspectives.[23]

Gurin and her colleagues argue that diversity in postsecondary education fosters cognitive disequilibria that ultimately produce tangible benefits for society, and democracy in general. Students come to understand and experience new social connections, and thus understand how their lives are ". . . necessarily shaped by others."[24]

Cognitive constructivism postulates that exposure to previously alien ideas and experiences constitute a precondition for cultivated thinking in one's political life. In relation to the topic at hand, if we cannot cultivate a critical orientation in our students, this inability may hinder our ability to collectively address the deficiencies of the economic system. In particular, "automatic thinking" may constitute a significant obstacle, blocking fundamental changes in attitudes and institutions. From this perspective, the present crisis constitutes a moment of opening, rather than imposing constraints upon our teaching. The recent economic circumstances are the very types of unprecedented experiences that break our complacency with the status quo, potentially fostering cognitive and intellectual growth. The crisis constitutes a moment of disequilibrium, from which we might begin to critically interrogate our understandings of the capitalist economy.

Thus far, the primary application of cognitive constructivism to higher education has examined the intellectual growth emerging out of new forms of interpersonal social interaction characterized by greater diversity. We agree that greater diversity can foster the types of intellectual enlargement which Piaget hypothesizes. We nevertheless feel that this sells the insights of cognitive constructivism short, focusing only on the *social* disequilibria and minimizing the *contextual*. Piaget posits that subjects transcend repetition of prior knowledge, gaining enlarged intellectual capacities, not simply through social exposure to diverse others. Rather, Piaget's point is diverse *experiences,* whether interpersonal or new circumstances, generate a desire to move beyond existing cognitive categories and seek new modes of understanding. On this basis, the crucial pedagogical insight is not merely to devise ways to expose our students to new voices and identities (though this is no doubt a crucial and enriching part of any contemporary pedagogical mission). Educators must also marshal those events and experiences alien for the majority of their students.

The current economic crisis is one such example. Traditional American university students are unlikely to have ever experienced a large-scale economic crisis. Having never endured a dysfunctional economy, these students may have never had reason to question capitalism's superiority as a mode of organization. We are all likely aware of the types of student responses such an orientation can produce: "Capitalism is the most efficient way to run the economy," or "State planning never works. That's why communism fell and capitalism won." We are not implying students offering such opinions are simply regurgitating information heard elsewhere, or dismissing that our students may have thoughtful reasons for holding these views. However, in light of the contemporary experience, such statements merit further scrutiny. Stylized binary oppositions between "capitalism" and "socialism" become problematic. Speaking in such terms drastically simplifies the varieties that either system might take. Given the present scale of government involvement, our students are forced to evaluate the ways in which significant levels of state control need not mean a centrally planned economy. Furthermore, when the economy fails to deliver in so many ways at once—credit, employment, symmetry of information for consumers and producers—we can rightly question its status as the most efficient option available.

While these sorts of realizations need not entail outright *rejection* of capitalism, they do create problems for existing assumptions and, hopefully, force a more critical and reflective attitude. They send our students scrambling for new ways of making sense of the capitalist economy. In short, they provide students with an impetus through which they might expand their intellectual capacities concerning capitalist economic relations. Enabling students to effectively take hold of this moment of disequilibrium and branch out beyond prior schemata and modes of understanding is the responsibility which economic "hard times" have thrust upon us as educators.

Past (im)possibilities and present potentialities—the role of utopian socialist literature

Utilizing disequilibrating moments to critically interrogate the underpinnings of the capitalist economy is a daunting pedagogical challenge. At the moment that students seek guidance, we are denying their impulse toward certainty, propelling them to embrace disequilibrium. Yet there are good reasons for this. Pragmatic approaches focusing strictly upon immediate policy options risk "shutting down" this moment of uncertainty. Additionally, pedagogical strategies where the professor acts as a "sounding board" for the students' questions about the crisis, seeking simply to "dispense expertise," will fail to inspire the type of *internal* questioning through which students reshape prior notions or ideas. Rather, the solution lies in creatively structuring exercises and settings that *preserve* this moment of flux and enable students to engage deeper questions that reside under the surface of the crisis. Admittedly, one could achieve this goal in many different ways. In this section, we examine utopian socialist literature as a means to do so.

To clarify at the outset, utopian socialism, as we employ it here, emerges out of a broad set of ideas originating in the nineteenth century. This strain of socialism took a different route than the "scientific socialism" which Marx and Engels were developing at the same time. In using the term, we are referring to the socialist tradition associated with the likes of Simon Linguet, Saint-Simon, Fourier, and Robert Owen, as well as the entire tradition of thinkers, literature, and utopian communities which followed in their wake. We are not referring to the nonutopian insights of late Marx, or those who later sought to implement state-socialist economies in practice.[25] One would be hard-pressed to call utopian socialism a "challenger" to capitalism, due to the minute scale of its real-world manifestations. In fact, utopian socialist thought offers promise in thinking about contemporary capitalism precisely because it avoids such questions. As Manuel and Manuel write, within utopian socialist thought, diagnosis of the social ills takes place on the moral and psychological levels, and the demonstration of the cure is on the same plane. Without great interest in or any understanding of the realities of the economic process . . . utopians focused upon the psychological consequences of the privatization of objects, both persons and things.[26]

Thus, utopianism fosters active consideration of the psychosocial impacts a capitalist society imposes on its members. Students may ultimately disagree with the critical view utopian socialist thought offers, but the hope is that they pause long enough to *critically engage* previously unconsidered elements of capitalist life.

Preliminary considerations: Reading utopian socialist literature

The characteristics which make utopian socialist thought a valuable resource also make it challenging terrain for students. Such are likely unknown to them, embedded in unfamiliar historical controversies. To avoid confusion, the professor must make clear to the students at the outset *why* they are reading this work, and the different ways they might read the text. This involves not only introductory information on the emergence of modern capitalism, but also exposure to the historical context of the work. Furthermore, it involves teaching students *how* to read such works. We suggest that there are essentially three ways for students (and educators) to approach utopian socialist thought. *First,* one could read utopian socialist thought as a **blueprint** for a new society or form of organization. By this framework, the text gives us particulars and a concrete vision of a better, even "perfect," alternative that overcomes the existing order's deficiencies. Ideally, though often with varying degrees of clarity, utopian blueprints offer us the concrete steps by which we transition from one mode of organization to another.

Second, we could read utopian socialist thought as **an attempt at moral judgement.** Reading utopian socialist thought in this way, we see it as an effort to shift our understanding of contemporary economic forms. Through this lens, the author problematizes the current system of economic organization, showing us that it is only one possible state of affairs, and drawing attention to its precarious nature. The author emphasizes to us that things could always be different. The best explanation of utopianism comes to us from political theorist Judith Shklar. She depicts utopian political thought as

an attack on both the doctrine of original sin, which imposes rigid limits on men's social potentialities, and on all actual societies which always fall so short of men's real capacities. The object of these models however, was never to set up the perfect community but simply to bring moral judgment to bear on the social misery to which men have so unnecessarily reduced themselves. For the fault is not in God, fate, or nature but in ourselves—where it will remain. To recognize this, to accept it, to contemplate and to judge: this is the function of utopian political thought.[27]

Shklar's eloquent insights suggest the liberating possibilities such works engender within the classroom, creating space for judgement and reassessment of our role in the prevailing state of affairs, denying convenient impulses to attribute blame to circumstances beyond human control.

One of the most valuable elements of reading utopianism in this light is to invite reflection upon conceptions of *human nature*. Our understandings of human nature, the potentialities and limitations of mankind, inform our notion of what is possible in systems of political and economic organization. To be clear, considering economic institutions in light of human shortcomings is a vital imperative. However, appeals to the limitations of human nature also taint our ability to think beyond that which exists and imaginatively construct normative political conceptions beyond the status quo. If we are engaged in a debate about reforming capitalism's excesses, and our opponent argues that these simply flow from what human beings *are*, the space for reflection dramatically shrinks. Appeals to human nature can act as a bludgeon for progressive alternatives, potentially trapping humanity within widespread suffering or injustice.

Third, and lastly, we can read utopian socialist thought as a **challenge to the reader**. Through this lens, utopian socialist thought is not simply about judgement. It is about action and agency. It attempts to jar the reader out of complacency, engaging them in efforts to change the existing system. It is an attack on the reader's contentment with the economic order's shortcomings. This is a more activist reading, frequently found within utopian works aiming at mass appeal, such as literature or film. Yet the goal is not simply to compel the reader to individualized moral judgement, though this is likely operative, but also to foster concerted political action.

Of these three possible modes of reading utopian socialist thought, the most promising for our efforts to teach the economic crisis is as moral judgement. The depiction of a society far-removed from our own forces students to step "outside" of the existing order, and by extension, "outside" of the schemata used to comprehend their economic system. It invites and sustains disequilibria as the writer ". . . has the capacity to achieve a measure of distance from the day-to-day controversies of the marketplace and to view the life of his society in light of its manifold possibilities."[28] By contrast, reading utopian socialist thought as a blueprint or as a catalyst for action risks premature suspension of such disequilibria. Such interpretations ground discussion in the pragmatic realm of what we can accomplish given existing societal structures. This pushes students away from the more critical, introspective realm whereby they engage underlying dynamics behind current economic realities, or ethical merits of current economic structures.

Thus, important responsibilities lay in the hands of the professor assigning such material. As educators, we must clarify that, while reading utopian thought as a "political blueprint" is one possible mode of interpretation, often the original authorial intent, there exist far richer rewards by approaching such works as calls for moral judgement. Absent careful guidance, such works can actually *reinforce* preexisting schemata in the eyes of the students. Without these preliminary explanations, reading about such fantastical ideal societies with "perfect" institutions may cause students to instinctively recoil, seeking stability in engrained ideas about human nature, the potentialities of their own societies, and "natural impulses" of humans. The benefit of fostering critical reflection of previously held schemata is a gratifying pedagogical reward.

Practical considerations: Utopian socialist thought in the classroom

In this final section of the chapter, we examine our classroom experiences with utopian socialist literature, occurring over five semesters during various stages of economic crisis. Here, we discuss how we integrated this material into our larger courses, and the insights and challenges occurring within the classroom. From Spring 2009 to Fall 2010, we taught five separate sections of an introductory course in political theory at a large state university in the northeastern United States. Throughout this period, the American economic system buckled under the stress of the economic crisis as policymakers tried to prevent economic collapse. With these developments unfolding in American life and deeply affecting our students, we thought it appropriate to focus extensively on political economy. The entire second half of these courses was devoted to competing perspectives on organization of the economy. The course began with works by Strauss, Wolin, and Berlin on the nature of political theory before surveying Western political thought, beginning with antiquity and leading up through the Enlightenment. The second half of the course opened with foundational works in political economy, beginning with selections from Adam Smith's *Wealth of Nations*, followed by the work of Marx and Engels. After an interlude with utopian socialism, and the screening of a film on which our students wrote a paper, we closed the course with the contemporary libertarianism of Nozick, the liberal interventionism of Rawls, as well as perspectives from critical theorists.

Much of the initial focus on political economy involved discussions about the contemporary capitalist economy in which the students reside. These initial classes entailed the students attempting to reconcile their own economic experience with the ideals offered by Marx and Smith. What we emphasized was that no *pure* economic system exists, that virtually any real-world system will incorporate elements of decentralized decision-making by individuals and centralized decision-making by state and corporate entities. Furthermore, we pushed them to compare theory and practice, targeting potential disjunctures between the hypothetical models offered by prior thinkers and eventual practice. Having established intellectual foundations, our classes could now begin to examine utopian socialist literature.

As mentioned at the outset, we assigned Edward Bellamy's utopian socialist novel, *Looking Backward: 2000–1887*.[29] In Bellamy's novel, we follow Julian West, an upper-class gentleman living in Boston in the late nineteenth century as his society endures the birth-pangs of industrial capitalism. While West is aware of inequality and inefficiency of his time, he feels that human beings are incapable of transcending these problems. For him, the world of 1887 is the only political, economic, and social order of which human beings are capable. Then, in an extraordinary turn of events, West falls asleep, awaking 113 years later. In the care of a family named the Leetes, he learns that Boston of 2000 is a socialist utopia. The state oversees production, commerce, and finance. Individuals perform compulsory industrial service for 24 years, collecting universal shares in the income of the nation, rather than individual wages. Democratic control over one's labor, hour reductions, and a system of nonmonetary adulation replace wages as incentives for hard work. An expansive state-funded system of education ensures that talent and tenacity, rather than wealth, are the means to social betterment. Due to these reforms, this utopian society eliminates neediness, inequality, even war, and criminality. While this is a novel about literal *awakening*, it is also a novel about intellectual awakening. Through his exposure to this alien future, West realizes that his prior society, to paraphrase Shklar, had fallen so short of its real capacities and unnecessarily reduced itself to social misery. Beyond the narrative itself, this is the realization which Bellamy seeks to instill in his readers. His work daringly asserts that nineteenth-century capitalist society is only one possible world. To paraphrase the contemporary alter-globalization movement, *other worlds are possible.*

Aside from an initial introductory lecture about the three ways in which we might "read" utopian thought and Bellamy's purpose in writing the novel, the format of these classes was free form and discussion-based. Though initially hesitant to introduce the students to complex new material while providing minimal direct guidance, this worked quite well within the classroom. We spent several classes working through the text. However, as suggested before, the purpose was not to assess whether such a sweeping set of proposals constituted a potential *solution* to the economic crisis in the United States today. Rather, Bellamy acted as a foil to sustain the disequilibria brought about by the economic crisis, and think about the inevitability of the economic order, as it exists in our society.

First, the story of Julian West is a literary presentation of the disequilibrium the students themselves are experiencing. West was lulled into complacency by an economic system which he thought to be unavoidable, and from which he garnered significant advantage. Upon waking, he struggles, adjusting to a different reality and recognizing the cracks in the façade of the nineteenth-century economy, insights virtually impossible while imbricated within that order. In the same way, many of our students had taken a stable (if inequitable) economy for granted. An extraordinary chain-of-events now forced them to confront its deficiencies and the ways in which they were potentially complacent with its stability. Prior schemata and modes of understanding were more likely to seem deficient.

In discussing the novel with our students, we asked, "Will we look back on the dawn of the twenty-first century in the same way that West looked back on his time?" This forced students to confront their *contemporary* experiences of disequilibria, yet in an analytical way, maintaining distance from the uncertainty occurring in their own lives. The cogent responses that this exercise provoked impressed us. Students would admit that while the late nineteenth century's inadequacies—lack of labor representation, violent strike-breaking, absence of social safety nets—were more severe, there are aspects of the contemporary economy which, one day, will seem obsolete to us. Of course, students differed considerably in which aspects they felt would eventually be obsolete, but the point is, it provoked the discussion. Coupling this question with Julian West's experience removed them from immediate and nonreflective questions of "what is to be done?" propelling them into the more imaginative, critical realm of how future generations will critically evaluate our contemporary economic practice.

Second, West's narrative engaged students in reflection regarding the role of the state. In the emergent moments of the economic crisis, a student asked whether the proposed government bailouts and takeovers meant "the end of capitalism." It was necessary to explain to him that while the capitalist ideal is limited state interference, there are always exceptions. Only a very rigid interpretation of capitalism would view more government involvement as "the end" of capitalism. *Looking Backward* provides the educator a means to demonstrate the wider spectrum of state involvement in the economy, yet it does so absent the negative connotations that accompany "real world examples" of socialism such as the USSR or Cuba. Furthermore, Bellamy's calls for reforms such as universal public education or an expansive network of collective bargaining for labor foretell later developments in the trajectory of American economic life.

In demonstrating how capitalism, in order to survive, must at times co-opt the platform of its challengers, *Looking Backward* enabled us to loosen students' tendencies to view greater state involvement with unreflective alarm. At the very least, they were able to recognize that such changes are not unprecedented and constitute an attempt to strengthen capitalism, rather than its death knell. While nearly all students considered Bellamy's proposals for complete state control of the economy undesirable, their discussions of when state involvement should occur were thoughtful and sophisticated. In the course of our classes, it became clear that simply arguing that government involvement naturally induced a slide toward oppression would probably not pass muster. At the very least, one would need to offer further justifications for this view. Some students grounded their arguments against Bellamy in the philosophical justifications of capitalism given by Smith. Others pointed to debates raging about the American government's response to the crisis as evidence that Bellamy's transition could not be voluntary or peaceful. Rather, initial collectivization and redistribution efforts would almost certainly have to employ state coercion, if not massacre. While students found ways to justify a measured version of Bellamy's suggestions, the majority found the likelihood of violence impossible to stomach, rejecting the scheme of centralization he proposed.

Our initial fears were that any such debates would generate largely "automatic" responses, to use Piaget's language, and that students would resort to prior, internalized ideas regarding the advantages or drawbacks of the American capitalist economy. Yet our students adapted their ideas when challenged, suggesting that in this setting, the class was able to move beyond automatic thinking. Furthermore, we were struck by the concessions and amendments which students were able to make to their own positions in the course of discussion. Only a handful of students took, and consistently held, positions in an "automatic" fashion. The introduction of Bellamy's radical utopian proposals seemed to soften ideological divisions in the room, as the alternative was no longer the position of one's fellow student. Though ideological difference persisted, the tone of the exchanges seemed less confrontational than we had seen earlier in the same courses.

Third, the classes utilizing Bellamy's text were able to foster an insightful discussion on the nature of incentives and the question of wage inequality in ways that would have been difficult without a radical utopian proposal to consider. At various stages in the economic crisis, commentators condemned gaps between CEO and lower-level employees, or the continuation of executive bonuses despite companies' insolvency. The crisis forced consideration of the structure of wages and benefits in the United States and many, particularly on the ideological left, did not like what they saw. Yet our discussion in the classroom delved deeper into this question. Bellamy's proposal forces us to think about the institution of wages itself: Why are we paid a wage? Why are some paid more than others? Is there an alternative form of incentivizing work, one that does not foster stark levels of inequality?

In the course of our discussions, the class frequently returned to questions of wages and incentives. In general, the students felt that wage labor was a desirable institution that would characterize economic life for the foreseeable future. Yet students probed the institutions of wages in intriguing ways. Many cited nonwage elements of their working lives that problematize notions that they were simply working for a paycheck—the importance of reputation, self-satisfaction, commitment to fellow employees, noneconomic recognition by family, friends, and co-workers. Thus, their rejection of Bellamy's nonwage-based system of incentives was not indicative of "automatic thinking." We had expected to confront the familiar refrain, "if everyone earns the same, where is the incentive to try harder?" and some students said just this. Yet even these students coupled their rejection with sentiments sympathetic to the viability of nonwage incentives, illuminating ways in which such structures already exist.

Consideration of wages, and the inequality which a wage-based labor system creates, produced discussions tapping into the character of American economic life generally. In addition to examining the procedural necessity of wages, students explored the *ethos* that drives wages structurally. What is more, they did so largely without our prodding. Students remarked that many of the contemporary problems associated with the economy were driven by the unrealistic expectations of economic actors, a set of expectations that they saw linked to the wage system. For wages to *continue* to effectively incentivize, workers must expect that there is upward mobility. Yet, as our students pointed out, workers often overestimate the upward wage mobility, which they, as individuals, possess. Individuals even take on financial liability as incentive to continue to labor. One student, for example, told of how he had bought a brand new car just a few years earlier, despite his limited means to finance it and successfully make his payments. Now, struggling to work full-time while going to school, and having already suffered repossession, he regretted that decision. He admitted he had bought the car for many reasons, but one resonated with the students and led to further discussion. He thought that a large monthly car payment would "keep him honest;" he would work long hours to meet his financial commitments. Our initial foray into the institution of wages, which we feared would be characterized by hackneyed, unthinking responses, instead produced critical reflection not only on the institution of wages, but also on the larger ethos which drives wages. For some, it even provoked personal reflection about their attitudes toward debt, consumption, and earning potential.

Fourth, and *lastly,* our discussion of Bellamy lead to numerous reflections upon the "inevitability" of capitalist structures. At the outset of this section of the course, we would ask students the open-ended question, "What do you associate with the word 'capitalism'?" What were striking were those aspects which students would *not* mention. Frequently, we would hear things like "markets," "money," "supply and demand," "production," "growth," and "freedom." Yet in asking what enables capitalism to function, students would be hard-pressed to flesh out its specifics. We initially thought that perhaps this was indicative of lack of information. Perhaps students only knew capitalism in the vaguest terms, not understanding its internal workings. Yet, as our subsequent discussions demonstrated this was not the case. Prior to reading Adam Smith, many students could already recite his central premises verbatim. Students already possessed a sense of what capitalist economic principles looked like in practice—being embedded within a capitalist society.

As we continued this exercise over several semesters, it became clear that some aspects of capitalism which the students experienced were so ubiquitous that they encountered them primarily as "facts of life" rather than malleable characteristics of the capitalist economy. The most glaring example we encountered was advertising. Through follow-up questions and prodding, we could usually get students to flesh out capitalism's other concrete dimensions such as currency, wages, capital, and credit. Yet we found ourselves struggling to get our students to introduce advertising as a vital dimension of capitalist economic life. Thankfully, in large public universities with shrinking custodial budgets, we nearly always had student-targeted advertising pasted on the wall, enabling us to simply point while asking students to identify the thing toward which we were gesturing. From there, we would often have engaging discussions about advertising and the ways in which it drives our economy, and affects our own lives. The problem was not lack of awareness; it is simply impossible to live within American society and not be acquainted with advertising. Rather, it was the recognition that advertising is *not* an inherent feature of our lives, and that other realities were possible.

The value of *Looking Backward* is that it brings those types of destabilizing realizations into sharper relief. The novel shows us that things we consider simply "part of the scenery" actually perform a function, uphold a purpose, and support a specific economic order. In this sense, Bellamy's novel forces disequilibrium, exposing the contingency of prior modes of economic functioning. Bellamy addresses this very example within his novel. Julian West, exploring twenty-first century Boston, is confused by the total lack of advertising, where once billboards and placards had been plastered onto nearly every visible public surface. In the context of the novel, it is no longer necessary. The existence of only one firm, the state, has eliminated competition. The state distributes information about its products according to a tightly regulated, transparent process. This is but one example of contemporary economic life which we might take for granted and which Bellamy exposes. There are numerous others: the behavior of salespeople, the logic of inheritance, desire for consumer objects, industrialization's externalities, the economic impulse behind specialization, the definition of public goods, or how many years we ought to devote to labor. Again, Bellamy's interjections remind us of the ways in which we naturalize what is still a product of human agency, something over which we retain control.

Conclusion

The contemporary "hard times" have brought unexpected challenges in making students understand their political responsibilities, and prepare them for those that they will inherit. Revitalizing our national economy, and rethinking our personal attitudes toward consumption, debt, and consumerism *will* constitute challenges that our students will face, even if they have not already begun to do so. It is incumbent upon us to devise ways of preparing them for these challenges. Yet every crisis engenders opportunity. While the novelty and complexity of the economic crisis makes our jobs "harder" in one sense, manifold pedagogical possibilities have opened with regard to engaging the assumptions underlying contemporary capitalism. Such moments suspend unquestioned assumptions and rupture our complacency with the status quo. In a realm of human affairs where cynics often caustically shun "ideals" as dangerous, moments such as these make us second-guess such dismissal. The current crisis is a moment of societal disequilibrium.

Yet such moments of rupture are hard to sustain. As Piaget's model shows us, we seek a return to consonance and harmony. We cannot reside in contingency and flux forever. Our moments of disequlibria, though the basis for cognitive and intellectual growth, are episodic. At some point, we all devise schemata and heuristics to make sense of complexity. The content of these new schemata in relation to capitalist economic life in the United States remains unclear. Our responsibility as educators is not to capitalize upon this moment to compel students toward the economic alternative we wish to see. Rather, we must ensure that the new incarnation of capitalism, which all observers seem to agree must emerge out of the crisis, is one about which our students have actively thought, both in its practicability and ethical desirability. Given the depth of the current crisis, and the scope of the challenges associated with rebuilding our beleaguered economy, it is not an exaggeration to suggest that our collective fate hinges upon our ability to achieve this goal.

[Please see the companion website for the book. Details are listed on the back cover of the book.]

Notes

1 Simply put, subprime mortgages are home loans granted to those who pose greater credit risks than borrowers traditionally eligible for such funds.

2 Kirk Shinkle, "Damage Report 2008: US Household Wealth Down $10 Trillion," *U.S. News and World Report* (December 12, 2008).

3 Robert Glaser, "Education and Thinking: The Role of Knowledge," *American Psychologist* 39(2) (1984): 93–104; Jean Piaget, *The Equilibration of Cognitive Structures: The Central Problem of Intellectual Development* (Chicago, IL: University of Chicago Press, 1985); Paul A. Frewen, Elspeth M. Evans, Nicholas Maraj, David J. Dozois, and Kate Partridge, "Letting Go: Mindfulness and Negative Automatic Thinking," *Cognitive Therapy and Research* 32(6) (2008): 758–74; Charis Psaltis, Gerard Duveen, and Anne-Nelly Perret-Clermont, "The Social and the Psychological: Structure and Context in Intellectual Development," *Human Development* 52(5) (2009): 291–312.

4 Diane Ruble, Ronda Eisenburg, and E. Tory Higgins, "Developmental Changes in Achievement Evaluation: Motivational Implications of Self-Other Differences," *Child Development* 65(4) (1994): 1095–110; Patricia Gurin, *Expert Report of Patricia Gurin – Gratz et al. v. Bollinger et al.,* No. 97–75321 (E.D. Mich.), *Grutter et al. v. Bollinger et al.,* No. 97–75928 (E.D. Mich.) (1999). Accessed December 9, 2009, from www.vpcomm.umich.edu/admissions/legal/expert/gurintoc.html; Patricia Gurin, Eric L. Dey, Sylvia Hurtado, and Gerald Gurin, "Diversity and Higher Education: Theory and Impact on Educational Outcomes," *Harvard Educational Review* 72(3) (2002): 330–66; Patricia Gurin, Biren A. Nagda, and Gretchen E. Lopez, "The Benefits of Diversity in Education for Democratic Citizenship," *The Journal of Social Issues* 60(1) (2003): 17–34.

5 Piaget, *The Equilibration of Cognitive Structures,* 10.

6 We should note that the goal is not fostering within students a "rejection" of capitalism. It is only to examine unquestioned assumptions with regard to its desirability. If a student unquestioningly supportive of capitalism, pauses to critically examine it only to return to supporting it, this would not be a "failure." On the contrary, it would be exactly the sort of reflection cognitive constructivism attempts to foster.

7 Robert L. Burden, "Psychology in Education and Instruction," in *International Handbook of Psychology,* ed. Kurt Pawlik and Mark R. Rosenzweig (London: Sage, 2000): 439.

8 Mark Windschitl, "Framing Constructivism in Practice as the Negotiation of Dilemmas: An Analysis of the Conceptual, Pedagogical, Cultural, and Political Challenges Facing Teachers," *Review of Educational Research* 72(2) (2002): 140.

9 Jean Piaget, "Problems of Equilibration," in *The Essential Piaget,* ed. Howard E. Gruber and Jean Jacques Voneche (Northvale, NJ: Jason Aronson, 1995 [1975]): 838.

10 Piaget, *The Equilibration of Cognitive Structures,* 10. Piaget argues that our initial state prior to actively seeking knowledge is one of "profound disequilibria."

11 Ibid., Ch. 1.

12   Jean Piaget, "Intellectual Operations and their Development," in *The Essential Piaget,* ed. Howard E. Gruber and Jean Jacques Voneche (Northvale, NJ: Jason Aronson, 1995 [1963]): 349.

13   Windschitl, *Framing Constructivism,* 132.

14   Piaget, *The Equilibration of Cognitive Structures,* 15.

15   Ibid., Ch. 1.

16   Ibid.

17   Ellen J. Langer, "Rethinking the Role of Thought in Social Interaction," in *New Directions in Attribution Research Vol. 2,* ed. John H. Harvey, William Ickes, and Robert F. Kidd (Hillsdale, NJ: Lawrence Erlbaum Associates, 1978): 36–58; Susan T. Fiske, "Social Cognition and Social Perception," *Annual Review of Psychology* 44 (February 1993): 155–94; James L. Hilton and William von Hippel, "Stereotypes," *Annual Review of Psychology* 47 (February 1996): 237–71; Frewen et al., "Letting Go."

18   Psaltis et al., "The Social and the Psychological," 300.

19   Windschitl, *Framing Constructivism,* 140.

20   See in particular the research of Patricia Gurin and her colleagues, "Diversity and Higher Education: Theory and Impact on Educational Outcomes."

21   Gurin et al., "Diversity in Higher Education," 338.

22   Ibid.

23   Ibid.

24   Ibid., 339.

25   In such practical settings, the utopian principles which once grounded such regimes are largely absent existing only in ". . . a recrudescence of futuristic utopian speech on ceremonial occasions." See Frank E. Manuel and Fritzie P. Manuel, *Utopian Thought in the Western World* (Cambridge, MA: Belknap/ Harvard University Press, 1979): 803.

26   Manuel and Manuel, *Utopian Thought in the Western World,* 557.

27   Judith Shklar, *Men & Citizens: A Study of Rousseau's Social Theory* (Cambridge, UK: Cambridge University Press, 1969): 2.

28   Manuel and Manuel, 24.

29   Edward Bellamy, *Looking Backward 2000–1887* (Oxford, UK: Oxford World Classics, 2009 [1888]).

PART TWO

Art and visual media

Introduction

Art and visual media, both in explicitly political forms (political cartoons), and more implicit political variants (graphic novels) present unique ways for educators to move beyond the written word. The use of such mediums harnesses the power of visually presented political phenomena, and brings to bear the immediacy of visual imagery on the educational experience. Through such methods, students engage the ubiquitous nature of political imagery over time, as well as the ways in which a startling or arresting image can shape political consciousness, while shifting political attitudes and values. The visual nature of this media also provides pedagogical opportunities by appealing to another form of learning, helping visually oriented learners intellectually access material that is frequently presented through text and discussion. The chapters in this section offer educators guidance in moving beyond the written word, and a pedagogical means for analyzing the political themes present in visual depictions of political relations and concepts.

History is full of visual depictions of political phenomena or the use of visual depictions for political purposes. From politically charged paintings to campaign posters, from *New Yorker* cartoons to *Doonesbury*, from the work of Banksy to the omnipresent Che Guevara t-shirts on college campuses, political imagery is everywhere. As students are inundated with the presence of political illustrations, the importance of studying these graphic representations increases. When the visual presentations of the political relate to themes and materials already covered in classes focusing on politics, the integration of art and other visual media makes sense. However, knowing how best to introduce, analyze, and discuss these depictions can be a tricky process often relying on repeated trial and error. When the political messages of any visual media are implicit, knowing how to integrate the visual media can be even more difficult, leaving curious educators wondering where to begin or too hesitant to even try. The chapters in this section offer practical guidance for introducing visual media into a college classroom.

In the first chapter in this section, Conners focuses her discussion on political cartoons. Conners discusses the means by which educators can use political cartoons to stimulate discussion, contextualize political events, as well as use political cartoons as part of course assignments. Her chapter presents both pedagogical guidance and justification for integrating political cartoons into college classrooms studying politics.

Worchester's chapter also looks at a comic medium, but instead of short-form political cartoons, he discusses the use of long-form comics (graphic novels) to teach political topics. Worchester discusses fiction, nonfiction, and historical-fiction graphic novels, emphasizing how these can be integrated into a classroom to cover a large variety of political topics. These graphic novels range from overtly political to those with much more implicit, but certainly present, political content, allowing for a variety of uses from alternative texts to complimentary readings.

Increasingly we live in a visual world. As politicians, pundits, and social commentators continue to embrace visual media, teaching students to evaluate the political messages within these media will be crucial to fostering a citizenry that is capable of evaluating the visual realm of politics. From televised political ads to politically charged YouTube videos, politics is becoming stunningly visual at a rate that is ever increasing. To focus on text at the expense of the visual is to ultimately do a disservice to the students we encounter in our courses. The chapters within this section provide guidance for educators to use art and visual media effectively within the classroom. Employing art and visual media effectively can lead to engaged students, and better retention of course material. Moreover, teaching students how to analyze visual messages, as well as textual ones, will leave them better prepared for the world in which we all live.

CHAPTER FOUR

Laughing and learning: Using political cartoons to teach politics

Joan L. Conners

If asked to think of the visuals of politics, a number of symbols may come to mind: images of patriotism such as the Statue of Liberty, the bald eagle, or Uncle Sam; different visuals of the American flag, perhaps seen flying over a government building or being waved at a parade, may be easily recalled; photographs of key political events, both American as well as international, may be the focus for others. Politics is an intensely visual medium and we use visual reference points to both recall and initially comprehend political life.

One form of political visual that will be the focus of this discussion is political cartoons. While still laden with symbolism, political cartoons serve the role not only of presenting a persuasive argument or opinion, but also doing so in a potentially entertaining and humorous way. The political symbols mentioned above often appear in cartoon imagery on a variety of topics, which provide the opportunity to utilize the cartoon images in discussion and analysis of political themes in class contexts.

Just as a slogan presents a memorable catchphrase to embody a much larger issue or topic, visual symbols, including political cartoon images, present similar opportunities. The adage that "a picture is worth a thousand words" applies to the visuals of political cartoons as well. In recalling a past presidential campaign, for example, one might recall a particular photograph demonstrating a conflict from a particular debate. Or in considering the tight contest between candidates, as well as the competitive game themes that frame much of the media coverage of an election, one might remember a political cartoon image featuring the political candidates in a very close race as jockeys in a neck-and-neck horserace. These visual symbols are filled with meaning, past and present, that the reader has the potential to experience when encountering political cartoon images. They can embody and demonstrate complicated issues of politics with an elegant simplicity, which makes them excellent resources in educational situations.

Political cartoons can be a valuable pedagogical tool in teaching politics. They offer the opportunity to explore political symbols that are not as readily available in other texts. They also present potential connections of contemporary images to long-standing political themes and issues. These connections to historic symbols and issues present the opportunity to contextualize contemporary issues, which could result in greater comprehension of politics content. Additionally, as they are typically presented as single-panel images, political cartoons provide an efficient presentation of an idea into a class discussion. They are, however, so visually rich that greater class discussion of symbols and related themes can develop as well. While the focus of a political cartoon is to express an opinion in primarily visual form, the nature of the image as a cartoon is an entertaining yet substantive way to enter conversations on related political themes. Although they may offer more complex content than comic strips, students may associate the two media forms with each other, and therefore be quite receptive to discussions of them.

This chapter will describe the use of political cartoons to discuss political themes and issues, and will present examples to demonstrate the relevance of using such visuals to teach politics. First, we will discuss Symbols Systems Theory as a basis for using political cartoons as a pedagogical tool in politics courses. Then two examples of political cartoon imagery will be presented to demonstrate how cartoons could be used to teach political themes and how they can contribute to students' learning political concepts. The chapter concludes with a discussion of additional suggestions of cartoon images to incorporate into classes, issues for consideration in using such images in classroom contexts, and the potential power of popular culture allusions and metaphor imagery in political cartoons to influence learning about politics.

Symbol Systems Theory and learning from political cartoons

Scholars of teaching and learning have long recognized a role for mass media in the learning experience. The teaching and learning theory that best supports teaching with political cartoons would be Salomon's Symbol

Systems Theory.[1] Symbol Systems Theory explores the influences on how information is selected from future messages as how it is interpreted in the context of prior messages, how it is categorized with other messages, as well as how it is stored and later recalled. Scholars of teaching and learning have long recognized a role for mass media in the learning experience. This theory also relates to other learning theories, specifically Gardner's Multiple Intelligences, specifically the visual-spatial intelligence;[2] additionally, Salomon himself acknowledges the connection of Symbol Systems Theory to Schema Theory in how messages are perceived and stored.

While Symbol Systems Theory has often been applied to studying learning through mass media such as television (e.g. *Sesame Street*) or film, the tenets of the theory also extend to the more fixed visual media of political cartoons. According to Salomon, mass media are "modes of expression and communication, based on technologies, that give rise to new symbol systems or to new blends of symbol systems. By focusing on the symbol systems of media, we are able to ignore the common characteristics of different media and can consider only the most essential or prototypical characteristics of each medium—or, what 'makes a difference'."[3] Therefore, in the processing of media messages, we rely on those symbols to help us comprehend messages, as well as associate those symbols with ones from previous messages. Salomon explains the theory by stating that media symbol systems:

> affect the acquisition of knowledge in a number of ways. First, they highlight different aspects of content. Second, they vary with respect to ease of recoding. Third, specific coding elements can save the learner from difficult mental elaborations by overtly supplanting or short-circuiting specific elaboration. Fourth, symbol systems differ with respect to how much processing they demand or allow. Fifth, symbol systems differ with respect to the kinds of mental processes they call on for recoding and elaboration.[4]

In applying the aspects of Salomon's theory to learning through political cartoons, we see a number of advantages of using such visual elements of political cartoons in learning about politics. The symbols contained in political cartoons will highlight specific themes related to political events. Across various political events students may discover similar political symbols being used, which may provide them an opportunity to organize and categorize political content together in meaningful and memorable ways for future recollection. Finally, the humorous nature of political cartoon messages presents an entertaining entry into discussions of political topics.

Salomon's conceptualization of learning by the use of symbol systems also suggests one's ability in doing so improves with repeated experiences.

So while students may not easily read the messages of a political cartoon initially, with practice, they may more efficiently and comprehensively acquire messages from such visual media. Such efficiency may also allow students to explore the visuals further for particular rhetorical devices and persuasive arguments conveyed in more subtle visuals. To this point of reinforcement or practice, Salomon says, "there should be little doubt that increased experience with coded messages improves one's skill in extracting information from such messages. However, one's experience with media's symbol systems may encompass more than the improved mastery of skills that serve better information extraction."[5] In the symbol-laden environment of contemporary politics, students need to attend to, and work to comprehend, visual political messages. While political cartoons offer perhaps a more entertaining approach than other visual political symbols, students can become attuned to the use and influence of political symbols through various "readings" of political cartoon imagery related to course content.

Gardner's categorization of visual-spatial intelligence reflects many similar concepts to Salomon's Symbol Systems in how we use this type of intelligence when encountering visual content. Gardner acknowledges visual-based intelligence as one of eight categories of intelligences or learning styles. Gardner identifies a number of skills with visual-spatial intelligence that are relevant to learning from visual images such as political cartoons: "the ability to recognize instances of the same element; the ability to transform or to recognize a transformation of one element into another; the capacity to conjure up mental imagery and then to transform that imagery."[6] These abilities directly relate to the potential learning that can occur from studying political cartoons. We will see in the examples presented below the repetition of similar visuals across political cartoons, which may then offer an individual the opportunity to categorize content together when storing it in memory. Additionally, political cartoons reinforce particular visual symbols by representing similar themes across different events, so the transformation of visual elements Gardner refers to can be studied in political cartoon imagery. Learning through the presence of allusions in political cartoons, as examined by Medhurst and DeSousa,[7] reflects not only the ability Gardner identifies of recognizing a transformation of a reference into a visual context of a cartoon, but also creating mental imagery and altering it to fit a particular message. Medhurst and DeSousa studied political cartoons specifically for their use of literary or cultural allusions, which they define as "any fictive or mythical character, any narrative form, whether drawn from legend, folklore, literature, or the electronic media."[8] Using political cartoons as part of learning about politics can provide students the opportunity to make connections to such cultural references, which may aid in their comprehension of political themes demonstrated in political cartoon visuals.

Example #1: Join, or Die

Benjamin Franklin's "Join, or Die" segmented snake image (seen in Figure 4.1) is the most familiar cartoon from American history, and the frequent subject of analysis.

The interpretation of this classic image, however, varies among sources, which could present the opportunity in a classroom setting to discuss not only different political events in history that may relate to the image, but also differing interpretations. In the American Government textbook *The Logic of American Politics* by Kernell, Jacobson, and Kousser, the "Join, or Die" image appears in the chapter on the Constitution. Accompanying the image is the following caption: "In what is recognized as America's first political cartoon, Benjamin Franklin depicts the colonies as caught in a classic collective action dilemma. If united, the colonies represent a formidable force for England to reckon with. But if any colony attempts to free ride, the collective effort will survive no better than a dismembered snake."[9]

The "Join, or Die" image was *later* used as a suggestion for the colonies to band together to confront the British.[10] However, Franklin's image was used by others to convey different interpretations of division or connection, but not Franklin's original message. "Because 'Join, or Die' " was circulated in opposition to the French and Indians, the serpent device was not initially a symbol of protest or rebellion within the British Empire, but rather it dramatically symbolized the need for well-orchestrated action against an outside threat."[11] Further analysis confirmed the earlier context for this image that "The quarrels among the colonies had long distressed Franklin for he saw, more clearly than most, that the future depended upon unity. When

FIGURE 4.1 *"Join, or Die." Pennsylvania Gazette, May 9, 1754. Benjamin Franklin.*
Source: Courtesy of the Library of Congress.

the unhappy struggle between the colonists and the French for possession of the lands west of the Alleghenies was about to break out, Franklin, urging the colonies to unite against their common foe"[12] published the "Join, or Die" cartoon. The visual importance of Franklin's persuasive symbols must also be considered; given illiteracy rates "the image itself sent a powerful reminder that should the colonies fail to join forces to fight against the Indians and the French, they would meet defeat."[13]

Regardless of the interpretation of the image, its persuasive message applies to both contexts, either facing the French or preparing to band together against the British. There is a common goal for its use: "By keying into the folk belief that a segmented serpent could reunite its parts and survive, the motto emphasized the most salient feature of [per]suasory appeal: both the colonies and serpent must join if they would live."[14]

While one context for the image is provided in a textbook description, we see other interpretations of the purpose of the "Join, or Die" image exist. An analysis of the symbolism of Franklin's image would be productive to examine how political symbols are not only created but used by others as well as interpreted in multiple ways by potential audiences. One could examine contemporary political campaigns to discover other examples of political symbols used for multiple purposes. Additionally, the interpretative differences of the same image or event, demonstrated in the use of Franklin's image would be relevant for a class discussion of related political events and issues. For example, we could compare how the Tea Party in 2010 and 2011 portrayed President Barack Obama's initiatives in health care reform to how the Republican Party portrayed those same initiatives. For the Republican Party, it may be one example among many to argue for the need for a Republican in the White House; for the Tea Party movement, the focus may be more narrowly on "Obamacare" and not linked as broadly with other concerns.

For those interested in a further focus on historical contexts of such political images, the "Join, or Die" image has also been contrasted to other early colonial images. For example, Olson conducts an extensive analysis comparing Franklin's 1754 "Join, or Die" cartoon image with his "Magna Brittania, or her Colonies Reduc'd" from 1765 that features the colonies as dismembered limbs from the female Britannia.[15] The notion of segments, and the reliance of the whole on the joining of the separate parts, is reflected in both of these images.

Beyond the introduction and context of the 1754 "Join, or Die" image, we can also compare and contrast those symbols to similar imagery reflected in cartoons addressing contemporary political issues. Two political cartoon examples are provided here as images involving different political current events that reflect Franklin's segmented snake.

If we consider Benson's cartoon of the segmented donkey (Figure 4.2) in the context of Salomon's Symbol Systems Theory, someone "reading"

FIGURE 4.2 *"Join, or Die." Arizona Republic, May 21, 2008. Steve Benson.*
Source: *By permission of Steve Benson and Creators Syndicate, Inc.*

this image might note the common language and visual symbol of the segmented snake. Given that Franklin's image was politically laden, one's schema might categorize other images in a similar manner, without needing to note any other political cues. Not all editorial cartoons are necessarily political in theme, but the snake imagery consistent in Figures 4.1 and 4.2 may automatically imply political connections for each.

To contrast the historic and contemporary images, Benson's snake does not identify specific states in the segments, as Franklin's image identified abbreviations of colonies, so the parties involved are less clear. If we consider the heads of the two images, the snake's tongue of Franklin's image is out as if ready to attack, while the donkey's wide-eyed expression in Benson's cartoon might be described as scared or uncertain.

Consistent in both images is the concept of disconnected parts that may need to join together to face a challenge or opponent. Benson's cartoon features the opponent in an image of a smiling John McCain, dressed similar to early colonial politicians, stating "Please, take your time." McCain's statement in Benson's "Join, or Die" cartoon implies the longer it takes for the Democratic voters to align themselves behind a candidate, either Barack Obama or Hillary Clinton during the 2008 Democratic primaries, the better his chances would be in the general election. The timing of this image is also relevant in order to understand the perceived discontinuity of Democrats in their vote choice. Published in late May 2008, approximately seven states had yet to hold their primaries or caucuses for the Democratic nominee for president; in the previous nine states, Barack Obama had won six races, while Hillary Clinton had won three. Depending on interpretations of past primaries and caucuses, either Obama was leading Clinton in delegates won, or Clinton had the lead in the popular vote. Obama claimed victory on June 3, 2008, when he had received a simple majority of delegates sufficient to win the Democratic nomination, which was followed by Clinton's concession of the race on June 7, 2008.

Between these two cartoon images there is already considerable material for analysis and discussion for a classroom context. In the context of Symbols System Theory, the presentation of multiple similar images would provide the opportunity for reinforcement of symbolic themes in different political contexts. Such reinforcement can provide students with a natural path for categorizing related information to use for later analysis or recollection in other political contexts.

These political cartoon images also present the opportunity for discussion of other themes in politics courses. For example, a comparison of these images would be a productive introduction to discussion of themes such as political unification, political division, the diversity of state perspectives within the collectivity of a nation, as well as persuasion and propaganda.

The second contemporary visual reflecting the segmented snake, Ariail's 2008 image (Figure 4.3), identifies various segments as issues related to energy politics, specifically alternative energy sources. The snake's head no longer represents an animal, but is instead a gas pump. Considering Salomon's Symbol Systems Theory for the context of learning from such images, the similarity in images might imply a shared political theme as well, and so these quite disparate issues might be categorized by our schema in related ways. The connection of newly learned content to previously learned content, which the visual continuity of these images offers, creates for students not only efficiency in learning, but also the opportunity to extend that understanding beyond any single isolated event. The concept of transformation of an image from visual-spatial intelligence could be practiced in this instance—what political themes are similar in these different

FIGURE 4.3 *"Join, or Die."* The State, *July 1, 2008. Robert Ariail.*
Source: *ARIAIL © 2008 Robert Ariail. Reprinted by permission of Universal Uclick for UFS. All rights reserved.*

contexts? These three political images all demonstrate the concepts of division and unification, although the parties involved is what transforms, from individual states or political groups of voters to, in Ariail's image, different arguments regarding energy politics and alternative energy resources. While the snake as segmented gas pump demonstrates a contemporary context of the image, its connection to historic images and those on other political themes situates this particular issue in a broader history of politics rather than treating it as a unique and unrelated issue from others.

While the imagery in Ariail's cartoon is similar to Franklin's and Benson's, the lack of the animal metaphor here changes the interpretation, and perhaps also the categorization of the symbols, of this cartoon when compared with the other two. What is contained in the snake-like segments here is not necessarily individuals or groups, although the segments may imply supporters of these different energy approaches. The "need to join" does not necessarily involve people, but perhaps alternative approaches to resolving the long-term energy issues of the United States. In using this cartoon image in a class discussion or project, students could examine alternative energy policies and proposals as a case study, and explore how groups in disagreement with each other may need to resolve differences in order to reach a comprehensive energy proposal. The Ariail cartoon not only encapsulates a broader set of issues in a single image, but it also provides a starting point for a discussion of those issues. This cartoon also offers a context for it in past political history with respect to divided opinions or contested solutions.

These two examples that reference Benjamin Franklin's original "Join, or Die" image demonstrate how political cartoon images can be used to raise and discuss political issues, but also to provide the opportunity to analyze broader political themes that transcend any single political issue. The use of political symbols, potentially beyond the political cartoons themselves, may also be valuable for class purposes in discussing political themes. Political cartoon images offer a concise idea on an issue, perhaps one that involves a number of competing perspectives and interests as demonstrated above. The visual shortcuts they offer to the reader can provide an efficient entry into a discussion of broader issues compared to more traditional types of texts. While the cartoons themselves may address very serious issues, they offer a potentially entertaining introduction into a topic for class discussion.

Example #2: Political party images

Discussions of partisanship and political parties present another natural connection to the use of political cartoons in class content. The donkey and elephant have evolved into iconic visual symbols of the Republican and

FIGURE 4.4 *"The Third-Term Panic."* Harper's Weekly, *November 7, 1874.*
Thomas Nast.
Source: *Courtesy of the Library of Congress.*

Democratic parties. The contemporary use of such symbols can be presented in a discussion of political parties in which the historic use of these animals, as presented in the following two images, could be incorporated. The Republican elephant originated in Thomas Nast's cartoon image "The Third-Term Panic" as seen in Figure 4.4.

Thomas Nast was a political cartoonist with *Harper's Weekly* who targeted politician William "Boss" Tweed in numerous cartoon images in the late 1860s for his involvement in corrupt politics, voter fraud during elections, and stealing public dollars. Nast's images were seen by millions of readers (who were also voters). In 1871 Tweed was voted out of office and his Tammany Hall "Ring of Thieves" collapsed, due in part to Nast's cartoon attacks, as well as negative coverage from *The New York Times*. Tweed reportedly stated the following about the potential influence of Nast's images: "Let's stop them damned pictures. I don't care so much what the papers write about me—my constituents can't read; but damn it, they can see pictures."[16] While other men involved in Tammany Hall were also featured as targets of Nast's images in cartoons, Boss Tweed embodied the corruptness of the New York City political system, and Nast "decided that in terms of stature and visual potential for mischievous menace, Bill Tweed as a target would provide the greatest opportunity for artistic development and effectiveness."[17] It was on the heels of the rise of Nast's prominence and influence in Tweed's downfall that his political party animal images rose in popularity, eventually to be adopted by the Republican and Democratic parties themselves.

The image of the elephant being connected with Republicans dates back to an Illinois newspaper's use of the image when Abraham Lincoln ran for president in 1860.[18] Nast, a Republican, adopted the elephant image for its reflection of the party as strong, intelligent, and dignified, although he had portrayed Republicans as a variety of animals previously, including a bull, an eagle, a horse, and a lamb.[19] Kennedy notes that Nast used the elephant to represent the Republican vote or party seven times in 18 months, starting with "The Third-Term Panic," and by the 1880 presidential election, other cartoonists had also adopted the political imagery of the Republican elephant.

The context for this image was presidential election politics, specifically concerns that Ulysses S. Grant might seek a third term as president. Restricting presidents to only two terms was not limited until the 22nd Amendment to the Constitution was passed in 1951, but the tradition had been that presidents served only two terms. Nast's cartoon is described as "a comment on fears that Grant would run for a third term as President that led some Republicans to vote with the Democrats."[20] While Nast's "The Third-Term Panic" image features a donkey (covered in a lion skin), this was not the animal image reflecting the Democratic Party in the political cartoon. Rather, the fox shown at the bottom edge of the image, about to step onto the board labeled "Reform," symbolizes the Democrats in this cartoon.[21] The image suggests that either the Democrat or Republican may fall into the pit, labeled "chaos," depending on the outcome of the 1874 congressional elections; the Democrats won control of the House of Representatives in that election year, the first time since prior to the Civil War. Nast featured the outcome in a subsequent cartoon later in November 1874, "Caught in a Trap—The Third-Term Hoax," in which the Republican elephant had fallen into the pit.[22]

Nast's reference to the Democratic Party in the image of a donkey had been introduced in the cartoon image, "A Live Jackass Kicking a Dead Lion," in 1870 (see Figure 4.5). The reference to a Democratic donkey did not originate in Nast's cartoon image; rather, it first appeared as a symbol of the Democratic Party when Andrew Jackson was President. According to a description of the symbols reported on the California Democratic Party website:

> When Andrew Jackson ran for president in 1828, his opponents tried to label him a 'jackass' for his populist views and his slogan, "Let the people rule." Jackson, however, picked up on their name calling and turned it to his own advantage by using the donkey on his campaign posters. . . .

"A LIVE JACKASS KICKING A DEAD LION."

And such a Lion! and such a Jackass!

FIGURE 4.5 *"A Live Jackass Kicking a Dead Lion."* Harper's Weekly, *January 15, 1870. Thomas Nast.*
Source: *Courtesy of the Library of Congress.*

The first time the donkey was used in a political cartoon to represent the Democratic Party, it was again in conjunction with Jackson. Although in 1837 Jackson was retired, he still thought of himself as the Party's leader and was shown trying to get the donkey to go where he wanted it to go.[23]

This earlier cartoon by caricaturist and publisher H. R. Robinson's "A Modern Baalim and his Ass" was published in 1837. The image contrasts Jackson to "the Old Testament story of a prophet who is reproached by an angel for beating his talking donkey when the animal stops to make way for a divine messenger"[24] and reflects the imagery of a 1493 *Nuremberg Chronicle* image by Hartmann Schedel of "Balaam and His Ass." One description of Nast's cartoon notes that a rooster also had been used as a symbol of the Democrats in other imagery, but the donkey became the popular symbol for the party in the 1880s.[25]

The context of the animals in Nast's donkey image includes a reference to Copperhead, a nickname for Northern Democrats, who rejected Abraham Lincoln's Secretary of War, Edwin M. Stanton, represented in this image by the deceased lion. The image of the donkey wearing a lion skin in "The Third-Term panic" image by Nast does not connect to this cartoon; rather, it reflects Aesop's fable of "The Ass in the Lion Skin" about using a disguise.[26]

This pair of cartoons, which demonstrate early representations of animal images related to the two dominant political parties in the United States, present examples that could easily be incorporated into a class discussion of political parties. The processing and recall of visual symbols such as these from historic political cartoons, according to Symbol Systems Theory, can help students associate these themes with other content areas, as well as help them process and store in memory the related concepts. The powerful visual symbols demonstrated in these images, even without the contextual background of their evolution, can help students relate and recall visual cues with those symbols when they encounter them again. In using these images as the starting point, educators can ask students to continue the analysis to present day, by having them discover contemporary political party symbols that reflect the elephant or donkey. These might involve images from the political party messages themselves, or from contemporary political cartoons about current elections and campaigns.

Other images, approaches, and issues

The two sets of examples above demonstrate a variety of issues that could be raised in the use of political cartoons for teaching different political themes. This final section will offer suggestions for other imagery that could be used for similar analysis, additional ideas for incorporating political cartoon images into class content and activities, as well as concluding thoughts on potential advantages and disadvantages of using such imagery in teaching politics.

The representation of political campaigns can be a rich environment for the use and discussion of political cartoon images. In reviewing highlights of late twentieth-century presidential campaigns, one could incorporate not only visual examples but also research on the cartoon imagery from the campaigns of Carter versus Ford in 1976,[27] Reagan versus Carter in 1980,[28] Bush and Dukakis in 1988,[29] Clinton and Bush in 1992,[30] Clinton and Dole in 1996,[31] Bush and Gore in 2000,[32] Bush and Kerry in 2004,[33] as well as Obama and McCain in 2008.[34] Other media sources such as news stories may lead to allegations or accusations of media bias for or against a political candidate or political ideology. However, political cartoons are a superior medium for analysis because of their inherently critical orientation. Therefore, we can easily find political cartoons that attack political candidates of all viewpoints, sometimes criticizing the broader political institutions by including both Democrats and Republicans in the same image in a similar manner. "To be featured in a political cartoon is traditionally to be criticized or the source of satire, as compared to other media messages."[35] Therefore, it would be unlikely to evaluate a political cartoon as being favorable toward a political candidate or politician. As Adler and Hill confirm, "Effective caricatures usually have a dynamic interaction with reality, whereby the distorted likeness depends upon a general awareness of what the subject actually looks like—physical features, movement and gestures."[36] While readers may recognize the likeness of a politician or political candidate in a political cartoon, it is the exaggeration and distortion of the person him or herself, or a characterization of the individual by what he or she says or does, that demonstrates the critique.

While not originating from a political cartoon image, the "Don't tread on me" snake image, would also be worthy of further analysis as a political symbol in, as well as apart from, political cartoons. The origins of the image could be examined in a political context for its connection to Continental Colonel Christopher Gadsden who represented South Carolina at the Second Continental Congress in 1775, and the consideration of the Gadsden flag (containing the "Don't tread on me" image) as an early flag of the United States, preceding the stars and stripes model flag. Embraced by the contemporary Tea Party movement, the image appears frequently, and in various adaptations, in political cartoons regarding the Tea Party. In a discussion of contemporary political parties, fragmentation of political opinion, and perhaps the development of social movements, this example might be profitable for a number of analyses. The Gadsden flag demonstrates a contemporary example of what occurred with Franklin's "Join, or Die" image historically—it evolved in its application over time, in this case to being used as a political symbol to demonstrate a contemporary political movement. While the themes may be similar to historical uses, it provides a basis for looking at how a contemporary movement borrows and employs political symbols for the advancement of its agenda.

The examples discussed above could be used in a variety of ways in a politics course, as could other historic or contemporary political cartoon images relevant to course themes. These may be the basis for class discussion as part of a lecture on relevant topics of unification, partisanship, campaigns, or political symbols. One could simply start a class session with an image from a political cartoon related to that day's course topic for an initial discussion, or to reflect the theme or mood of that class session. If introduced for discussion in class, an essay exam question could be constructed to involve analyzing a political cartoon image in the context of a political event studied as part of the course. Students could be directed to conduct their own analysis assignments of political cartoon images, perhaps gathering a contemporary sample from online resources such as www.cagle.com[37] that provides collections to both American as well as international political cartoon content. Perhaps in addressing different methodologies in a Research Methods course, students could conduct a pilot project using content analysis of political cartoon images. Such an analysis could be useful to demonstrate to students the concept of variables, different types of measurement that could be utilized, and even issues of validity and reliability in research. The use of such images might merit a class discussion on the possible effects of mass media in politics, if appropriate to address in one's politics course, or the more general influence of media in the political arena, beyond political cartoons themselves. Students could also be asked to compare different forms of political opinion content such as political cartoons versus opinion columns or editorials for how persuasive political messages are constructed, what issues or themes they address, and what potential impact such messages may have on political elites as well as citizens. While students may examine the language of persuasion of other types of political messages, political cartoons offer the opportunity to focus on political symbols, the meanings they may offer to the reader, as well as the historical (or popular) context for the symbols. They offer students to make connections with other issues or events that can be easily understood and associated with symbols they have previously encountered or studied.

One drawback to the use of such opinion-laden imagery for class discussion is the polarizing nature of political cartoons. Students may make conclusions about the educator's political ideology, as well as their classmates', based on the images presented (if the images are neutral or unfavorable toward the President, for example). And if students perceive an inconsistency in their own political beliefs with those of their instructor, that might frame other assessments of the course, its content, and their potential for succeeding in it. One solution that may control this would be to include images from a variety of political positions and opinions, whether within the same class session or perhaps across multiple classes. If including political cartoons to discuss some aspects of a political campaign, one could include imagery that presents both major party candidates, or perhaps an image of a Republican candidate that is critical in some way as well as a separate negative image of a Democratic candidate, to offer balance in the opinions incorporated through these visual images.

Another challenge to the use of such cartoon imagery, even those presented in the chapter, is the context for the political situation an educator or students might lack. Given how political cartoons are often laden with allusions to current events and popular culture references, the "I don't get it" response may arise in response to some political cartoon images. Research on the use of allusions in political cartoons confirms this reaction, in their claim that "to decode the cartoon, one must be somewhat familiar with the literary or cultural source to which it refers."[38] Therefore, contemporary readers of past political cartoons may need to examine the broader political and current event context to comprehend fully and analyze a political cartoon image. When presenting them in a classroom context, the educator should be prepared with some background information to provide in the discussion of political cartoon images. One could first see what connections students make, what symbols and signs they identify, what they think those refer to, and how they "read" the cartoon. Then background information about the allusions in the cartoon image, or the relevant political events of the time period could be incorporated into the discussion.

In relation to the concerns raised above, I contend elsewhere[39] that the use of popular culture references of current films, advertising themes, and other media-oriented events can facilitate the comprehension and appreciation of a cartoon representation of a political event or issue. "Political cartoons that reflect popular culture references . . . focus on potentially provocative political issues, but tie them to imagery and references from entertainment that may unexpectedly draw in readers to politics."[40] While a future student may not have a full recollection of the events or relevance of the Arab Spring of 2010–11, for example, he or she may appreciate the notion of social movements when incidents of political unrest are compared to an American reality television program. Rather than recall details of the revolutions in Yemen, Tunisia, Egypt, and Libya, among others, a student may understand the association among them, and which governments have fallen versus those that persist, in a political cartoon portraying the individual countries as contestants in an endurance competition on a program like *The Biggest Loser.* Or as cartoonist Osama Hajjaj demonstrated in his August 2011 cartoon "Angry Birds Syria," with Syrian President Bashar Al-Assad being launched by slingshot against citizens. Such popular images may enhance a student's attention to and engagement with a political cartoon image, and potentially create an opportunity to discuss relevant political issues. My previous research confirmed that political cartoonists themselves may consider including popular culture references in their work either due to their own appreciation of American popular culture or due to their hope that such references may assist readers in understanding the message of the cartoon.

The potential value of popular culture imagery reflects my perspective of the value of using political cartoons in teaching: that they help students connect broader course themes with particular symbols and imagery. And those visual symbols may help students relate those themes to others they have previously examined and perhaps categorized in memory by similar symbols, as Symbol Systems Theory suggests. The provocative nature of many political cartoon messages, inherent to their role in mass media of expressing opinion in a predominantly visual approach, can stimulate lively discussion and debate, can be useful in analysis and interpretation, and can potentially aid student learning and connections of political content.

Notes

1 Gavriel Salomon, *Interaction of Media, Cognition, and Learning* (Hillsdale, NJ: Lawrence Erlbaum Associates, 1994).
2 Howard Gardner, *Frames of Mind: The Theory of Multiple Intelligences* (New York: Basic Books, 1983).
3 Salomon, *Interaction of Media, Cognition and Learning*, 61.
4 Ibid., 226–7.
5 Ibid., 113.
6 Gardner, *Frames of Mind*, 176.
7 Martin J. Medhurst and Michael A. DeSousa, "Political Cartoons as Rhetorical Form: A Taxonomy of Graphic Discourse," *Communication Monographs* 48 (1981): 197–236.
8 Ibid., 201.
9 Samuel Kernell, Gary C. Jacobson, and Thad Kousser, *The Logic of American Politics*, 5th edn (Washington, DC: C.Q. Press, 2012): 43.
10 Lester C. Olson, "Benjamin Franklin's Pictorial Representations of the British Colonies in America: A Study in Rhetorical Iconology," *Quarterly Journal of Speech* 73 (1987): 26.
11 Ibid., 26.
12 Isabel Simeral Johnson, "Cartoons," *The Public Opinion Quarterly* 1 (1937): 33.
13 S. Suzan J. Harkness, Mohamed Magid, Jameka Roberts, and Michael Richardson, "Crossing the Line? Freedom of Speech and Religious Sensibilities," *PS: Political Science & Politics* 40 (2007): 275–6.
14 Olson, "Benjamin Franklin's Pictorial Representations," 25.
15 Ibid., 25–31.
16 Adler John and Draper Hill, *Doomed by Cartoon: How Cartoonist Thomas Nast and the New York Times Brought Down Boss Tweed and His Ring of Thieves* (Garden City, NY: Morgan James Publishing, 2008): 3.
17 Ibid., 80.
18 Ohio State University Libraries, "Thomas Nast Portfolio," 2002. Accessed January 4, 2012, from http://cartoons.osu.edu/nast/kicking_lion.htm.
19 Robert C. Kennedy, "On This Day: Nov. 17, 1874," *New York Times* (November 17, 2001). Accessed January 4, 2012, from www.nytimes.com/learning/general/onthisday/harp/1107.html.
20 Ohio State University Libraries, "Thomas Nast Portfolio."
21 Kennedy, "On This Day: Nov. 17, 1874."
22 Ibid.

23 California Democratic Party, "History of the Democratic Donkey," 2005. Accessed January 20, 2012, from www.kintera.org/site/pp.asp?c=fvLRK7O3E&b=33708.

24 Jessica Lepler, "Pictures of Panic: Constructing Hard Times in Words and Images," *Common-Place*, April 2010. Accessed January 20, 2012, from www.common-place.org/vol-10/no-03/lepler/.

25 Ohio State University Libraries, "Thomas Nast Portfolio."

26 Kennedy, "On This Day: Nov. 17, 1874."

27 Ernest G. Bormann, Jolene Koester, and Janet Bennett, "Political Cartoons and Salient Rhetorical Fantasies: An Empirical Analysis of the '76 Presidential Campaign," *Communication Monographs* 45 (1978): 317–29; Alette Hill, "The Carter Campaign in Retrospect: Decoding the Cartoons," in *Rhetorical Dimensions in Media: A Critical Casebook*, ed. Martin J. Medhurst and Thomas W. Benson (Dubuque, IA: Kendall/Hunt, 1984): 182–203.

28 Michael A. DeSousa and Martin J. Medhurst, "Political Cartoons and American Culture: Significant Symbols of Campaign 1980," *Studies in Visual Communication* 8 (1982): 84–97.

29 Emmett H. Buell, Jr. and Mike Maus, "Is the Pen Mightier than the Word? Editorial Cartoons and 1988 Presidential Nominating Politics," *PS: Political Science & Politics* 21 (1988): 847–58; Janis L. Edwards, *Political Cartoons in the 1988 Presidential Campaign: Image, Metaphor, and Narrative* (New York: Garland Publishing, 1997).

30 William Koetzle and Thomas L. Brunell, "Lip-Reading, Draft-Dodging, and Perot-noia: Presidential Campaigns in Editorial Cartoons," *Harvard International Journal of Press/Politics* 1 (1996): 94–115; Chris Lamb and Joseph E. Burns, "What's Wrong with this Picture? The Anti-Incumbent Bias of Cartoon During the '92 Campaign," Presented at the Association for Education in Journalism and Mass Communication Southeast Colloquium, Roanoke, VA (1996).

31 Edward H. Sewell, Jr., " 'Torture-by-Tedium' or Editorial Cartoons During the 1996 Presidential Campaign," in *The 1996 Presidential Campaign: A Communication Perspective*, ed. Robert E. Denton, Jr. (Westport, CT: Praeger, 1998): 161–77.

32 Janis L. Edwards, "Running in the Shadows in Campaign 2000: Candidate Metaphors in Editorial Cartoons," *American Behavioral Scientist* 44 (2001): 2140–51.

33 Joan L. Conners, "Visual Representations of the 2004 Presidential Campaign: Political Cartoons and Popular Culture References," *American Behavioral Scientist* 49 (2005): 479–87.

34 Joan L. Conners, "Barack vs. Hillary: Race, Gender and Political Cartoon Imagery of the 2008 Presidential Primaries," *American Behavioral Scientist* 54 (2010): 298–312; Janis L. Edwards, "Presidential Campaign Cartoons and Political Authenticity: Visual Reflections in 2008," in *The 2008 Presidential Campaign: A Communication Perspective*, ed. Robert E. Denton, Jr. (Lanham, NJ: Rowman & Littlefield, 2009): 191–208; Eileen L. Zurbriggen and Aurora M. Sherman, "Race and Gender in the 2008 U.S. Presidential Election: A Content Analysis of Editorial Cartoons," *Analyses of Social Issues and Public Policy* 10 (2010): 223–47.

35 Conners, "Visual Representations of the 2004 Presidential Campaign," 480.
36 Adler and Hill, *Doomed by Cartoon*, 80.
37 Faculty as well as students should be aware that copyright permission for many cartoon images is required even for classroom presentation use. Some may involve nominal fees, and some syndicating organizations may waive or reduce copyright fees for different uses.
38 Medhurst and DeSousa, "Political Cartoons as Rhetorical Form," 201.
39 Conners, "Popular Culture in Political Cartoons."
40 Ibid., 261.

CHAPTER FIVE

Graphic novels in the social science classroom

Kent Worcester

Introduction

Over the past couple of decades there has been a notable upswing in the number, and overall quality, of graphic narratives that address significant historical and political topics. While illustrators have been combining words and pictures in sequence to comment on political figures and social mores since the eighteenth century, if not earlier, only recently has there been a critical mass of long-form comics that explore significant social issues. Not coincidentally, in the same period there has been a boom in the scholarly study of comics. In addition, a growing number of articles and books are concerned with comics and cartoons as pedagogical tools. The bulk of this literature is focused on primary and secondary school classrooms, however. The available material on comics and college-level pedagogy is aimed at faculty in the arts and humanities rather than political scientists or social scientists more generally. For members of our discipline who might be interested in bringing comics into the classroom, there is very little in terms of substantive published sources.[1]

This chapter addresses this lacuna by exploring the ways in which long-form comics, otherwise known as graphic novels, can be incorporated into courses dealing with political themes. It is a companion piece to the chapter on political cartoons by Joan Conners, which concentrates on short-form editorial cartoons and comic strips.[2] In this context, the term "graphic novel" applies to longer, more ambitious works of graphic narrative that may be fictional or nonfictional in nature. First coined in the

1960s, the term was popularized by Will Eisner and others in the 1970s and 1980s. Many noteworthy graphic novels could be more accurately described as graphic memoirs, or graphic nonfiction, but the label has proved popular with publishers, critics, and booksellers seeking to differentiate recent approaches to illustrated narrative from the pamphlet-style comic book format that remains associated with superhero, fantasy, and related genres. While the graphic novel/comic book distinction can be problematic—for one thing, superhero and fantasy stories have the potential to convey sophisticated ideas—it nevertheless makes sense to distinguish the serial fiction of the type produced by the major comic book companies from standalone graphic narratives.

As this chapter will show, graphic novels can be usefully introduced into a range of offerings in political science and other social scientific disciplines, from first-year courses to upper-level undergraduate and graduate courses. The chapter opens with a brief survey of the history and form of the graphic novel, and suggests reasons for why the comics medium has taken a creative leap in recent years. It then takes up the question of whether and to what extent graphic novels belong in course syllabi. After that, it provides an annotated guide to 12 graphic novels that members of the discipline, as well as social scientists more generally, should find intriguing. The names of a few of these titles, such as *Maus* and *Watchmen*, will be familiar to many readers. Others are more obscure, but merit serious consideration. The guide identifies widely offered politically themed courses for which each selection may be especially appropriate, and lists related graphic novels that could also be plausibly incorporated into course syllabi. The chapter goes on to incorporate these recommended readings as case studies for a general discussion of teaching strategies for faculty interested in assigning graphic narratives. It additionally offers examples of comics-related assignments that allow faculty to meaningfully evaluate students' learning outcomes, and closes with a few general observations.

Words and pictures

The story of narrative art reaches into human prehistory and encompasses such well-known artifacts as Trajan's Column in Rome (second century CE) and the Bayeux Tapestry (eleventh century CE). Many surveys locate the origins of modern visual commentary in the nineteenth century, however, when advances in printing, paper production, and periodical distribution facilitated the emergence of mass-circulation illustrated newspapers and magazines. The most famous of these publications, in the English-speaking world, was *Punch*, which was founded in 1841. Indeed, the editors of *Punch* were responsible for coining the modern meaning of the word "cartoon." But the tradition of combining words and pictures as a means of contributing to public controversies can be traced back to at least the eighteenth century, when artists such as John Collier, Isaac Cruickshank, James Gillray, William Hogarth, and Thomas Rowlandson fashioned satirical prints that were sold by printshops and displayed in shop windows, taverns, and private homes. These prints blended visuals and prose, and some arranged panels in sequence to tell a story.[3] Comics and cartoons have long enjoyed a reputation as a marginal and slightly disreputable form of outsider art. But many people find the amalgamation of words and pictures intrinsically appealing. The production and consumption of narrative art constitutes a long-established means by which we interpret the social world and communicate that understanding to others.

That said, comics and graphic novels are easy to discount. Even those who appreciate the work of, say, Herbert Lawrence Block (Herblock) or Garry Trudeau (*Doonesbury*), or read Hergé's *Tintin* to their children, often assume that uninterrupted text is inherently more serious-minded than material that fuses words and images in sequential form. Logocentrism has deep roots in our educational system, and even in our language. The term "comics," after all, connotes humor and entertainment rather than artfulness or critical analysis. Yet, at least in the hands of talented creators, the comics medium can be a multifaceted mode of cultural expression. As the literary scholar Charles Hatfield has argued, comics are "characterized by a plurality of messages. They are heterogeneous in form, involving the co-presence and interaction of various codes . . . comic art is composed of several kinds of *tensions*, in which various ways of reading—various interpretive options and potentialities—must be played against each other."[4] The formal elements of the comics page—most notably panels in sequence, word balloons, and gutters (i.e. the spaces between panels)—work in tandem with the drawings and the prose. The quality of the compositions, and the writing, is up to the artist, or the creative team. But the reading experience is in the hands of the reader, who faces the task of integrating an entire ensemble of languages, codes, symbols, and subtexts as he or she transforms static, two-dimensional pages into meaningful narrative.

The history of comics is closely interwoven with the history of anticomics campaigns. From their inception, literary gatekeepers and moral authorities have warned against the insidiousness of mixing words and pictures. In 1846, in a poem titled "Illustrated Books and Magazines," William Wordsworth inveighed against the popularity of what he deemed "a dumb Art": "A backward movement surely have we here/From manhood—back to childhood; for the age/Avaunt this vile abuse of pictured page!/Must eyes be all in all, the tongue and ear/Nothing? Heaven keep us from a lower stage!"[5] Wordsworth's concerns regarding this "backward movement" were echoed in the early twentieth century, when editorialists and religious leaders raised fierce objections to the vulgarity of the newspaper comic strip, and were revived after World War II, when Fredric Wertham,

Gershon Legman, and others expressed alarm concerning the social impact of the crime, horror, and mystery comics that could be readily purchased at newsstands and drugstores in the 1940s and early 1950s. The triumph of superhero, funny animal, and adventure comics in the postwar period reflects the success of anticomics campaigners who insisted that comics should be suitable for all readers, including young children. A kind of cultural division of labor took hold, in which fine art pointed the way toward beauty, and books expressed ideas, and comics represented a crutch for readers who were not quite prepared for the rigors of the unsullied image or the unadorned text.

A key moment in the redefinition of the medium came with the rise of underground comics in the 1960s and 1970s, which offered brazenly countercultural images and storylines. In the 1980s and 1990s a new generation of self-described "alternative" cartoonists took advantage of the trail blazed by underground cartoonists to address social and political themes. Art Spiegelman's *Maus*, which received a Pulitzer Prize in 1992, was the first canonical work of this alternative comics movement.[6] The commercial and critical success of Spiegelman's masterpiece offered convincing proof that comics is an expressive medium rather than merely a menu of commercial genres.

In the wake of *Maus*, a subset of comics publishers, from Fantagraphics and Drawn and Quarterly, to First Second and Picture Box, have concentrated on publishing thoughtful graphic texts that elide genre-based categories. In the past decade or so, several trade publishers, including Pantheon, FSG, Houghton Mifflin, and Henry Holt, have introduced their own graphic imprints. While the University Press of Mississippi has played a pivotal role in promoting comics scholarship, the roster of university presses with books on comics continues to expand. The emergence of a scholarly infrastructure is further indicated by the founding of the Comic Art and Comics area of the Popular Culture Association in 1992, the launching of the *International Journal of Comic Art* in 1999, and the more recent establishment of online journals such as *Image and Narrative*, *ImageText*, and *Signs: Studies in Graphical Narratives*. The website that accompanies this volume includes a supplementary "List of Resources" that provides links to these journals and other online resources in comics studies.[7]

Comics in the classroom

Many professors show movies in their classes, and tape cartoons to their office doors. Yet the idea of placing a graphic novel on a course syllabus will strike some educators as beyond the pale. As we have seen, this anxiety may reflect concerns that comics and graphic novels are by definition inferior to other modes of expression, and that the medium is the sum of its best-known genres. It is conceivable that a faculty member without tenure, whether adjunct or tenure track, may be reluctant to jeopardize his or her position by assigning picture books. To the extent that comics remain entangled with the culture wars, the response of chairs and deans to the presence of graphic novels on course syllabi may speak to the location, affiliation, and demographics of a particular campus. Those educators who teach at community colleges, art schools, or liberal arts colleges presumably enjoy greater freedom to experiment with unconventional teaching materials than their colleagues at, say, research universities. In some contexts, assigning a graphic novel may be viewed as needlessly provocative; at others, it may be encouraged. All of these factors have implications for faculty members who are considering introducing graphic novels into their classrooms.

Perhaps the most obvious reason for assigning graphic novels is that they can excite student interest. Faculty looking to motivate undergrads who have tuned out conventional textbooks and monographs may be impressed by the response that comics and graphic novels can inspire. The fact that textbooks themselves have become increasingly stuffed with images and short bursts of prose presumably reflects the disaffection some students feel with more traditional approaches. Textbooks are becoming more like comics, in other words. This is a trend that many professors regard with a deep sense of regret or ambivalence. The idea of incorporating graphic novels into college-level courses may offend colleagues who are already dismayed with the sheer razzle-dazzle of many best-selling first-year textbooks. But these are in fact two separate questions. Just because publishers are sometimes manic about deploying visuals does not mean that a serious work of graphic literature, memoir, or nonfiction cannot contribute to a serious-minded course. Course materials that are rich in visuals may encourage students to take a closer look, but a parade of images neither guarantees nor precludes an intellectually meaningful educational experience.

The quality and contribution of the assigned text remains paramount. The strongest argument for assigning graphic novels is not that visuals are neat but that a growing cadre of illustrators and cartoonists are using the medium to investigate and make sense of the world around them. The goal is not to elicit "wows" from students, but "hmm, that's interesting." Dropping a graphic novel into a syllabus—that is, a long-form comic that actually addresses the needs of a specific course—may encourage students to read the assigned material, and speak up in class. As with showing a movie, or taking a field trip, the very experience of stepping beyond the familiar can make the semester more meaningful. At the same time, unlike with movies and field trips, a graphic novel has a physical form that allows for the same kind of sustained interactions that motivated readers enjoy vis-à-vis traditional texts. Students can bring a graphic novel to an "open book" midterm or final exam, just as they might consult conventional readings. They can quote from the material in research papers, and even mark up selected passages with yellow highlighters. The point of assigning a graphic novel is not to provoke enthusiastic responses from hardcore aficionados but to have other students report, at the end of the semester, "At first I didn't understand what you were thinking, but I learned a lot from the assignment and am delighted you made such a bold choice."

Setting aside the powerful anxieties that comics and graphic novels can sometimes provoke, the biggest challenge is that most educators within the social sciences simply do not possess the kind of background knowledge that can facilitate the importation of graphic novels into the college classroom. Given their visual nature, their distinctive internal logic, and their long and complex genealogy, graphic novels raise pedagogical issues that graduate training in the discipline never confronts. Speaking as a political scientist, we are taught how to probe texts for hidden meanings, but are not taught how to make sense of aesthetic or formal issues. For this reason, most political scientists who currently assign graphic novels are probably comics fans. Assigning graphic novels arguably requires extra work, such as consulting *Understanding Comics*, and/or *A Comics Studies Reader*, before the semester begins.[8] It could also involve perusing reviews of relevant graphic novels and seeing what scholars and critics have pulled out of particular graphic texts. The new comics scholarship makes it abundantly clear just how dense with meaning comics and graphic novels can be. The good news is that some basic familiarity with how comics work—what distinguishes them from other media, and how they have evolved over time—can make an enormous difference to the teaching and learning experience.

There are a small number of topics where assigning more than one graphic novel might make sense, such as courses on Propaganda, the Politics of Popular Culture, or even the Politics of Superheroes. These kinds of thematic courses are rarely taught by political science faculty, however, and are probably mostly offered at liberal arts colleges rather than larger institutions. Interestingly, courses on "the sociology of culture" are far more widely offered than courses on "the politics of culture," even though many students are keenly interested in the political dimensions of mass culture. Departments concerned with student enrollment and "growing the major" could do worse than to think about developing courses on pop culture politics. It is perhaps revealing of the discipline's complacency on this score that there is no political science analogue to the commercially successful "Psychology of Popular Culture Series" and "Blackwell Philosophy and Pop Culture Series," both of which place their books in regular bookstores as well as on psychology and philosophy course syllabi. A comparable series on "The Politics of Popular Culture," with titles like "The Politics of Star Trek," or "The Politics of Spider-Man," is arguably overdue.

In most cases, assigning a single graphic novel is audacious enough. Comics can supplement, rather than supplant, conventional reading assignments. The challenge is to find the right graphic novel, one that can help students see the semester, and the other assigned readings, in a fresh light.

Recommended titles

A social scientist whose awareness of comics is limited to scanning the occasional *New Yorker* cartoon could be forgiven for finding the new wave of comics publishing and scholarship a bit overwhelming. If he or she visited their local Barnes & Noble, they would find *manga*, superhero collections, horror comics like *The Walking Dead*, coffee table books on comics, and standalone graphic novels jammed together in the same aisle. (And, if they visit their local comics shop, there is a good chance they will be bombarded with superhero imagery and perhaps puzzled or put off by the vicissitudes of fan culture.) Apart from *Maus*, they would be hard pressed to know where to begin. Many beautifully produced volumes lack substance, and some of the most intellectually significant books slip in and out of print. Titles that a store clerk might recommend may not address the needs of college faculty, who are not looking for what's visually dazzling but for what can advance specific pedagogical goals.

The following is an annotated guide to 12 graphic novels that both political scientists and those in other social scientific disciplines may find particularly noteworthy, from biographies and travelogues to historical surveys and political polemics. While the emphasis is on memoir and nonfiction books, the list includes a comic strip collection, a political allegory, and a revisionist superhero tale. If it inspires readers to explore the field for themselves, and to consider what kinds of graphic novels might make sense for their own courses, then it has served its purpose. An expanded version of this list can be found on this volume's companion website.

The 9/11 Report: A Graphic Adaptation. Written and drawn by Sid Jacobson and Ernie Colón. Alternate: *After 9/11: America's War on Terrorism*[9]—This somber adaptation of *The 9/11 Commission Report* became a national best seller. It skillfully deploys an array of devices, from silhouettes and cinematic close-ups to splash pages, timelines, and a restrained use of color, to transform an unusually high-profile document into a visually appealing text. Jacobson and Colón hew closely to the original source material, but adopted a more critical approach in their follow-up volume, *After 9/11*. These are just two of the many nonfiction graphic novels published in the past decade that have inspired a broader reevaluation of the comics medium. Suitable for courses on political violence, international relations, and US foreign policy.

A.D.: New Orleans after the Deluge. Written and drawn by Josh Neufeld. Alternate: *War in the Neighborhood*[10]—This emotionally resonant graphic memoir tells the real-world story of six New Orleans residents as they confront Hurricane Katrina and live through its tragic aftermath. Portions of the book were first serialized on the web and then collected in a handsome hardback volume. It is one of the most impressive works of recent comics journalism and one of the best books of any type on the impact of Katrina on ordinary people. *War in the Neighborhood* depicts the gripping conflict between squatters, police, and city officials on New York's Lower East Side in the 1980s and 1990s, and tells the story from the perspective of the squatters. Suitable for courses in urban politics, southern politics, and US politics.

Birth of a Nation: A Comic Novel. Written by Aaron McGruder and Reginald Hudlin, and drawn by Kyle Baker. Alternate: *King: A Comics Biography of Martin Luther King, Jr.*[11] —This scathing political satire imagines what would happen if impoverished East St. Louis—"the inner city without an outer city"—seceded from the United States. Whimsical, cartoony, and politically astute, its creators use this improbable scenario to explore the ideological and sociological fault lines within the African American community as well as the gap between urban America and lawmakers in Washington, D.C. Ho Che Anderson's *King* offers a sympathetic, carefully researched, yet not uncritical account of the contribution of Martin Luther King, Jr. to the civil rights movement. Suitable for courses on black studies, social movements, and African American politics.

The Complete Maus: A Survivor's Tale. Written and drawn by Art Spiegelman. Alternate: *We Are On Our Own*[12]—This famous memoir uses anthropomorphic animals to tell the heartbreaking story of a concentration camp survivor (Spiegelman's father) and his family. A comics scholar recently quipped that 50 per cent of the serious writing on comics is about *Maus*. While this is an exaggeration, its impact on the current graphic novel boom is hard to overstate. Few if any comics have been as widely assigned in high school and college classes. Miriam Katin's moving account of how her mother and she survived the Nazification of their country of origin is obviously more obscure but offers a thoughtful and unsettling portrait of the war's horrific impact on Hungarian Jews. Suitable for courses on the Holocaust, and World War II.

The Complete Persepolis. Written and drawn by Marjane Satrapi. Alternate: *Palestine*[13]—This prize-winning memoir uses woodcut-like images and generous quantities of black ink to present one young woman's coming-of-age story in modern Tehran. Raised in a politically minded household, Satrapi shows what it was like to take part in mass protests under the Shah and how clerical authority transformed the country in the 1980s and beyond. The book was subsequently turned into an animated film that undergraduates interested in international relations and the Middle East can relate to and learn from. Joe Sacco's *Palestine* draws on the author's extended visits to Gaza and the West Bank in the 1990s and provides a nuanced portrait of the Israel–Palestine conflict from a humanistic and broadly pro-Palestinian perspective. Suitable for courses on Iran, modern revolution, and Middle Eastern politics.

The Essential Dykes to Watch Out For. Written and drawn by Alison Bechdel. Alternate: *Fun Home: A Family Tragicomedy*[14]—A handsome collection of comic strips that tracks the romantic and political ups-and-downs of a small circle of mainly lesbian friends. As a reviewer for *Ms.* magazine noted, it provides a "permanent cartoon record of modern lesbian-feminist history." Students interested in feminist politics will be fascinated by the honesty and irreverence of Alison Bechdel's closely observed micro-history. Bechdel is perhaps best known for her highly praised memoir of growing up with a closeted gay father, *Fun Home.* Suitable for courses on gay and lesbian politics, social movements, and contemporary political culture.

Footnotes in Gaza. Written and drawn by Joe Sacco. Alternate: *War is Boring: Bored Stiff, Scared to Death in the World's Worst War Zones*[15]—Joe Sacco is the unrivaled master of war-reportage comics. In this beautifully crafted book he uses oral history and archival records to dramatize a dimly remembered episode in Gaza's history—the 1956 massacre of civilians in the towns of Khan Younis and Rafah. In the course of his research he talks to shopkeepers, farmers, aid workers, high-level militants, and despondent cynics. He makes a point of stressing his commitment to the facts and refuses to paint the people he meets as pure-hearted idealists. David Axe and Matt Bor's *War is Boring* uses comic book imagery to convey the smell and feel of contemporary warfare in places like Iraq and Afghanistan. Suitable for courses on Middle Eastern politics, and international relations.

How to Succeed at Globalization: A Primer for Roadside Vendors. Written and drawn by El Fisgón. Alternate: *A People's History of American Empire*[16]—A witty dissection of neoliberalism's promises told from the perspective of a roadside vendor and free market enthusiast. One-sided, of course, and well argued. El Fisgón is the pen name of Mexico's leading political cartoonist, Rafael Barajas Durán. *A People's History of American Empire* adopts a similarly dyspeptic view of the strengths and limitations of the Anglo-American model of market-driven political economy. Suitable for courses on globalization, US foreign policy, and international relations.

Pyongyang: A Journey in North Korea. Written and drawn by Guy Delisle. Alternate: *Burma Chronicles*[17]—Guy Delisle's minimalist pen and ink sketches capture his impressions of one of the most secretive places on the planet, the North Korean capital. Based for a time in Pyongyang as a result of his work for a French film animation company, Delisle uses comics to record everyday life in a police state where Western-style journalism is strictly forbidden. Another one of his books, *Burma Chronicles*, takes the reader into a similarly remote and heavily monitored setting where foreign travelers rarely venture. Suitable for courses on East Asian politics, and international relations.

Stuck Rubber Baby: A Novel. Written and drawn by Howard Cruse. Alternate: *Students for a Democratic Society: A Graphic History*[18]—One of the best memoirs of the 1960s is also a graphic novel. *Stuck Rubber Baby* presents the story of Toland Polk, whose adventure takes him from a racially segregated town in the Deep South to civil rights protests and big city gay culture. Cruse's highly detailed, almost pointillist linework offers a distinctive look that meshes nicely with a tale of coming-of-age and coming out. The *SDS* collection revisits the radical sixties by focusing on the legendary student-based organization that crashed and burned at the end of the decade. Suitable for courses on gay and lesbian politics, social movements, and the politics of the sixties.

The United States Constitution: A Graphic Adaptation. Written by Jonathan Hennessey and drawn by Aaron McConnell. Alternate: *A Cartoon History of the United States*[19]—A carefully researched, handsomely drawn introduction to the intellectual and social conflicts that contributed to the making of the US Constitution. Unlike most of the titles on this list, this book was explicitly designed for classroom use. Larry Gonick's cartoon history covers a lot more ground but offers a similarly optimistic perspective on the capacity of the political system to respond to its citizenry and adapt to changing times. Suitable for courses on US politics, and law and government.

Watchmen. Written by Alan Moore and drawn by Dave Gibbons. Alternate: *Superman: Red Sun*[20]—One of the most influential superhero stories ever published, *Watchmen* offers a self-consciously deconstructive critique of the political psychology of costumed vigilantism. Rated by *Time* magazine as one of the 100 best novels of the twentieth century, Moore and Gibbons significantly raised the bar for genre storytelling and thereby reshaped mainstream comics. Mark Millar's well-received *Superman: Red Sun* provides a counterfactual literary history in which the orphan from Krypton lands in the Ukraine rather than Kansas, and puts his considerable talents at the disposal of the Soviet fatherland. Suitable for courses on the Cold War, and politics and literature.

Teaching strategies

Comics and graphic novels can serve a variety of pedagogical purposes. They can be used the same way that movies and field trips are, that is, to add an extra dimension to the classroom experience. They can be deployed as supplemental sources of information on history and culture. They can add a bit of sparkle and novelty to the proceedings, but they can also usefully convey facts and data. They can help faculty engage students who seem immune to more traditional approaches, and they can inspire new ways of assessing learning outcomes.

The graphic novels highlighted above help illustrate some of the ways in which comics can serve the needs of faculty in political science and other disciplines. Books like *Birth of a Nation,* or *How to Succeed at Globalization,* have a light-hearted quality even as they tackle serious issues. Assigning these kinds of texts can lighten the mood and provide a counterweight to assignments that focus, for example, on policy debates or political economy. They can also be used to reward students after a difficult midterm or research paper assignment. At the same time, books like *The 9/11 Report,* or *The United States Constitution,* can help students absorb and retain large quantities of information that may be useful later in the semester. Their visuals can encapsulate valuable background material and provide a foundation for subsequent readings that dig deeper. Students in a first-year course on US politics, for example, might appreciate the opportunity to read Hennessey and McConnell's thoughtfully organized summary before delving into the political essays of, say, the Constitution's framers.

Graphic novels can recreate experiences that are very different from those that may be familiar to most college students in the United States. They can convey what it was like to be a teenager during the Iranian revolution, a southerner living through the tumultuous 1960s, or a poor person trying to survive Hurricane Katrina. Books like *Persepolis, Stuck Rubber Baby,* and *A.D.: New Orleans after the Deluge* offer a kind of you-are-there immediacy that is difficult for conventional textbooks and monographs to emulate. Collections like *The Essential Dykes to Watch Out For,* or *Students for a Democratic Society,* offer rich sources in social history that can help recreate for students the conditions and sensibility of the receding past.

At the same time, graphic novels can provide a window onto different cultures and world regions. This is obviously true of Joe Sacco's war reportage, as well as Guy Delisle's books. Even now, reporters and academics rarely spend significant chunks of time in the North Korean capital, as Delisle did. First-hand, English-language accounts of life in Pyongyang remain scarce. Comics can be an effective way of gaining insights into societies that remain closed off to journalists and photographers, since even the most repressive-minded officials are more likely to confiscate cameras and laptops than notepads filled with sketches. North Korea may be an extreme case, but not an unimportant one given that country's bellicose foreign policy and demonstrated nuclear capability. We sometimes forget how much of our knowledge about social conditions prior to the industrial revolution comes from drawings. To take just one example: the modern-day recreation of Shakespeare's Globe Theatre, situated on the south bank of London's Thames River, relied heavily on a handful of illustrations that survived the centuries. Delisle's *Pyongyang* helps the reader appreciate the extent to which North Korea's decades-long program of industrialization has bypassed the information revolution.

In addition, graphic novels can offer an engaging way of exploring historical counterfactuals. What if the Watergate scandal had never been uncovered, and the superpowers were headed toward all-out nuclear war in the 1980s? That is precisely the premise of *Watchmen*, which is set in an alternate version of 1985. What sort of public morality is acceptable in the face of nuclear conflagration? How would legal and political authorities respond if vigilantism became a familiar feature of everyday life? *Watchmen* may be a superhero drama, but it nevertheless raises fascinating questions about morality and the law. It's hard to picture a classroom in which students would rather sit on their hands than debate the radically divergent perspectives that *Watchmen*'s main characters articulate and represent about truth, justice, and the American way.

As the example of *Watchmen* suggests, graphic novels can help students gain a deeper appreciation for strongly held points of view. From their inception, comics and graphic novels have been created for the purpose of advocacy and propaganda. Given that they are inexpensive to produce, easy to distribute, and popular with all kinds of readers, political movements of various stripes have long enlisted the aid of cartoonists and illustrators to promote their cause. Comics have a "small-d" democratic quality that distinguishes them from, say, novels or movies, which are labor-intensive to create. In the right hands, an effective cartoon, comic strip, or short graphic story can be completed and even printed in a few hours. As noted earlier in Joan Conners' chapter on using political cartoons to teach politics, one of the first cartoons published in the United States was Ben Franklin's "Join or Die," which appeared in the *Pennsylvania Gazette* in 1754.[21] It offered a simple but effective call for colonial unity and went on to become a symbol of the revolution. It took less time to complete, and probably reached a larger audience, than the numerous articles and pamphlets that revolutionists drafted in the run-up to the Declaration of Independence. From the eighteenth century onwards, social and political movements have used images in general, and comics in particular, to get their point across. Not surprisingly, the list of graphic novels that express an explicitly political agenda is growing.

As this brief discussion suggests, comics and graphic novels can serve a range of teaching goals. They can provide a break from the routine and inject a welcome jolt of humor into the classroom. They can help students gain a more finely grained appreciation for specific times and places, and for particular milieu. They can help history come alive, and can help students envision counterfactual scenarios. They can function as windows, time machines, and portals. And they can convey the political passions of people who lived in the past, who hold minority views, and/or who live outside the global north. They can reenergize class discussions, pull in disaffected students, and encapsulate important insights about the world we live in and the political and social conflicts that helped get us here.

Assignments and outcomes

Graphic novels can play an integral part in both oral and written assignments. They can also contribute to the larger expectations, and learning outcomes, of a productively organized course on political themes and concepts. Assigning a graphic novel does not mean that it needs to be central to the semester, however. A graphic novel or comic strip collection could be included on a list of recommended readings, for example. As noted above, it could give students a respite from an especially demanding set of readings. A graphic novel could play a constructive role even if it does not feature on the final exam. A well-chosen graphic novel could flesh out certain themes, just as assigning a novel, short story, or documentary film might help clarify for students what it felt like to live in Moscow in the early 1920s or to be a Freedom Rider in the early 1960s. An appropriately chosen graphic novel can lend color and texture to the study of different times and/or locales.

Graphic novels can be used for extra credit assignments. A professor could invite volunteers to introduce a graphic text and talk about the specific nature of the medium and the ways in which drawings, words, and formal elements interact to produce a distinctive reading experience. This might provide an opportunity for artistically inclined students to share their cultural expertise. The professor might also learn from the presentation. At a college or university with a sizable art program it might even be possible to invite students to prepare their own graphic short stories that comment on the assigned reading(s). The compressed nature of panel-based storytelling can help students appreciate the importance of word choices and apt quotations. The best examples could be distributed to the entire class or even more widely via a course website.

Graphic novels can in fact be incorporated in a variety of ways into course assignments. A review essay assignment, in which students critically analyze two or more secondary sources, could scrutinize a graphic novel along with more conventional readings. A research paper assignment could draw on graphic material in a way that encouraged students to insert visuals into their papers. After all, the current generation of word-processing programs makes it much easier to place images alongside prose than ever before. Alternatively, for the right kind of course—such as a course that revisits the social movements of the 1960s—the proliferation of high-quality graphic histories and memoirs would make it possible for a professor to ask students to prepare a review essay or research paper that looks at *either* graphic novels or standard sources. At the same time, a major assignment for a historically minded course, on twentieth-century revolutions for example, could ask students to consider how cartoonists and illustrators responded at the time to certain epochs and critical junctures. Artistic expression can offer a tangible way of understanding how specific social groups and subcultures experienced and processed world-historic events.

While it might not make sense for faculty in such settings to quiz students about the artistic merits and formal qualities of assigned graphic material, comics and graphic novels can inspire similar kinds of questions about plot, characterization, and dialogue that movies and novels can. In what sorts of ways do specific characters represent and articulate distinct points of view? Can we connect the ideas and actions of specific characters with larger social groups, classes, political parties, and/or social movements? To what extent do conflicts between, say, a father and son, or an estranged couple, reflect wider political and social cleavages? What are the ideological underpinnings of particular arguments and plot points? What are the broader implications of someone's heartfelt reminiscence? Can students establish meaningful linkages between a specific graphic novel or memoir, and economic or political data provided by official sources, or between a graphic history of the Constitution, and the Federalist Papers? Graphic memoirs can highlight important questions about the relationship between macroeconomic and macro-social dynamics and everyday experience, just as graphic histories can raise interesting questions about how historical events are remembered and the extent to which historians and social scientists rely on narratives, metaphors, and (mental) images to frame and advance their arguments.

Carefully selected comics and graphic novels can contribute to the process of assessing student learning in the same way that other, more conventional texts can. Course syllabi and classroom lectures can be used to establish explicit learning goals for assigned readings, whether comics-based or not. What kinds of questions should students consider as they review the assigned material? How are these questions connected to the overall learning goals of the semester? Writing assignments, tests and exams, and oral presentations can all provide opportunities for students to demonstrate that they have grasped these learning goals and can relate the specificities of the assignment to larger intellectual concerns. The output of students, as reflected in a variety of assignments that are identified on the syllabus, can provide evidence for what students are learning and where there is room for improvement. By the semester's end the faculty member should have acquired a great deal of information about whether and to what extent the learning goals of the course have been met. This information can then provide a foundation for reflecting on how readings, assignments, lectures, and guided discussions can be tweaked or reformed so that the learning experience can be substantially enhanced the next time around. Done right, outcomes assessment is a deliberative, ongoing process that combines the patient accumulation of relevant empirical information with the scholarly and pedagogical wisdom that is needed to interpret this information and to think creatively about how the lessons of a particular semester can be used to improve future outcomes.[22] Comics and graphic novels can offer a tool for measuring student learning just as more familiar kinds of primary and secondary readings can.

Conclusion

Humans are innately visual creatures, and we find meaning in and derive pleasure from pictures, images, and drawings. Contemporary life is in fact crammed with screens, monitors, billboards, posters, photographs, visual propaganda, visually stimulating advertising, and so on. The internet itself has become a crucial aspect of our visually centered culture. We are confronted and bombarded with manufactured and informally generated images on a daily basis, to an extent to which even our recent ancestors would have found bewildering. With the help of YouTube and similar websites, today's undergraduates can retrieve a near-century's worth of commercials, speeches, programs, clips, and interviews with historical figures. They can take snapshots with their smart phones, and instantly upload the results to their Facebook pages. Whether they are sitting in classrooms, hanging out with friends, or attending concerts, they are increasingly likely to be engaged in, or thinking about, sharing the experience with others, via visually centered technologies. Our students have acquired a facility for entering and navigating dense visual environments that leaves the rest of us speechless.

Given this reality, it makes sense for faculty to consider whether and to what extent imagistic learning materials belong in their syllabi and in their classrooms. As we have seen, many textbook publishers have responded to the changing expectations of our students by filling their books with ever-greater quantities of images. But the results are not always pretty, or edifying. A witty cartoon or comic strip can certainly spruce up a syllabus or course website, and many students will appreciate almost any effort that faculty make to incorporating visual elements into traditional forms of pedagogy. Visual learning is here to stay. The question is how faculty can make the most of these shifting cultural tectonics.

Adding a graphic novel, memoir, or work of nonfiction can add a whole new dimension to the learning process. For some students, this relatively simple step can make an enormous difference in how they relate to the classroom experience. For others, it can help them understand the extent to which a newly energized comics medium can serve our shared intellectual and scholarly agendas. The contemporary reevaluation of comics, and the graphic novel boom, in both publishing and scholarship, reflects a larger process of cultural transformation. In a world where the internet fuses words and pictures, sounds and moving images, homepages and vast data sets, the idea that there is something disreputable or inherently juvenile about the underlying logic of the comics medium is passé. Words and pictures, in combination and in sequential form—the graphic novel, in other words—can usefully contribute to serious-minded pedagogical ends.

[Please see the companion website for the book. Details are listed on the back cover of the book.]

Notes

1 Many readers will have noticed that trade publishers, booksellers, book critics, and literary festivals are taking a greater interest in graphic literature than ever before. For this new scholarship on comics, see Matthew P. McAllister, Ian Gordon, and Edward H. Sewell. *Comics and Ideology* (New York: Peter Lang, 2001); Bradford W. Wright, *Comic Book Nation: The Transformation of Youth Culture in America* (Baltimore, MD: The Johns Hopkins University Press, 2001); Charles Hatfield, *Alternative Comics: An Emerging Literature* (Jackson, MS: University Press of Mississippi, 2005); Thierry Groensteen, *The System of Comics* (Jackson, MS: University Press of Mississippi, 2007); Matthew J. Costello, *Secret Identity Crisis: Comic Books and the Unmasking of Cold War America* (New York: Continuum, 2009); Jörn Ahrens and Arno Meteling, *Comics and the City: Urban Space in Print, Picture and Sequence* (New York: Continuum, 2010), and others. For recently published textbooks, see Randy Duncan and Matthew J. Smith, *The Power of Comics: History, Form and Culture* (New York: Continuum, 2009); Jeet Heer and Kent Worcester, eds, *A Comics Studies Reader* (Jackson, MS: University Press of Mississippi, 2009). Cartoonists themselves have contributed to comics scholarship. See Will Eisner, *Comics and Sequential Art* (New York: Norton, 2008); Scott McCloud, *Understanding Comics: The Invisible Art* (Northampton, MA: Tundra, 1993). Key sources on comics-based pedagogy include James Bucky Carter, ed., *Building Literacy Connections with Graphic Novels: Page by Page, Panel by Panel* (Urbana, IL: National Council of Teachers of English, 2007); Nancy Frey and Douglas B. Fisher, *Teaching Visual Literacy: Using Comic Books, Graphic Novels, Anime, Cartoons, and More to Develop Comprehension and Thinking Skills* (Thousand Oaks, CA: Corwin Press, 2008). For a pedagogical text aimed at faculty who teach courses in art, composition, drama, literature, and popular culture, see Stephen E. Tabachnick, ed., *Teaching the Graphic Novel* (New York: The Modern Language Association, 2009).

2 See Joan Conners' chapter in this volume.

3 The best source on eighteenth and early nineteenth century satirical prints is Vic. Gatrell, *City of Laughter: Sex and Satire in Eighteenth-Century London* (New York: Walker and Company, 2006). Of course, establishing what and who came first, in the arts in general, and comics in particular, is notoriously difficult. For many years historians of comics mainly focused on late nineteenth- and early twentieth-century antecedents. More recently, a scholarly consensus has coalesced around the fascinating figure of Rodolphe Töppfer, a Swiss painter and essayist whose illustrated humor stories appeared in the 1830s and 1840s. Töppfer's efforts were explicitly informed by the work of William Hogarth and other eighteenth-century illustrators, however. The art historian David Kunzle links the emergence of the comic strip, if not long-form graphic narratives, to the printing revolution of the fifteenth and sixteenth centuries. See David Kunzle, *The Early Comic Strip: Narrative Strips and Picture Stories in the European Broadsheet*

from c. 1450 to 1825 (Berkeley, CA: University of California Press, 1973). Identifying the earliest comic book, comic strip, or editorial cartoon turns out to be as difficult as trying to establish who played or recorded the first jazz tune or pop song.

4 Charles Hatfield, *Alternative Comics: An Emerging Literature* (Jackson, MS: University Press of Mississippi, 2005): 36.

5 Jeet Heer and Kent Worcester, eds, "Introduction," *Arguing Comics: Literary Masters on a Popular Medium* (Jackson, MS: University Press of Mississippi, 2004): vii.

6 Art Spiegelman, *The Complete Maus: A Survivor's Tale* (New York: Pantheon, 1996).

7 Please see the companion website for the book. Details are listed on the back cover of the book.

8 Scott McCloud, *Understanding Comics: The Invisible Art* (Northampton, MA: Tundra, 1993); Heer and Worcester, *A Comic Studies Reader* (2009).

9 Sid Jacobson and Ernie Colón, *The 9/11 Report: A Graphic Adaptation* (New York: Hill and Wang, 2006); Sid Jacobson and Ernie Colón, *After 9/11: America's War on Terror* (New York: Hill and Wang, 2008).

10 Seth Tobocman, *War in the Neighborhood* (New York: Autonomedia, 2000); Josh Neufeld, *A.D.: New Orleans after the Deluge* (New York: Pantheon, 2010).

11 Kyle Baker, Reginald Hudlin, and Aaron McGruder, *Birth of a Nation: A Comic Novel* (New York: Crown, 2004); Ho Che Anderson, *King: A Comics Biography of Martin Luther King, Jr* (Seattle: Fantagraphics, 2005).

12 Spiegelman, *The Complete Maus* (1996); Miriam Katin, *We Are On Our Own* (Montreal: Drawn and Quarterly, 2006).

13 Joe Sacco, *Palestine* (Seattle: Fantagraphics, 2002); Marjane Satrapi, *The Complete Persepolis* (New York: Pantheon, 2004).

14 Alison Bechdel, *Fun Home: A Family Tragicomic* (New York: Mariner Books, 2007); Alison Bechdel, *The Essential Dykes to Watch Out For* (New York: Houghton Mifflin, 2008).

15 Joe Sacco, *Footnotes in Gaza* (New York: Metropolitan Books, 2009); David Axe and Matt Bors, *War is Boring: Bored Stiff, Scared to Death in the World's Worst War Zones* (New York: New American Library, 2010).

16 El Fisgón, *How to Succeed at Globalization: A Primer for Roadside Vendors* (New York: Metropolitan Books, 2004); Paul Buhle, Mike Konopacki, and Howard Zinn, *A People's History of American Empire* (New York: Metropolitan Books, 2008).

17 Guy Delisle, *Pyongyang: A Journey in North Korea* (Montreal: Drawn and Quarterly, 2005); Guy Delisle, *Burma Chronicles* (Montreal: Drawn and Quarterly, 2010).

18 Howard Cruse, *Stuck Rubber Baby: A Novel* (New York: Paradox Press, 1995); Paul Buhle, Gary Dumm, and Harvey Pekar, *Students for a Democratic Society: A Graphic History* (New York: Hill and Wang, 2009).

19 Larry Gonick, *A Cartoon History of the United States* (New York: Collins Reference, 1991); Jonathan Hennessey and Aaron McConnell, *The United States Constitution: A Graphic Adaptation* (New York: FSG, 2008).

20 Alan Moore and Dave Gibbons, *Watchmen* (New York: DC Comics, 1987);
    Mark Millar, *Superman: Red Son* (New York: DC Comics, 2004).
21 See Joan Conners' chapter in this volume.
22 Barbara D. Wright, "More Art than Science: The Postsecondary Assessment
    Movement Today," American Political Science Association (APSA). Accessed
    August 23, 2011, from www.apsanet.org/content_13026.cfm.

PART THREE

Musical/theatrical media

Introduction

Going back at least as far as Plato's *Republic*, music and theatre have been seen as innately political. In this section of the volume, the authors describe how music and performative in-class simulations can effectively expose students to powerful political expressions and experiences. Music and performance offer a means to speak to the students in a language that resonates with their own life experiences. Furthermore, such media can effectively integrate the students into the educational experience in direct ways, as they literally perform the actions which other educational models would only have them observe, usually from a considerable intellectual distance. Moving beyond textbooks and into such performative and artistic realms can be intimidating, and educators may face a challenge in attempting to connect such unorthodox pedagogical techniques to the substance of their courses, and the subject matter of politics. The selections in this section offer a guide for effective integration of media long-acknowledged to have a role in political education.

With the proliferation of iPods, and various other technologies, music is an ever-present part of most students' lives. Consequently, effective integration of music into a college classroom harbors profound pedagogical potential to reach students through a medium in which they are ensconced.

Gosa's chapter provides an in-depth discussion of the use of rap music within the classroom. He offers practical insights from his own experiences, focusing on students' reactions to music, and how these reactions can generate resistance when it comes to analyzing the politics within students' favorite music. Gosa discusses numerous helpful suggestions for encouraging students to critically evaluate the political dynamics within rap music, regardless of whether these messages are overt or deeply embedded within the lyrics and content.

Similarly, Sriram also engages students in politics through music. The core of his chapter explores an innovative assignment that asks students to integrate music of their choosing with various political topics and ideas from course material, in short, create a "mix tape." His reflections indicate how the use of music aids students' understanding of political ideas, and also encourages more robust class participation and engagement with course material. Gosa's and Sriram's chapters establish a blueprint for embracing music as a nontraditional medium suited for integration into many courses covering political subjects.

Theatre, much like music, has the potential to engage students' affective and emotional sensibilities. However, participatory theatre within the classroom (i.e. simulations) offers a different instructional benefit. In most cases, music is passive. Use of music in class, even asking students to pick and discuss music relevant to the course, does not mean that students *produce* the music in question. Simulations, however, are active. In simulations, students are asked to play a role relevant to some aspect of the class. Requiring students to participate in a simulation can lead them to think about course material from perspectives other than their own, as they are asked to personify the positions of others. Alternatively, simulations can force students to do research and really think through their own perspectives before engaging in a collective endeavor with their peers. Much like music, carefully considered simulations offer educators a means to push students outside of their comfort zone to better evaluate course ideas.

Kasniunas's chapter reflects on an interdisciplinary simulation she conducted about the United States Supreme Court. She explains the simulation, while distilling her experience into useful guidance for other educators seeking to use similar pedagogical methods. The simulation she discusses has students argue real cases before individuals pretending to be real political figures (the justices on the Court).

Whereas Kasniunas focuses on having students simulate actual cases before an extant political institution, Williamson takes us on a trip into the fictional. Williamson's inventive simulation utilizes the fictional idea of a "zombie apocalypse" to have students portray political decision-makers responding to a crisis. The nature of this specific simulation makes it applicable to a number of courses studying various political institutional structures. The expanded discussion within his chapter offers various suggestions for how this simulation, or similar simulations, can be used to engage students in a manner that effectively demonstrates concepts central to a class about politics. Both Kasniunas's and Williamson's discussion of simulations provide useful models and suggestions for how to engage students through simulation in a manner that advances the exploration of course material rather than tacks on an unrelated facet.

Music can lead to critical reflection about politics spurred on by music's emotional core. Simulations can lead to critical reflection through active engagement, perhaps while requiring students to fictionally adopt viewpoints that are not their own. As the chapters in this section of the volume suggest, both media harbor great pedagogical potential and the chapters in this section offer guidance in successfully utilizing these nontraditional "texts" within the college classroom.

CHAPTER SIX

Why do students resist hip hop studies?

Travis L. Gosa

Introduction

The pedagogical use of rap music provides a case study for thinking about the shifting fields of culture and power in the American academy.[1] In the 1970s, hip hop represented cultural survival for undereducated, criminalized Black and Latino youth.[2] Since the early 1990s, hip hop has migrated from urban ghettos, to corporate boardrooms, to the corridors of the ivy tower.[3] Under the auspices of "hip hop studies" or "rap pedagogy," the symbolic representations of society's most marginalized citizens are being recast as valuable knowledge in the educational marketplace.[4] The nation's elite universities (i.e. Harvard, Stanford, and Cornell) boast hip hop library archives, and at last count, hip hop-related books have appeared on more than 700 college syllabi.[5]

Political scientists are now using social-realist, "gangster-rap" lyrics to discuss contemporary politics. Given the explicit themes of poverty, conflict with the criminal justice system, or limited educational opportunities, rap music can potentially serve as a supplementary text for accessing the themes of urban politics or racial inequality. In English departments, reading these lyrics as poetry might serve the dual purpose of developing writing skills and social justice awareness. Educators can use popular representations embedded in music, film, and television to help move students from common knowledge to the specialized jargon of academia. Hip hop's unique pedagogical value is that entertaining performances often contain a serious analysis and critique of global apartheid, patriarchy, and class exploitation. Thus, in the college classroom, hip hop provides a framework for teaching about the social problems facing marginalized people in the United States and abroad.

The quantifiable impact of hip hop on student achievement is beyond the scope of this essay. Instead, I am concerned here with the *hidden politics of rap pedagogy*: how the use of rap music antagonizes the construction of higher education as a privileged space, including the meaning of nondominant narratives and professorial authority. This chapter examines the micro- and macro-politics of using hip hop as an educational tool in the college classroom. In particular, I explore why academic hip hop texts can complicate efforts to teach contemporary politics, and how educators might use alternative strategies to benefit student learning.

The analysis is predicated on the belief that the academy is not a sterile, neutral site of learning. In education, Michael Apple observes, "cultural struggles and struggles over race, gender, and sexuality coincide with class alliances and class power. Education is a site of struggle and compromise. It serves as a proxy as well for the larger battles over what our institutions should do, whom they should serve, and who should make these decisions."[6] As an African American, male professor who regularly uses hip hop in social science courses, it is my experience that the successful use of rap pedagogy requires addressing these hidden power imbalances of elite, predominantly White institutions.

By highlighting the difficulties of making hip hop meaningful, this chapter contributes to a growing body of literature on hip hop and critical pedagogy. Potentially, hip hop can be part of an exciting college experience. It can be used to create educational spaces that encourage critical engagement and social justice.[7] As proponents imagine, hip hop can be used to destabilize commonsense understandings of society, to highlight marginalized voices, and to disrupt the entrenched "whiteness" of the American academy.[8] I contribute to the literature by explaining why some students resist the inclusion of hip hop in the curriculum.

The section titled "Hip hop is read: Text in the college classroom" focuses on the use of hip hop text in the college classroom. Through a synthesis of courses taught in US universities, the review demonstrates how academics typically approach the intellectualization of hip hop. The section titled "Getting real about hip hop in the classroom" describes why some students oppose the intellectualization of hip hop culture via text. I argue that the inclusion of rap textbooks is likely to raise questions about linguistic politics, generational gaps in music consumption, and racial authority. Instead of feeling empowered by the inclusion of hip hop, some students react with dismay when their favorite Jay-Z songs are deconstructed as political text. One goal of this chapter is to explain the nature of the complaints voiced by students. These objections, I believe, are not unreasonable.

The chapter concludes with recommendations for best practices that may help professors overcome the obstacles of bringing hip hop into the classroom. Based on the discussion, I argue for a need to de-privilege academic texts and point to alterative writings that might facilitate student learning. The use of popular texts and informal writing and listening assignments, in addition to emphasizing multiculturalism, can help overcome student resistance. When done deliberately, hip hop pedagogy can be used to explore a wide range of topics such as urban politics, inequality, the political economy of the music industry, and identity politics.

Hip hop is read: Text in the college classroom

The cliché "hip hop is dead" is often invoked to lament the transformation of ghetto protest music into a highly corporatized popular culture product.[9] There is an extensive literature that unpacks the meteoric rise of hip hop as popular music culture and consumer culture.[10] Less attention has been paid to the academic appropriation of hip hop culture over the past 20 years. In the American colleges, hip hop is commonly "read" as part of the formal curriculum.

The dominant currency of knowledge in institutions of higher education is text. For academic status and promotion, professors write journal articles and books, while students are expected to read books, and to provide written "answers" on tests. Outside the performance arts, such as musicology and dance, text dominates college life. So it is no surprise that the educational value of hip hop is often imagined as hip hop in its textual form. In social science and humanities classrooms, student engagement with hip hop typically involves reading and writing about hip hop lyrics, articles, and books.

Text-based engagement with hip hop is evident in the syllabi of college courses. Currently, the best source of information about how colleges are using hip hop is "The Hip Hop Archive." An initiative of Harvard University's W. E. B. Du Bois Institute, "The Hip Hop Archive" indexes hundreds of hip hop-related graduate theses and more than 800 book manuscripts. Their repository of hundreds of academic syllabi, known as the "Hip Hop University," provides insights into how professors are using hip hop to teach politics. Examination of this archive reveals four important observations about the role of text.

First, there has been an explosion of academic, hip hop-related texts written since the early 1990s. This interest in writing about hip hop corresponds with the aging-in of young faculty of color into the academy. The first cohort of hip hop scholars grew up in the late 1970s and 1980s "golden-age" of hip hop, categorized by the music of Afrika Bambaataa, KRS-One, Public Enemy, and Queen Latifah. They listened to rap music of that era, which, according to political theorist Jeffery Ogbar, was defined by the "hip hop intelligentsia."[11] These explicitly political artists believed that rap music should be used as "edutainment," that is, the music was intended to address the political realities of post-Civil Rights America, including the War on Drugs, dissolution of traditional community life, and racial profiling by the police. In addition, the hip hop intelligentsia understood hip hop as part of a global political movement comprised of youth in Western Europe, Africa, and Asia, who all faced similar economic and social problems. Thus, when young academics began using hip hop as part of their teaching repertoires, they used the music to address the themes of urban politics and social movements. Likewise, the first critical texts about the music emphasized hip hop's political significance beyond the music.

Second, review of these materials suggests that hip hop in the college classroom tends to be "text-centric." Courses in the diverse fields of education, psychology, English, African American Studies, music (ethnomusicology), theater, and art all appear to incorporate major scholarly texts on hip hop. For example, *That's the Joint!*, a textbook edited by Murray Forman and Mark Anthony Neal, is the most commonly assigned book in all undergraduate courses containing hip hop content.[12] The textbook emphasizes the political significance of hip hop history, with sections organized around the politics of graffiti and breakdancing, interpersonal politics (i.e. race, gender, social class), spatial politics and urban studies, political messages in the music, and the political economy of rap music. Therefore, there is a good chance that when college students encounter hip hop it comes in the form of political text.

Third, colleges appear to embrace a "rap-centric" conception of hip hop, with the emphasis being placed on the politics surrounding rap music performance, famous rappers, and their lyrics. Students are often assigned to read rap lyrics outside of class. Many syllabi contain lyrical appendices, or web links to online lyrical repositories such as "The Original Hip-Hop Lyrics Archive." *The Anthology of Rap*, a 900-page collection of rap lyrics published by Princeton University Press, is becoming popular in classes.[13] Advanced courses structured around the lives of Tupac Shakur, Jay-Z, and Nas can even be found in the course catalogue. These courses seek to situate the careers of rap celebrities within the larger socio-political landscape (e.g. American capitalism or patriarchy), and examine how these artists critique the government's lack of concern for poor communities, or antagonize gender relationships through heteronormative lyrics. Less evident is a desire to develop student appreciation for the creative, aesthetic, or visual aspects of hip hop culture, such as graffiti art or breakdancing.[14]

Fourth, the works by a small set of authors are widely used in courses. For educators unfamiliar with the field of hip hop studies, scholars such as Tricia Rose, Michael Eric Dyson, Jeff Chang, Baraki Kitwana, and Mark Anthony Neal have acclaimed books related to various political topics, and

regularly provide political analysis on national news and television outlets. Their influence on hip hop pedagogy is further enhanced by large academic conferences like University of Wisconsin-Madison's "Getting Real:
The Future of Hip Hop Scholarship" in 2009 and Chicago's University's
"Feminism and Hip Hop" conference in 2005. By looking at syllabi alone,
it is not possible to know exactly how the texts by these authors are used in
day-to-day operation of classes. But the centrality of these authors provides
some clues as to how hip hop is likely to be conceptualized and legitimated
as useful knowledge. Rose's *Black Noise* and Chang's *Can't Stop, Won't
Stop* are both treatises on rap music as Black-Afrodiasporic expression in
response to postindustrial segregation and joblessness.[15] Kitwana's *Hip Hop
Generation* treats hip hop as post-Civil Rights generational status, a way
to frame the crises facing Black communities, including family breakdown,
urban unemployment, and incarceration.[16] Works by Dyson and Neal cover
the gamut of Black cultural production and the importance of using hip
hop to understand race-gender identity.[17]

This review suggests that when college professors assign hip hop texts,
they are usually requiring that students read serious academic tomes on contemporary politics. That is to say, the most popular books listed on course
syllabi all frame hip hop within traditions of empirical methodologies such
as historical analysis and textual categorization. Hip hop text, when read
in the college setting, is informed by rap lyrics meant to illuminate and crit-
icize how power operates in society. The existing hip hop studies literature
contains exemplars of cutting-edge scholarship in political science. These
texts attempt to frame rap music as an externalized, objective extension
of African and Black Atlantic diasporic aesthetics which holds the key to
understanding racism, politics, or even state power without the trappings
of Western, colonial, or capitalistic logic.

Getting real about hip hop in the classroom

One might expect that the theoretical funk of savvy rappers will disrupt
the orthodoxy of stuffy disciplines. Resembling the Hollywood movies
like *Dangerous Minds* or *Freedom Writers*, we would like to imagine that
when educators use hip hop they will magically transform the hierarchical
teacher–student relationship into an organic "rap cypher" that privileges
group learning, experimentation, fun, and mutual understanding. In real
life, using hip hop to enhance learning or student participation is far more
daunting. Rap pedagogy can puzzle and anger students.

It is my experience that many students are ambivalent about the educational value of hip hop. Some actively oppose the ways in which the intellectualization of hip hop culture occurs via academic books, and react with

dismay when their favorite rap songs are deconstructed as political text. In this section, I draw upon the voices of past students, educational theory, and a critical reading of hip hop culture to rearticulate the difficulties of rap pedagogy. I point to three challenges that can arise from use of hip hop in the classroom, including the issues of language, student consumption of rap music, and racial identity.

Lost in translation: The strange language of academic hip hop

One matter of concern is the peculiarities of language use in academic spaces versus that of hip hop culture. As a number of works on the socio-linguistics of rap indicate, the explicit use of street slang, "profanity," "Ebonics" (or Black English) define the language of empowerment in hip hop culture. As Alim puts it, "language is far more than linguistic variables, polysyllabic utterances, and turn-taking in conversion . . . language is the revolution, a powerful discourse in and of itself."[18] Language is part of the various styles and identities attached to different rap spaces, as verbal dexterity or "flow" and regional dialects are significant beyond the content of what is being said. The concept of "discursive space" denotes that hip hop has significance beyond *content*, what is actually being rhymed.

Accordingly, the power dynamics of curse words, especially the embrace of the dreaded "N-Word," is made meaningful through subtle pronunciation ("er" versus "a") and biographical authenticity. Likewise, much of the emphasis on wordplay owes to the African American vernacular tradition of "cultural inversion" or "signifying," in which alternative meanings are used to voice dissent, tease, and poke fun at White America—all without White people or the general "Other" catching on.[19] Importantly, language is forwarded as quickly changing "manias" to prevent outsiders from mastering hip hop lingo. Thus, hip hoppers quickly abandon words like "phat/fat" (a positive affirmation) or "swagger" (notable aesthetics or personal style) as soon as old people and/or White people catch on.

The use of language as oppositional discourse creates a challenge for the classroom. When academics get a hold of hip hop, the result can be reconstruction of popular culture to fit the language, norms, and values of elite, White privileged spaces. Professorial text production and the testing of students through related exams and essays can lead to making hip hop palatable within the existing norms of academia.

How nondominant narratives get lost in translation can be seen in the ways professors talk about hip hop. The following is a short excerpt from my lecture notes from a sociology course entitled "The Hip Hop Generation: Power, Identity, and Social Change." After assigning readings from *That's*

The Joint! and other hip hop studies articles, I provide an academic reading of the song "Gin & Juice" by Snoop Dogg:

> The song is an example of a black, oppositional soundscape that is at odds with the melodic and harmonic structures of Western classical music. Through its African sound organization, obsession with break beat repetition, riffs, call-and-response, and dense rhythmic percussion loops, the sonics are attempts to create protective and resistant spaces from general whiteness and the negatives of collapsing late capitalist industries. This anthem calls attention to hip hop as the new black youth culture that rejects many of the values that have sustained black communities of the aging Black Power and Civil Rights eras. Under the guise of "simplistic" and "repetitive" nonsense sound, Snoop Dogg is constructing a powerful discursive space that has significance beyond content, beyond what is actually being rhymed. In the logic of post-structuralism, bragging about access to expensive Tanqueray Gin becomes an important resource for the disadvantaged, as power and control over consumer goods and black women provides a place for "alternative truths" to circulate that might challenge racism and sexism. Using the refrain, "with my mind on my money/and my money on my mind," Snoop disrupts normal discourse by rearticulating values and norms of capitalism widely accepted by most Americans. He reframes (or "remixes") dominant ideals under the illusion of defiant blackness, causing American ideals to be problematized as delinquency. The tension between the hybrid identity of rap as popular (white) culture and (black) counterculture exposes the normal social practices of valuing money over women in society. Free market capitalism and male-dominance are not contentious cultural norms. But when Snoop vocalizes these customs with pithy slogans and dope beats, he exposes the boundaries of unreasonable talk and accepted behavior.

This critical reading of Snoop Dogg is representative of the language used to make rap music significant in textbooks and peer-reviewed journals. The goal of the lecture is to get students thinking about the politics of identity, such as race, social class, and gender norms in contemporary society. The problem with this approach is obvious to many students, and perhaps to anyone who is familiar with the song. When most listeners *hear* "Gin & Juice," they hear a celebratory song about drinking liquor and having sex. But in the echo chamber of the ivy tower, academic speak renders the song unrecognizable.

Elite institutions tend to be quite hostile to using the lower-class, popular language of rap. As Pierre Bourdieu notes, educational spaces reflect power relationships in society, with schools codifying elite forms of "cultural capital"—such as language, knowledge of music, and literature—in order to preserve the class advantages of upper and middle class children.[20] Using the language of rap would likely make the curriculum more culturally relevant and realign the learning process to eliminate the "cultural gap" between colleges and students from disadvantaged backgrounds. However, the transmigration of hip hop in colleges has required an increasingly complex language of academic hip hop suitable for preparing students for success in privileged work spaces.

Students with mastery of academic jargon can and do excel at translating hip hop in the dominant language of the academy, though some appear uncomfortable with this practice. The latter students complain, perhaps rightly so, that intellectuals "don't get it," or that professors "don't feel (truly understand) what rapper X is really saying." But, the linguistic mismatch can make facilitating a discussion of hip hop almost impossible. For example, Georgetown Professor Michael Eric Dyson, known for his large classes on the political significance of rappers, observes that the norms of academia caused divisions among students in his "Sociology of Tupac Shakur" course. The problem, he says, is that students disagreed as to whether anyone, especially White students, should be allowed to repeat Tupac's lyrics or song titles. Uttering the "N-Word" or "B-Word" in a classroom setting is a nonstarter, so these words get translated into obtuse phrases like "counter hegemonic discourse."

All about the beat: Rap lyrics don't really matter to students

The incorporation of hip hop into the classroom usually arrives in the form of reading rap lyrics as political text. Most subgenres of rap music are obsessively lyrical, and even rappers known primarily for their party songs have lyrics that critique elected officials or social inequality. In my "Sociology of Race and Education" course, for example, I quote lyrics from Kanye West's *The College Dropout* album or Dead Prez's "They Schools" as a way to discuss the disproportionate placement of Black males into special education courses and high dropout rates. Both of these works contain straightforward lyrics about the sad state of America's public schools. Ironically, it is a daunting task to convince students—even those self-proclaimed "hip hop fans"—that the lyrics of their favorite rappers could help us understand what is occurring in schools.

At Cornell University's "Born in the Bronx" hip hop conference in 2008, noted hip hop scholar Tricia Rose provided a succinct story about how today's students actively disregard rap lyrics.[21] Similar to students who appear in my classes, Rose described students who say that they do not care about or listen to the actual words of rap songs. For this generation of students, rap is all about the beat. As such, they resisted her attempts to use the lyrics of popular rap songs as a way to discuss interpersonal politics or inequality. Frustrated, she provided the following hypothetical to students: "What if the Klu Klux Klan—the racist hate organization—released a track about lynching black people and burning crosses; but the song had a great beat. . . . Would you keep dancing and ignore the lyrics?"[22]

To understand why students may have a hard time dealing with lyrics, it is important to first understand how and why academics read lyrics as text, and then to rethink how millennial youth (those born in the 1990s) actually engage rap music. There are two basic approaches to the academic reading of rap lyrics: lyrics can be read with an emphasis on "poetics" or "political significance." The *poetics of rap music approach* suggests that lyrics can be read like poetry. How lyrics are delivered, including verbal dexterity, intonation, humorous sounds, imagery, and texture can be examined in union with the literal meaning of a song.[23] Like regular poetry, this perspective encourages students to conduct multiple readings of the same song to produce more complex interrogations of potential meanings by looking at rhyme schemes, wordplay techniques, and narrative forms of individual songs.

The *rhetorical politics approach* involves analyzing the social and political critiques offered by rappers. The approach implies that there is a "message in the music," and students only have to listen to hear artists "kick knowledge" about social problems. Rap songs, supposedly, are an alternative news source ("the black man's CNN") and provide a stage for speaking inconvenient truths to power. For example, the stories about police brutality and prison life told by rappers might be used to learn about the criminal impact of mass incarceration on communities of color. In my "African-American Families" course, I attempt to use the lyrics to Outkast's "(Sorry) Ms. Jackson" to discuss whether states should incarcerate absentee fathers who refuse to pay child support. The track is a narrative about a father who wants to support his children, but threatens to stop providing money once the relationship with his "baby's mama" becomes hostile.

Whether the focus is on poetry or message, treating rap music as text is based on the belief that lyrics reflect power relations and hidden assumptions of society that can in effect be "read" or deconstructed as an exercise in knowledge production. In addition, professors assume that rap lyrics are "mediated narrative," that youth rely on the lyrics of rap songs to navigate institutions and social networks, thus what rappers say are part of the performative identities of youth.

After several semesters of failed attempts to reference rap lyrics in class, one brave undergraduate finally told me the awful truth: "Lyrics matter to professors because professors are old." Indeed, my frame of reference is embedded in rap of my youth, the late 1980s and 1990s, but this does not resemble the rap worlds of today. This generational gap means that professors mistakenly assume that rap music is lyrically angry, spiritual, and political. Likewise, I want to use hip hop in teaching because rap is immensely personal and relevant. The analytical positioning of *hip-hop-as-biography* means that rap lyrics relate to an authentic, self-reflective lived experience that cannot be captured in studying statistics. In the spirit of KRS-One's signature phrase, "I Am Hip-Hop." While I see hip hop as an inherently important aspect of the social, political, and historical milieu, my students usually think about rap as only music.

Some of the problem is nostalgia on the part of aging professors. Though, there are real reasons why today's students tend to be less invested in the content of rap music. First, they have no real life experience with hip hop as community culture. Since the early 1980s, public ordnances spurred by the "Broken Windows Thesis" of crime have prohibited graffiti, block parties, loitering and cruising, and loud music in public space that nurtured hip hop as community culture.[24] The criminalization of nonrap has exacerbated an institutionalization of graffiti in fine art museums, and dance as a professional aspect of fine arts colleges. Second, the commodification of rap by multinational corporations has replaced emcees and DJs with pop culture celebrities and computer drum machines.

It is clear that students are still consuming music, but this consumption practice may or may not involve listening to music, especially with a critical concern for the lyrics. The third reason students struggle with lyrics is due to the social revolution in internet music. In the late 1990s, college youth, once the cash-cow of the media industries, began "sharing" (or "stealing") compressed MP3 music files. The "Napster Revolution" has made music "free" and "unlimited." Thus, today's students spend little time *really* listening to music. Instead, they are preoccupied with creating elaborate screen names ("avatars") on file sharing sites and trading massive file collections and generated playlists. Students in my classes regularly admit to having tens of thousands songs on their phones and music players, but have little attachment to this content.

Asking students to seriously think about music reveals a generational shift of hip hop as *youth culture* to hip hop as *popular culture consumer lifestyle*. The shift from culture to lifestyle implies the decreasing significance of a hip hop politic or ideology, and an increasing importance of tastes and buying habits. This point has been articulated by hip hop scholar S. Craig Watkins who describes hip hop as a "media environment" filled with branding and purchasing opportunities.[25] For many college students, hip hop entails purchasing Sean Jean designer jeans, drinking Nelly's "Pimp Juice" caffeinated energy drinks or Jay-Z's vodka, and playing 50 Cent's video games on the Playstation 3. Given the relative insignificance of rap songs, students are likely to be more familiar with the movies of rappers like Ludacris or Common, than the ideas found in their music.

These changes in hip hop culture mean that professors have to work hard to provide a reorientation for students. Even though they "own" thousands of songs, many are more familiar with the lines of sixteenth-century poetry than with what rappers say. Convincing them that rap might provide a useful analytic and methodological approach, in which rap could become an instrument used to interrogate and conceptualize social phenomenon, can be a daunting task.

Black culture, White space: Racial performance of hip hop

Last, hip hop in the classroom is likely to raise concerns over interpretive authority and cultural ownership. Rap pedagogy can result in accusations that professors are "stealing Black culture." The use of hip hop for academic purposes places teachers and researchers in the larger culture wars of racial representation, specifically the politics of Black cultural production. An uncritical framing of hip hop as Black culture can raise serious questions about whether upper-class, and/or White academics have a legitimate right to engage hip hop. Likewise, it can place minority academics in the position of having to perform conflicting, and insincere racial performances to convince students that they should be allowed to talk about hip hop.

Professors have degrees in formal academic disciplines such as communications, American studies, or sociology. But none can claim expertise about hip hop through formal credentials. When deploying rap pedagogy, students often inquire about the professor's "real" proficiency in the subject, that is, besides reading or writing books. The belief that there is something inauthentic about academic hip hoppers is articulated by one of Anthony Kwame Harrison's students who observed that, "there was a 'big difference' between people who knew all about hip hop because they had 'read every book ever published on it' and those who actually 'lived it'."[26] In the absence of formalized expertise, some students rely on racial and social class clues to assess whether professors know what they are talking about.

Rap is typically imagined as inner-city, Black culture, making the use of hip hop by White academics on college campuses problematic. In the extreme, this can become the basis of an argument that non-Black professors and students have no right to use hip hop in academic (read: White) spaces. This complaint contains what political philosopher Tommie Shelby refers to as a "Black cultural nationalism," the belief that "blacks must become the primary producers, purveyors, and beneficiaries (financial or otherwise) of their culture" and "blacks are (or must become) and should be regarded as the foremost interpreters of the meaning of their cultural ways."[27]

The anxiety surrounding the racial identities and social class motives of professors is based on concerns about cultural rights and interpretive authority. In his interview with Meta DuEwa Jones, Michael Eric Dyson says that issues of race and representation are at the forefront of academic hip hop. He provides the following assessment of "who is authorized to interpret and articulate hip hop's past, present, and future":

> Some outside the [black] race think that if they study the culture and learn from its artists and thinkers, they are qualified to interpret and analyze black culture. I don't disagree with that conclusion. Color can't be the basis for analyzing culture. . . . But there is something to be said for the dynamics of power, where nonblacks have been afforded the privilege to interpret . . . and to legitimate or decertify black vernacular and classical culture in ways that have been denied to black folk.[28]

The nuanced statement provided by Dyson avoids the trap of forbidding non-Blacks from using hip hop in the classroom, but his response also reflects what seems to be a widespread belief that we should be cautious about White academics using hip hop. At minimum, his argument suggests that Blacks be the ultimate arbitrators or certifiers of "legitimate" hip hop study.

To be sure, this concern is part of a larger history of guarding against what is often seen as the White appropriation of Black culture. The fear is that, White universities, White-controlled disciplines, legions of tuition-paying, White undergraduates, and White publishing houses might turn hip hop studies into an ivory-tower minstrel show. That White people have always loved hip hop and might have claims as legitimate creators and contributors can be a distressing proposition to some students who read hip hop as the property of inner-city Blacks.

The phrasing of hip hop as Black culture can also place unreasonable expectations on minority professors and Black students. Because of racial background, some students come to class expecting that professors will "keep it real" by wearing Sean Jean jumpsuits, rapping in class, tagging the faculty lounge, and hanging out with a rap posse. When rap videos are shown in class, some minority students might feel pressure to relate and enlighten their privileged classmates about what's going on in the "streets."

In predominately White universities, what professors say about hip hop can be restricted by political correctness. Likewise, some students appear afraid to say anything critical about hip hop's nihilistic violence, materialism, homophobia, or sexism for fear of being perceived as a racist. Classroom discussions can grind to a halt when *hip hop* gets misconstrued as code for *Black people*. As cultural critic Adam Sexton observed of the early attempts to intellectualize hip hop, it is hard to avoid the dichotomy of "cheerleading" or "ill-informed rap bashing."[29] Because hip hop is performed "predominately by young black males, our society's least-trusted, least respected element by a long shot, and you have a recipe for not just defensiveness but clinical paranoia."

Strategies for the successful use of hip hop

By examining the appearance of hip hop in college courses and the themes appearing in major hip hop studies books, this chapter highlighted how academics intellectualize the topic as text. This chapter has also explored the challenges of using hip hop as an educational tool in the college classroom. Based on past teaching experiences, theory, and research on hip hop, I showed how the issues of language, student consumption of rap music, and racial identity can hamper rap pedagogy. It is not always obvious how educators can translate this material into useful knowledge. The chapter concludes with three recommendations that may help professors overcome the obstacles of bringing hip hop into the classroom.

De-privilege academic texts

It is possible to build an entire hip hop class around scholarly texts published on academic presses such as Oxford University or Cambridge Press. Academics regularly claim that they and their books are an important and authentic part of hip hop culture, and I agree that there is much value in utilizing these works. Journal articles, anthologies, and textbooks provide students with a familiar academic experience, and there are obvious ways to design day-to-day assignments around these materials. However, the academic jargon and intellectualization through the language of the academy can alienate students and encourage the reading of rap in ways that are ultimately unproductive.

For those wanting to use texts in the classroom, one strategy is to draw upon both academic and nonacademic sources. Journalistic essays, newspaper articles, and blogs can provide accessible entry into the world of hip hop. Journalists such as Bill Adler, Steven Hager, Nelson George, and Joan Morgan, provide writings about hip hop from an authoritative, yet comprehensible point of view. These authors write as fans of the music—they draw insights from riding the tour buses and interviewing the artists—while also addressing the larger socio-political and historical context of the music. These alternative texts can help students uncover both the artistic poetics and political significance of hip hop.

One exciting possibility is utilizing books and articles (co)written by hip hop artists and those with insider knowledge of the music industry. Books such as Jay-Z's *Decoded* or Prodigy's (of Mobb Deep) *My Infamous Life* are examples of recent books authored by popular rappers.[30] Both offer autobiographical narratives of the impact of inner-city life, crime, and fatherlessness on young people. Musical giants of hip hop's "golden age," including KRS-One and Chuck D (of Public Enemy), have published manuscripts that address Black leadership, public education, and religion. While the market for intelligent raps about world politics and Black Nationalism seems marginal in today's music market, these rapper-authors have discovered success in the text world. For classes about politics, *The Tao of the Wu*, authored by RZA of the the Wu-Tang Clan, is part memoir and philosophical treatise that is endorsed by Cornel West.[31] This new genre of books by rappers contains explicit political discourse usually supported with first-person accounts and annotated rap lyrics, which can further help students decode the meanings of songs.

These popular texts can also serve as the basis of lessons on the political economy of the music industry. 50 Cent's *The 50th Law*, published on his G-Unit Books press, offers business strategies and personal finance planning based on his criminal and music career.[32] To examine the business of hip hop, educators might assign *Make It Happen*, written by Kevin Liles, who rose from unpaid intern at Def Jam Records to Vice President of Warner Music Group.[33] These materials provide an alternative intellectualization of hip hop culture that is accessible and closely linked to the rap music students know and love. Importantly, this can be a way to engage students in the related legal subjects that surround popular culture, such as copyright law, sampling, and intellectual property.

Consider informal writing assignments

Even for students familiar with hip hop, making sense of the music, reading lyrics, and drawing connections to topics of political significance can be a daunting task—especially when they are being asked to do so in the very public and status conscious space of the classroom, or in response to a formal test. Informal writing and listening assignments can help ease students into the new territory of thinking critically about hip hop.

In undergraduate courses involving hip hop, I require that students compile a hand-written (or hand-produced) journal called a "rhyme book." Throughout the semester, students are given short, informal writing assignments about rap songs, music videos, and classroom discussion. One of the only requirements is that the rhyme book is based in autobiography— the writing must be personal and self-reflective. I also suggest that students should feel free to include "art, sketches, poetry, random thoughts, observations, concert ticket stubs, rhymes, rants, magazine clippings, and photography," as long as it reflects an engagement with hip hop. Last, I tell the students that they could use it as a music listening journal, to record and make note of songs that they hear on the radio. This is a graded assignment, though students who write it in regularly and demonstrate creatively are assured an "A."

Instead of transcribing academic speak, I find that this exercise causes students to offer sincere and thought-provoking analyses of hip hop. In addition, they show an ability to use their personal reactions to rap as a way to translate complex issues of power and identity into meaningful text. That is, they build the capacity to translate both hip hop culture and social science concepts into something they understand. In open classroom discussions, students are often hesitant to talk about violence or homophobia, but this exercise can create a safe, semi-private space for students to grapple these subjects.

Informal writing assignments can also be a useful way for educators to assess course progress and measure learning outcomes. In their rhyme books, students usually take the liberty to critique hip hop, the class, and even my performance as professor. In fact, many of the ideas in the essay come from feedback students have written in their rhyme books, not what they put on official course evaluations. Multiple-choice exams might be appropriate for measuring student comprehension of facts. But when hip hop pedagogy is used to teach social justice, self-reflective student writing can be used to determine if students have begun to think critically about injustice or their own privilege. Evidence of successful use of hip hop in the classroom is often found in student self-assessments that they have become active consumers of popular culture, no longer passively "ignoring" racist or sexist lyrics. Likewise, it is rewarding to read that hip hop caused students to rethink the boundaries of sociology or academic inquiry.

Highlight diversity in hip hop

When dealing with college students in elite spaces, hip hop can be seen as being about the disadvantaged "other," or the cultural possession of only Black people. This can prevent any real engagement with hip hop, as students use politically correct responses to avoid dealing with complex social issues. Hip Hop pedagogy is successful when the silence surrounding the various –ism's (i.e. racism, sexism, etc.) is disrupted. I typically know when I have been effective when the framing of classroom discussions about inner-city America or crime shift from "those poor or Black people" to "we" and "I."

A useful strategy is to reiterate the multicultural and multiracial aspects of hip hop. Students may not be immediately ready to talk about race, so having students consider instead regional differences can be a start. Exploring the differences in sound and language in southern hip hop, versus West Coast and East Coast, can start the consideration of more political modes of difference. Likewise, a small project on global hip hop can lead students to explore Australian, Japanese, and German hip hop scenes. The global view of hip hop cultures, plural, can do much to help students think about big ideas such as globalization. The emphasis in this approach should be placed not only on differences, but also on how hip hop provides a universal language of youth empowerment, creative expression, and resistance. Conversely, this exercise can be used to help students reconnect these same issues back to local political issues on campus.

Hip hop conceptualized as only Black culture can work to silence non-Black students and create claims of cultural theft. And relying on one-dimensional notions of Black identity and authenticity can further stifle the benefits of hip hop pedagogy. Pointing out the significance of Latino music, dance, art, linguistics, and expressions in formation of early and contemporary hip hop can bring more students into the conversation. Few students realize that pioneers of hip hop in the early 1970s such as DJ Kool Herc and Grandmaster Flash were Jamaican and Barbadian immigrants. From the 1980s forward, many of hip hop's most popular acts including Heavy D, Notorious B.I.G., Big Punisher, The Fugees, and A Tribe Called Quest have drawn on their Caribbean immigrant culture to influence hip hop. Raising awareness of these facts can help create an atmosphere in which students of various backgrounds can begin seeing themselves as having a legitimate voice in conversations about hip hop. A related successful strategy is to make college students aware that many of their favorite rap groups were formed on college campus, with many self-proclaimed gangster rappers having advanced degrees. Doing so can help students begin thinking about themselves as part of hip hop culture.

Conclusion

In this chapter, I have described several potential benefits for incorporating hip hop into the college classroom experience. Substantively, hip hop can provide a novel way to approach traditional political themes and serve as a springboard for teaching students about the topics of urban politics, inequality, or identity. Moreover, hip hop, when part of a larger critical pedagogical framework, lends itself to encouraging political awareness and social justice. Embedded in hip hop culture is an inherent critique of the status quo, and a desire to challenge injustice.

While hip hop studies is a relatively recent addition to the pedagogical toolkit for educators, this chapter demonstrated that there are already a large number of academic texts available for adoption in courses across the various disciplines, and hip hop scholars are increasingly present on college campuses. However, I have argued that successful rap pedagogy should go beyond translating hip hop into the safe language and logic of the academy, as doing so can undermine the true potential of hip hop. Rap pedagogy can be used to both teach politics and challenge the hidden politics of the classroom.

Engaging students through hip hop does not require elaborate classroom performances. Based on past teaching experiences, I would recommend that most professors stay away from trying rap or dance in class. Equally problematic is casting rap music in such overly academic jargon as to render it unrecognizable. Rather, successful rap pedagogy requires that educators acknowledge how issues of language, generational differences, and racial performance can complicate teaching. Possible strategies for addressing these issues include de-privileging academic text in favor of alternative forms of knowledge, and fostering student expression beyond formal writing and tests. In addition, embracing a multicultural approach can improve the odds that students will experience hip hop as a constructive aspect of the college curriculum.

Notes

1 The author acknowledges the poignant debates over the terminology of "rap" and "hip hop"/"hip-hop." I use these terms interchangeably to refer to music, artistic aesthetics, and the broader identity and culture. The boundaries of rap music genre are notably permeable, and the word rap is not intended to suggest a subgenre of music that is more "intense" or "controversial" than hip hop.

2 Jeff Chang, *Can't Stop, Won't Stop: A History of the Hip-Hop Generation*, 1st edn (New York: St. Martin's Press, 2005).

3 The intellectualization of rap music is marked by the first academic conference on the topic at Howard University in 1991.

4 Murray Forman and Mark Anthony Neal, *That's the Joint!: The Hip-Hop Studies Reader* (New York: Routledge, 2004).

5 Bakari Kitwana, *Why White Kids Love Hip-Hop: Wankstas, Wiggers, Wannabes, and the New Reality of Race in America* (New York: Basic Civitas Books, 2005): 105.

6 Michael Apple, "Whose Markets, Whose Knowledge," in *Sociology of Education: A Critical Reader*, ed. Alan R. Sadovnik (New York: Routledge, 2007): 195.

7 Marc Lamont Hill, *Beats, Rhymes, and Classroom Life: Hip-Hop Pedagogy and the Politics of Identity* (New York: Teachers College Press, 2009).

8 Houston A. Baker, *Black Studies Rap, and the Academy, Black Literature and Culture* (Chicago, IL: University of Chicago Press, 1993).

9 "Real hip hop," critics say, continues to be tied to grassroots, local artists, while top-40 urban radio and mainstream rap represents the inauthentic "fake."

10 S. Craig Watkins, *Hip Hop Matters: Politics, Pop Culture, and the Struggle for the Soul of a Movement* (Boston: Beacon Press, 2005).

11 Jeffrey Ogbonna Green Ogbar, *Hip-Hop Revolution: The Culture and Politics of Rap* (Lawrence: University Press of Kansas, 2007): 17–18.

12 Forman and Neal, *That's the Joint!: The Hip-Hop Studies Reader*.

13 Adam Bradley and Andrew DuBois, *The Anthology of Rap* (New Haven, CT: Yale University Press, 2010).

14 Scholars typically credit Afrika Bambaataa as inventor of the phrase "hip hop" and one of the first to argue that music, rhyme, dance, art, and his fifth element—"knowledge" of self via the Zulu Nation political and social movement—comprises the core elements of hip hop culture. These elements of music, art, dance, poetry, and interpersonal politics, respectively, are usually the basis of the claim that hip hop is more than just beats and rhymes.

15 Chang, *Can't Stop, Won't Stop: A History of the Hip-Hop Generation*; Tricia Rose, *Black Noise: Rap Music and Black Culture in Contemporary America* (Hanover: Wesleyan University Press, 1994).

16 Bakari Kitwana, *The Hip Hop Generation: Young Blacks and the Crisis in African American Culture*, 1st edn (New York: Basic Civitas Books, 2002).

17 Mark Anthony Neal, *Soul Babies: Black Popular Culture and the Post-Soul Aesthetic* (New York: Routledge, 2002); Michael Eric Dyson, *Know What I Mean?: Reflections on Hip-Hop* (New York: Basic Civitas Books, 2007).

18 H. Samy Alim, *Roc The Mic Right: The Language of Hip Hop Culture* (New York; London: Routledge, 2006): 9–10.

19 Imani Perry, *Prophets of the Hood: Politics and Poetics in Hip Hop* (Durham, NC: Duke University Press, 2004).

20 Pierre Bourdieu, *Outline of a Theory of Practice* (Cambridge, UK; New York: Cambridge University Press, 1977).

21 Tricia Rose, "Keynote Address," Paper presented at the *Born in the Bronx*, Cornell University, Ithaca, NY (2008).

22 This rhetorical question was met with nervous laughter, but no one said they would refrain from listening to the KKK song.

23 Alexs D. Pate, *In the Heart of the Beat: The Poetry of Rap, African American Cultural Theory* (Lanham, MD: Scarecrow Press, 2009).

24 Chang, *Can't Stop, Won't Stop: A History of the Hip-Hop Generation*.

25 S. Craig Watkins, "The Hip Hop Lifestyle: Exploring the Perils and Possibilities of Black Youth's Media Environment," Paper presented at the *Getting Real: The Future of Hip Hop Scholarship*, University of Wisconsin-Madison (2009).

26 Anthony Kwame Harrison, *Hip Hop Underground: The Integrity and Ethics of Racial Identification* (Philadelphia, PA: Temple University Press, 2009): 86.

27 Tommie Shelby, *We who are Dark: The Philosophical Foundations of Black Solidarity* (Cambridge, MA: Belknap Press of Harvard University Press, 2005): 166–67.

28 Dyson, *Know What I Mean?: Reflections on Hip-Hop*, 3–4.

29 Adam Sexton, *Rap on Rap: Straight-Up Talk on Hip-Hop Culture* (New York: Delta, 1995): 2–3.

30 Jay-Z, *Decoded* (New York: Spiegel & Grau, 2010); Prodigy and Laura Checkoway, *My Infamous Life: The Autobiography of Mobb Deep's Prodigy* (New York: Simon & Schuster, 2011).
31 RZA, *The Tao of Wu* (New York: Riverhead Books, 2009).
32 50 Cent and Robert Greene, *The 50th Law*, 1st edn (New York: HarperStudio, 2009).
33 Kevin Liles and Samantha Marshall, *Make it Happen: The Hip Hop Generation Guide to Success* (New York: Atria Books, 2005).

CHAPTER SEVEN

To be a rock and not to roll: Promoting political literacy through music and mixtapes

Shyam K. Sriram[1]

It has to start somewhere, it has to start some time/
What better place than here? What better time than now?

"GUERILLA RADIO" BY RAGE AGAINST THE MACHINE (1999)

Popular music meets popular politics

During the 2008 presidential campaign, both the Democrat and Republican challengers used popular music to a large degree in their campaigns. The idea of theme music is not a new one to American politics; Schacter noted that presidential candidates as early as George Washington used music to generate popular support.[2] Yet, in the last few election cycles, there has been a more pervasive use of music to accompany public appearances of candidates and a larger role played by the artists themselves, so much so that the parties and candidates have claimed a sort of "issue ownership" with certain songs. Heart's "Barracuda" became Governor Sarah Palin's theme song and was played when she was introduced at the RNC's convention and also after Senator John McCain's acceptance of the GOP nomination.[3] In a similar fashion, two very different songs accompanied then-Senator Barack Obama's introduction and exit at the DNC convention—U2's "City of Blinding Lights" and Brooks and Dunn's "Only in America," respectively.[4]

All of these might simply be attempts at creative campaigning by using popular music, but the truth of the matter is that music is as important as ever in how people, especially young people, identify themselves, that is, it is not just a political thing. Although the method of obtaining popular music might have drastically changed—LPs to tapes to CDs to iTunes—music still forms an integral part of how people identify themselves and their interests.

Research has shown the hugely important role music plays in the lives of youth the world over. In a 2007 New American Media survey of 16- to 22-year-olds in California, 27 percent of those surveyed said that music and/or fashion defined their identity more than religion, or race.[5] In a similar study conducted in the United Kingdom, the authors found that those surveyed listened to music an average of 2.45 hours daily and preferred listening to music over all other indoor activities.[6] What was even more interesting was why the respondents listened to pop music in the first place. The most popular reasons were "to enjoy the music;" "to be creative/use his/her imagination;" "to relieve boredom;" "to help get through difficult times;" "to relieve tension/stress;" "to express his/her feelings/emotions;" and "to reduce loneliness."[7]

If politicians and candidates are using music to reach new audiences and if young people are identifying with music more and more, then is it not plausible to suggest that music can be used to teach politics or at the very least, used as a medium to *write* about it? The question is how. Academics have been working on creative ideas to use music as a vehicle of instruction and as a way to stimulate debate. Yet, they continue to have the same challenges in teaching students to appreciate politics. Notes Deets, "I have found it challenging to teach students to truly see different sides of contentious issues, appreciate how political science insights can illuminate many aspects of the world around us and really delve into issues of political culture and the power of identity."[8] He notes two particular challenges. Students either bring too much of their own biases and passions to class or conversely, are simply overwhelmed by the unknown, unwilling to understand how politics happens. Echoing a similar sentiment, Soper had this to say:

> There are several challenges to teaching an introductory American politics course . . . Chief among these obstacles are a growing indifference to or cynicism about politics among our students, a pervasive feeling that politics does not relate to their lives, a lack of passion for the study and practice of politics.[9]

But, what if an assignment could be crafted that did both? Allow students to bring their individual passions to class, but also make them confront the unknown by having them question the very selection of these passions? What about a writing assignment on music *and* politics? The "mixtape" essay is a unique and stimulating take-home essay that I incorporate in three different classes I teach at Georgia Perimeter College—POLS 1101, "American Government;" HEDS 1011, "Guide to College Success;" and GPCS 1010, "First Year Seminar." Students are challenged to pick five songs from any genre of music—or language for that matter—and write their version of liner notes, but emphasizing the political significance or symbolism of the music they have chosen. Choosing the songs is moderately difficult, but writing about the political significance of each selection is far harder. This assignment is one for critical thinking, listening, reading, and writing.

A unique assignment melding music and politics could be especially consequential for international students who face particular challenges related to critical thinking and writing in the American classroom. A key point brought up by Centellas is how too often, international students are at a gross disadvantage during in-class discussions and with writing assignments.[10] The disadvantage is evident when students are expected to have some basic understanding of American politics before even stepping into the classroom.

This chapter outlines my experiences using the political mixtape assignment over the last 4 years at Georgia Perimeter College, a multicampus, 2-year access institution in the State of Georgia (24,000 students at last estimate). Over 600 students have completed the assignment and chosen music by almost 800 different artists representing a myriad of languages and 34 countries. This chapter explores similar pedagogical techniques used in political science and other disciplines, trends in popular music, and the powerful way students are able to break out of their shell and write about politics in a cogent and articulate manner. I feel strongly that this "experiment" in music-focused literacy can be adapted for a myriad of academic disciplines, as well as student populations.

What are mixtapes?

A standby from the 1970s, "mixtapes" were cassettes with multiple songs from different artists recorded on them. There is some dispute about the origins of mixtapes—and even the name, with some suggesting "mix tapes" and "mix-tapes"—with many hip hop purists arguing that the tapes grew out of the New York disco culture where early rap pioneers like Grandmaster Flash and Afrika Bambaataa put together "party tapes" that included hard-to-find music, sampling, shout outs and allowed the consumer to recreate the party and club atmosphere, albeit at home.[11]

Mixtapes have gradually evolved with the advent of file sharing and disc burning software, into CDs, ushering in, what Gallagher, has called "the golden age of the mix CD."[12] As Sante eloquently put it in *The New York*

Review of Books, "The maker dubs onto cassette or burns onto CD a group of songs by other hands, the selection and sequence intended to compose a billet-doux . . . It is a natural outcome of home-recording technology, and represents a back-porch, scaled-down amateur version of the highly competitive art of the DJ."[13] According to Schantz[14] and Ciccariello-Maher,[15] mixtapes have a particular significance for fans of hip hop and rap as anyone with the simplest software and CD duplication hardware can produce cheap CDs with demos, unreleased material, radio edits, or just music for the masses.

An alternative theory is that mixtapes grew out of the "bootleg 8-track" era and "were largely found for sale at truck stops and flea markets in the 1960s."[16] This gave way to the exhaustive, do it yourself (DIY) ethic of the 1970s and 1980s where billions of songs were copied from LPs, radio, live records, and other tapes onto new compilation cassettes, which came to be known as mixtapes.[17] For Jansen, "Mix taping became a widespread practice between the late 1970s and early 1990s, after which its popularity declined, gradually giving way to digital forms of rerecording."[18]

Mixed media in the classroom: The research so far

In the following section, I outline some of the scholarship on using multimedia in the classroom to teach concepts and issues relating to the social sciences. Although it is not an exhaustive list, it is encouraging to read about faculty experimentation with using media and popular culture ranging from *The Daily Show* to graphic novels to make the subject matter more palatable for students. Deets has referred to the power of novels and films that force students to ponder questions about "complex power relationships, tensions over communal identity, issues of responsibility and institutional behavior."[19] Yet, he also laments the incredible "disservice" that educators do to students by not bringing popular culture more in to the teaching space. As Soper has similarly noted, educators must "make an effort to understand the world from the standpoint of our students, attempt to increase the cultural relevance of our courses and explore the benefits of using music to make students feel more engaged in the study of politics."[20]

To be fair, there have been several attempts by political scientists in the last decade to harness popular culture as a pedagogical tool. Film has achieved particular success as a medium for teaching political topics. Brozek notes that film-related politics courses have been offered at the University of Texas, the University of Connecticut, New York University, Duquesne University, and the University of Pittsburgh.[21] Certain films have also achieved widespread use as teaching tools—particularly Stanley Kubrick's

1964 film, *Dr. Strangelove (Or How I Learned to Stop Worrying and Love the Bomb)*.[22] Lindley suggest that this "black comedy" can be used to discuss key concepts in US foreign policy and international relations including "deterrence, mutually assured destruction, preemption, the security dilemma, arms races, relative versus absolute gains concerns, Cold War misperceptions and paranoia and civil-military relations (in this order)."[23] *Dr. Strangelove* was also used in a political science class by Garcia Iommi who discussed its portrayal of deterrence, in conjunction with her use of the films *Paradise Now* to discuss Alexander Wendt's social constructivist international relations theory and *Syriana* on Antonio Gramsci's theory of hegemony.[24] "Our students learn in an increasingly visual culture," writes Garcia Iommi, "of which, they are sophisticated consumers, which makes film a comfortable medium for them to reflect on the artifice of these ideas."[25]

Political scientists have also looked at other media for enhancing learning on politics including competition-based reality shows like *Survivor*[26] and American Idol;[27] the *Harry Potter* films and books;[28] and *The West Wing*.[29] The use of reality television can achieve different goals based on the educators' expectations. Centellas used *American Idol* as a basis for allowing students to think critically about Alexis de Tocqueville and Karl Marx.[30] Since "students rarely deconstruct their own social context," when asked to do so through the material of a popular social experience like *American Idol*, students were able to unscramble political scenarios more easily, which made it easier for the educator to engage them on political theory.[31]

Arguing that the current crop of American college students are far more likely to watch and be engaged in shows like *Rock of Love Bus* and *I Love Money* than hard news, Dreyer has suggested an alternative technique for teaching political concepts.[32] Why not channel this new form of reality television programming into the classroom? According to the author:

> I am not suggesting that the reading of academic texts should be replaced with television viewing. Nor do I believe that students can learn everything they need to know about politics through watching reality shows. Nonetheless, popular culture can at times be references in discussions of course material, providing students with alternative ways to think about certain concepts, thereby facilitating learning.[33]

He suggests that reality shows like *Survivor: Cook Islands, Survivor: The Australian Outback* and *Wife Swap* can be used to teach a variety of political science concepts including strategic behavior, balancing power, bandwagoning, alliance behaviour, and the prisoner's dilemma.

Three additional essays also look at the use of comic television as a teaching tool by building on the research about the significant effect of comedy-news shows on political efficacy.[34] In a similar project, though aimed at a decidedly younger population, Allen and Brewer[35] examined portrayals of Governor Sarah Palin on *Saturday Night Live* and its effects on high school students' opinions of the candidate and about government. More recently, Beavers incorporated *The Daily Show* in her classes using a two-step process: comedy clips were screened in class to contextualize current events and then, students were given related assignments using the comic material to engage critical thinking and writing.[36] She asks, "Could comedians such as Jon Stewart, Tina Fey and Stephen Colbert succeed where generations of political science professors and high school civics teachers have often struggled? Could such figures make it [politics] 'cool' (or perhaps even 'sweet' as my own young nephew might say)?"[37]

Another unexplored medium for teaching politics is through comics and graphic novels like Art Spiegelman's *Maus*, Alan Moore and Dave Gibbons' *Watchmen*, Joe Sacco's *Palestine*, and the titles published by India's Amar Chitra Katha publishing house. Brozek has suggested that understanding and appreciating comics is an acquirable skill like critical thinking and listening and one that can make students more perceptive consumers of graphic novels, particularly when they have applicable political content.[38] He writes, "Artists and authors start with a blank, white sheet of paper, which means there are an infinite number of ways to fill the page. Unlike a film or written work, there are virtually no limitations on the artist's imagination."[39] A recent work by Sriram has looked at the titles on religious figures and national heroes in India published by Amar Chitra Katha and how these comics frame Hindu–Muslim tensions through retellings of history, politics, and culture.[40] For a much more detailed discussion of the usage of graphic novels and comics in the classroom, please see Chapter 5 by Kent Worcester in this book.

When it comes to using music to teach concepts in social sciences classes, the research pickings are even slimmer. I was only able to locate three political science papers in the area. In one experiment, Soper conducted an extra-credit project with students choosing songs and videos that compliment the class material for the day.[41] Students were given extra credit to suggest a song to begin every lecture with and asked to mail the educator the song title, the complete lyrics, and one paragraph of liner notes. The student whose song is chosen receives a very small amount of extra credit, but as the author points out, that's not the point—he wants students to feel like they have individually set the tone for the class. Soper explains, "I believe that the assignment is a way to engage students in learning about politics, and that it can ultimately help them become better political scientists . . . I have no intention of abandoning textbooks, but music can often be a successful way to highlight topics to which students only give a cursory glance in the book."[42]

In another experiment, Burgess used popular music in the classroom to raise awareness of and educate about potentially controversial topics like domestic violence, racism, and inequality.[43] Some of the songs used were Billie Holiday's "Strange Fruit," Elvis Presley's "Hound Dog," and the Chrystals' "He Hit Me (Felt Like a Kiss)." Lastly, Stein offered an innovative approach to tackling racial identity and white privilege in the political science classroom through a music video by hip hop group, the dead prez.[44] The author did a pretest first to examine students' knowledge about rap music and their thoughts about rap lyrics. Then the instructor screened the video, "Hell Yeah," and allowed students to reflect on what they had seen. After a moderated discussion, students were asked to complete a post-test questionnaire which gauged their ideas on white privilege and whether those ideas had changed after seeing the video. All of these assignments show great promise, as well as ingenuity, in their use of music as mechanisms for teaching and learning. Whether used as extra credit or vehicles of social change, each experiment allowed students to utilize their interest in popular music as a form of experiential learning.

Clarkston: "Small Town, Big Heart"[45]

I carried out my political mixtape project on the Clarkston campus, unique among all the Georgia Perimeter College (GPC) campuses as well as a location for a college. Since the 1980s, the majority of refugees in Georgia have been resettled in Clarkston, a small city in DeKalb County, approximately 11 miles east of Atlanta. According to St. John,[46] Clarkston's biggest selling point was an over-abundance of affordable housing built in the 1970s to accommodate middle-class workers. Coupled with easy access to MARTA, Atlanta's public transportation system, and the presence of several refugee aid agencies like the International Rescue Committee (IRC), Refugee Family Services (RFS), and World Relief, Clarkston became a refugee resettlement hub for the Southeast United States. This incredible diversity—it is more common to hear Amharic, Somali, and Dzongkha sometimes than English—has also affected the student population of the Clarkston campus of GPC. Most classes have at least one refugee student, across all majors—some have more.

The 2010 Census estimates that Clarkston is one of the most ethnically diverse cities in Georgia. The United States Census Bureau estimated that 2,301 of Clarkston's 7,231 residents (or 33.7 percent) were foreign-born, compared to 11.1 percent for the entire United States. Forty-one percent of Clarkston's residents also speak a language other than English at home, compared to 17.9 percent for the entire United States.

The assignment

The inspiration for this assignment came to me while I was in graduate school at Georgia State University and supplementing my assistantship stipend by spinning records at bars and parties around town and working at the student-run college radio station, WRAS-Atlanta, 88.5 FM.[47] Music and politics formed such a big part of my life and music seemed to be such an integral part of my students' existence that the mixtape assignment seemed to come almost naturally. What if students made mixtapes for me with their favorite political songs? That might be a fun and creative way to get their minds chugging about politics in song. But how was that generating critical thinking and writing on their part? The answer, I thought, was in the lost tradition of the record/tape/CD liner notes that accompanied most music until the twenty-first century. What if students were challenged to write liner notes about their favorite political music for a hypothetical mixed tape? Thus, the mixtape essay was born!

There are three components to the assignment—the in-class discussion; the mixtape essay; and the mixtape presentation. For the introduction to the assignment, I spend about 30 minutes of class time going over the idea behind this paper; the broad types of music, students can choose from (countries, languages, cultures, genres, etc.); and some samples so they get a better idea of what I expect. Borrowing an idea from Soper, I show two music videos in class to get students in the correct mindset for this assignment and to make them really think about what makes music political, and also to showcase some the diversity of musical genres.[48] The two videos I screen are "Ekhtelaaf" by Hichkas, an Iranian artist who raps in Farsi (with English subtitles) and Bruce Springsteen's "Streets of Philadelphia." "Ekhtelaaf" is from the 2010 Iranian film, *No One Dreams About Persian Cats*. The choice of a foreign song seems to matter a great deal for my Non-Native English Speakers (NNES) who seem to light up when they see an artist on the screen, singing in a language other than English.[49] In this case, the song also features gritty lyrics and footage of life in Tehran, the capital of Iran. The latter, a hit song from the film *Philadelphia* (1993), allows younger students to think about how music can showcase important political and cultural issues, and make them understand that political music does *not* have to include references to politicians or war, but can, as in this case, touch on socio-political issues like HIV and AIDS.

After a detailed in-class discussion of the assignment, I post more directions online. These include an introductory paragraph on the relationship between music and politics; formatting guidelines (font, page numbers, citations, etc.); and due dates. I also share *my* five favorite political songs with them so they understand how much this assignment means to their instructor on a personal level. I include the countries of origin to make students, especially the international ones, feel comfortable with international music so that they are encouraged to draw from diverse sources: the Rolling Stones' "Paint It Black" (UK); Jay-Z and Alicia Keys' "Empire State of Mind" (USA); the Procussions' "Little People" (USA); Hichkas's "Ekhtelaaf" (Iran); and A. R. Rahman's "Kanaalinae" (India).

I also provide a sample paragraph of my own and let my students know that this is what *I* would submit if I was doing this assignment. For example, this is the sample paragraph I post about Jay-Z and Alicia Keys' "Empire State of Mind":

> I first heard this song in 2009 when my sister, who used to live in NYC, started raving about it and how it was her anthem. It is definitely a New Yorker's song and in the purest sense, an homage to the Big Apple. But, it is also very political. Specifically, I think of the lyrics, "And since I made it here/I can make it anywhere/yeah they love me everywhere." New York has always represented the successes—and downsides—of the American Dream and these lyrics point to that. Jay-Z represents success and he is inviting other people to share in his dream. But, he also mentions that New York can be too tough, too competitive for some. He raps, "Eight million stories out there/ And they're naked/Cities is a pity/ Half of y'all won't make it." I think this contradiction makes the song political because he is letting folks know that New York is the place to be, but also cautioning that not everyone survives or attains their dream.

Students are asked to write at least 100 words per song, in a similar format to what I provided. They are encouraged to include sample lyrics and some history about the first time they heard their musical selections. The emphasis is on how these songs make them feel. Some students also burn CDs for me, but it is not required and students do not receive extra credit for making CDs in conjunction with their liner notes. Non-English songs must be translated into English.

The third and final component of this assignment is an in-class presentation of any one song from the students' mixtapes. After grading their essays and returning them, I ask each student to email me one song they would like to present in class and I assign songs on a first-come-first-serve basis to avoid artists being represented more than once and in general, to diversify the song selection. The presentation is usually not graded as strictly (or for as many points) as the essay, but since it is a graded component of their overall class grade, students know they have to take it seriously. Since one of my foci is making sure students improve their critical thinking and speaking skills—an expectation I make very clear on the first day of the semester—this final component of the political mixtape assignment ensures those learning outcomes by forcing students to adapt their writings into a short, but cogent presentation on why they chose that certain song and why it is political. On a side note, the presentation part of the assign-ment is a recent addition and was added on the suggestion of a conference discussant. However, it has become an enjoyable part of the assignment for my students, as well as myself, because the students are able to personalize their song selections even more during their presentations and add mate-rial that did not make it to the essay. I have seen some genuine emotion in these presentations—even tears—as students from Nepal to Nebraska have bared their souls in class while discussing songs that mean so much to them.

What has been interesting to observe are the trends in students' song choices. Though the average age of my students is 23 years, the most pop-ular artists continue to be older artists like Marvin Gaye (1st) and Bob Marley (2nd). Second, rap and hip hop artists have the most appeal for students with acts like Tupac Shakur, Young Jeezy, Eminem and Lil' Wayne in the top ten. Lastly, the most common songs chosen were "What's Going On" by Marvin Gaye; "Buffalo Soldier" by Bob Marley; "Changes" by Tupac Shakur; "Man in the Mirror" by Michael Jackson; and "Where is the Love" by the Black Eyed Peas.

One presentation that really stood out to me was made by a student who had served two tours of duty as a Marine sniper in Afghanistan. His song was "Rooster" by Alice in Chains. I had enjoyed reading his written mate-rial on the song in his mixtape essay, but it was his presentation that really shook the roof for the other students and me. He recounted how the song was a homage to the father of one of the band members who had gone by the nickname "Rooster" during Vietnam. My student said that during one of his tours, his squad had come under attack during a routine reconnais-sance mission. In that moment, as he was being pinned down by gunfire, the student mentioned that the only thing going through his head was this song and that he started whispering it to the other Marines—"Here they come to snuff the rooster/Yeah, here come the rooster, yeah/You know he ain't gonna die." In that moment, that student made the class and American foreign policy real for the rest of us and justified to me why the mixtape assignment "works" so well in class.

The real power of this assignment is, of course, in the students' responses and statements about the power of music. It is clear to see that if students are taught to *think* critically then those skills can be transferred to *write* critically as well. In the following four samples, my students are able to write about military service and foreign policy; government accountabil-ity and natural disasters; the internment of Asian Americans; and refugee reflections on genocide, in a way that I believe is unique and refreshing and perhaps, *only* possible through the mixtape assignment:

> He [John Fogerty] is talking about politicians who often use the flag to hide behind it. As a 10 year veteran of the United States Marine Corps,

this touches a deep nerve in me. I often question politicians who are in a position to send troops into harm's way without any military service . . . I expect this as a minimum from my superiors and my troops look at me for the same, so why would I expect nothing else from the suits on Capitol Hill? (a student writing about **Creedence Clearwater Revival's "Fortunate Son"**).

"This song is personal to being a victim of Hurricane Katrina. When I think back to the events of that time period, the lyrics touch a sensitive spot . . . This song just shows that as poor people, we don't count, but as a people we matter to each other. Tie my hands, I can't do anything, so I need help and that is what we didn't get. Relying on each other is how we made it (a student writing about **Lil Wayne's "Tie My Hands"**).

"The song features clips from an interview with the father and aunt of lead singer Mike Shinoda, who tell the vivid story of the life of Shinoda's family before, during and after World War II including their internment at Manzanar . . . Every time I listen to this interview, I can picture the insecurity, feeling and emotion of the Japanese people in the United States caused by bloody war and politics. Can you imagine when you waking up one morning and your family are told to be locked away in a camp?" (a student from Indonesia, writing about **Fort Minor's "Kenji"**).

"As soon as I heard this song I felt like understood what he was feeling and he was trying to say. You can easily tell this song is political because of the lyrics: 'Ain't no way to explain the pain/ That I went through in the rain/ They tried to terminate my kind by putting babies in graves/Man the women got shot and their bodies decay/ They had us running for our lives, man hiding in caves/ Kurdistan I represent I'm from the land of the brave." These lyrics talk about the Kurdish struggle and the oppression that is imposed on the Kurdish people by dictators to further achieve their political agendas. (**Refugee student** from **Iraq** writing about **Brothas From Tha Gutta's "Life Story."**)

Conclusion: Thoughts for the future

There is no denying the influence of popular music on American politics and vice versa, whether manifested in the election slogans or campaign efforts of candidates for higher office or the political messages conveyed by folk, rap, and rock artists in songs and videos. The question of course is how to channel this kinetic relationship into the classroom and create an environment of learning where music opens doors toward a better under-standing of politics. There are some exciting projects, courses, and peda-gogical techniques being employed by educators to use music as a vehicle of expression for students, but clearly the subject area is wide open for further exploration and experimentation.

I believe that the mixtape assignment is enjoyed by my students because it is unusual, which brings a certain shock value, but more importantly because students actually feel like they can express more of themselves through frank discussion of music than any other writing assignment or class discussion. As one student recently said in an email, "I just wanted to let you know I'm super pumped about this writing assignment. I am very passionate about music and was so exciting [sic] to see a writing assign-ment allowing me to freely choose and write about songs that I like and can connect to politics." Looking back at the level of introspection and honestly that accompanies these assignments, I simply do not believe that this level of critical thinking can be manifested simply or in many other assignments.

With that said, however, there are still a couple of potential drawbacks to this assignment. The first is that like many classroom experiments, this one requires a lot of preparation work from educators. Most students will "get" the idea behind the assignment right away, but they will also need detailed instructions on how the assignment should be submitted, as well as the educator's expectation and grading rubric. The second is that because of the nature of this experiment, that is, a hybrid assignment that melds dif-ferent learning objectives, determining if the assignment is a success may be difficult. It is really up to each educator to structure the mixtape project in a way that meets institutionally specific learning objectives.

It is also important to note that this particular assignment, though origi-nally intended for political science educators, can easily be adapted to any number of disciplines. For example, a history professor could ask students to write and/or speak on songs from a certain era or that deal with specific events like the Civil War. Students might choose "The Night They Drove Old Dixie Down" by The Band, "Civil War" by Guns N' Roses, or "When the Roses Bloom Again" by Wilco and Billy Bragg. On the other hand, a professor of geography might utilize this assignment by having students choose two to three songs that deal specifically with place (like "Home" by Edward Sharpe and the Magnetic Zeroes or "Back to Memphis" by Chuck Berry). Students would have to locate the songs (promoting research skills); listen to them with an ear to lyrics (critical listening); analyze the lyrics and write creative liner notes tied to the specific theme (critical writing); and then present the material to class in a confident manner, while maintaining eye contact, and explaining the importance of the songs (public speaking).

In future semesters, I plan on controlling for the students' sex and age, to determine how that might affect the selection of certain songs. I might also insist students provide me with the years of release for the songs to keep better track of generational shifts to look at potential correlations between students' age and that of the songs. I hope this research inspires my colleagues in disciplines across the board to embrace music as not just a teaching tool, but as a potential avenue for the development of critical reading and writing skills.

Notes

1 Thanks to my wife, Shahbana, for being supportive of my career; Robert King, Will Miller, and Chris Soper for their inspiration and direction; Matt Rosensweig, Farbod Kokabi, and Farzad Moghaddam at WRAS-Atlanta; and finally, Jim Henson, for creating "The Muppet Show" and populating my childhood with Kermit, Fozzy, Miss Piggy, and many musical memories.
2 Sarah Schacter, "The Barracuda Lacuna: Music, Political Campaigns and the First Amendment," *The Georgetown Law Journal* 99 (2011): 571–604.
3 Ibid., 571.
4 Christopher Soper, "Rock and Roll Will Never Die: Using Music to Engage Students in the Study of Political Science," *PS: Political Science & Politics* 43 (2010): 363–7.
5 New American Media, "California Dreamers: A Public Opinion Portrait of the Most Diverse Generation the Nation Has Known," Last modified March 1, 2011. Accessed March 9, 2012, from http://news.newamericamedia.org/news/view_article.html?article_id=a4449ee6c67f1191 537a19781c2293fd.
6 Adrian C. North, David J. Hargreaves, and Susan A. O'Neill, "The Importance of Music to Adolescents," *British Journal of Educational Psychology* 70 (2000): 255–72.
7 North et al., "The Importance of Music," 264.
8 Stephen Deets, "Wizarding in the Classroom: Teaching Harry Potters and Politics," *PS: Political Science & Politics*, 42 (2009): 741–4.
9 Soper, "Rock and Roll," 2010.
10 Miguel Centellas, "Pop Culture in the Classroom: *American Idol*, Karl Marx and Alexis de Tocqueville," *PS: Political Science & Politics* 43 (2010): 561–5.
11 Meredith Schantz, "Mixed Signals: How Mixtapes Have Blurred the Changing Legal Landscape in the Music Industry," *The University of Miami Business Law Review* 17 (2009): 293–324.
12 David F. Gallagher, "For the Mix Tape, A Digital Upgrade and Notoriety," *The New York Times* (January 30, 2003).
13 Luc Sante, "Disco Dreams," *The New York Review of Books* (May 13, 2004).
14 Schantz, "Mixed Signals."
15 George Ciccariello-Maher, "Brechtian Hip Hop: Didactics and Self-Production in Post-Gangsta Political Mixtapes," *Journal of Black Studies* 36 (2005): 129–60.
16 Michael Resnick, "Burnlists: The Digital 'Mix Tape' Comes of Age," last modified March 1, 2012. Accessed March 4, 2012, from www.events-in-music.com/burnlist-mix-tapes.html.

17 James Paul, "Last Night a Mix Tape Saved My Life," *The Guardian* (September 25, 2003).

18 Bas Jansen, "Tape Cassettes and Former Selves: How Mix Tapes Mediate Memories," in *Sound Souvenirs: Audio Technologies, Memory and Cultural Practices*, ed. Karin Bijsterveld and Jose van Dijck (Amsterdam: Amsterdam University Press, 2009): 43–54.

19 Deets, "Wizarding," 741.

20 Soper, "Rock and Roll," 363.

21 Jason Brozek, "Boom! Thwak! Teaching War with Comics," presented at the Annual Meeting of the Midwest Political Science Association, Chicago, IL (March 30–April 3, 2011).

22 Dan Lindley, "What I Learned since I Stopped Worrying and Studied the Movie: A Teaching Guide to Stanley Kubrick's *Dr. Strangelove*," *PS: Political Science & Politics* 34 (2001): 663–7; Lucrecia Garcia Iommi, "Let's Watch a Movie! Using Film and Film Theory to Teach Theories of International Politics from a Critical Perspective," presented at the Annual Meeting of the Midwest Political Science Association, Chicago, IL (March 30–April 3, 2011).

23 Lindley, "What I Learned," 663.

24 Garcia-Iommi, "Let's Watch a Movie."

25 Ibid., 3.

26 David R. Dreyer, "Learning from Popular Culture: The 'Politics' of Competitive Reality Television Programs," *PS: Political Science & Politics* 44 (2011): 409–13.

27 Centellas, "Pop Culture in the Classroom."

28 Deets, "Wizarding."

29 Staci Beavers, "*The West Wing* as a Pedagogical Tool," *PS: Political Science & Politics* 35 (2002): 213–16.

30 Centellas, "Pop Culture in the Classroom."

31 Ibid., 561.

32 Dreyer, "Learning from Popular Culture."

33 Ibid., 413.

34 Jody Baumgartner and Jonathan S. Morris, "The *Daily Show* Effect: Candidate Evaluations, Efficacy and American Youth," *American Political Research* 34 (2006): 341–67; Paul R. Brewer and Xiaoxia Cao, "Late Night Comedy Shows as News Sources: What the Polls Say," in *Laughing Matters: Humor and American Politics in the Media Age*, ed. Jody C. Baumgartner and Jonathan S. Morris (New York: Routledge, 2008): 263–77; Xiaoxia Cao, "Political Comedy Shows and Knowledge about Campaigns: The Moderating Effects of Age and Education," *Mass Communication and Society* 11 (2008): 43–61.

35 Meg Allen and Paul R. Brewer, "*Saturday Night Live* Goes to High School: Conducting and Advising a Political Science Fair Project," *PS: Political Science & Politics* 43 (2010): 767–71.

36 Staci Beavers, "Getting Political Science in on the Joke: Using *The Daily Show* and Other Comedy to Teach Politics," *PS: Political Science & Politics* 44 (2011): 415–19.

37 Beavers, "Getting Political Science," 415.

38 Brozek, "Boom! Thwak!"

39 Ibid., 5.

40 Shyam K. Sriram, "Review of Karline McLain's 'India's Immortal Comic Books: Gods, Kings and Other Heroes'," Reviewed in Pop Matters (August 28, 2009). Available from: www.popmatters.com/pm/review/110238-indias-immortal-comic-books-gods-kings-and-other-heroes-by-karline-m.

41 Soper, "Rock and Roll."

42 Ibid., 366.

43 Susan Burgess, "See Jane Rock: Using Popular Music in Political Science and Women's Studies Classes," presentation at the Annual Meeting of the Western Political Science Association, San Francisco, CA (April 21–24, 2010).

44 Robert Stein, "Seeing White through Rap: A Classroom Exercise for Examining Race Using a Hip-Hop Video," *Journal of Political Science Education* 7 (2011): 312–28.

45 Official town motto (www.cityofclarkston.com).

46 Warren St. John, "The World Comes to Georgia and an Old Church Adapts," *The New York Times*, September 22, 2007.

47 www2.gsu.edu/~www885/.

48 Soper, "Rock and Roll."

49 Margareta L. Larsson, *Tips for Teaching Non-Native English Speaking Students* (Atlanta: Center for Teaching and Learning, Georgia State University, 2011).

CHAPTER EIGHT

The case is submitted: Re-enactment theater and US Supreme Court oral arguments

Nina Therese Kasniunas

Student engagement and interdisciplinary study are core elements of a liberal arts education. *The Case is Submitted* is a project that emerged out of an effort of myself and a colleague[1] to engage students in an interdisciplinary manner. Too often students in a particular field of study never have an opportunity to grapple with problems and issues alongside students from outside of their discipline, particularly in upper-level courses. While we are careful to introduce diverse viewpoints into the classroom, seldom do we make a concerted effort to include perspectives of those from other disciplines. Interdisciplinary studies are attractive, particularly in a liberal arts setting, because they offer diversity of perspectives. The goal of this interdisciplinary unit, designed by myself and my colleague, was to engage in a discussion of citizenship and civil rights. Because theater has a long history of breaking barriers and making difficult topics more accessible to the masses, we felt a theatrical re-enactment (a simulation) would be an exciting way for students to approach the topic. By bringing together two distinct groups of students, a Political Science class and a Theater class, we hoped to create an environment in which different points of view on the topic would be heard, and to underscore the idea that citizenship includes all members of a society, not just those who are politically engaged. Additionally, attempts were made to discern any connection between student learning style, receptivity to the project, and whether the project effectively imparted knowledge on the students.

Active learning and student engagement

Student engagement and active learning are terms commonly heard in the hallways of colleges and universities. Particularly at liberal arts colleges, professors are closely evaluated to determine how well they engage students when they are being considered for promotion. Mission statements proclaim the engagement of students. Faculty members participate in "Teaching Circles" and other activities all gauged toward improving teaching skills. And increasingly academic conferences are convened on the topic of teaching within the discipline. All point to recognition within the academy that engaged learning improves the educational experience of the student.

Some professors participated in programs as graduate students that served to introduce them to different pedagogies and teaching methods, others encountered programs during their tenure as junior faculty members geared toward strengthening teaching skills. For others, though, we became creative and improvised when we recognized traditional lecture style teaching did not seem to be that effective. Regardless of how we get to the place where we are seeking ways to better engage students, once there, we find an overwhelming library of books offering different active learning strategies and methods.[2] Not to mention the numerous journals devoted to pedagogy and the many articles written on the topic.

A simulation is a teaching method designed to not only transfer knowledge and develop a skill set, but to teach students the application of skills and knowledge.[3] Active learning can be transformative, "a process by which previously uncritically assimilated assumptions, beliefs, values, and perspectives are questioned and thereby become more open, permeable, and better justified."[4] Simulations are a specific type of active learning that "has the power to recreate complex, dynamic political processes in the classroom, allowing students to examine the motivations, behavioral constraints, resources and interactions among institutional actors."[5] Active learning approaches more generally seek to give students greater insight into political processes, to have them be more active in their learning, to retain information for longer periods of time, to sharpen their critical thinking skills and to develop stronger speaking skills.[6]

Much advice can be found in the literature when designing a simulation. First, the instructor should generate a set of learning objectives and goals.[7] But as Hertel and Millis point out, it is not enough to have a set of learning objectives and goals, they need to be part of a carefully thought out syllabus that clearly states the nature of the simulation along with the goals and objectives.[8] Having objectives and goals will give some structure to the simulation; students will at least have an understanding of why they are undertaking the project. Learning objectives and goals are also an essential component of assessment. The instructor cannot adequately assess the simulation if there are no objectives and goals; without assessment the simulation falls to simply being an activity that potentially breaks the monotony of a class that might otherwise consist of traditional lecture format. It should be noted however, that at least one study found that whether students actually were aware of the learning objectives had no impact on their ability to gain knowledge from the simulation.[9] Cunion was perhaps testing Ramsden's belief that the quality of student learning is in part dependent on how students perceive an instructor's reason for choosing a given teaching method.[10] In either event, it would not be wise from a structural or assessment standpoint to forego identifying the goals and objectives of a simulation.

A number of articles call for written assignments leading up to or worked within the simulation.[11] For some, this is a guarantee of some level of preparation on the part of students,[12] while for others it is one area where gains in student learning are made. Others have recognized that students do not want to be embarrassed in front of their peers and that written preparation goes a long way in easing their discomfort.

Another important component within a simulation, aside from the activity itself, is a debriefing following the simulation. Debriefing can involve "open ended questions that identify processes, goals, motivations, constraints and resources, [an] interview of the major players about their goals, motivations and frustrations, questions on communication, or questions about the reality of the game."[13] The debriefing session allows for the instructor to be sure students are making the connection between their game and the course material.[14] Debriefing also involves an opportunity for students to reflect on the simulation and assess their experience.[15] The debriefing is a follow up to having stated goals and objectives, in order to be sure students are understanding how the activity did (or failed to) meet them. Part of the debriefing following the simulation could be an evaluative component in which the students provide the instructor feedback on their experience.

Of the advice given regarding how to structure simulation activities, curiously some fail to include a seemingly important step—assessment.[16] Although some authors make references to positive course evaluations, they do not explicitly discuss assessment.[17] Scholars have recently acknowledged the assessment void as is evidenced in the literature focused on the empirical testing of whether simulations and active learning are an effective method of knowledge transfer.[18] It also begs the question of how an instructor should assess the effectiveness of an activity. Is it adequate to point toward course evaluation or debriefing comments written by students indicating how much they enjoyed and learned from the activity? Should there be more rigorous testing in the form of an exam in which students are then asked substantive questions about the subject material in order to discern how well they learned the material? For many instructors, assessment likely has taken the shape of the former and if one's teaching is being evaluated through course evaluations, this makes sense. We should not, however, fail to recognize the importance of a more rigorous testing if indeed one of our objectives of the activity is to impart knowledge about some subject matter.

Learning style inventory

One of the reasons instructors turn to simulations, active learning strategies, or some other teaching approach is because of an understanding that a variety of methods in the classroom will help reach more students; not all students learn in the same way. Within the pedagogical literature there is much written about learning styles. One such learning model was developed by Kolb.[19] According to Kolb, learning occurs in four stages: (1) concrete experience, (2) reflective observations, (3) abstract conceptualization, and (4) active experimentation. Extrapolating from these stages of learning, learners have been categorized in four ways. The "diverger" combines concrete experience and reflective observation;[20] divergers like to reflect on learning experiences in which they are able to engage their senses. In other words, they enjoy "hands-on" activities. The "convergers" combine abstract conceptualization and active experimentation.[21] These students begin by thinking about a problem, and then experiment to find a solution. "Accomodators" combine concrete experience and active experimentation.[22] "Accomodators have the most hands-on approach, with a strong preference for doing rather than thinking. They like to ask 'what if?' and 'why not?' to support their action-first approach. They do not like routine and will take creative risks to see what happens."[23] The last learning style is the "assimilator" which combines abstract conceptualization and reflective observation.[24] This represents the most cognitive of the learning styles, those who prefer to think than act; they prefer to listen to information presented to them in a logical and thoughtful, predictable manner.

What Kolb acknowledges is that students range in preferences from concrete experience to learning from abstract conceptualization; from active experimentation to reflective observation. Assimilators learn more effectively in traditional lecture-style formats while accommodators much prefer to be engaged in ways encouraged by active learning advocates. In a study of students enrolled in political science courses, Fox and Ronkowski administered a Kolb-learning style inventory.[25] They found all learning styles were evenly distributed among the students, leading them to recommend instructors to incorporate a variety of teaching styles.

An alternative to the Kolb styles is the VARK model developed by Neil Fleming.[26] The VARK model maintains learners tend to be some combination of four prototypes: visual, aural, reading-writing, and kinesthetic. Visual learners like to see information presented in graphs, pictograms, flow charts, pictures, diagrams, and the like. Students who learn best by hearing and talking, the aural learners, tend to prefer lectures, discussions, and even email. Readers/writers prefer to see information presented in words, therefore they learn through reading, with PowerPoint presentations and information presented as lists. Lastly are kinesthetic learners who prefer to perceive information using their senses; they like to "do" things. While most students will prefer some combination of the styles, inventories can be given to students to determine their preferences. Since most classrooms are filled with students with a range of learning styles, a variety of methods would do best to reach all students.

In recent literature written on simulations and active learning, an attempt is being made to determine whether these activities are better received and more effective with some types of learners than others. For example, those who are largely kinesthetic on the VARK model, or accommodators under the Kolb model are purported to learn better through hands-on activities. Does this stand up to empirical testing? One recent study found it does. In the study, Robbin Smith created a pre- and post-test to give students surrounding a simulation on Congress.[27] The largest gains in acquiring information by participating in the simulation were made by students who were classified as kinesthetic learners according to a VARK inventory.[28] They scored on average more than 19 points on the post-test. The Smith study not only demonstrates the effectiveness of active learning to reaching a certain population of learners, it reminds us that different activities and methods should be used to reach the most students based on their varied learning styles.[29]

Theater and politics

The relationship between theater and politics is as old as Western civilization. The ancient Greeks developed the art form of drama; the earliest playwrights included Aeschylus, Sophocles, and Euripides. These dramas often were influenced by and reflected the politics of the days. The history between theater and politics is extensive and cannot be properly treated in this space. However it should be noted that political issues such as power and dominance have received extensive treatment on stages throughout history in all parts of the world. Theater allows us to interact and deal with difficult or sensitive topics in a space distinctively unique from reading a story or news account.

Augusto Boal is a playwright who recognized this distinctive space. Through his experiences on the stage he recognized how theater allowed the audience to interact with the subject presented to them in the play, recognizing the instantaneous (sometimes visceral) feedback from the audience. Boal would change the actor/audience dynamic by inviting members of the audience to interrupt a play at particular moments and offer alternative responses or directions than indicated in the script. As this drama form progressed he would invite audience members to come up, not only change the direction of the script, but to act out how the member felt the play should proceed. Boal continued to explore the dynamic of acting and came to draw heavily upon the thought and writings of Paulo Freire. Freire wrote *The Pedagogy of the Oppressed* calling for a revolution in classrooms in which the hierarchical power structure between professor and student would be dismantled.[30] He advocated for an environment in which learning was entered into by the professor and students on an equal plane. Leaving the students as an "empty vessel" to be filled with the professor's knowledge only served to reinforce the oppressive power structures present in colonialism. Augusto Boal then applied Freire's thoughts about the classroom to the stage. For Boal the stage should be a space wherein power structures did not exist and actors and "spect-actors" can enter into a pure dialogue grappling with difficult political issues. In fact, Boal went on to create legislative theater, which he enacted while he was in elected office, wherein communities, through acting identify issues of concern and locate potential causes and solution.

Another variant of this, but with a tradition older than the legislative theater, is community theater. Community theater is an important vehicle for change in marginalized communities. The theater enables community members to confront the dominant ruling class' values systems and negotiate different structural relationships within and beyond the existing regime.[31] Again, the stage is a distinctive space which allows participants to engage with and confront difficult issues. The notion that individuals are freed to explore oppressive and sensitive issues on the stage rests on the idea that role-playing allows individuals to take on another's perspective and evaluate themselves from the other's viewpoint.[32] This is also the premise or rationale for employing simulations in the classroom. Having the student leave one's own self and take on the role of another enables the student to explore a topic or issue from a different vantage point. It also forces the student to see her own actions and thoughts through the viewpoint of the other.

Theater and politics come together naturally and in retrospect it is surprising that more interdisciplinary activities between Political Science and Theater are not developed. Students within both disciplines have both encountered the political realm but up until this point most of the political science students had not interacted with it in the distinct place of the stage.

The Case is Submitted

The Case is Submitted thus was a collaborative effort between myself and a colleague in the Theatre Department. Teaching at a small liberal arts college, we conceived this to be an interdisciplinary unit which would bring together my Introduction to American Government class and his Introduction to Dramaturgy class. Our goals and objectives were very much aligned with the philosophy of a liberal arts education. We hoped to impart on our students a lesson on citizenship. We wanted students to see that citizenship is not the exclusive domain of those interested in politics. It is, at a minimum, the responsibility of all members of a community. We also hoped bringing the two classes from different disciplines together, would demonstrate a diversity of viewpoint likely to be found within any community, and the richness such diversity provides to the discussion at hand.

Another objective of ours was to actively engage our students in a discussion on discrimination. While the relevance and magnitude of civic issues become clear to students in the course of this project, it is role-playing that turns this intellectual inquiry into an educational activity that accomplishes more objectives. Role-playing encourages students to engage their personal passions and beliefs in the constitutional debate. It builds character by asking students to play roles that have authority and consequence, roles they do not normally play in their daily lives. It also presents students with a unique acting challenge: they must express themselves in the particular rhythms and hesitations of another person's thought and speech. This can be an extremely demanding challenge, but when successfully achieved by students, the irregular and interrupted speech patterns of Supreme Court Justices and high-powered lawyers add tremendously to the authenticity and humanity of the debate.

Our project is comprised of five pedagogical components:

- Study of and attendance at Supreme Court oral arguments— Goucher College is located in Baltimore, which is 45 miles from Washington, DC.

- Selection of a case with research and review of the case briefings.

- Re-enactment of the oral arguments with improvisational elements.

- Debate and decision-making among student participants.

- Analysis and comparison of the participant decision with the majority opinion of the Court.

Step one: Preparation

There is much planning to do in the early stages. First, ideally both classes involved in the project would be scheduled to meet on the same days and times during the semester in which the project is to be executed. Our classes were not so instead, over the 2-week period we canceled some classes and scheduled special meeting days and times for the project. We planned only two shared experiences among the students: the field trip and the re-enactment performance. In lieu of more shared classes, I spent additional time in my colleague's Theatre class and he spent time in mine. In retrospect we believe sharing the entire 2 weeks would have enhanced the experience for all students.

We planned a field trip to inaugurate our interdisciplinary unit. The field trip would serve to generate excitement for the project, give students an opportunity to witness the event they would be re-enacting, and give students an opportunity to interact with one another prior to the simulation. All three elements prepare students for the simulation, helping to increase their comfort level entering into such a unique and perhaps foreign experience. If you have the resources to go on a field trip to witness the activity your class will be re-enacting, this should be your kick-off event. Planning for the field trip should occur during this initial stage of preparation, particularly if you need to secure funding.

Next, you need to choose a case to re-enact. We wanted a case dealing with some aspect of civil rights. *Boy Scouts of America v. Dale* (2002) quickly emerged as our choice case because we believed students would be able to relate to it, it centers on discrimination, the case was narrowly decided, and it was ruled in a way we believe would be contrary to how our students would have liked it to be. We steered away from unanimous Court decisions because we wanted our students to learn there are different perspectives among the justices of the Court and that there is more than one way to argue how a case should be ruled. In this instance, the ruling (which we believe would be unpopular) could either serve as a provocateur pulling students into the discussion or at the very least serve as a lesson in learning and understanding an alternative perspective.

You also need to be sure you can locate transcripts of the oral arguments for the case you selected.[33] This will not pose a problem unless you select a "historic" case that goes back far enough that we do not have audio recordings of the oral arguments. If you are re-enacting some other event or activity, you will need to find transcripts and read through them to identify whether they will need to be edited in any manner because of time constraints.

Step two: The field trip

For many, the Supreme Court is shrouded in mystery. It is the branch of government with which we have the least contact and the only one that is not accessible to television cameras. What better way to introduce students to the Supreme Court than to bring them to oral arguments. There is one difficulty in trying to attend oral arguments—observers are seated on a first come, first served basis. This means individuals begin lining up early in the morning to be able to get in to see oral arguments. If you do not get seated you have an opportunity for a "5 minute viewing" where you can be brought in to the very back of the gallery and watch the oral arguments for 5 minutes. After arriving by train into Washington DC, we realized we would not make the cut for getting seated for oral arguments. We therefore opted for the 5-minute viewing deciding to spend the rest of our time in DC visiting Capitol Hill and the House of Representatives office buildings.

The quick 5 minutes was well worth the trip. There were gasps of excitement heard when my students first saw the justices and much animated talk about what they saw and heard afterward. But the greatest benefit of this inaugural event revealed itself on the train ride home. Students were bonding with one another—they were becoming friends and forming a shared identity. Baker identifies this as a benefit of simulations more generally.[34] She said, "Students become acquainted during the exercise, leading to increased student participation through the rest of the semester."[35] But for my students, mostly freshmen, it was the first time they identified themselves as a unit, a class of political scientists. Due to an issue that arose weeks prior to the scheduled trip, the Theatre class canceled their participation in the field trip. This was regrettable, seeing the bonding experience it provided for those who did attend. The bonding experience also further cemented the likelihood that this was an event they would not forget any time soon.

Step three: Lead up to performance

At the end of our class meeting prior to our field trip, we distributed copies of the briefs submitted by the petitioner and respondent and asked students to begin reading and identifying the important questions being asked of the Court as well as the precedents on which each argument was based. After our field trip we spent a class discussing the briefs, the precedents used, and the questions presented. A variation on this could involve having students read and discuss amicus curiae briefs filed by third parties. While they are not typically represented in oral arguments, including these briefs could enhance the discussion for more advanced classes. During this class we also informed those students who would take on a role in the re-enactment who they would portray.

The theater class in preparation not only read through the briefs, but they also found YouTube videos of the Supreme Court justices in order to observe their comportment, to see their mannerisms, and hear them speak. They also read through parts of the transcript in rehearsal. Future implementations of this simulation will have the Political Science students spend some time observing the justices, although we would have them do this on their smart phones on the field trip train ride into Washington, DC to observe oral arguments.

Step four: The re-enactment

The keystone event of the project is the re-enactment performance. We scheduled our event for the evening and held it in a special meeting room which was set up with podia for the counselors and a long table with name placards for the justices. We found black robes which all of the justices donned and had a viewing area set up for the audience, not unlike the gallery in the Supreme Court. It is advisable to find a special location for the event to heighten the distinctiveness surrounding the re-enactment. We planned on an hour for re-enactment of the oral arguments and 30–45 minutes for small group discussion following. During the re-enactment scripts were used, but read-throughs of it prior to the event ensured students would be able to handle irregularities in speech, difficult pronunciations, and the like.[36] Audience members consisted of students not playing roles and interested visitors. Scripts were made available to them to follow along or take notes as necessary. A short break was taken after the re-enactment with subsequent discussion in small groups in which students were asked to decide the case and present the reasoning behind their decision. All participants (role-players and audience alike) were involved in the small group discussions and they were designed to mix Theatre students with Political Science students. The event culminated in the small groups presenting their rulings to the others and us (the instructors) handing down the real ruling of the Court. On the way out, students were given the opinion of the Court along with the dissent and instructed to read them for the following class.

Step five: Debriefing

In class following the performance, we dissected and discussed the Court's ruling comparing it to how the students had originally ruled. These discussions happened in separate classrooms although my colleague and I were present for one another's class. We then talked about why we chose to do this project and gave students time to write down their thoughts and reactions about the project. In my class, students had an additional reading assignment on political theater and had a short discussion surrounding it with my colleague.

Assessment

Students were assessed with an essay question on the final exam about the majority and dissenting opinions of the Court. Additionally, the reflection writings collected during the debriefing served as feedback on the project. Students appear to have gained knowledge from the simulation; all (with one exception) demonstrated this on their final exams. They also enjoyed the experience and were enthusiastic about it as illustrated on the reflection comments and course evaluations. Whether this was a more efficient teaching method than a standard lecture/discussion model is not able to be discerned as there is not a comparison group of students who were subjected to a lecture/discussion model instead. Ideally there could be an empirical testing of the effectiveness of the simulation versus the lecture/discussion model however only one section of Introduction to American Politics is offered each year with enrollment only around 15–25 students. Understanding the difficulty we would have in testing this, we decided to distribute a VARK learning inventory to students the first day of the semester. Our thought was that the feedback would not only give a better understanding of their learning needs, but then allow us to see if indeed certain types of learners (such as kinesthetic) are more receptive to and better served by simulation activities.

The results of the VARK assessment indicated learning styles were fairly evenly distributed. Some students were more suited to kinesthetic learning and others toward aural. Overall, the class tended to lean strongest toward aural learning and second toward kinesthetic learning. We had suspected, coming into this project, that kinesthetic learners would be more evident. However, the results are interesting and do not conflict with the assumption that the oral argument simulation would be effective. Not all students were active in the role-play to the extent they played one of the characters, everyone else sat in the "gallery" and listened to the re-enactment. This would work well for aural learners. Using the VARK inventory was an interesting exercise (and we will likely use it again) but really the size of our sample was too small to detect any meaningful patterns to offer evidence on the effectiveness of the project for kinesthetic learners.

Although scholars are necessarily concerned about assessment, and determining whether the activity enhanced the attainment of knowledge, this is not the only goal. An equally important outcome consists of having put the students into the distinctive space of the stage. Putting students into roles other than their own allows them to step outside of themselves, explore other perspectives as well as seeing their own perspectives from the viewpoint of the other. There is no clean, empirical way to assess what is gained from the exercise, but we would suggest that doing the exercise itself is a strong enough outcome on its own.

Alternatives to "The Case is Submitted"

While this project was planned and originally implemented as an interdisciplinary unit, it can also be implemented within your course without collaborating with another department. At our institution, the interdisciplinary element was important from a normative perspective, but it also had a practical benefit. We are a small school with small class sizes. Typically there are only 15 students enrolled in the Introduction to American Politics course, so having a larger group of students (a larger audience) made this feel more like an "event." However, if you teach a course with 30 or more students, this can easily be done with your students alone. Active learning activities such as simulations or re-enactments can be used in any class size; you may just have to modify certain elements. For example, if you teach a class of 150 students you might consider scheduling a separate re-enactment for each discussion section. If you do not have a scheduled discussion section for the course, during the planning stage you could arrange to have a week of evening sessions and have students sign up for the session that best fits their schedule. The re-enactments could occur in smaller groups of 25–30 students while the debriefing session could be held with the entire class as one. As long as you use the preparation stage accordingly, there is no reason to think it is too complicated or difficult to create a simulation or re-enactment for your course.

Another alternative already mentioned is substituting the kick-off event, which in our case was a field trip to attend oral arguments at the Supreme Court. Substitutions, again, can include a field trip to the closest federal district court or watching a documentary on the Supreme Court. We would recommend the latter over the former because it increases the specialness of the whole project. This would require additional lessons on the procedural differences between the two types of courts, but lessons students would have needed anyway. It also raises the level of excitement within the students. The greater the level of excitement and anticipation for the actual re-enactment, the more care and consideration students will turn toward it.

Should you have the opportunity to make the trip to Washington, DC to attend oral arguments, you might consider re-enacting one of the cases you witnessed in person. Doing so would put students in the position of deciding the case long before the actual opinion on the Court is handed down. This could elevate the quality of student work that goes into rendering a decision, and require more critical thinking on the part of students.

Lastly, the re-enactment we conducted stayed fairly close to the script, the transcripts. An alternate approach is to use the transcripts in the preparation classes leading up to the re-enactment, reading through the transcripts at the same time you are exploring the arguments and precedents presented in the briefs. Then, rather than re-enact the oral arguments, you can have students do a simulation in which they, as the counsel for the petitioner and respondent, are ready to face questions and answers by the justices about the briefs submitted. The justices would be free to explore the arguments presented in the briefs with their own formulated questions. This alternative approach would require much more preparation and thought by the students beforehand, but the students would be forced to engage at a much higher level of thinking and the payoffs in terms of developing the students' critical thinking skills would be very great. We would perhaps recommend using this alternate approach with upper-level courses rather than with an introductory course.

Conclusion

Political theater has a long history and we should therefore not be surprised at how well Theater and Political Science students came together for a lesson in citizenship. For 2 weeks out of the semester these students embarked on a distinctive project in which re-enactment of Supreme Court oral arguments gave them access to the judicial process and immersed them in a moral and legal conversation about discrimination in our society.

Increasingly, college and university professors are turning to simulations and role-playing as pedagogical tools. Simulations are touted as bringing lessons to life for students, challenging them to be flexible and swift in their thinking, and leaving them with skills which can be applied in the practical field of study. Theater has an enduring history of breaking down barriers and making difficult subjects accessible to the masses; role-playing does the same, on a much smaller scale in the classroom. Allowing students to take on roles not only enlivens material for them and sharpens their thinking skills, but it also gives them an opportunity to practice speaking in public.

Our students used a re-enactment of Supreme Court oral arguments to engage in a discussion about civil rights, all the while learning much about the legal process and reasoning behind the opinions of the Court. This lesson could have been delivered in a number of other ways, but we chose an approach that also reinforced other lessons regarding the broad reach of politics and the importance of including all citizens in a discussion of issues such as discrimination, not solely those involved in politics. Individuals have different experiences and ideas depending on their interests. School teachers will have a different perspective on discrimination than will the business woman, computer programmer, or the local elected council member. Because issues like discrimination impact on all members of a community, all members of a community have a responsibility to enter into the discussion on the issue, in the hope the issue will be resolved in a way most beneficial to all members of community. Choosing a venue (the Supreme Court) often thought to be the most mysterious in politics only heightened the enthusiasm and interest of the students; this lesson likely will be remembered far into their futures.

Looking forward, we see that this project can be moved beyond the classroom. Just as many professors are increasingly using more engagement techniques in the classroom, more colleges are offering experiential learning experiences or opportunities for students to partner with local community organizations and groups. There is an opportunity to identify interested parties in the community with whom students can use oral argument re-enactments to stimulate conversations on a variety of topics of interest: civil rights, freedom of speech, freedom of religion, individual rights to privacy, to name a few. Theater as an art brings many benefits to a community, but small-scale theater re-enactments can bridge partnerships between students and the community which serve to generate dialogues centered on important civic issues.

[Please see the companion website for the book. Details are listed on the back cover of the book.]

Notes

1 Many thanks to Michael Bigelow Dixon for developing this project with me.
2 See for example, Alexander W. Astin, *Achieving Academic Excellence* (San Francisco, CA: Jossey-Bass, 1985); Linda A. Baloche, *The Cooperative Classroom: Empowering Learning* (Saddle River, NJ: Prentice Hall, 1998); Elizabeth F. Barkley, *Student Engagement Techniques: A Handbook for College Faculty* (San Francisco, CA: Jossey-Bass, 2009); John C. Bean, *Engaging Ideas* (San Francisco, CA: Jossey-Bass, 2001); John Paul Hertel and Barbara Millis, *Using Simulations to Promote Learning: An Introduction* (Sterling, VA: Stylus, 2002); David A. Kolb, *Experiential Learning: Experience as the Source of Learning and Development* (Upple Saddle River, NJ: Prentice Hall, 1984); Wilbert James McKeachie and Barbara K. Hofer, *Teaching Tips: Strategies, Research and Theory for College and University Teachers* (Lexington, KY: Houghton Mifflin, 2001); Chet Myers and Thomas B. Jones, *Promoting Active Learning: Strategies for the Classroom* (San Francisco: Jossey-Bass, 1993).
3 Hertel and Millis, *Using Simulations to Promote Learning*.
4 Patricia Cranton, *Understanding and Promoting Transformative Learning: A Guide for Educators of Adults* (San Francisco, CA: Jossey-Bass, 2006) as quoted in Barkley, *Student Engagement Techniques*, 6.
5 Elizabeth T. Smith and Mark A. Boyer, "Designing In-Class Simulations," *PS: Political Science* 29 (1996): 690.
6 Ibid.
7 See for example, Victor Asal and Elizabeth Blake, "Creating Simulations for Political Science Education," *Journal of Political Science Education* 2 (2006): 1–18; Rebecca Glazier, "Using Current Events to Design Classroom Simulations," Paper presented at the *APSA Teaching and Learning Conference*, San Jose, CA (February 22, 2008); Hertel and Millis, *Using Simulations to Promote Learning*; Smith and Boyer, "Designing In-Class Simulations."

8 Hertel and Millis, *Using Simulations to Promote Learning.*

9 William Cunion, "Learn this," Paper presented at the *APSA Teaching and Learning Conference*, Baltimore, MD (February 6–8, 2009).

10 Ibid. Paul Ramsden, *Learning to Teach in Higher Education* (New York: Routledge, 2003).

11 See for example, Nancy Baker, "The Trials of Teaching the Supreme Court," *PS: Political Science* 27 (1994): 253–5; John Fliter, "Incorporating a Sophisticated Supreme Court Simulation into an Undergraduate Constitutional Law Class," *Journal of Political Science Education* 5 (2009): 12–26; Brian Frederking, "Simulations and Student Learning," *Journal of Political Science Education* 1 (2005): 385–93; Smith and Boyer, "Designing In-Class Simulations;" Laura VanAssendelft, " 'It's the Supreme Court, Stupid': A Simulation Approach to Feminist Thinking," *Feminist Teacher* 16 (2006): 216–24.

12 VanAssendelft, ibid.

13 Smith and Boyer, "Designing In-Class Simulations," 693.

14 Glazier, "Using Current Events to Design Classroom Simulations."

15 Frederking, "Simulations and Student Learning;" Smith and Boyer, "Designing In-Class Simulations."

16 Asal and Blake, "Creating Simulations for Political Science Education;" Baker, "The Trials of Teaching the Supreme Court."

17 Fliter, "Incorporating a Sophisticated Supreme Court Simulation into an Undergraduate Constitutional Law Class."

18 Frederking, "Simulations and Student Learning;" Chad Raymond, "Do Role-Playing Simulations Generate Measurable and Meaningful Outcomes? A Simulation's Effect on Exam Scores and Teaching Evaluations," *International Studies Perspectives* 11 (2010): 51–60.

19 Kolb, *Experiential Learning.*

20 Richard L. Fox and Shirley A. Ronkowski, "Learning Styles of Political Science Students," *PS: Political Science & Politics* 30 (1997): 732–7.

21 Ibid.

22 Ibid.

23 http://changingminds.org/explanations/learning/kolb_learning.htm (last accessed October 29, 2011).

24 Fox and Ronkowski, "Learning Styles of Political Science Students."

25 Ibid.

26 N. Fleming, *VARK: A Guide to Learning Styles* (2001), at www.vark-learn.com/english/index.asp (last accessed October 29, 2011).

27 Robbin Smith, "Simulations, American Government, and Student Learning Styles," Paper presented at the *APSA Teaching and Learning Conference*, Baltimore, MD (February 6–8, 2009).

28 Ibid.

29 Information about the Kolb and VARK inventories can be found on the website accompanying this text.

30 Paulo Freire, *Pedagogy of the Oppressed* (New York: Continuum Publishing, 1970).

31 Shulamith Lev-Aladgem, "Remembering Forbidden Memories: Community Theatre and the Politics of Memory," in *Social Identities* 12 (2006): 269–83.

32 George Herbert Mead, *Mind, Self and Society* (Chicago, IL: University of Chicago Press, 1934).
33 Resources to help you find transcripts to oral arguments can be found on the companion website.
34 Baker, "The Trials of Teaching the Supreme Court."
35 Baker, "The Trials of Teaching the Supreme Court," 254.
36 Most transcripts of oral arguments can be found at www.oyez.org/.

CHAPTER NINE

The comparative politics of zombie attack

Steven Williamson[1]

Introduction

In the fall of 2010 I incorporated a semester-long classroom exercise into an introductory course in comparative politics. The student cohort was 35 students, which I hoped to divide into small groups of six students or fewer. The class had a mixture of traditional and nontraditional students, and many were in their Freshman or Sophomore year. The exercise centered on the concept of zombie apocalypse as an example of state collapse and the subsequent reconstitution of the state. Using a fictional catastrophe as the starting point for a discussion of how real-world states face crises is not necessarily obvious, yet the proliferation of zombie imagery in popular culture is undeniable. I contend that this proliferation says something about our underlying anxieties over the fragility of our social order and the state. I am not alone in making this connection. In June of 2011, a resident of Leicester, England, used a freedom of information statute to force the city council to admit that they were unprepared for a zombie attack. Within a week hordes of zombie impersonators staged a mock attack, overrunning the city.[2] Similarly, the CDC discovered that zombie apocalypse was both useful as an eye-catching hook to advocate disaster preparedness, and as an engaging platform for ongoing discussions about public health crises.[3] Zombies are therefore interesting as a topic of discussion in themselves and illustrative of various aspects of crisis management and societal collapse. The popularity of the zombie genre also provides a great "hook" to capture the interest of students.

The value of active learning, such as role-play and collaborative exercises, has been well documented in the literature both in terms of improved student interest and improved grasp of the material.[4] The purpose of this chapter is to explore the specific potential for the idea of a zombie apocalypse to further our understanding of the state and our relationship to it as citizens.

The chapter is broken into three sections: the first consists of a brief deconstruction of the exercise that I actually implemented in 2010, the second discusses how the zombie concept relates to theoretical conceptions of the state, and the third section outlines a briefer version of the zombie exercise to target the specific questions raised in the second section. My intention in this chapter is to demonstrate how the implicit anxiety manifested in popular culture can be explicitly harnessed to fuel a deeper understanding of the concepts undergirding the modern state. While the chapter concludes with a ready-made exercise that can be used without modification, I hope that the chapter might also prove useful in generating ideas for lectures, in-class discussions, or alternative exercises.

The "Apocalypse of 2010" and theories of teaching and learning

The concept for the initial exercise was to treat the class as one large committee (a committee of the whole) that had for mysterious reasons been contacted with the information that a zombie apocalypse would occur at the end of the semester. No other information was given, and the class was instructed to divide into a series of subcommittees that would think through all of the stages of the crisis, from the initial outbreak to the eventual reconstruction of society and the state. Seven subcommittees formed the overarching Zombie Committee (or ZomCom): Zombie Intelligence, Crisis Prognosis, Safe Zone, Community Planning, Legal and Constitutional, Longterm Defense, and Rebuilding and Colonization. Each subcommittee was assigned a series of questions, which were to be addressed in a report to the class as a whole. The exercise then anticipated that each subcommittee would incorporate the evolving understanding of the crisis into its own responses. The ZomCom met every other week and would begin with a report from the subcommittee responsible for that week's report, followed by debate and any necessary actions/votes. The meetings typically used 20–30 minutes of class time every other week. As the class met twice weekly for an hour and fifteen minutes, approximately one tenth of class time was dedicated to the exercise. I did consult with each of the subcommittees independently as their report was approaching, but this was ordinarily possible in the time immediately before or after the regular class meetings.

I had anticipated that there would be some contention, particularly when the exercise moved to the reconstruction of society and the state. The questions addressing the law and constitution of the new state were in fact intended to generate controversy by asking, for example, whether or not zombies might have rights. Such difficult questions not only make the activity more interesting, but also have potentially important functions for learning.

The use of simulations and role-play exercises in the classroom has a number of theoretical pedagogical justifications. These justifications center on the ability of such exercises to fundamentally alter the dynamic between the teacher and the student. Morrone and Tarr argue that a variety of theoretical perspectives can be useful in the classroom, provided the designer chooses the theoretical perspective appropriate to the educational goal.[5] By this argument, the most traditional approach to education, the "behavioralist" perspective, assumes a fixed body of knowledge that the teacher communicates to the student. This would be the theoretical foundation appropriate to a traditional lecture, for example. The less traditional "information-processing" perspective assumes that the role of the teacher is to train the student in effective learning strategies. These would include exercises designed to provide templates and structures for learning in general. Moving still further from the traditional model is the Piagetian "constructivist" model, which sees learning as a process of internal conflict resolution. In this model the student constructs knowledge by assimilating new information and reworking existing knowledge in the process. Even more radical is the "social constructivist" account wherein knowledge is the product of social interactions rather than internal processes. By this account interactions between students are as essential as interactions between instructor and student.

Clearly each of these perspectives assumes a different relationship between teacher and student, becoming less hierarchical as they progress away from the traditional model.[6] Role-play and simulation best serve the constructivist and social constructivist perspectives—students interact in order to define the field of knowledge to be assimilated rather than relying entirely on the instructor. The body of knowledge accessed in these exercises is not assumed to be entirely fixed and external to the learning process itself. Students can arrive at new understandings of contested concepts. Conflict over the material is therefore to be understood as beneficial, as it provides challenges to existing beliefs. Some also point out that this type of problem-based learning encourages meta-cognition, thinking about thinking.[7]

Fictional circumstances, such as zombie attack, inherently depend on constructivist and social-constructivist perspectives, as students are pushed not only to examine the actual concrete practices that embody political concepts today, but also to envision how the world would look without those practices or with altered forms of the concepts. In the Piagetian framework this pushes students to engage their higher-order, formal-operational cognitive capacities.[8] For example, if we discuss property rights today we can make various assumptions that will not necessarily be possible after the zombie apocalypse. Whereas today we can talk meaningfully of property deeds and law courts, these are not likely to survive in their present form after the event. The constructivist perspectives invite the students to build a fresh understanding of the concepts, given the changed circumstances. The call for theoretical eclecticism, however, does not require us to abandon more traditional theoretical foundations. Locke, for instance, did write specific things about property rights that should be understood and taken into account. Thus, a lecture on Locke's perception of property rights is completely appropriate alongside less traditional exercises. The key difference between a traditional lecture and a simulation or role-play undertaken with a social-constructive perspective, is that the lecture assumes certainty about some area of knowledge, while the less traditional exercises rely on doubt, questioning, and conflict. Without conflict there is no need to rethink existing knowledge and belief, the primary mechanism for intellectual growth by the Piagetian account.[9]

Overall, the zombie committee generated a fair amount of enthusiasm and did work well in building from each subcommittee report to the next. However, the exercise did not generate much controversy on the subject of reconstituting the state, and in fact the class seemed to settle on an illiberal and militarized state without much debate. Thus the contentious issues were tactical, rather than ideological. This was not a complete surprise, as the literature within political science suggests that crisis-based decision-making is not conducive to democracy, particularly under low state capacity.[10] Furthermore, insofar as the zombie genre does contemplate an ongoing role for the state, it is frequently the military alone that proves useful. These points will be explored further below, but they underscore that the exercise was largely a success. The students successfully articulated a complete vision of the zombie apocalypse, the postapocalypse reality, and the type of regime that they felt would fit that reality. The shortcoming of the exercise, which I realize was a problem of my design rather than their execution of it, was that it did not allow for the creation of competing visions of the threat posed by zombies and a resulting postapocalyptic reality that might in turn inspire competing visions of the state.[11] Some might justifiably assert that the postapocalypse reality does not provide fertile ground for a liberal conception of the state or for the extension of human rights to the living dead. While this is ostensibly true, the zombie genre is not monolithic and the postapocalyptic world does not necessarily preclude the emergence of a liberal state or a rethinking of the zombie as an inhuman other.

The following section of this chapter addresses the relationship of the zombie genre in general to the concept of the state. It then explores three particular films that provide different insights into the postapocalyptic reality and our relationship to the living dead. This provides the theoretical framework that underpins the final section of the chapter, which outlines a scaled-down version of the original exercise designed to maximize ideological contention.

What the zombie apocalypse can teach students about the state

The state, according to Weber, is characterized not by its ends but by its means.[12] That is to say that various entities that could be termed "states" might have a variety of ends, but all states function through the same mechanism—a monopoly over the legitimate use of force in a given territory. Zombies undermine that very nature of the state under this conception, insofar as legitimate violence during the apocalypse is universal and certainly not state-directed. The state loses its ability to be the arbiter of violence. The violence of the zombies is a given and creates an atmosphere of chaos, but the violence of the living is instantly legitimated, both as a response to violence in itself and in particular to violence from a nonhuman or semi-human "other" that is incapable of anything else. The inherent reasoning here is syllogistic. All zombies are violent, those who are violent are legitimate targets of violence, therefore all zombies are legitimate targets of violence. We do not need permission from the state or case-by-case analysis to justify human-zombie violence, it is inherently legitimate. This is the same kind of thinking that keeps us wary of all rattlesnakes, rather than trying to get to know them as individuals.

But zombies are not animals as such. They are our neighbors, friends, family, and co-workers who happen to be dead and transformed into hideous monsters. This tension between the recognition of the human past and the horror of the zombie present is frequently and inevitably exposed when the survivors must address the fate of an infected comrade or loved one who then becomes part of the threatening "other." This sets the zombie crisis apart from other apocalyptic disasters. After an earthquake your mother is still your mother. The zombie crisis lets loose incredible violence and the state in its Weberian conception is overwhelmed. But beyond the collapse of the state the social order itself is destroyed and with it, the normative foundations of our daily lives. The advent of the apocalypse signals not just the advent of war between zombies and the living, but also the specter of violence and chaos among the living.

How zombies help students to understand the state of nature

Those who conceive of a social contract (e.g. Hobbes, Locke, and Rousseau) define the state not by its means, as in the Weberian conception, but by its ends. For Locke, the state uses its capacity for violence to assure us our liberty and our property. For Hobbes, the state is formed to "overawe" us and to convert the state of nature (the state of war) into civil peace. For Rousseau, the state of nature is idyllic but denies man his full potential, so that the social contract allows men to become fully themselves. The collapse of the state within the zombie genre clearly produces a return to something like a state of nature, but it is in no way what Rousseau had in mind. It is instead the Hobbesian state of nature, but on steroids.

The implication is that civilization itself is called into question, and with the destruction of the social and political order the concept of "property" becomes almost instantly outmoded. Remarkably, a zombie apocalypse inverts completely the traditional Anglo-American value structure of our world. Ordinarily we spend most of our time working to buy things and keep them—we expend our time (our lives) to gain things. In the zombie movie we see valuable homes and cars, the largest purchases most people make during their lifetimes, left idle or destroyed in order to gain a few more precious moments of life. We therefore dispose of things to gain time (life). Two dynamics make this so. First, there are few living left during the apocalypse so that there is an enormous surplus of goods. Second, the value of continued life suddenly outweighs the value of any given object, particularly given the surplus of objects.

In this ultra-Hobbesian world we do see the emergence of a semi-Lockean sense of ownership, as in *Zombieland* when a character complains of being robbed. The things stolen from him were not his in the preapocalypse sense of ownership, but rather in the sense that he had been using them and had perhaps modified them to his tastes. The concept of ownership emerges then, if at all, in the sense that all people have an equal claim to all things and appropriate them to themselves through some labor (even if that labor is simply picking the thing up). Of course whereas Locke makes this argument in reference to the fruits of nature, the zombie film makes it in reference to a world filled by the flotsam of the sinking human species.

In Marxist terms, the means of production has become scavenging. Humans have become vultures picking at the carcass of their former lives, and we might expect that if anyone survives and civilization is rebuilt that the new society might look completely different. The preceding discussion covers the significance of the zombie apocalypse for the collapse of society, which was incorporated into the initial exercise under the responsibilities of the first few subcommittees. These groups were charged with forming a picture of the collapse of the state/society and the organization necessary for survival (see appendix[13]). However, I am convinced that this groundwork might be just as easily and perhaps more effectively covered by a brief lecture and classroom discussion. The exercise proposed here really focuses on the period after the collapse, when the few survivors attempt to move forward into the postapocalyptic realm.

In the original exercise the notion was that the work of each subcommittee would provide the basis for the work of subsequent subcommittees. Thus, the work of Zombie Intelligence was to construct a fairly detailed picture of the zombie threat and this provided a rough guide for future subcommittees. As mentioned above, I was particularly excited to see what the subcommittee dealing with legal and constitutional order would devise, as they had been assigned some provocative questions, for example, "Do zombies have rights?" When writing that question I certainly had in mind the films that really begin to question the nature of human–zombie relations postapocalypse, such as *Fido*, *Land of the Dead*, and *Shaun of the Dead*. I expected that the students would engage this controversy but instead they adhered unquestioningly to the assessments provided by Zombie Intelligence. What resulted was a legal order that resembled the Salem witch trials with a dash of liberal property rights. The lesson for me was, ask a Hobbesian question, get a Hobbesian answer.

Still, the exercise was certainly a success in terms of the interest generated by the theme and the experience of working as a committee to resolve real-world problems in a hypothetical setting. If anything the students succeeded in working together too well. What was absent was actual controversy. Upon further reflection and feedback from academics more experienced in the field of classroom role-play and simulation, I decided to redesign the exercise to focus exclusively on the process of establishing a legal and constitutional order in a postapocalyptic environment and to promote discussion and dissent by creating competing factions.

Rethinking the exercise with contention in mind

In the following exercise, three groups will be assigned a different movie and a packet of readings as primary sources to "front-load" their conception of the world. This does not, of course, predetermine the conclusions of the discussions, but it does create the probability of dissent between the factions. Additionally, given the range of issues raised by the primary sources, the questions asked will also be expanded from the original exercise. Overall this increases the focus of the exercise on the process of incorporating abstract concepts into a fictional, socially constructed reality.

Primary sources

All of the films listed here might be considered "campy" zombie movies. Three are comedies and the fourth is ostensibly serious, but "over the top." There are two reasons for this. First, it so happens that these films all raise serious questions about the nature of zombie–human relations in a way that is not possible for pure horror movies, which must use the unqualifiedly mindless zombie as a plot tool. Second, these movies are more accessible to students who might not care for the zombie genre. Perhaps it should go without saying, but it is important to remember that some students might find the kind of graphic violence depicted in zombie films (even over-the-top campy ones) too disturbing. It is therefore worth asking any students who feel they might be overly impacted by the movies to contact you for an alternative assignment (such as taking additional reading responsibility for articles that would complement the primary materials package). Other films might be chosen as well, but I recommend the following.

Fido (2006): In this film the title character is a zombie owned by an archetypal suburban family from the 1950s, with the twist that in this version of the past a zombie apocalypse has left a radioactive field that reanimates the dead almost instantly. A benevolent monopoly, Z-Corp, has however developed a special collar that keeps the zombies under control as something between a pet and a slave. The film has a *"Leave it to Beaver"* feel to it, but this masks some deep and perhaps disturbing questions. Funerals where the head is buried separately from the body have become a symbol of status, the elderly are considered inherently dangerous (given the likelihood that they might suddenly die and be reanimated), and the relationships between zombies and humans can at times assume an emotional dimension that may or may not be completely platonic.

Shaun of the Dead (2004): In this film the title character, Shaun, and a small group of friends and relatives face the typical zombie meltdown with a good deal of humor and style. Several scenes stand out as important: at the outbreak of the zombie crisis Shaun goes about his morning routine oblivious to the emerging chaos around him; during the crisis he must face the fact that his own mother has become infected; the crisis ends as the state reemerges (in the guise of the armed forces) to reestablish law and order; and in the end the zombies are converted to a subhuman laboring class, which includes Shaun's best friend Ed, who is kept in the garden shed playing video games. *Shaun of the Dead* therefore implicitly argues that the state is durable enough to survive the crisis and furthermore that the existence of zombies is not necessarily an unmanageable threat. Moreover, zombies might be useful to society and social bonds between zombies and humans, though greatly altered, may ultimately survive.

Zombieland (2009): Another humorous take on the postapocalyptic reality, *Zombieland* follows the adventures of a group of survivors who go only by the names of cities, Columbus, Tallahassee, Wichita, and Little Rock as they travel across country looking for Twinkies and amusement parks. The central tension in this film is whether it makes any sense to form any relationships in a world where anyone might turn on you and no one is guaranteed survival. The film ends on a somewhat positive note, however, as the small band of survivors ultimately decides to stick together. This film is interesting because it very consciously lays out the notion that survival requires rules. In the beginning these are practical and antisocial-Columbus writes rules for himself that include "double tap" (shooting a zombie twice to make sure it is dead) that reflect an environment where trust and confidence are dangerous. Nevertheless during the course of the film the characters do come to rely on each other, signaling the possibility that society may survive and that a new world may yet be possible.

Land of the Dead (2005): Written and directed by the master of the genre, George Romero, this is the most serious of the films suggested here and represents the evolution of the zombie genre toward a consideration of the postapocalyptic reality. Here some vestiges of state authority have survived and the humans have achieved some level of (at least temporary) security within the confines of a walled city. However, the political order that has survived here is no longer the relatively benevolent state we see in *Shaun of the Dead*, but is instead oppressive and oligarchic. Here the living are not much more trustworthy than are the dead, and the dead themselves are not the mindless creatures seen in other films, but are capable of emotion, learning, and evolution. This presents the idea that the zombies are a rival form of humanity rather than merely nonhuman.

As a primary source of information, these films vary on key points: the survival of the state, the form of the postapocalyptic state, the role of property, the ability to make agreements/trust, and the nature of the zombie–human relationship (Table 9.1).

The choice of these four films is clearly not arbitrary, as each provides a different vision for what the survivors of the zombie apocalypse will face. The legal and constitutional framework of the new society will require different starting points in each case and the answers to new problems (such as the nature of zombie–human relations) will be impacted by the way these problems are presented. The degree to which the state collapses dictates the maneuvering room allowed for subsequent legislation, so while the residents of *Zombieland* are really free to innovate a new regime or to live as anarchists, those in the *Land of the Dead* must contend with entrenched interests controlling the remnants of the state or choose to go it alone.

These films can then be paired with appropriate readings to emphasize the distinctions between the differing zombie ontologies presented. The redesign of the exercise seeks to expand on the original issues presented to

TABLE 9.1 Summary of the films discussed and the theoretical positions they offer for the assignment

Film	State survival	Form of state	Property	Contracts/trust	Zombie as "other"
Fido	Yes	Corporatist state dominated by a single monopolistic conglomerate	Yes but property rights are not secure against the security apparatus	Contracts honored but elements of paranoia in social interactions	Domesticated zombies treated as property, but possibility of limited reason and affection between zombies and humans
Zombieland	No	Nonexistent	Semi-Lockean or Hobbesian	Doubtful but possible	State of total war (Hobbesian state of nature) with zombies that are incapable of reason
Shaun of the Dead	Yes	Presumably liberal-democratic	Property rights as preapocalypse with additional possibility of owning zombies	Restored to preapocalypse levels	Zombies are kept as subhuman servants or pets, incapable of reason but may retain some vestiges of former identity
Land of the Dead	Partially	Oligarchic security state	Property rights persist but the division of wealth is highly uneven	Contractual obligations enforced but social/class division persists and trust in society is limited	State of total war between zombies and humans, but zombies are capable of limited emotion, reason, and learning

TABLE 9.2 Summary of reading and film pairings, and the themes presented in these pairings

Subcommittee	Movie(s)	Core readings	Overall theme
One	*Land of the Dead*	*The Communist Manifesto*, Marx (All)	Class conflict and elite control
Two	*Zombieland*	*Leviathan*, Hobbes (Chapters 13–21)	Animalistic human/ zombie nature
Three	*Fido* and/or *Shaun of the Dead*	*Second Treatise on Government*, Locke (Chapters 2–9)	Possibility of building trust among people/ zombies

the Legal and Constitutional Subcommittee in order to highlight these differences. The following is not intended to be an exhaustive list, but if students are asked to watch one movie and to read the short passages suggested or others of similar lengths, then the overall preparation should not be too burdensome. While the readings listed here highlight some of the clear tensions in the films with which they are paired, any readings questioning the nature of the state, property, and individual liberty might be interesting to consider in the context of a zombie apocalypse. Since students are working in groups it is always possible to expand on the overall theme with additional readings and to divide the labor within the group (Table 9.2).

The exercise

The original exercise was not designed to maximize contention, but rather to illustrate the concepts of state collapse and reconstruction while the whole class worked as a committee. Thus the Legal and Constitutional Subcommittee was charged with devising a new framework for the postapocalyptic state. The original mandate to the subcommittee was as follows.

Legal and constitutional

This will address the legal and constitutional considerations appropriate to the new community and draft recommendations in a five- to seven-page report. These recommendations will cover: the best form of government for the new community, the relationship of the community to other survivor communities, personal and property rights within and outside the community, the administration of justice, and the rights of zombies.

The exercise made several assumptions that the current exercise does not (e.g. the existence of other survivor communities) that are not necessary in the current framework. More importantly, this initial formulation of the exercise did not spell out what was involved in the questions of "personal and property rights . . . justice, and the rights of zombies." This omission became apparent to me in the course of the exercise and was the driving force that motivated its retooling. Specifically, I wanted the new exercise to draw out the legal status of zombies, the legal status of private property, and the possibility of a return to a democratic order. Furthermore, the challenge presented by each of these questions is compounded when we consider them in tandem. For example, can zombies organize themselves democratically? Such questions were lost in the initial project because it did not focus on them in particular. The following exercise is intended to capture these lost pedagogical opportunities by making the legal and conceptual issues surrounding zombies, property, and the state the primary concern of the exercise for the entire class. In this exercise the students will all face identical questions, but will begin from different ideological frameworks. It is intended as both a ready-made exercise that may be used in its current format and a general framework that might be usefully altered or adapted as needed to probe some of these thorny issues.

Once the students have been separated into three groups and given their list of primary materials, they should be given some generic instructions such as these.

Small group assignment

You have been contacted by a mysterious but well-informed scientific network known only as Z-web. They have very reliable information, from sources they cannot divulge, that a zombie apocalypse is imminent. As such, they have assembled planning councils to determine the best survival strategy for the human species and the best long-term plans for the future rebuilding of society. There is broad agreement in Z-web about the nature of the early phases of the zombie threat and the best survival strategies. However, there is strong disagreement over projections for the long-term nature of the threat and the likely form of society in the wake of the apocalypse. Three factions have formed within Z-web and they cannot reach any agreement. The resultant discord is threatening the mission itself. As such they are appealing to you to help them resolve this controversy. Your class will be the committee that resolves the dispute. Each of the three subgroups formed has been asked to view a movie which closely mirrors the predictions of one of the Z-web factions. It is your job to argue for the legal and constitutional order that makes the most sense, given what you have learned from the film. The following questions must be explicitly answered, specifying the arguments invoked in your discussion. If anyone from the group dissents (does not agree with the decision of the subcommittee) then they have the right to have their objection entered into the record. Your answers will be the platform or proposed program of your team. You should think of this platform as the basis of a new postapocalyptic constitution that anticipates potential conflicts before they arise. It is therefore crucial that you answer all of the questions, even if they seem unlikely to arise immediately after the apocalypse.

Review the following questions before watching the assigned movie and reading the other assigned material for your group. Try to think about these issues as you watch the film and do the readings. What scenes or passages would you cite to back up your argument? When your group reconvenes, be prepared to discuss these questions and come to agreement as a group.

Questions

Property rights

1 Do individuals have the right to keep property that they had before the apocalypse?
2 What if that property is necessary to someone else's survival?
3 How is property acquired after the apocalypse?
4 If someone has become a zombie, is their property open to be claimed by anyone or does it belong to their rightful heirs?
5 Can the state seize property for the good of the community?
6 Will money be worth anything?
7 How will goods and services be exchanged?
8 Will it be possible or necessary to work?
9 Can people own zombies?

Zombies

1 What do we do with survivors who become infected?
2 What if a loved one becomes infected (a parent, child, or spouse)?
3 Is it ever appropriate to use zombies or the threat of zombies as a punishment (for criminals or enemies of the state)?
4 If so, can criminals/enemies only be expelled from the safety of the community or could you actually throw them to the zombies?
5 Do zombies have any emotions?

6   Can zombies think?

7   Can they learn?

8   Could zombies ever form their own society?

9   If so, how would that society be organized? Would it have "natural" leaders or would it be democratic?

10   If zombies had their own society could humans and zombies ever reach a truce?

11   Should zombies have any rights within human society?

12   Should zombies have any rights within zombie society?

The state

1   After the zombie apocalypse, will the state (meaning the institutions of government) reassert itself?

2   Will society become democratic again? Will power be shared equally?

3   If power is not shared equally, who will be in charge?

4   What role should wealth play in deciding who governs? If not wealth what should decide?

5   If a state can be maintained what is its job so far as zombies are concerned?

6   Can the state ultimately provide us with security once the initial crisis is over?

Typically this type of assignment will require the small groups, or subcommittees, to meet at least once after they have each done whatever reading and viewing is required. There is no reason why this meeting could not be done during class time, but it could also be done outside of class or even online. In any case there should be sufficient time between the dissemination of the assignment and the subcommittee meeting for the students to do the work and reflect on it. Finally, when the small groups have prepared reports the entire class should meet to see if they can reach an overall consensus on the questions presented. In the original exercise I found that 2 weeks between meetings allowed the subcommittees to have enough time to do their work without losing momentum. Using that schedule the entire exercise outlined here would take one month. The initial discussion and dissemination of the assignment can be done in the last 15 minutes of a regular class, the subcommittee meeting does not necessarily need to be done in class, and an entire class period should be dedicated to the final full-class discussion.

Assessing outcomes

Assessment of this type of assignment is always difficult, particularly the work done as a subcommittee. It seems reasonable to assign each student a grade based on the overall performance of their group in using the assigned materials to answer the questions, the participation of that student in the full-class discussion, and an additional short reflection paper to be completed after the exercise. Using this format, the work of each subcommittee is factored in, but the individual grade is also based on the student's success in rethinking the political concepts challenged by the simulation. There is not a single right or wrong answer, but the ideas presented by the student need to be defended with reference to the assigned materials and the exercise itself. The success of the student is therefore not determined by the absorption and regurgitation of a preordained understanding of what the state, property, or rights mean. Instead the exercise anticipates that students will come to see these concepts as complex, interrelated ideas that are challenged when the status quo is altered. It is on that basis that the exercise and the individual performance of the students ought to be assessed. (The actual grade breakdown should be specified in the syllabus.) The guidelines for the reflection paper can be distributed after the conclusion of the exercise. Some suggested questions:

1 How do differing perspectives on the nature of the world/humanity lead to differing perceptions of legal rights?
2 What groups have historically been excluded from participation in democracy because they were seen as "others" or outsiders?
3 How does trust/mistrust of other people influence political preferences?
4 How do you feel about the value of this exercise? How would you assess your own participation?

Conclusion

The preceding chapter is intended to scratch the surface of what I suspect is a very deep vein of anxiety in our popular culture over the fragility of our apparently stable states and societies. In this vein, we can view the success of the zombie genre as a manifestation of that anxiety, which is implicit in the films themselves. Additionally, at town councils in Britain and at the CDC in the United States, that connection has been made explicit. My intention in conducting the original exercise and in presenting the revised version outlined here has been to harness the anxiety and issues inherent in the zombie genre to assist students in rethinking political concepts.

Specifically, I have focused on the implications of these films for our conceptual understanding of the state; the difficulty of reestablishing normal politics in the wake of state collapse; and the fragility of individual rights. The popularity of the genre allows zombies to be accessible for today's students while capturing socially relevant anxiety, which necessitates the resolution of cognitive conflict and facilitates the assimilation of new knowledge. This chapter demonstrates these potential uses of contemporary film as a new tool for teaching political concepts. I hope this will prove both useful and inspiring for others.

Notes

1 I would like to acknowledge the editors of this volume and the participants of the 2011 APSA T&L Conference panel on Role Play and Simulations in Comparative and International Politics for their input on the original version of this exercise and suggestions for its improvement.
2 British Broadcasting Company, "Zombie Attack: Leicester City Council Overrun by Undead." Accessed September 1, 2011, from www.bbc.co.uk/news/uk-england-leicestershire-13823427.
3 Centers for Disease Control, "Zombie Preparedness." Accessed September 1, 2011, from www.cdc.gov/phpr/zombies.htm.
4 J. Patrick McCarthy and Liam Anderson, "Active Learning Techniques versus Traditional Teaching Styles: Two Experiments from History and Political Science," *Innovative Higher Education* 24 (2000): 279–94.
5 Anastasia S. Morrone and Terri A. Tarr, "Theoretical Eclecticism in the College Classroom," *Innovative Higher Education* 30 (2005): 7–21.
6 Ibid.
7 Luann Wilkerson and Wim H. Gijselaers, *Bringing Problem-Based Learning to Higher Education: Theory and Practice: New Directions for Teaching and Learning, no. 68* (Hoboken, NJ: Jossey-Bass Inc., 1996).
8 Morrone and Tarr, "Theoretical Eclecticism," 7–14.
9 Ibid; see also Bevevino, Mary M. Joan Dengel, and Kenneth Adams, "Constructivist Theory in the Classroom: Internalizing Concepts through Inquiry Learning," *The Clearing House* 72 (1999): 275–8.
10 Giovanni Sartori, *The Theory of Democracy Revisited* (Chatam, NJ: Chatam House, 1987); Charles Tilly, *Democracy* (New York: Cambridge University Press, 2007).
11 This exercise was discussed in greater depth in a paper presented at the *2011 APSA Teaching and Learning Conference*.
12 Max Weber, *Politics as a Vocation* (Philadelphia, PA: Fortress Press, 1968).
13 Please see the companion website for the book. Details are listed on the back cover of the book.

PART FOUR

Film and television

Introduction

From the inception of the moving image, political actors have recognized its communicative power. As early as 1915, D. W. Griffiths' *The Birth of a Nation* achieved mass appeal and impact with his racially charged presentation of the Klu Klux Klan as a heroic force in the post-Civil War South. Leni Riefenstahl's 1935 *Triumph of the Will* depicts the Nazi consolidation of power with vivid imagery and cinematography. Though the Nazi ideology contained within is likely repugnant to most, few deny that the visual landscape in Riefenstahl's film is stunning. Political actors have sought to harness this power, in pursuit of both benign and malign objectives. The ubiquitous nature of modern visually oriented technologies has only amplified the political impacts of film and television.

Thus, film and television present educators and students with rich "texts" to utilize in understanding contemporary political life. Many movies, from documentaries to political propaganda, from independent films to Hollywood blockbusters, contain arresting depictions of political phenomena. In addition, we live in a "renaissance age" of television. Hastily assembled and crude "variety hours" of decades past are gone. Modern television dramas such as *The Wire* or *Mad Men* possess dense, novelistic structures and methodical character development, often harboring many layers of intensely political meaning. The contemporary proliferation of news networks, though sometimes short on meaningful, objective journalism, nevertheless assaults us with images for consideration and critique. Lastly, political satire—often directed at the above-mentioned networks— has reached a remarkable level of sophistication and impact. As a testament to this, the lines between such satire and the "real world" frequently become blurred.

Luckily, this decades-long accumulation of visual media coincides with an age where it is vastly easier to incorporate film and television into our learning environments. It no longer means rolling a VCR and television into the classroom, painstakingly fast-forwarding to relevant sections, and begging for our students' patience as they squint at the small, occasionally jumpy image in front of them. The modern classroom is a thing of wonder, possessing technology that enables instantaneous access to digital media, high-quality projection and sound systems, and the ability to instantly pinpoint relevant film or television segments. Furthermore, online learning environments enable us to host digital media or provide links to video that supplement themes in our courses. In this sense, educators can become "co-authors" of the visual experiences of their students.

Yet we must proceed with caution. A modern world in which we are awash in political imagery can be overwhelming. We may experience a "saturation effect" where our minds cannot process this information beyond the most superficial of levels. We must be cognizant of this as we deploy visual media in the classroom.

The authors in this section explore pedagogical uses of film and television, examining ways to bring politics to the students in forms they inherently understand, yet perhaps do not consciously interpret, or even recognize, as political. Dannagal Young's chapter engages the political satire of Jon Stewart and Stephen Colbert, pinpointing how humor can be a rich resource that facilitates comprehension and retention of complex political phenomena. However, her chapter is cautionary in that it also explicates how humor, if misused, can actually undermine these objectives. Similarly, Miller and his co-authors examine numerous films by the animated giant Pixar, to demonstrate the ways that these seemingly innocuous, digitally animated films with loveable characters unlock challenging political questions.

This section also engages visual media as a means to reach beyond one's society and understand the complex dynamics of foreign political systems or contemporary international affairs. Cook examines recent films that engage the fascinating internal dynamics of African politics. Yet he warns that those who utilize them must be mindful of the ways they can reinforce preconceptions or stereotypes about the characteristics of these states. Lantis explores the use of film to understand war and peace in an upper-level course on international security. He then reflects upon his experiences teaching the course in both a film-centric and a traditional format, providing valuable guidance for those considering similar curricular innovations.

The common thread emerging from these pieces is that visual media possess significant potential pedagogical value, but should not be incorporated into curricula haphazardly or without precise attention to the learning objectives one wants to achieve. If we do the latter, we can actually undermine intellectual growth and comprehension in our students. As educators puzzle over how to best utilize a new set of visual possibilities in the classroom, such thoughtful examinations can serve as an essential and valuable guide.

CHAPTER TEN

Entertainment, satire, and the big questions of our political world

Dannagal G. Young

While the role of humor in educational activities has a long and complex history the question of how televised political satire might facilitate classroom discussion and critical engagement with politics has rarely been explored.[1] Political satire programs like those hosted by Jon Stewart and Stephen Colbert offer political and media satire in a format well-suited to the enhancement of classroom discussion and to the illumination of central course concepts. Yet, the research examining humor and satire's effects on attention, recall, and comprehension is mixed. In this chapter, I explore this body of research, synthesizing findings from education, psychology, neuroscience, and communication regarding humor's impact on attention, recall, comprehension, and cognitive elaboration. To help instructors understand the micro-level processes through which humor affects these key outcomes, the chapter then offers a reflection on the psychological mechanism underlying humor construction and appreciation. By dissecting the mechanism responsible for creating humor, satire, and irony, instructors can better pinpoint what element of a text or lecture will be affected by the use of a specific humorous stimulus in the classroom. Three examples from *The Daily Show* and *The Colbert Report* on the topics of journalistic norms, campaign finance law, and the logic of scientific research, are presented and deconstructed. Using these examples, I illustrate how, if used *correctly*, televised political and media satire can not only promote attention and engagement among students, but can also enhance recall and comprehension of large concepts, propositions, and critiques.

Humor as a pedagogical tool: Mixed findings

Research on the role and impact of humor in education has centered on two important categories of outcomes, student satisfaction (an affective evaluation of the course or instructor) and student performance (usually measured through comprehension or recall).[2] In general, students give higher evaluations to instructors who use humor over instructors who do not, though only when the humor is deemed constructive or relevant to course materials.[3]

More important than humor's impact on student satisfaction, perhaps, is the relationship between instructor's use of humor and rates of student learning. Here, research indicates a positive association between humor and student comprehension and retention.[4] Yet again, this relationship depends on the relevance of the humor to the course lesson.[5] In fact, Wanzer, Frymeir, and Irwin's *Instructional Humor Processing Theory* (IHPT) posits that for humor to foster student learning, it must be found appropriate and relevant and must be met with positive affect. In addition, the humorous component of the text must be tied directly to course materials to foster cognitive processing of concepts central to the course curriculum.[6] If the humor is irrelevant, the enhanced attention given to the humor will serve to distract from (and hence undermine) the cognitive processing of curriculum-centered concepts.

A recent review by Banas and colleagues concludes that the successful use of humor in the classroom requires that it be topical, related to course materials, not overused, and congruent with the instructor's natural teaching style.[7] In fact, Banas and his colleagues provide detailed guidelines to help instructors implement humor in a way that will maximize engagement and learning. Rooted in the work of Ziv,[8] the authors advocate that, "The instructional humor should illustrate a concept that has just been taught, and instructors should then paraphrase the material again after the laughter subsides."[9] Such a method will maximize student performance by taking advantage of the humor's ability to foster recall of "concept material" and its ability to foster attention and interest.

Evidence from psychology: Humor's effects on attention, recall, and message processing

These observations from education scholars are remarkably consistent with findings from psychology and communication regarding the cognitive mechanisms involved in humor processing. Studies of message attention and encoding consistently demonstrate that people engage in deeper processing in the face of unexpected events, hence privileging encoding and later retrieval of such events in memory.[10] Because humor often involves the intersection of an established frame of reference with an incongruous, unexpected one, scholars have posited that the comprehension and appreciation of humor fosters attention and recall by default.[11]

Due to such enhanced attention, humorous messages tend to receive greater cognitive elaboration and deeper processing compared to nonhumorous messages,[12] a finding that has been replicated using eye-tracking studies.[13] Importantly, most studies of this kind also find that attention to nonhumorous components of a message suffers when humor is present. Earlier work by Schmidt using nonphysiological measures found similar patterns, with humor enhancing attention at the *expense* of attention to nonhumorous content.[14] Strick and her colleagues explicate how these findings relate to the deliberate use of humor in communication and learning contexts:

> Although privileged attention for humor may benefit learning when used to illustrate important concepts, the present research indicates that humor that is unrelated to the study material may impair learning. In summary, whether humor could be successfully applied in communication depends on the importance of explicit memory (above and beyond implicit memory) and the relevance of the humor in the learning context.[15]

Research from cognitive psychology and advertising echo these sentiments. Wyer and Collins posit that humor will have the strongest beneficial impact on elaboration and recall when it is both unexpected—hence fostering attention—and relevant—hence fostering attention to the "correct" elements of the message.[16] In a study of humor's impact on advertising effectiveness, Kellaris and Cline state simply, "unexpected information is superior to expected information, relevant information outperforms irrelevant information, and expectancy and relevancy interact to produce differential effects on recall."[17]

In addition to studies of attention and recall, research from neuroscience has employed fMRI studies, finding that humor comprehension is associated with the activation of the frontal cortex and involves the activation of those regions of the brain associated with the anticipation of reward, joy, and euphoria as well as appraisals of uncertainty.[18] Indeed, these studies reinforce the notion that humor's effects on message elaboration and processing depth operate (at least in part) through attention; since it is attention that is enhanced through the anticipation of reward and in the navigation of the unexpected. However, these studies also point to a more complex form of cognitive processing in response to humor than we witness in response to nonhumorous stimuli.

As neuroscientists Coulson and Lovett assert, "Jokes presuppose the speaker's ability to interpret language against background knowledge."[19]

Coulson and Williams have referred to humor comprehension as "a high-level language phenomenon . . ."[20] Recipients of humor are involved in a sophisticated—yet largely automated—process. They encounter new information that they hold in working memory, activate old information from long-term memory, interpret the new in light of the old information, encounter an unexpected gap, then attempt to reconcile it through cognitive contributions, all of which happens in working memory. The nature of such processing is akin to complex mental gymnastics. Evidence from neuroscience demonstrates that humor is associated with increased activity in the right hemisphere of the brain which governs information processing involving the manipulation of information in long-term memory.[21] Additional studies have identified high working memory load among those most adept at comprehending humor as well as brain activity indicative of the processing of incongruity and the active reprocessing of information.[22]

While these complex cognitive tasks might signal enhanced processing that could lead to higher comprehension and recall, some scholars propose that such higher-order cognitive phenomena might actually drain resources available to engage in critical thinking or message scrutiny.[23] While the underlying mechanism is still in question, studies show that arguments presented in a humorous way generate fewer counterarguments from the audience than when presented seriously.[24] Regardless of whether this signals a reduction in one's ability to cognitively elaborate on message arguments, or a willingness of the listener to apply different rules ("discounting" the message as "just a joke"), it deserves noting that humor appears to enhance some forms of cognitive processing while diminishing others.

Understanding the mechanisms of political satire and irony

This growing body of research leaves instructors with a roadmap and a set of challenges. If humor fosters attention to the humorous element of a text, while undermining attention paid to other elements of a text (or a lecture), and if the reconciliation of humor enhances processing of some elements of a text, while disrupting the scrutiny of other aspects of a text (or lecture)— then the use of humor in the classroom is a potentially precarious activity. A consideration of the nature and construction of humor itself will help us understand the precise ways in which televised political satire, in particular, could affect student learning in a classroom environment.

While psychological and sociological theories of humor abound, the humor theory most frequently integrated in cognitive psychology is that of incongruity. According to incongruity theory, humorous texts contain two frames of reference (or schema): an initial expository schema (a set of concepts, people, places, beliefs) and second frame of reference (or schema) that is incongruous with the first and only makes sense through the cognitive leaps of the listener. Through reconciliation, the listener "bridges the gap" and makes sense of the humor.[25] While different disciplines use different terminologies to describe this process, the underlying mechanism is largely the same—the listener makes the cognitive contribution that ultimately gives meaning to an otherwise incomplete text.

In contrast to the humorous texts that use an explicit "read-in" or exposition, followed by a punchline, the nature of the incongruity in ironic or parodic texts often involves the juxtaposition of two concurrent frames of reference, though not necessarily in an unexpected way. The use of concurrent incongruous frames is inherent in the satirical political skits, headlines, and commentary on *The Daily Show* with Jon Stewart and in the content of *The Colbert Report*, whose entire premise is founded on irony. The comprehension of these texts typically involves the integration of seemingly incompatible schemas and the active extrapolation of the author's underlying proposition—usually an argument or valenced observation about the state of the world or our political reality. In such instances of satire or parodic irony, the juxtaposition is not so much between an original frame of reference and the introduction of an unexpected incompatible idea, but rather the simultaneous existence of two competing realities: The real and the ideal. The nature of such propositions is inherent in Dustin Griffin's definition of the satirist, as one who ". . . insists on the sharp differences between vice and virtue, between good and bad, between what man is, and what he *ought to be*."[26]

Example 1: Exploring the nature and value of scientific inquiry through irony

A *Daily Show* segment from October 2011 provides an illustration of the complexities of such ironic satire. In the wake of various claims from Republican candidates regarding the threat of global warming, the danger of the HPV vaccine, and other science-related fear appeals, *The Daily Show* aired an ironic segment entitled, "Science. What's it up to?" In it, *Daily Show* correspondent, Aasif Mandvi, ironically depicts science as the enterprise of self-serving, money-hungry, elite scientists. In an interview with Mandvi, conservative strategist Noelle Nikpour criticizes the process of scientific research, arguing that since only scientists are qualified to critique such research, it should call their integrity into question. Mandvi ironically assumes his guest's position on the issue, offering an exaggerated extension of her argument.

Mandvi: Yes. It's like, why are surgeons the only ones allowed to perform surgeries and other surgeons are the only ones who get to say if the surgery is necessary or not, right?

Nikpour: Absolutely!

Mandvi: It doesn't make any sense!

Nikpour: It never makes any sense.

Mandvi then goes "under cover," depicting the ritual of the "school science fair" as a deliberate attempt to corrupt our children, and ends the segment with Nikpour's take on the relationship between fact, science, and common sense.

Nikpour: It's very confusing for a child to be only taught evolution to go home to a household where their parents say, "Well, wait a minute . . . God created the Earth!"

Mandvi: What is the point of teaching children *facts* if it's just going to confuse them?

Nikpour: It confuses the children when they go *home*. We as Americans—we are paying tax dollars for our children to be educated. We need to offer them every theory that's out there. It's all about choice; it's all about freedom.

Mandvi: It should be up to the American people to decide what's true.

Nikpour: Absolutely! Doesn't it make common sense?

Mandvi's ironic suggestion that "it should be up to the American people to decide what's true," clearly presents several dysfunctional propositions if taken to its logical conclusion. But Nickpour's *agreement* with this statement reframes *her* position on science as illogical at best and dangerous at worst. The absurdity of Mandvi's conclusions forces us to acknowledge the need for a competing reality—that is, a perspective advocating that science *is* an enterprise of objective, knowledge-seeking scholars. That it *does* provide us with verifiable facts. That society *does* need a professional class of experts to provide insight into the truth value of claims about the universe. In this example, the "real" (what certain conservative politicians are arguing) is offered in exaggerated form by Mahndi's character, while the "ideal" (the truth) is extrapolated by the viewer as its logical opposite.

Although such multilayered humorous messages might reduce a listener's ability and/or motivation to scrutinize its underlying proposition,[27] the classroom context provides a wonderful opportunity to circumvent these "humor side effects" (counterargument disruption or discounting cue effects) while still capitalizing on humor's beneficial processing implications: enhanced attention at message encoding and deeper processing of the humorous component of the text. Imagine how this clip and its fundamental premise could be integrated into the teaching of the scientific method, the logic of social science, the concepts of falsifiability, reliability, and verifiability. Through this ironic inversion, students could explore the implications of a world without the scientific method, of what happens if observations and conclusions about the world are driven by common sense and intuition, rather than by deductive reasoning and the scientific process. Students could consider other ways in which Mandvi's argument could be extended and critique the implications of both of these perspectives.

Example 2: Highlighting the problematic aspects of postmodern journalistic practices through satire

Let us now consider an example that would serve instructors of journalism, media, and political communication courses. In this particular *Daily Show* episode (October 12, 2009), Jon Stewart highlights how a recent *CNN* segment had "fact checked" the accuracy of claims made in a *Saturday Night Live* sketch about President Obama's accomplishments. Puzzled by the cable news network's decision to fact check a sketch comedy show, Stewart then considers whether *CNN* imposes that same scrutiny on the claims of political officials. What follows is a scathing critique of contemporary cable news programming. Namely, the news media's unnecessary coverage of entertainment, the absence of critical inquiry, its failure to challenge partisan talking points, the striking lack of knowledge and research on the topic in question, the lack of journalistic accountability, and the failure of such news shows to follow-up and examine previous claims once additional information becomes available.

Stewart: [To be fair . . .] fact checking *is* the function of news. That is the public service they provide. . . . You can't get away with shit on *CNN*. For instance, a mere *day* before the *SNL* fact check, Arizona Republican Senator Jon Kyl tried to sneak a whopper past [*CNN* anchor] John King. Watch! . . . [Cut to Jon Kyl making statistical claims about the savings to the government if congress passed malpractice reform.]

Stewart: Holy 1 to 200 billion just for malpractice reform? That is an impressively high, citation-free, *completely made up number*! And Kyl had a bunch of 'em. King wasn't going to let that stand.

[Cut to a montage of Kyl reciting numerous statistics and monetary amounts].

[Cut back to host John King]

CNN's King:	We will talk more about this as it reaches the floor, I assure you. We are out of time on this day . . .
Stewart [Incredulous]:	Out of time on this day??? Your show is four fucking hours long! Actually, John King was probably just biding his time for the CBO report which said 'malpractice savings would only amount to 11 billion.' Even over 10 years, that's only 54 billion off the deficit, not the 1–200 billion claimed by Kyl. I'm sure that after the report came out, they had a *HUGE* fact check segment on the. . . .

[Jon pretends to receive a report in an invisible earpiece]. I'm being told they did not. . . . [Continuing to speak to imaginary person in his ear] I'm sorry . . . how about if [*Saturday Night Live's*] Fred Armisen learned a Jon Kyl impersonation? Would they cover it then?

[Jon listening in to the earpiece] I'm being told there is no one talking to me.

This particular segment illustrates a favorite satirical tool of Stewart: ironic deadpan delivery of his idealistic assumptions. By proposing that *CNN*'s John King was "probably just biding his time" for the more detailed CBO report, Stewart offers King his ironic benefit of the doubt, which we quickly see deflated through information received through Stewart's fictional earpiece. Even the fact that Stewart "receives" fictional fact-checking input from an imaginary higher entity reveals a striking contrast to the lack of journalistic interrogation that he is critiquing. Stewart then asks the invisible earpiece "higher-up" if *CNN would* fact check these claims if an *SNL*'s comedian could impersonate Senator Kyl, intimating that *CNN* is more driven by the pursuit of ratings-friendly entertainment news than in the pursuit of truth and the public good.

Stewart then cuts to a montage of GOP spokespeople issuing broad claims about the implications of health care reform, to which the host responds, "Alright, well, we'll leave it there."

Stewart:	Why would you leave it there? There is a terrible place to leave it! Unless somebody's gonna pick it up later? Does anybody pick it up later?

[Cut to montage of nine different *CNN* programs with hosts reciting various iterations of, "We'll leave it there."]

Stewart: "AGGGH! [tears up script] You have 24 hours in a day! How much more time do you need? Well, I guess that explains *CNN*'s new slogan: Nobody leaves more things there . . .

Stewart: Actually *CNN* does have a non-*SNL* fact-checking mechanism. It's called balance. It works like this: Basically you get two crazy bald people [Cut to reveal Democratic strategist James Carville and Republican operative Ari Fleischer] one representing the right and one representing the left and since those are the only two functional and rational points of view, the anchor [Cut to reveal *CNN*'s Anderson Cooper] helps them come to a golden consensus. [Cut to montage of shouting match between Carville and Fleischer which Cooper interrupts with, "We're going to have to leave it there."]

Stewart: Leave it where? [pleading] I don't even know where we were! What exactly did you have to leave it there to get *to*?

[Cut back to Anderson Cooper] "Next up, meet the next *youtube* star. His name is Josh Sacco. Just 5 years old. He recites a monologue from his favorite movie. The film is called Miracle . . . [Cut to footage of little boy on *youtube* video].

The opportunities to integrate this segment into course curricula are numerous. Stewart has presented a scathing critique of the norms of postmodern journalism: fragmentation of news coverage, the pitfalls of "objective" journalism, and the implications of pressures of time and money in the newsroom. Such concepts are central to countless texts: From Neil Postman's popular qualitative critique of television culture *Amusing Ourselves to Death* to W. Lance Bennett's seminal textbook on the relationship between politics and media, *News: The Politics of Illusion*; from David Mindich's exploration of why young people have abandoned news, *Tuned Out*, to Timothy Cook's examination of the news media as a political institution, *Governing with the News*.

By assembling a montage of reporters engaging in almost identical use of "We'll leave it there," the show reveals that this tactic is not isolated, but is a normative practice in cable news. This example echoes Postman's criticisms of television news from his chapter titled, "Now This . . .," in which he suggests that the structure of television news leaves stories, events, and issues disconnected from one another.

[By saying 'Now . . . this' . . .] The newscaster means that you have thought long enough on the previous matter (approximately forty-five seconds), that you must not be morbidly preoccupied with it (let us say, for ninety seconds), and that you must now give your attention to another fragment of news or a commercial.[28]

The Daily Show's extensive montage illustrates that by systematically leaving debates and policy conversations unresolved and underexplored, the viewer is either left with little understanding of the policy in question, or worse, with misperceptions caused by the dubious claims that now remain unchallenged. As described by Bennett "News fragments exist in self-contained dramatic capsules, isolated from each other in time and space."[29] The result, argues Bennett, is that

> . . . people are invited all the more to project their own interpretations onto the world. In place of new information about situations, information is either cast adrift or assimilated into old plot formulas. In either case, the world is reduced time and again to myriad encapsulated happenings, each with its own emotional coherence, but isolated from the others.[30]

In Stewart's description of the concept of "balance," the humorous juxtaposition resides in the incongruity between Stewart's ironically optimistic observations and the aggressive shouting match between Carville and Fleischer. Because the norms of journalism prevent Anderson Cooper from probing the guests' underlying propositions or from bringing them to a "golden consensus," Cooper is ultimately forced to shut down the conversation by "leaving it there." This one segment would serve as a fruitful springboard for a discussion about the origins and functionality of the practice of objectivity, complementing such work as Mindich's (1998) *Just the Facts: How Objectivity Came to Define American Journalism*. Students in journalism courses could engage in a critical examination of the press norm of objectivity, as well as related concepts such as fairness and balance. Do these professional norms increase the ability for political operatives to spin news stories to their own advantage? Is Bennett correct in his assertion that "reporting the claims from both sides in a balanced fashion as though they have equal weight factually may leave audiences confused and unable to distinguish the credibility of any side?"[31] Does objectivity necessarily reduce a journalist's capacity for critical interrogation? Or are there other iterations of "fairness" and "truth" that do not hinge so heavily on symmetrical viewpoints or "equal time?"

Finally, the revelation that Anderson Cooper is actually transitioning from the Carville/Fleischer "conversation" to give time to a 5-year-old who recites movie lines serves as the perfect punctuation to Stewart's segment, particularly as Stewart concludes with the ironic observation, "To be fair, there was probably *no* other way people could have seen that . . . *Youtube video*." So, while Stewart never comes out and says it, the viewer is implicitly invited to hypothesize about the origins of such dysfunctional practices. The answer? because news producers are covering what they think viewers *want* to see and hear (not what they *need* to see and hear—after all, we could all have seen that video on *YouTube*), highlighting the preeminent role played by production constraints in a ratings-driven news media environment. This particular observation, and others that accompany it, are central to a rich body of literature on the consolidation of media ownership and the implications for journalism.[32]

A word of caution: Humor as high reward and high risk

Given the broad range of concepts and arguments presented in this *Daily Show* segment, it might be helpful to consider situations in which this clip might *seem* appropriate, but could actually *undermine* student comprehension and recall. Given that the clip starts with a conversation between *CNN's* John King and Senator Kyl about how malpractice reform might affect health care costs, it would be tempting for instructors in courses on public policy or health policy to integrate this segment into lecture. After all, Kyl makes several claims about the level of government savings through malpractice reform. Stewart himself introduces factual details from the CBO regarding the projected savings through these kinds of reforms. However, Stewart is merely using this particular debate as a context in which to expose a pointed criticism of certain journalistic practices. The incongruity inherent in the humor does not hinge on the details of health care policy. Instead, it hinges on the contrast between how King *should* be interrogating Kyl, and how King is *actually* interrogating Kyl. Not only might this clip not enhance learning of health policy details, it might actually foster recall of the underlying premise of the clip (the criticism of *CNN's* lack of critical interrogation) at the *expense* of these health policy details. Indeed, research suggests that the encoding of neutral information is interrupted by the introduction of particularly surprising or emotionally charged information, hence reducing recall of the neutral information that was being encoded at the outset.[33] So, while unexpectedness may increase attention to the unexpected construct and often enhances recall of information encoded *after* the emotional arousal the information that was being encoded just prior (in this case, the nuanced details of health care costs and malpractice reform) is likely to be disrupted. Hence, it is essential to dissect the humorous mechanism in a given text and its underlying propositions before integrating it into course instruction.

Example 3: Stephen Colbert: Political power, campaign finance laws and performance art

In June 2011, Stephen Colbert, host of *The Colbert Report* on Comedy Central, announced that he was launching a "SuperPAC," an "independent-expenditure only committee" (see OpenSecrets.org) to, in the words of Colbert's PAC, "make a better tomorrow, tomorrow." In January 2010, the US Supreme Court issued a landmark decision in *Citizens United v. the Federal Election Commission* effectively allowing corporations, unions, associations, and individuals to engage in "electioneering communications," a kind of campaign financing that had been prohibited under McCain-Feingold.[34] Since the *Citizens United* decision, creative campaign financing mechanisms, including the "Super PAC," have been established to channel funding from corporations and unions to support or oppose individual candidates. One of these mechanisms involves the joint creation of a registered nonprofit 501(c)(4) organization, which does not have to disclose the names of its donors. When anonymous donors give funds to the 501(c)(4), *that* nonprofit organization can then donate in its own name to the corresponding Super PAC, hence permitting SuperPAC "funded" campaign activities without the limitations of individual donor disclosure.[35]

While the inner workings of these campaign finance organizations are both tedious and complex, by launching his own SuperPAC in the summer of 2011, Stephen Colbert opened the door to a form of satirical performance art that has rendered these intricacies at once interesting and understandable. Most importantly, perhaps, by illustrating the various *legal* financial transactions and devices Colbert is able to employ with his SuperPAC, he has also shown that the current campaign finance laws deserve scrutiny, as they provide opportunities for the further conflation of money and political power in US elections. On the September 29, 2011, episode of *The Colbert Report*, the host featured a segment about the impressive earnings of Karl Rove's conservative Political Action Committee (PAC), "American Crossroads" and its sister organization, American Crossroads GPS. "Shocked" by the huge amounts of money Rove has been able to raise through these organizations, Colbert set out to learn how he did it—by eating a portion of Karl Rove's head (a ham loaf wearing glasses). Colbert explains,

> . . . You see, Crossroads GPS isn't a PAC, it's something called a 501(c)(4) which does not require donor disclosure. It's like a Secret Santa . . . if Santa wanted to weaken environmental regulations. And while American crossroads raised only 200 dollars in May, in June of that year Crossroads GPS brought in 5.1 million dollars. That's an increase of 2,550,000%. Those are growth numbers usually only seen in in emails for boner pills. Clearly these c4s have created an unprecedented, unaccountable, untraceable cash tsunami that will infect every corner of the next election . . . And I feel like an idiot for not having one.

Enter Trevor Potter, "former general counsel to the McCain campaign," Stephen Colbert's "personal lawyer" and a reoccurring guest on *The Colbert Report* since the launch of his Super PAC.

Colbert to Potter:	So, I've got all these people that have been giving me money. Individual Americans. But I haven't gotten any of the big corporate money! That's why I have a Super-PAC! Why wouldn't a corporation give money?
Potter:	They would be nervous about giving in a way that their name was publicly disclosed. People might object to what they've done: their shareholders, their customers.
Colbert:	That's where a c4 comes in. A corporation or an individual can give to a c4 and nobody gets to know that they did it. So how do I get one?

Potter explains that he has created an anonymous shell corporation registered in Delaware that Colbert can then use as his c4. They sign documents (pulled from Potter's briefcase) that appoint Colbert as his own "board of directors." Potter explains that the documentation authorizes the corporation to file paperwork with the IRS in May 2013.

Colbert:	So I could get money through my c4 and nobody knows *anything* about it until 6 months *after* the election? [Incredulous and happy] That's *my* kind of campaign finance restriction! . . . So now I can get corporate and individual donations of unlimited amounts for my c4. What can I do with that money?
Potter:	That c4 could take out political ads and attack candidates or promote your favorite ones as long as it's not the principle purpose for spending its money.
Colbert:	No. Its principle purpose is as an educational entity. I want to educate the public that gay people cause earthquakes.
Potter:	There are probably some c4s doing that.
Colbert:	Can I take the c4 money and donate to my SuperPAC?
Potter:	[head tilted and eyebrow raised] . . . You can.
Colbert:	[stunned] But wait. SuperPACs are transparent. And the c4 is secret! So I can take secret donations from my c4 and give it to my supposedly transparent SuperPAC?
Potter:	And it'll say, "Given by your c4!"
Colbert:	What is the difference between that and money laundering?
Potter:	. . . It's hard to say . . .

Throughout the summer and into the fall, Colbert featured numerous segments highlighting the use of his SuperPAC and accompanying 501(c) (4) to advance certain issues, and to promote and attack individual candidates. In November, Rove's American Crossroads made a request of the Federal Election Commission (FEC) that furthered Colbert's performative campaign. American Crossroads sought the FEC's approval to allow SuperPACs to feature individual candidates in "issue ads" *without* violating existing campaign laws prohibiting so-called coordinated communications between PACs and individual campaigns. Once again, Colbert turned to Trevor Potter for advice on how he could help influence the FEC decision. Potter explained that Colbert could write a letter to the FEC indicating his "approval" of Rove's request, and could include visual aids to demonstrate the kind of campaign ads that would be legal if Rove's request were granted. With long-shot Presidential contender, former Louisiana Governor Buddy Roemer, as his exemplar, Colbert showed how such SuperPAC-funded ads could engage in the kind of "uncoordinated" "coordinated communications" that would be possible were the FEC to grant Rove's request.

The nature of the humor inherent in Colbert's ongoing SuperPAC campaign is quite different from the self-contained satirical segments discussed earlier. Through his ironic persona, parodying a power-hungry, ethics-free conservative politico, Colbert operates within existing campaign finance regulations to highlight the inherent flaws within them. By engaging in egregious—yet legal—behaviors, from concealing corporate donations to his "transparent" SuperPAC, to campaigning for individual candidates in "issue ads," Colbert exposes the weaknesses of what *is,* while inviting viewers to speculate about what *ought to be.* When Colbert explained that his c4 was designed to "educate" the public that gay people caused earthquakes, for example, he was highlighting a plausible action that could legally be taken under current campaign finance law, inviting the audience to conclude that such misleading persuasion campaigns *ought not* to be considered "educational."

The impact of Colbert's SuperPAC has extended far beyond isolated instances of learning or comprehension on the part of the audience. In fact, in deliberations over Rove' request in December 2011, Federal Election Commissioners invoked Colbert repeatedly and thanked him for his efforts.[36] Commissioner Ellen Weintraub explained that due to Colbert's attention to the issue, they had received over 500 comments regarding Rove's request.

> We can count on one hand the number of issues that have come before the commission that have generated more public interest and public comment and that is, of course in part, thanks to our friend Stephen Colbert, and I do thank him for shining a little light on this obscure corner of the federal government.[37]

This kind of impact of political entertainment—affecting political attention, interest, discussion, and participation—is something that political communication scholars have explored extensively over the past decade, with all signs pointing to positive correlations between the viewing of political satire and healthy democratic behaviors. Scholars from the humanistic tradition describe how humor's accessibility and emotional resonance offer a more appealing form of political information than alienating elite political discourse.[38] Quantitative studies indicate that viewers of these shows are more participatory and attentive to politics than nonviewers.[39] Similar analyses have found that viewers of The Daily Show discuss politics with friends, family, and co-workers more often than nonviewers.[40] Another promising line of research on the impact of political satire programs suggests that viewing these shows fosters subsequent information seeking behaviors, particularly among the less politically involved.[41] Rooted in Baum's gateway hypothesis, these studies demonstrate that consumption of political satire is associated with increased rates of information seeking and attention to traditional news on the very topics covered in the political satire programming.

If these relationships emerge as a function of mere exposure to political satire, imagine the possible implications for political attention and engagement if augmented by classroom discussion and instruction. With the added benefit of political, historical, and economic context through complementary lecture materials, something as tedious as campaign finance reform could suddenly take on real-world meaning and resonance. Through the integration of Colbert's SuperPAC activities into political science courses, students could become familiar with the origins of "corporate personhood," the implications of the relationship between corporate personhood and the first amendment, as well as broad questions about the role of money in American politics.

Again, the reason such curricula are likely to be successful stems from the humorous mechanism at the heart of Colbert's commentary. Aside from the details about FEC requests and campaign finance laws, Colbert's underlying premise holds the meaning that students will likely recall long after class has ended. That premise is found at the intersection of two competing realities that Colbert exposes. The first is our current reality: the campaign-related activities and financial transactions permitted under current campaign laws. The second reality is an alternate vision of what *ought to be*—and here Colbert merely operates through implication, not instruction. Should Colbert be able to "hide" corporate donations through the creative use of his (c)(4)? Should he be able to include candidates in ads funded by his SuperPAC while claiming that he has not "coordinated" with the candidate? Should he be able to use these funds to attack candidates on character-based charges? What other kinds of actions might be "legal" yet potentially problematic under current campaign finance law? What does it mean that corporations are "people?" What are the benefits and disadvantages of "corporate personhood" for democracy? Such critical inquiries would provide rich fodder for class discussion, bolstered by the possibilities presented through Colbert's performance art.

Discussion

In today's teaching environment where instructors are encouraged to employ multimedia presentations, often transforming classrooms into audio-visual extravaganzas, the integration of televised political humor and satire is a tempting route to take. And while the use of such content in the classroom often generates positive affective responses, the question guiding instructors in their content selections must be: "Will this content enhance attention to, comprehension, and recall of the *central concepts* of this course?" To answer that question, instructors must become quasi-experts in the psychology of satire; dissecting the message, unpacking its incongruous elements, and identifying its main underlying proposition. When used correctly, segments like those of Colbert or Stewart will not only foster attention to and recall of that underlying proposition, but will likely promote subsequent attention and information-seeking behaviors, as well as political discussion and engagement. Through the added context provided by class discussion and course materials, the potential for critical examination, debate, and long-term reflection is great.

I will close with an anecdote from my own experience teaching a course in Politics and Popular Culture. Students read Postman's *Amusing Ourselves to Death,* and worked in groups to discuss his arguments about television news as impotent, incoherent, and irrelevant. We discussed Bennett's news content biases like fragmentation and dramatization, and engaged in a critical discussion of press objectivity, its origins, and purpose.[42] We considered how the evolution of media regulation and economics had affected the production of news and what it meant for the kind of content citizens received. After several weeks of these discussions, I opened class one day with the *Daily Show* segment, "CNN leaves it there," described earlier. Students were asked to work in groups to connect the segment to Postman and Bennett and to explore the implications of Stewart's critique. Six weeks later, at the end of the semester, I asked students to take a moment to write down what from the course had made an impact on them. And while Stewart's clip occupied only 10 minutes of the 13-week class, of the 50 students, 12 included the "CNN leaves it there" clip in their lists. One student stated, "CNN Leaves it there" and that Jon Stewart used these CNN clips to illustrate the Postman's concept of incoherence. Another student wrote that ". . . Stewart's criticism of CNN ending stories with 'Let's leave it there' exposes the lack of depth in news coverage." It is my hope that such critiques and concepts will stay with my students out in the world—with much thanks to my colleagues, Professors Stewart and Colbert.

Notes

1 Jennings Bryant and Dolf Zillmann, "Using Humor to Promote Learning in the Classroom," *Journal of Children in Contemporary Society* 20 (1988): 49–78.
2 John Banas, Norah Dunar, Dariela Rodriguez, and Shr-Jie Liu, "A Review of Humor in Educational Settings: Four Decades of Research," *Communication Education* 60 (2011): 115–44.
3 Jennings Bryant, Paul W. Comisky, Jon S. Crane, and Dolf Zillmann, "Relationship between College Instructors' Use of Humor in the Classroom and Students' Evaluations of their Instructors," *Journal of Educational Psychology* 72 (1980): 511–19; Randall L. Garner, "Humor in Pedagogy: How Ha-Ha can Lead to Aha!" *College Teaching* 54 (2006): 177–9; Sarah E. Torok, Robert F. McMorris, and Wen-Chi Lin, "Is Humor an Appropriate Teaching Tool?: Perceptions of Professors' Teaching Styles and Use of Humor," *College Teaching* 52 (2004): 14–20; Melissa B. Wanzer and Ann Bainbridge Frymier, "The Relationship between Student Perceptions of Instructor Humor and Students' Reports of Learning," *Communication Education* 48 (1999): 48–61.
4 Robert M. Kaplan and Gregory C. Pascoe, "Humorous Lectures and Humorous Examples: Some Effects upon Comprehension Retention," *Journal of Educational Psychology* 69 (1977): 61–5; Avner Ziv, *L'humor en education: Approche psychologique* (Paris: Editions Social Francaises, 1979). Avner Ziv, "Teaching and Learning with Humor: Experiment and Replication," *Journal of Experimental Education* 57 (1988): 5–15.
5 Debra Korobkin, "Humor in the Classroom: Considerations and Strategies," *College Teaching* 36 (1988): 154–8.
6 Melissa Wanzer, Ann Bainbridge Frymier, and Jeffrey Irwin, "An Explanation of the Relationship between Instructor Humor and Student Learning; Instructional Humor Processing Theory," *Communication Education* 59 (2010): 1–18.
7 Banas et al., "A Review of Humor," 140–4.
8 Ziv, "Teaching and Learning," 5–15.
9 Banas et al., "A Review of Humor," 136.
10 Reid Hastie, "Causes and Effects of Causal Attribution," *Journal of Personality and Social Psychology* 46 (1984): 44–56.
11 Arthur Koestler, *The Act of Creation* (London: Hutchinson and Co., 1964); Lawrence La Fave, "Humor Judgments as a Function of Reference Groups and Identification Classes," in *The Psychology of Humor*, edited by Jeffrey H. Goldstein and Paul E. McGhee (New York: Academic Press, 1972): 195–210. Stephen R. Schmidt, "The Humour Effect: Differential Processing and Privileged Retrieval," *Memory* 10 (2002): 127–38.
12 Stephen R. Schmidt, "Effects of Humor on Sentence Memory," *Journal of Experimental Psychology: Learning, Memory, and Cognition* 20 (1994): 953–67;

Marc G. Weinberger and Charles S. Gulas, "The Impact of Humor in Advertising: A Review," *Journal of Advertising* 21 (1992): 35–59.

13 Madelign Strick, Robert W. Holland, Rick Van Baaren, and Ad Van Knippenberg, "Humor in the Eye Tracker: Attention Capture and Distraction from Context Cues," *Journal of General Psychology* 137 (2010): 37–48.

14 Schmidt, "Effects of Humor on Sentence Memory;" Stephen R. Schmidt, "Can we have a Distinctive Theory of Memory?" *Memory and Cognition* 19 (1991): 523–42.

15 Strick et al., "Humor in the Eye Tracker," 45.

16 Robert S. Wyer and James Collins, "A Theory of Humour Elicitation," *Psychological Review* 99 (1992): 663–88.

17 James Kellaris and Vincent Kline, "Humor and Ad Memorability: On the Contributions of Humor Expectancy, Relevancy, and Need for Humor," *Psychology and Marketing* 24 (2007): 506.

18 Goel Vinod and Raymond Dolan, "The Functional Anatomy of Humor: Segregating Cognitive and Affective Components," *Nature Neuroscience* 4 (2001): 237–8; Karli K. Watson, Benjamin Matthews, and John Allman, "Brain Activation During Sight Gags and Language-Dependent Humor," *Cerebral Cortex* 17 (2007): 314–24.

19 Seana Coulson and Christopher Lovett, "Handedness, Hemispheric Asymmetries, and Joke Comprehension," *Cognitive Brain Research* 19 (2004): 277.

20 Seana Coulson and Robert Williams, "Hemispheric Asymmetries and Joke Comprehension," *Neuropsychologia* 43 (2005): 128.

21 Goel and Dolan, "Functional Anatomy," 237–8; Amy Bihrle, Hiram H. Brownell, John A. Powelson, and Howard Gardner, "Comprehension of Humorous and Nonhumorous Materials by Left- and Right-Brain Damaged Patients," *Brain and Cognition* 5 (1986): 399–411; Prathba Shammi and Donald Stuss, "Humour Appreciation: A Role of the Right Frontal Lobe," *Brain* 122 (1999): 657–66; Yves Joanette, Pierre Goulet, and Didier Hannequin, *Right Hemisphere and Verbal Communication* (New York: Springer Verlag, 1990).

22 Robert Kluender and Marta Kutas, "Subjacency as a Processing Phenomenon," *Language and Cognitive Processes* 8 (1993): 573–633; Seana Coulson and Marta Kutas, "Getting it: Human Event-Related Brain Response to Jokes in Good and Poor Comprehenders," *Neuroscience Letters* 316 (2001): 71–4.

23 Dannagal G. Young, "The Privileged Role of the Late-Night Joke: Exploring Humor's Role in Disrupting Argument Scrutiny," *Media Psychology* 11 (2008): 119–42.

24 Robin L. Nabi, Emily Moyer-Guse, and Sahara Byrne, "All Joking Aside: A Serious Investigation into the Persuasive Effect of Funny Social Issue Messages," *Communication Monographs* 74 (2007): 29–54.

25 Koestler, *Act of Creation.* LaFave "*Humor Judgements.*"

26 Dustin Griffin, *Satire: A Critical Reintroduction* (Lexington: The University Press of Kentucky, 1994): 36.

27 Nabi et al., "All Joking Aside," 29–54. Young, "Privileged role," 119–42.

28 Neil Postman, *Amusing Ourselves to Death* (New York: Penguin, 1985): 99.

29 W. Lance Bennett, *News: The Politics of Illusion* (New York: Longman, 9th edn 2012): 59.

30 Ibid., 59.

31 Ibid., 193.

32 Ben Bagdikian, *The New Media Monopoly* (Boston: Beacon Press, 2004); Robert McChesney, *Rich Media, Poor Democracy: Communication Politics in Dubious Times*. Paperback edition, with a new preface by the author (New York: The New Press, 2000).

33 Douglas K. Detterman and Norman Ellis, "Determinants of Induced Amnesia in Short Term Memory," *Journal of Experimental Psychology* 95 (1972): 308–16; Douglas K. Detterman, "The von Restorff Effect and Induced Amnesia: Production by Manipulation of Sound Intensity," *Journal of Experimental Psychology: Human Learning and Memory* 104 (1975): 614–28; Marisa Knight and Mara Mather, "Reconciling Findings of Emotion-Induced Memory Enhancement and Impairment of Preceding Items," *Emotion* 9 (2011): 763–81; Mara Mather, "Emotional Arousal and Memory Binding: An Object-Based Framework," *Perspectives on Psychological Science* 2 (2007): 33–52.

34 Adam Liptak,, "Justices, 5–4 Reject Corporate Spending Limit," *New York Times* (January 21, 2010): A1.

35 Josh Boak, "Enter the Era of the Super PACs," *Campaigns and Elections Magazine* (September 8, 2011).

36 Robin Bravender, "Colbert Gets Love at the FEC," *Politico.com* (December 1, 2011). Accessed December 10, 2011, from www.politico.com/news/stories/1211/69536.html#ixzz1fxbpr9P5.

37 Ibid.

38 Jeffrey P. Jones, *Entertaining Politics: Satire Television and Political Engagement* (Lahman, MD: Rowman & Littlefield, 2009). Liesbet Van Zoonen, *Entertaining the Citizen: When Politics and Popular Culture Converge* (Boulder, CO: Rowman and Littlefield, 2005).

39 Xiaoxia Cao, "Hearing it from Jon Stewart: The Impact of *The Daily Show* on Public Attentiveness to Politics," *International Journal of Public Opinion Research* 22 (2010): 26–46; Lindsay H. Hoffman and Dannagal G. Young, "Satire, Punch Lines, and the Nightly News: Untangling Media Effects on Political Participation," *Communication Research Reports* 28 (2011): 1–10.

40 Kristen Landreville, R. Lance Holbert, and Heather LaMarre, "The Influence of Late-Night TV Comedy Viewing on Political Talk: A Moderated-Mediation Model," *International Journal of Press/Politics* 15 (2010): 482–98; Dannagal G. Young and Sarah Esralew, "Jon Stewart a Heretic? Surely you Jest: Political Participation and Discussion among Viewers of Late-night Comedy Programming," in *The Stewart/Colbert Effect: Essays on the Real Impact of Fake News*, ed. Armarnath Amarasinga (Jefferson, NC: McFarland and Co. Publishers, 2011): 99–116.

41 Matthew A. Baum, "Soft News and Political Knowledge: Evidence of Absence or Absence of Evidence?" *Political Communication* 20 (2003): 173–90; Lauren Feldman and Dannagal G. Young, "Late-Night Comedy as a Gateway to Traditional News: An Analysis of Time Trends in News Attention among Late-Night Comedy Viewers during the 2004 Presidential Primaries," *Political Communication* 25 (2008): 401–22; Lauren Feldman, Anthony Leiserowitz,

and Edward Maibach, "The Science of Satire: *The Daily Show* and *The Colbert Report* as sources of public attention to science and the environment," in *The Stewart/Colbert Effect: Essays on the Real Impact of Fake News*, ed. Amarnath Amarasingam (Jefferson, NC: McFarland and Company, 2011): 25–46. Michael A. Xenos and Amy B. Becker, "Moments of Zen: Effects of *The Daily Show* on Information Seeking and Political Learning," *Political Communication* 26 (2009): 317–32.

42 Bennet, "Politics of Illusion."

CHAPTER ELEVEN

The politics in Pixar: The underlying messages of America's animated favorites

William J. Miller, Jeremy D. Walling, Jill D. Miller, and Patrick F. Vining

Teaching abstract concepts such as political socialization can be difficult in American government courses. While students may be able to relate the political preferences of their parents and some of their own experiences to their opinions and views, they are less likely to be able to explain how various media potentially shaped their beliefs during childhood. In this chapter, we look at the socializing elements of Pixar films. Given the tremendous popularity of these films with children today, it is important to understand how the underlying messages may shape the belief patterns of the next generation of American students and citizens.

Political socialization and American youth

Political socialization is a concept that students struggle to understand in the abstract. Socialization, after all, is not something we actively experience in our childhood when many of our views and opinions are first engrained. Instead, we are merely passive participants as school, religion, and our parents influence us in ways we fail to always realize. At an early age, we learn to respect our country through reciting the Pledge of Allegiance at school. We learn to honor our nation's history through stories of figures like Johnny Appleseed and the good works and intentions of presidents such as George

Washington. At home, the general conversation and worldly outlook of our guardians predispose us to think a certain way about particular issues. Yet kids simply do not play an active role in these occurrences.

In preschool, children learn that police are helpful, benevolent authority figures.[1] As they enter elementary school, they become aware of presidents and tend to view them in a positive light given that they are presented as honest, trustworthy figures.[2] Moving along in their development, kids experience more actors—including firemen, mayors, and even governors.[3] More importantly, they begin to understand the difference between actors and institutions,[4] Further learning helps them to distinguish between the different institutions and their roles in government.[5] As they age in elementary school, students begin to hold different feelings for different actors, including an overall less rosy disposition toward authority in general.[6] Beyond actors and institutions, young children learn the expectations of being a good citizen—particularly keeping an interest in what happens around them.[7] They are taught that voting is important and that they should support individuals who would do well in office regardless of the party to which they belong.[8]

These views are enforced through various agents of socialization. First and foremost is their family—especially parents or guardians. Parents spend the most time with children and are also far more likely to express their own political beliefs in their presence as compared to the other agents we will discuss below.[9] Parents have the greatest influence on their children when communication about authority, government, and politics is clear, regular, and stressed as important. The most reliable area of socialization between parent and child is party identification.[10] As with vote choice, it is far easier for younger children to understand that a parent is a Democrat or Republican than it is to begin understanding the policy beliefs that make them so. Beyond parents, religious traditions and institutions work as actors of socialization. Given that different religions prescribe dissimilar approaches to punishment, social justice, and equality, it is clear how religious growth can alter political development.[11] A child's peers can serve as socializing agents as well. This impact in this situation is relatively minor and tends to occur more in adolescence than childhood but is worth mentioning regardless.[12] Schools work to socialize children—especially at a very early age. In educational settings, kids are shaped to support the American political system and the tenets of good citizenship, but are not directed toward any particular partisan or issue stance.[13]

The media as agent of socialization

The final regularly discussed agent of socialization is the media. American media play a complex role in shaping the worldview of its citizens.[14] For children, various media take different approaches to socialization. As they grow and begin to more fully understand their own beliefs, they will act differently and seek out media that aligns with their beliefs. Until they are able to do that, however, they are seemingly at the mercy of children's programming. From this perspective, a valuable classroom lesson can be drawn. College students—in both introductory courses and upper-level political behavior courses—occasionally struggle to understand how many of their favorite childhood films contained governmental and political undertones which potentially altered their thoughts and attitudes. By asking students in their late teens and early twenties to revisit these films, we aim to help them look beyond the surface in watching their favorite movies.

Through our experience, we have found Pixar films to be the best avenue through which to demonstrate the potentially socializing ability of children's movies. Classic Disney cartoon movies possess many of the same attributes but are more muted in their presentation compared to Pixar, which seems more willing to be direct in their depictions and intent. There are several resources for methods of using videos in the classroom and examples of clips for those methods. Numerous scholars have demonstrated the usefulness of film in helping students to understand various concepts within political science.[15] Ronal Berk has generically examined how videos can be used in a college classroom and devised 12 pedagogical techniques.[16] Faculty, for example, can utilize video to provide content and information, illustrate concepts or principles, present alternative perspectives, apply content to real-world applications, serve as stimuli for learning activities, exaggerate a point, and snap students to a point.

In the following section, we will look at all of the feature-length Pixar films produced thus far and discuss the underlying themes present in each. It is important to note that not all movies are created equal in this sense. The synopses of the films are presented in chronological order. Some are more direct and detailed while others have little more than a few scenes. With time, Pixar has seemingly become more brazen in their approach. The underlying themes have become clearer to the untrained eye, yet the packaging remains the same—Pixar movies are fun and mean to appeal to American families. Two trends will emerge from the synopses: (1) Pixar movies tell us what we should think about our government and (2) Pixar tells us what we should do as citizens. In this way—intentional or not—Pixar potentially socializes its young viewers.

Elements of socialization in Pixar films

In this section, we will provide synopses of Pixar films, highlighting the underlying elements of socialization in each that can be used to help students comprehend the concepts in your classes.

Toy Story

The political themes present in *Toy Story* focus mainly on the structure and function of a set political hierarchy, and what happens when a stress is placed on the system. A secondary focus on the flow of information through a population is also present, as well as how changes in public opinion follow this information flow.

When *Toy Story* begins, Woody is the single head leader of the society of toys. He has the respect of the other individuals in the society and, by virtue of this respect, holds considerable legitimate political power. The hierarchical structure of the society is put under pressure, however, when Buzz Lightyear, a popular, flashy toy joins the society. His presence as a second figure with growing popularity in the population challenges Woody's standing as the leader. In depicting the story of what happens to the society when this challenge occurs, Pixar is illustrating the idea that when a political order is disrupted, the society will devolve into anarchical chaos until a new one is set. When Woody tries to rid the society of Buzz and is himself removed from the society, the other toys adopt a Lord of the Flies type of justice system, and an oligarchy follows as Mr. Potato Head, Hamm, Slink, and Rex become the bickering opinion leaders of the group. When Buzz and Woody return, harmony is only achieved again when a new power system is adopted, with Woody and Buzz sharing the responsibility for care of the society.

The focus on public opinion is even more pronounced than the political systemic focus. Everyone in the population is supportive of Woody, the single leader, in the beginning of the movie. Soon, however, public trust in him falls to a low. When Buzz falls out Andy's bedroom window, many of the toys are quick to blame the entire incident on Woody, without giving him a chance to refute the charges. This concept shows how easy it is for opinion to spread rapidly and intensely through a population. Similarly, the alien toys in the machine at Pizza Planet illustrate how easy it is to brainwash a society when there is nothing to prevent the spread of misinformation. The alien toys all believe the Claw is the ultimate religious leader, and have fear and respect for its "decisions." This likely started with one alien speculating as to the importance of the Claw and the misinformation spread through the group at a rapid pace.

A Bug's Life

Pixar followed the breakout success of *Toy Story* with *A Bug's Life*, a tale of an individualist oddball ant protecting his colony from marauding grasshoppers. The political content of *A Bug's Life* is apparent, although extraordinarily subtle. *A Bug's Life* is clearly an amalgam of the classic Aesop fable

"The Ant and the Grasshopper" and Akira Kurosawa's masterpiece *The Seven Samurai*. In the fable, the ant harvests diligently to store adequate food for winter, while the grasshopper pursues leisure. Of course, the grasshopper starves and endures reproof from the ant upon asking for food. The twist in *A Bug's Life* is that the grasshoppers are executing a protection racket, extorting food from the ants in exchange for perceived safety. In the Kurosawa film, oppressed villagers seek protection from seven ronin, offering the samurai only meager provisions and gratitude. In *A Bug's Life*, the protagonist, the innovative entrepreneur Flik, mistakenly assumes that a ragtag group of bugs in a traveling circus are great warriors. The circus bugs agree to follow Flik, as they believe he is offering them a performance job. In the midst of obvious themes such as the value of hard work and planning for the future, the importance of pursuing one's calling, and a basic story of good versus evil, shrewd viewers will take note of the more subtle themes of the tension between the individual and the collective and the clash between the safety of tradition and the promise of innovation.

Early in the film, the ant colony prepares "the offering" for the grasshoppers, harvesting grain manually. Meanwhile, Flik is shown with a machine that removes and collects all grains from stalks, dramatically improving productivity and efficiency. After demonstrating a telescope crafted from a blade of grass and a bead of dew, one of the colony elders shouts at Flik: "Get rid of that machine, get back in line and pick grain like everybody else . . . we've harvested the same way since I was a pupae." This single line of dialogue illustrates the two major political themes of the film: the lure of the status quo against the potential benefits of progress and the struggle of the individual against the will of the collective. Tradition conspires with fear of the grasshoppers. Their leader, Hopper, describes the meaning of existence as: "The sun grows the food, the ants pick the food, the grasshoppers eat the food . . ." This line is comically completed by Hopper's brother, who continues: ". . . and the birds eat the grasshoppers." This telling insight reveals the fragility of nature's order, at that point unseen by the ants. Later in the film, Hopper reveals his own fear: "If you let one ant stand up to us, then they all might stand up. Those puny little ants outnumber us 100 to one and if they ever figure that out, there goes our way of life. It's not about food. It's about keeping those ants in line." Of course, this foreshadows the events that comprise the climax of the film.

Flik is portrayed as the outcast of the colony, shown physically and psychologically distanced from society. Flik's innovativeness and entrepreneurial spirit lead him to propose building a mechanical bird to scare away the grasshoppers. When the colony believes the plan to build the bird was hatched by the warrior group/circus bugs, they support it. Once it is revealed that it was Flik's idea, they rebuke him. Their fear of change is reinforced by Hopper who claims that "ideas are very dangerous things." In the end, it is Flik's individuality and willingness to stand up to Hopper, violating every cultural norm cherished by the colony, which produces the independence of the colony from the oppression of the grasshoppers. In the closing scenes of the film, the ants are seen embracing Flik's ideas and inventions, bringing harmony to the collective.

Toy Story 2

More than any other Pixar film, *Toy Story 2* lacks political socialization cues and instead is a simple action movie. There is, however, one scene with clear political implications. During the movie, the toys sit down to watch an episode of "Woody's Roundup"—starring their very own Woody. After Jessie shuts off the television at the conclusion of an episode, Woody asked what future episodes held. Stinky Pete the Prospector had to explain that the show was immediately canceled in the middle of a season. Woody asked: "What about the gold mine and . . . and the cute little critters and the dynamite? That was a great show! I mean, why cancel it?" Stinky Pete replied "Two words: Sputnik. Once the astronauts went up, children only wanted to play with space toys." What the example shows is how world events can alter seemingly unrelated aspects of our culture. In this specific case, the launching of Sputnik diverted American attention from Western shows and toys and introduced young children to the wonders of space exploration.

Monsters, Inc.

Monsters, Inc. presents a prime example of the potential negative elements of government control for citizens living within a society. The movie takes place in Monstropolis—a city run and occupied entirely by monsters. Through closet doors, monsters are able to travel to the bedrooms of human children where they gain the city's power supply extracting energy from their helpless screams. As a result of how the city collects power, monsters with strong scaring abilities are considered extremely valuable. The best scarer in the city is James Sullivan (Sulley) who is assisted by Mike Wazowski and their chief rival is Randall Boggs. The power company CEO—Henry J. Waternoose III—likes Sulley due to his strong ability to scare yet is extremely worried about how difficult it is becoming to scare children. As Waternoose despaired early in the film, "Kids these days. They just don't get scared like they used to." Without their screams, the city will likely suffer from an even greater energy crisis.

The emergent crisis comes to a head when Sulley and Mike accidently allow a small girl to return to Monstropolis with them. While they are originally scared of Boo since humans are allegedly toxic, they grow to care for her. They feel the need to return her to her home and protect her from Randall, who has set his aim at attaching her to a machine through which he can extract her screams. Once Boo is discovered, Sulley and Mike are banished to the Himalayas by Waternoose as punishment for risking the well-being of their entire civilization. Once they work their return to Monstropolis, Sulley and Mike set out to determine a way to return Boo and also demonstrate the corrupt nature of Waternoose. To do so, they trick Waternoose into believing he has entered Boo's room where he confesses "[he] would kidnap a thousand children before [he] let[s] this company die, and [he'll] silence anyone who gets in [his] way."

Finding Nemo

Unlike some other films discussed, *Finding Nemo* does not present as direct of a socializing message. Instead, it relies on underlying tones to demonstrate the role of authority and underlying issues of family structure. In the film, two clownfish—Marlin and Coral—move into a new home in the Great Barrier Reef. When a barracuda attacks, Coral attempts to protect her eggs but is ultimately eaten along with all but one egg and Marlin. This egg becomes Nemo. When we first meet Nemo, he is headed off to his first day of school. He has clearly suffered injuries due to the barracuda attack (namely a small right fin) and this in turn has led to Marlin being quite overprotective of Nemo. At school, however, Marlin is unable to monitor Nemo's every move. Ultimately, Nemo sneaks away toward a boat off of the reef where he is captured by a scuba diver. The remainder of the movie follows Marlin's efforts to find his son and Nemo's attempts to return to the ocean.

While the movie can be superficially said to have an environmental element to it given the setting and discussion of marine biology scattered throughout and even depicts the struggles of addiction (made evident by a shark attempting to get past his love of eating fish), the true socializing element is the focus on authority and the quest for freedom. For Nemo, the linkage is clear. Born to a single parent who has lost a loved one, Nemo finds himself unable to be like other children. His father keeps tight control over his every move and fails to realize the potential impact of his actions. Consider the following exchange:

Marlin: "Now, what's the one thing we have to remember about the ocean?"
Nemo: "It's not safe."
Marlin: "That's my boy."

Nemo—given the parameters set by Marlin—revolts and swims toward the boat despite his father's regular warnings about the dangers of the ocean. Marlin's authoritative stance leads to Nemo's defiant activity and ultimately risks his well-being. The irony of Nemo's quest for freedom from the reef is that he ultimately ends up in a fish tank in a dentist's office in Sydney where he encounters the "tank gang." This group has lived in a protected state where necessities are provided for them within the tank but spend their time determining ways to achieve freedom in the ocean. Their desire to leave demonstrates that despite living in a secure environment, autonomy is still the ultimate goal.

The Incredibles

The Incredibles was Pixar's sixth film, following up the critically successful and commercially lucrative *Finding Nemo*. *The Incredibles* was unique in that it was the first Pixar film in which the main characters were human (technically, superhuman), rather than animals, monsters, or inanimate objects. Comic book fans will identify archetypal superhero motifs and recognize the Parr family as analogous to Marvel Comics' Fantastic Four, another family of superpowered heroes. *The Incredibles* seems to represent an idealized 1950s vision of the future. The setting seems somehow both contemporary (much of the technology present in the film) and also nostalgic (the cars in present-day scenes appear to be based on 1950s and 1960s models). The obvious major theme of the film is the success and contentment enjoyed by a strong family that supports each other and acts as a unit. However the film is replete with political allegory and insight. The predominant political theme is similar to that of *A Bug's Life*: individualism strengthens, rather than damages, the collective.

Early in the film, Mr. Incredible (Bob Parr) attempts to catch a supervillain, Bomb Voyage. In the process, he saves the life of a man attempting to commit suicide. In television newscasts, the victim's attorney argues: "Mr. Sansweet didn't ask to be saved." When Mr. Incredible retorts that he saved Sansweet's life, Sansweet cries: "You didn't save my life. You ruined my death." As Mr. Incredible is an agent of the government (although the nature of this relationship is not explicitly explored), the government faces lawsuits from Sansweet and the injured passengers on an elevated train who were saved from derailment. It is hardly a stretch to suggest that this is a comment on the litigious nature of American society. Public pressure and financial strain lead the government to institute a Super Relocation Act, which provides amnesty for past actions in exchange for cessation of superhero activity. A graphic is shown that reveals that 85 percent are in favor of the measure. In the aftermath, Mr. Incredible/Bob becomes an insurance agent who tells policy holders how to legally circumvent the rules. Bob's boss is aghast that Bob would attempt to help his clients, shouting: "What I can't handle is your customers' inexplicable knowledge of Insuricare's inner workings. They're experts! Exploiting every loophole! Dodging every obstacle! They're penetrating the bureaucracy!"

The character of Dash led several libertarian critics to praise the film. After a meeting with Dash's principal, the following exchange occurs between Dash and Helen:

Dash:	"You always say do your best, but you don't really mean it. Why can't I do the best that I can do?"
Helen:	"Right now honey, the world just wants us to fit in. And to fit in, we just gotta be like everybody else."
Dash:	"But dad always said our powers are nothing to be ashamed of. Our powers made us special."
Helen:	"Everyone's special, Dash."
Dash:	"Which is another way of saying no one is."

Later, Helen rebukes Bob for lack of eagerness toward attending Dash's fourth-grade "graduation." Bob replies: "It's psychotic! They keep creating new ways to celebrate mediocrity, but if someone is genuinely exceptional . . ." As Bob dismisses the relativism that he believes oppresses Dash, his anger reflects the fact that his own excellence was extinguished by the Super Relocation Act. Whether intentional or not, *The Incredibles* champions the classic liberal ideal of the sovereignty of the individual. Having said that, it also demonstrates how individual excellence can strengthen the collective, as demonstrated by the Parr's defeat of Syndrome.

Cars

In *Cars*, the small town of Radiator Springs, once a flourishing city along the nation's busiest roadway (Route 66), has become an afterthought in the nation due to the creation of a high-speed interstate designed to bypass the city. Cars that are not residents of Radiator Springs seem only to end up in the town by mistake. This creates a severe drain on the city's economy, with many of the businesses closing down and residents suffering greatly. The film seems to be making the point that urban sprawl and creation of the interstate system have caused some of America's greatest gems to be overlooked. When visitors do finally begin to pass through Radiator Springs, they are pleased with what the quaint city has to offer, and learn the value of slowing down to experience the unexpected pieces of the country. Overall, Pixar seems to stress the importance of rebuilding small town America to avoid a loss of history and culture important to the nation since its formation.

Cars also tries to teach the lesson that small town America is looked down upon by many people in urban centers. Lightning McQueen displays feelings of contempt for the town when he is sentenced to pave the road as a punishment for speeding. As a city-born racecar, McQueen sees the residents of Radiator Springs as unintelligent and lacking ambition. He is surprised to learn Doc, the town's judge, and Sally, a local car with strong attachment to the town, were both formerly city cars as well. They both chose to remain in Radiator Springs after experiencing all the positives small-town life had to offer. McQueen learns the value of friendship and co-dependence that is present in Radiator Springs and absent in his city life. Pixar seems to be expressing the importance of respect for all people, regardless of region of the country or economic standing.

Ratatouille

Pixar's *Ratatouille* examines the political and economic ideas of upward mobility, comparative advantage, and the effectiveness of free-market principles in an economy. Each of these themes works together to help create a better situation for all of the characters in the movie.

In the beginning of this movie, Remy is stuck in a social situation with which he is dissatisfied; all of the other rats are content to eat garbage, but Remy wishes to become a chef. The other rats are dismissive of these ideas but, after being separated from his clan, Remy pursues his dream by assisting an aspiring chef, Linguini, at Gusteau's, a Parisian restaurant. This illustrates the idea of upward mobility—the movie's ever-present phrase "anyone can cook" is reminiscent of the idea that anyone can succeed. Remy, through hard work and dedication, is able to make a better life for himself. Simply working hard was not enough, however; Remy had to isolate himself from the naysayers around him in order to be successful. The movie seems to argue that if a person removes himself or herself from negative influence and works tirelessly, most goals are accomplishable in the real world.

Comparative advantage and the division of labor are also stressed in *Ratatouille* as ideals for an effective economy. Remy has a comparative advantage in cooking knowledge. Working with Linguini, who has a comparative advantage in the human elements of implementing this knowledge, the two are able to create popular dishes much more effectively than either could alone. This is indicative of the fact that for a society to be successful, division of labor must occur—not everyone is talented in every area, but working in areas in which one has strengths is enough to produce an efficient economy.

Free-market principles are a final political and economic element of this movie. In a free-market, firms produce only goods and services deemed desirable by the public. Prior to Remy's arrival at the restaurant, Gusteau's produces dishes that are not considered very popular, causing the restaurant's image and profitability to fall. When Remy arrives, new dishes are produced, and the public demands them. Production of these new, desirable dishes helps bring the restaurant back to its former glory. The free-market is also observable in the fact that even though Linguini's entire cooking staff leaves en masse after learning of Remy's role in the restaurant, and that the restaurant is closed because of rodent infestation, the market still provides a way. Demand existed in the public, so the restaurant was re-opened under a different name and with Remy a named-partner in the endeavor and the former cooks replaced.

WALL-E

WALL-E is the Pixar film with the most explicit political message. Distinct environmental and anticonsumerist messages are apparent. Based 700 years in the future—on a version of Earth destroyed by garbage and lacking plant and animal life, the film shows the human race living on the Axiom, an enormous spacecraft administered by the corporate-government hybrid Buy-n-Large. WALL-E (Waste Allocation Load Lifter-Earth Class) is the only robot left of a fleet designed to restore Earth so humans could return and resume their normal lives. While the assumed overtones suggest that the socialization element of the movie depict calls for Americans to care more for the environment and to make decisions and sacrifices to prevent our planet from becoming what is depicted in the movie, the film contains a more subtle underlying commentary about human dignity and self-reliance.

Acquiring human curiosity after 700 years of toil cleaning up the Earth, WALL-E discovers and becomes emotionally attached to a seedling and whisks it away to his hovel. Eventually the lonely WALL-E is visited by EVE (Extraterrestrial Vegetation Evaluator), an overtly biblical reference. As WALL-E falls in love with EVE, EVE's programmed objective is to retrieve WALL-E's plant and abscond to the Axiom. Upon the ship, humans are revealed to have become bloated and essentially immobile, transported around the spaceship by hover-chairs. Human faces are situated inches away from holographic screens that advertise products and services such as cupcake in a cup. Robots and machines groom humans, feed them, and play their sports for them. The captain of the Axiom is shown to be a shiftless blob, barely capable of reading. With all essential and nonessential tasks completed for them and no conceivable objective beyond instant gratification and consumption, humans in the film are portrayed as well-meaning but dim, lazy slobs.

When the captain sees WALL-E's plant and attempts to initiate the directive to return to Earth, it is revealed that humans are intended to remain on the Axiom in perpetuity, thereby abandoning Earth entirely and sustaining Buy-n-Large. Only after the captain reveals the corrupt plot to keep humans in space and the subsequent robot mutiny do the humans organize and work to return to Earth. Although *WALL-E* is a sweet, sentimental tale of a Chaplinesque robot finding a greater purpose than cleaning garbage, its political content is overt. To be sure, *WALL-E* presents a stark vision of environmental calamity and consumerism. However, it is a mistake to ignore the more subtle theme of humanity. Addressing questions about the portrayal of humans in the film, *WALL-E* director Andrew Stanton asked: "What if everything you needed to survive—health care, food—was taken care of and you had nothing but a perpetual vacation to fill your time?" In a subtle way, *WALL-E* seems to challenge the utopian ideal in which all material possessions are provided and egalitarianism reigns.

Up

Up focuses on the struggles of Carl Fredricksen, an elderly man struggling to cope with the loss of his partner in adventure. After Ellie, his wife, passed away, Carl maintained their simple home as the world built up quickly around him. The last holdout, Carl tried to live a simple existence and fondly remember his Ellie. He had to fight off developers wanting to move him out to build more skyscrapers, telling them that they can have his house "when [he's] dead." One day, a construction worker was directing a vehicle to back up and hit the mailbox Carl and Ellie had worked on together early in their marriage. Agitated, Carl rushed to fix it and ask the worker not to touch it. Unfortunately, the worker—attempting to assist—continued reaching toward it until Carl hit him on the head with his cane, drawing blood.

Carl knew immediately that what he did was wrong and would have an impact on his future. He was called to court over the assault and it was decided he would need to move into a retirement village since he was a public menace. When the nurses from Shady Oaks Retirement Village showed up the next morning to transport him, he asked for one last walk through of the house and stated he would then be out to the van. Instead, a large shadow emerged and the house began to pull away from its foundation. Carl yelled out from his balloon-lifted house, "Ah, ha ha ha! So long, boys! I'll send you a postcard from Paradise Falls!" The old man opted to live out his final years fulfilling a fantasy adventure he had long shared with his wife rather than simply adhere to the governmental edict that he move into a nursing home. Ultimately, *Up* characterizes government as coercive and intrusive into the lives of citizens; it forces individuals to alter their lives to avoid its demands.

Toy Story 3

Like the other movies in the franchise, *Toy Story 3* is not thematically political. However, elements of the film clearly demonstrate political meaning. In the movie, Andy is preparing to go to college and needs to clean his room—where he must decide whether to keep, store, throw away, or donate all of his toys to Sunnyside Daycare. All of the favorite toys from earlier movies ultimately end up at Sunnyside. When the toys arrive, they are placed in their box in the Butterfly Room where they notice happy children playing with all of the available toys. As the students left for recess, Andy's toys moved out of their box and were met by a group of resident toys excited to meet them. As the group leader—Lotso—stated, "Welcome to Sunnyside, folks. I'm Lots-o-Huggin Bear. But please, call me Lotso."

Lotso goes on to tell the toys that they will be taken care of and will always have someone to play with. Ultimately, Andy's toys find their way to the Caterpillar Room where they will await their first opportunity to play. As the children come back, the toys quickly realize the stark difference between the Butterfly and Caterpillar rooms. The children are screaming and rough—scaring and harming the toys. The toys manage to survive the day, but as the daycare closes, they approach Lotso to discuss the obvious mistake of their room assignment. Buzz, who leads the discussion, is invited to join the Butterfly Room but is not permitted to bring any of his friends along. When Buzz refuses the invitation, he is held down and returned to his demo mode—stripping him of his personality and existence. Lotso's actions make it clear that those who fail to act as he wishes will face repercussions for stepping out of line.

Herein lays the politics of *Toy Story 3*: the toys in the daycare operate largely as a political machine with Lotso leading the way. Toys all begin in the Caterpillar Room when they arrive at Sunnyside and if they are able to survive, they eventually are able to enter the Butterfly Room. Only by paying their dues and being abused by toddlers are the toys able to earn the right to be treated well. Sunnyside's rigid hierarchy reflects both a classic Tammany Hall-style machine and a statement on bureaucratic politics and structure.

Cars 2

The first *Cars* film was a character-driven piece. The thin plot, that of the arrogant self-absorbed race car learning to slow down and value friendship, allowed for the development of many likable characters and established their relationships. *Cars 2* was a critical and commercial disappointment. Conservatives argued that it was the most blatantly political Pixar film yet. Although *Wall-E* clearly advanced political notions, it appealed to both liberals (who championed the environmentalist notions) and conservatives (who noticed that the humans of the future become bloated, shiftless blobs when everything is provided for them). A child might define the theme of *Cars 2* as the value of friendship. For all others, the overarching theme of alternative fuel will be apparent throughout the film. John Lasseter, the film's director, told the *Wall Street Journal* that big oil is the "uber bad guy" of *Cars 2*.

The film centers around a race conceived by Sir Miles Axelrod in which the contestants will use his alternative fuel, Allinol. In a media interview, Axelrod states: "Big oil. It costs a fortune. Pollution is getting worse . . . Alternative energy is the future." In reality, Axelrod is "big oil" and is using the race to dismiss the validity of alternative fuel. Allinol is gasoline treated to ignite when hit with an electromagnetic beam. As each car flames out, the reputation of Allinol is further damaged and traditional fossil fuels look more attractive. Mater, the film's beloved tow-truck, unwittingly becomes a spy and uncovers the plot. When asked why Axelrod would do such a thing, Mater replies: "To make Allinol look bad so everyone'd go back to using oil." Lightning McQueen, the film's other major protagonist, curiously did not ignite when hit with the beam. McQueen's hippie friend Fillmore, a member of McQueen's pit crew, reveals that he did not trust Axelrod and used his own organic alternative fuel. In response, Sarge, a tacitly conservative military-issue Jeep and ideological counterpoint to Fillmore, states: "Once big oil, always big oil." If the film is meant to act as propaganda to advocate alternative energy, its success in doing so is debatable. The film advances alternative fuel by portraying oil companies as villainous, implying the virtue of alternative energy by default.

Classroom integration

Undoubtedly, students will greet the idea of watching animated films in a college classroom with skepticism. Yet, we suggest, that this assignment helps make a rather nebulous concept concrete for optimal learning.

When considering the assignment we utilize in our courses, we ask students to select two to three Pixar films (out of all produced) and to watch them with a critical eye for potentially socializing elements. They are then asked to explain (through a short paper) the messages they observe and most importantly to discuss whether this was something they remember noticing when they first watched the film as a child. On average, a vast majority of students admit to never noticing the political themes in prior viewings—mainly due to their interest in simply being entertained in earlier viewings.

By engaging in this activity, we can accomplish different outcomes depending on the class. In an introductory course, the activity works well to show how pervasive socialization can really be. Children's movies are largely assumed to be beacons of innocence and free from potentially corrupting influences. Once students become aware of the underlying tones present in these films, it serves as an alert to think more critically about how other ignored influences can still be shaping their beliefs and attitudes.

For upper-level students examining political behavior and public opinion, the assignment works to help evaluate the amount of influence different agents have on socialization. Likewise, it can be used as a way to introduce the ideas of lifetime effects and show how our thinking can change over time.

After having students complete the paper assignment, we devote a few class periods to discussing the assignments and asking students to bring in favorite clips for the class to discuss through informal presentations. In the presentation, students are asked to lead a discussion of their clip by having fellow students point to potentially socializing themes within it. They are then asked to talk about whether the clip would have influenced them as children or not. The in-class portion seems to energize students and lead to thoughtful discussion. However, when they start to understand the underlying tones, they begin to look at all of the movies differently. Most surprising to many students is the fact that many of these underlying themes are fairly conservative in nature. Student discussion turns in many cases to discussing the likelihood that children watching the movies pick up on the themes even accidently and what effect it can potentially have on citizen attitudes toward government as they grow. Further, discussion swirls on why these types of movies have such political tones if truly being designed for children. Through these discussions, our students begin to fully understand the concept of political socialization while doing little more than reassessing movies they know from their childhoods.

Most importantly, Pixar films can be used in other areas of courses. Beyond socialization, the films can be used to discuss specific policy issues (energy or the environment, for example) or political ideology in general. When used with these different topics, the overall impact of utilizing Pixar can be increased as students become more comfortable with the concept of animated children's films serving as alternative texts in their quest to understand government and politics in the United States. The key is to assure the usage is genuine. If you simply choose to play Pixar clips in an effort to attract student interest but fail to use them as a tool for actual pedagogy, students will likely fail to appreciate the full potential effect.

Conclusion

What the synopses suggest is that all Pixar films hold socializing messages. While some are pervasive throughout entire films and others are evident for only a few select scenes, they are always present. When it comes to helping students to understand a complex concept like political socialization, the use of Pixar movies (written with children and families in mind) helps to add elements of comfort through familiarity and allows students to relate material they know with a concept they may not. Even if students are entirely unfamiliar with Pixar films, they will be able to relate class materials to the movies upon their first viewing (regardless of whether they watch full-length or just selected clips). In our own experience, students have found scenes that could be viewed as potentially socializing that we failed ourselves to see in our many viewings. There are rarely any wrong answers. Innovative texts work in the modern college classroom—but faculty must work to assure that they show students something that is actually innovative.

The danger for faculty looking to use innovative texts, such as Pixar films, is to make sure they force students to work through their ideas completely. Without this, educators are doing little more than asking students to complete extra work with no additional value added to the course material. Students are less likely to respond when alternative texts are used in the classroom simply because they are different. The learning goals and opportunities must be genuine and clear. With our classrooms, we have found one successful way to assure this level of commitment is to volunteer our own example analyses of one Pixar film per semester so students understand how detailed and sophisticated papers and presentations based on animated films can be. Only by setting the bar high in terms of expectations can we fully expect students to take this alternative approach as seriously as they would the traditional mechanisms. Turning to Pixar films for homework is undeniably different for students but that does not mean expectations should be lower or the work any more challenging.

[Please see the companion website for the book. Details are listed on the back cover of the book.]

Notes

1 David Easton and Jack Dennis, *Children in the Political System* (Chicago, IL: University of Chicago Press), 1969.
2 Ibid. It goes without saying that this is not a universal claim. Many subgroups within the American population fail to hold government officials—or government itself—in high regard at any point in their development.
3 Fred Greenstein, *Children and Politics* (New Haven, CT: Yale University Press, 1965); Robert S. Erikson and Kent L. Tedin, *American Public Opinion* (New York: Pearson, 2005).
4 Greenstein, *Children and Politics*; Easton and Dennis, *Children in the Political System*.
5 Easton and Dennis, *Children in the Political System*, 1969.
6 Greenstein, *Children and* Politics; M. Kent Jennings and Richard G. Niemi, *The Political Character of Adolescence* (Princeton, NJ: Princeton University Press, 1974).
7 Robert D. Hess and Judith V. Torney, *The Development of Political Attitudes in Children* (Chicago, IL: Aldine, 1967).

8 Robert W. Connell, *The Child's Construction of Politics* (Melbourne: Melbourne University Press, 1971).

9 Roberta S. Sigel, *Learning about Politics* (New York: Random House, 1970).

10 Kenneth P. Langton, *Political Socialization* (New York: Oxford University Press, 1969).

11 Hess and Torney, *The Development of Political Attitudes*; Frank J. Sorauf and Paul Allen Beck, *Party Politics in America* (New York: Harper Collins, 1988).

12 Hess and Torney, *The Development of Political Attitudes*; Erikson and Tedin, *American Public Opinion*.

13 Hess and Torney, *The Development of Political Attitudes*.

14 Hanna Adoni, "The Functions of Mass Media in the Political Socialization of Adolescents," *Communication Research* 6 (1979): 84–106; M. Margaret Conway, Mikel L. Wyckoff, Eleanor Feldbaum, and David Ahern, "The News Media in Children's Political Socialization," *Public Opinion Quarterly* 45 (1981): 164–78; Steven H. Chaffee, Clifford I. Nass, and Seung-Mock Yang, "The Bridging Role of Television in Immigrant Political Socialization," *Human Communication Research* 17 (1990): 266–88; David Buckingham, "News Media, Political Socialization and Popular Citizenship: Towards a New Agenda," *Critical Studies in Mass Communication* 14 (1997): 344–66.

15 D. J. Self, D. C. Baldwin, and M. Olivarez, "Teaching Medical Ethics to First-Year Students by Using Film Discussion to Develop their Moral Reasoning," *Academic Medicine: Journal of the Association of American Medical Colleges* 68 (1993): 383–5; M. Lynn Kuzma and Patrick J. Haney, "And . . . Action! Using Film to Learn About Foreign Policy," *International Studies Perspectives* 2 (2001): 33–50; Cynthia Weber, "The Highs and Lows of Teaching IR Theory: Using Popular Films for Theoretical Critique," *International Studies Perspectives* 2(3) (2001): 281–7; Byongji Ahn, "The West Wing as an Inspiring Teacher," Paper presented at the *Annual Meeting of the American Political Science Association,* Boston, MA (2002); David Caroll Cochran, "Using the Godfather to Teach the Prince," in Annual Meeting of the American Political Science Association, Boston, MA, (2002); Elisabeth Anker, "Subversion and Satire in the 'Manchurian Candidate': Aligning Political Context and Historical Reception," Paper presented at the *Annual Meeting of the American Political Science Association,* Philadelphia, PA (2003).

16 Ronald A. Berk, "Multimedia Teaching with Video Clips: Tv, Movies, Youtube, and Mtvu in the College Classroom," *International Journal of Technology in Teaching and Learning* 5 (2009): 1–21.

CHAPTER TWELVE

American students, African conflicts, and Hollywood: The advantages and unintended consequences of using film to teach African politics

Christopher R. Cook[1]

Introduction

There is a small but growing body of literature about the pedagogy of film in the classroom.[2] For many political scientists, films have become integral in showing real life application to abstract concepts. Films like *Dr. Strangelove* (dir. Stanley Kubrick, 1964) can be found on the syllabi of international relations courses. Screenings of *Mr. Smith Goes to Washington* (dir. Frank Capra, 1939) can be found in introductory courses of American politics. Some of the more adventurous have used documentaries like Michael Moore's *Fahrenheit 911* (2004) to provoke a wider discussion about American foreign policy. However, there is a hole in this literature about the complexity of using film to teach American undergraduates about the political, economic, and ethnic issues facing the developing world.

This chapter examines the use of film as a teaching tool in an upper-level African politics course at Penn State Erie, The Behrend College. The course consisted of 25 students, primarily History and Political Science majors from Western Pennsylvania. For many of the students Africa was the proverbial "heart of darkness." They were exposed to the continent in its most negative terms: genocide, famine, AIDS, and poverty. Kenneth Cameron contends that by the nineteenth century a "conventional" Africa was formed in the minds of the West. He states this message was often "sparse in information and that depended on a few repeated motifs, especially 'jungle,' 'darkness,' and 'savagery' . . ." Africans, Cameron notes were seen as "childlike, violent, and superstitious."[3] These problems are exacerbated in the classroom because the gaze of academia is far more likely to focus on the politics of military coups, wars, grinding poverty, and genocide than the normalcy of everyday life. I admit that my course is conflict driven as well. However, if presented properly, popular films about African conflicts can become an important educational tool to show students that conflicts in Africa are modern and not the result of tribal warfare.

The films examined here include: *Lumumba* (dir. Raoul Peck, 2000) for its emphasis upon decolonization and independence to the formation of the African state; *Hotel Rwanda* (dir. Terry George, 2004) for helping students understand communal violence and confronting tropes like ancient tribal hatreds. Finally, the commercially successful *Blood Diamond* (dir. Edward Zwick, 2006) creates awareness that conflict is no longer super power intrigue (which to some extent is the story of *Lumumba*) but caused by globalization and the privatization of natural resources.

These films were incorporated into the curriculum through specific readings that tied course text to film. Assignments were given in two stages: first, before the film to raise awareness about certain topics, and then afterwards to reinforce comprehension, and to see if students noticed other kinds of content. Students were also given assignments to view the film critically for its thesis, historical inaccuracies and whether it perpetuated negative African stereotypes. I would argue that overall this was a positive experience and something that could be duplicated in other courses besides African politics.

The literature of teaching Africa and the use of film in the classroom

Paul Beckett once stated that it was intellectual hubris to think that one person can teach the politics of every African nation in one semester.[4] The pedagogical problem is compounded by the fact that no other continent is so misunderstood. Africa seems distant and strange. Students are routinely amazed by its size and cultural variety of 54 nations. Maybe this lack of classroom knowledge is not surprising considering that the media coverage of the continent has often lacked sophistication and exposition.[5] It can be argued that Africa is both ignored and exoticized. Instead of seeing the rich panoply of cultures and life, Africa remains a cliché. This view has been reinforced by the historical racism within the United States.

The second hurdle is the inherent bias in how Americans frame African political and economic problems. This bias leads to simplistic mono-causal explanations that fall on two ends of a spectrum: either colonialism or primitive ethnic brutality. One cannot tell the story of African nations (or most of the developing world) without the context of colonialism. But this approach denies African's agency. Furthermore, we cannot discuss African politics without an honest account of the role modern tribalism plays in political violence. For example, the roots of the Rwandan genocide and the tension between the Hutus and Tutsi are deeper and more systemic than a simple story of Belgian colonialism or the idea of age-old ethnic hatreds.

So how does one balance these competing demands in the classroom? J. J. Ayoade discusses three strategies for teaching African politics. First, one could, in his opinion, base a class around African sensationalism. In order to grab student attention, content would revolve around atrocities and genocides (Rwanda); insane dictators (Idi Amin in Uganda); famine (Ethiopia), etc. While such an approach can be factual and pique student interest it may fall into the trap of dehumanizing Africans. Second, Ayoade notes that one could focus on exhaustive single-country case studies that examine the formal, legal, or historical characteristics of nations. Finally, the popular approach, and one used by a new set of textbooks, is to look at the continent thematically.[6] Texts like Alex Thomson's, *An Introduction to Africa Politics*, and William Tordoff's, *Government and Politics of Africa* break up African politics into separate themes: the role of colonialism, political parties, the military, African socialism, regional organizations, economics, ethnic and social class, etc. But even this approach has its drawbacks for teaching about distinct nations.[7]

But if the complexity of teaching Africa to Americans was not enough another problem presents itself in the classroom. Students today are more likely to be visual learners. Stacy Ulbig argues in her American politics course, "the use of simple visual images can enhance students' impressions . . . and boost their interest."[8] Thus it is only natural to assume that visual images, and by extension film, can enhance a course on a distant subject such as Africa Films help students share experiences, "he or she might otherwise find remote and therefore puzzling."[9] Lynn Kuzma and Patrick Haney argue that the use of films create rich opportunities for students to learn. They "stimulate the senses, ground abstract concepts, engage the emotions, contextualize history, and facilitate an active-learning classroom environment."[10]

The use of film is not without its setbacks. It is difficult for students to understand that films operate on different levels than just entertainment. The films selected here were for the most part created and produced for

Western audiences. While they are dramatizations of real events, they have been altered by creative license. *Lumumba* has been accused as being overtly hagiographic. The President of Rwanda, Paul Kagame, has criticized *Hotel Rwanda* as flawed. *Blood Diamond* has been called nothing more than a tourist film. Students should realize that "movies reflect political choices, not with looking glass clarity, but often as shadowed, displaced, and distorted."[11] Michael Kellner and Douglas Ryan argue in *Camera Politica* that films are political texts that "operate to legitimate dominant institutions and traditional values." In the same vein Stewart Samuels contends that films, "symbolize existing ideologies."[12] But Kellner and Ryan go on to argue that people are not passive watchers. Films are a dynamic and interactive process shaping how social reality "will be perceived . . ."[13] We want students to actively engage the film as text and not passively accept what they see as truth. I argue that the best way to teach these films to American students is to address these cinematic shortcomings inherent in film head on. The pedagogical hope is to create a dialogue between the course text and the films they watch to enrich the classroom experience.

Themes of sovereignty and independence in Lumumba

I think it is imperative when teaching about the developing world that students understand the importance of independence and sovereignty. There are still many Africans who remember a Belgian Congo, or a British Kenya, or Portuguese Angola. This recent colonial background has shaped African politics across the continent in a myriad of ways, but none more powerful than the right to control their own destiny. How does one present this idea on the silver screen? It is not an easy task considering most films are made by the West. However, I have selected Raoul Peck's *Lumumba* (2000) as a jumping off point for a discussion of the troubles concerning colonialism, economic exploitation, and independence. The film tells the troubled story of the first Congolese Prime Minister Patrice Lumumba, a man invariably described as a nationalist, or a communist depending on whom you ask. The film concentrates on his final months before his brutal murder. Georges Nzongola-Ntalaja has stated his death was one of the most important assassinations of the twentieth century.[14]

The film presents us with many possible avenues of classroom discussion. First, it provides a visual image of colonialism and the racial stratification in Belgian Leopoldville (now Kinshasa). European colonialism in Africa was economic exploitation on the cheap. At the time of Congolese independence in 1960 barely half of the 13 1/2 million Congolese could read and write, and only 16 individuals were university or college graduates. There were no Congolese doctors, lawyers, or engineers, and no African officers in the 25,000-men Congolese Army.[15] The film accurately portrays a fledging nation imploding on its birth. But the centerpiece of this film is the fiery speech Lumumba gave for the Congolese Independence Day ceremonies on June 30, 1960. Special classroom attention should be given to this speech. In front of the Belgian King and other international diplomats, Lumumba railed against colonial injustices and talked about a bright future for Africa. According to the contemporary coverage by Harry Gilroy in the *New York Times*:

> He asserted that no Congolese would ever forget the struggle in which "we have not spared our strength, our privations, our sufferings or our blood." He commented that colonialism had left wounds too keen and too painful to be wiped from memory. Premier Lumumba reminded the members of the new Parliament of "the ironies, the insults, the blows that we had to submit to morning, noon and night because we were Negroes."[16]

The article also wryly notes that, "Premier Lumumba's speech produced comments of surprise and disappointment among Belgian and other Western representatives." Lumumba's Leftist rhetoric is a powerful piece of cinema. To reinforce its importance to themes in the course, I pass out a transcript of the speech and then show students a short clip from an obscure 1961 conspiracy documentary called *Katanga: The Untold Story of U.N. Betrayal*. This film uses actual footage of the speech but with an important difference, Lumumba is cast as a communist. Instead of Peck's presentation of an anticolonial hero, the narrator of *Untold Story* states an ungrateful Lumumba chose this solemn occasion to heap insults on the beloved King. By presenting this speech from a variety of different perspectives, we want students to understand the difficulties Africans had winning their independence, and the struggle they faced trying to forge their own destiny.

Was Lumumba a communist? No more than any other first-generation African leader, like Tanzania's Julius Nyerere, and Ghana's Kwame Nkrumah, who were also considered socialists by the West. But this African socialism has to be qualified with an understanding that Lumumba's economic viewpoints are forged with the memory of a repressive colonial economic system. Lumumba's generation feared Western economic domination. President Nkrumah argued whether sovereignty was even important if you did not control your own economic life.[17] After watching this film, I have found that students intuitively understand this. *Lumumba* humanizes the independence struggle.

Much of Lumumba's short political life and death revolved around the secession of the Katanga province. It is useful to give students the background information on the conflict before the film. Katanga was home to most of the Congo's natural resources and wealth. Lumumba was convinced (and he was right) that there was a level of Belgian duplicity involved in the conflict. The film serves as a historical reminder of Africa's position in the global Cold War and the exploitation of African resources (something we will discuss further in *Blood Diamond*). However, Lumumba never lived to see the end. He was deposed in a coup (carried out by his former friend Mobutu) and handed over to the Katangan government who tortured and executed him. Indirectly, and depending on how you want to teach the class, the film can also teach students the limitations of the United Nations. The United Nations eventually ended the conflict with accusations of human rights atrocities. The Congo Crisis set back the idea of humanitarian intervention in Africa for years to come.

The film also sheds light on other abstract concepts of decolonization, namely the European policies of divide and conquer that empowered rival centers of power (like Katanga) at the expense of a central government. Lumumba's party was one of the few nationalist parties in the Congo. His leadership in the Assembly was predicated on balancing a coalition of 12 different parties mostly regional and built on tribal lines. This is a good example of how one can integrate course text with film. Donald Rothchild and Jean Francois Bayart argue that the only way African governments could win legitimacy was by negotiation with rival political (and ethnic) groups and forming uneasy ruling coalitions over state-controlled resources.[18] Students watching *Lumumba* can see the Congolese government's inability to "impose its will" on society and the difficult negotiations needed to produce a viable state.[19] The film ends with the kleptocratic President Mobutu, sporting his trademark leopard skin hat, holding an ironic celebration for the "Zairian hero" Patrice Lumumba, a man he helped to kill.[20]

But there are drawbacks to showing this film. Raoul Peck states at the beginning: "this is a true story." But as David Moore argues Peck makes an assumption that "Lumumba was the complete hero" and that everything he said "was an automatic reflection" of the people.[21] Plenty of people in the Congo did not like him. Contemporary accounts reveal a charismatic, intelligent, but naïve man involved in a situation over his head. One has to caution students that Peck might be engaged in creating a hagiography. Films require creative license. The time frame is collapsed at the expense of important historical details. The Katanga secession, so crucial to the plot is left underdeveloped. Peck's mythmaking also downplays Lumumba's mistakes and intellectual evolution. For example, his political views toward independence and Belgian colonialism changed over time.

Depending on the course you may want to briefly examine the role the United States had in the coup that toppled Lumumba. Peck makes clear that US officials knew of the assassination plot.[22] What is known is that even if Washington was not directly linked to the coup they were glad it happened.

Mobutu was an American ally who would go on to help fight communism across Southern Africa.

Once students have the necessary information and historical context to critically examine Peck's thesis, the film can serve as an excellent jumping off point on a range of subjects discussed in an African politics course: decolonization, economic interdependence, Cold War intrigue, and the rise of the corrupt African leaders. One can even use the film to discuss the role of the United Nations. Overall the students enjoy the film (even with its subtitles). *Lumumba* accomplishes the pedagogical goals of visualizing what decolonization, independence, and sovereignty looked like for the Democratic Republic of the Congo in 1960, and how difficult it was. It is also important to note that some of the same themes in this film are present in the next one that focuses on the neighboring country of Rwanda.

The theme of ethnicity and tribal violence in *Hotel Rwanda*

Teaching the causes of the Rwandan genocide to American students is harder than people think. For example, it has been noted that students have a general awareness of the Holocaust but not why it happened.[23] For many Americans the Rwandan genocide is simply associated with primitive Africa and the negative stereotype of tribes. However, the Hutu genocide of the Tutsi population is not a simple story of age-old hatreds. To this end, I have selected the film *Hotel Rwanda* (2004, dir. Terry George), a powerful and accessible movie based on the true story of Paul Rusesabagina, who was able to shelter Tutsi refugees in Kigali. Student learning objectives for *Hotel Rwanda* are to grasp the political, economic, and social causes behind the genocide. Students will find a richer understanding of the tragedy exploring the reasons why Hutu politicians chose violence to solve their problems. Second, the events of April 1994 can also be used in the classroom to continue the exploration of ethnic differences on the continent and challenge popular American stereotypes about tribalism.

Hotel Rwanda is not the only film on the subject, but it is the most American and student friendly, with some well-known actors. The film is not without its critics; Mohamed Adhikari argues it is a missed opportunity, "more likely to perpetuate rather than dispel stereotypes of Africa as a place of senseless violence" because it lacks historical context.[24] So how do we get students to understand modern African tribes and not the clichéd stereotypes? For many Americans the concept of ethnicity is either based on the myth of the American melting pot or a rigid and unbending racial classification system. If *Hotel Rwanda* is to be a success in the classroom it is imperative for the educator to provide students the necessary context of ethnicity in Africa before the screening.

As with *Lumumba,* part of the answer of the Rwandan genocide lies in understanding how Europeans and Arabs engaged the continent. To be sure tribes existed before colonization, but the Europeans manipulated those distinctions for their own benefit. They discovered that many parts of Africa had a fluid concept of ethnicity based on loose kinship communities. Imperialism replaced this ethnic fluidity with rigid definitions. The Europeans needed indigenous allies to help protect the "thin white line."

However, students should also understand that Africans embraced this colonial definition of ethnicity because they benefited from it. These groups could enjoy the spoils of the state by accepting and maximizing the European definition of tribes. Alex Thomson wryly notes: "while the colonial authorities were busy assigning Africans to 'tribes,' Africans were busy building 'tribes' to belong to."[25] Rene Lemarchand argues that "ethnicity" in Africa is partially the politics of memory, myths, and imagined identities. "Violence does not come from the primordial mist—it is the product of the modern rapid mobilization of ethnic identities unleashed by a democratization built on the premise of inequality."[26] Mythmaking is central to the construction of the modern Hutu and Tutsi identity.

When discussing the history of Rwanda in the classroom one should start with the Germans, followed by the Belgians' choice of having the minority Tutsi rule over the Hutu to serve their colonial interests.[27] The colonial powers based their decision on the simple fact that the Rwandan Kingdom was a weak Tutsi monarchy with a small accompanying aristocracy. While there *are* ethnic differences, identity was often a fluid category in the Great Lakes area to designate social class not ethnicity. Thus social mobility within Rwanda was not strictly based on ethnic lines, and after years of intermarriage and changing economic fortunes plenty of people who looked "Hutu" were being treated as "Tutsi" and vice versa.

But to make matters worse the Europeans couched their political maneuverings in the racist ideology of the Hamitic hypothesis: the idea that the Tutsi were superior and exhibited the potential for modern nation building unlike the Hutu. The Belgians also pushed for an inflexible ethnic classification and systematically entrenched it into the apparatus of the state— shutting off social mobility and destroying the carefully built-in dispute resolution systems between communities. Gerard Prunier argues that the end effect was the development of a Hutu oppositional identity of inferiority.[28] Lemarchand notes that radical Hutu actually embraced the Hamitic myth as a badge of victimization and sharpened it as a rhetorical weapon against the Tutsi.

Hotel Rwanda tries to capture some but not all of these ethnic dynamics. One way an educator can try to engage the classroom about ethnicity in Africa is the counterintuitive method of having them examine ethnicity and race in the United States. In one scene a journalist is trying to understand the ethnic dynamics of Rwanda. He is told about the Belgian manipulation for political purposes and the Hamitic myth that since the Tutsi people were taller, had lighter skin and straight noses they had to be more like the Europeans. For Mohamed Adhikari the scene is not enough.[29] But as an educator it is important to stop and realize how new these concepts might seem to a group of American students with no previous knowledge of Africa. Most of my students come from a mixed European ethnic heritage. Instead of showing African tribes as foreign and primitive constructs, students can see these examples of ethnic and racial construction in American history. For example, Homer Plessy (of the landmark *Plessy v. Ferguson)* was 7/8 White but would have been legally required to sit in a colored car. In this case race becomes a construct. I often ask students before the screening: who is Irish on St. Patrick's Day; or German during an Oktoberfest festival? Construction of identity does not have to be a foreign concept.

But Rwanda is more than just ethnicity. The educator must also provide students the historical context of the years leading up to 1994 when Rwanda faced an increasing amount of internal and external pressure. In 1973 Hutu ultra-nationalist General Juvenal Habyarimana came to power and created a corrupt regime that revolved around his "kitchen cabinet," which comprised his wife, family, and close friends called the *akazu.*[30] While Habyarimana spoke in Hutu ethno-centric terms he really was concerned about his iron grip on the economy. In 1987 Tutsi and Hutu exiles formed the Rwandan Patriotic Front (RPF) and invaded Rwanda. The Civil War created a strain on society and sharpened in some a radical hatred of the Tutsi.

If that was not enough pressure, global economics played a role as well. Rwandan economic stability during the 1980s was based on the rise in coffee prices. By the 1990s the bottom fell out of that market which in turn threatened Kigali's international debt servicing and the regime's external funding and aid. Rural Rwanda was overcrowded without the necessary infrastructure to sustain agriculture output for its population and the growing lack of economic means to import food. A reluctant Habyarimana started negotiations with the RPF in Arusha, Tanzania, to end the war. The Arusha Accords would give the RPF a role in the new government. But not all of the *akazu* and rival Hutu groups had the intention of sharing the spoils of the weakened state. Furthermore, Hutu extremists saw the accord as surrender.

Instead of age-old hatreds, students see that the Hutu elite faced with losing their grip on power meticulously planned for a final solution. They trained and armed the Interahamwe, a private nonstate group that allowed the Rwandan government, and army the legal fiction that it was not directly involved in the slaughter. The Hutu goal was to reassert their dominance in Rwandan society and the uninterrupted access to the spoils of the modern state. By going over this crucial information before the screening students understand the modern reasons the genocide occurred.

In *Hotel Rwanda,* Paul Ruseabagina, George Rutaganda, an Interahamwe leader, and the drunken and corrupt Army Chief of Staff General Augustin Bizimungu serve the cinematic purposes of being stereotypes about the range of opinion within the Hutu community toward the killings. Rutaganda, the private citizen, is a corrupt Hutu fanatic. He knows what Rusesabagina is up to and warns him that someday the Hotel refugees will suffer. Meanwhile the powerless Bizimungu, the representative of the regime, is morally conflicted and chooses to look the other way. The film has little of the RPF. The President of Rwanda, and RPF leader Paul Kagame derisively called Rusesabagina, a "Hollywood made hero."[31] The RPF were able to end the genocide and the Civil War in the face of Western indifference.

Hotel Rwanda is a popular film with students. It presents a well-written and compelling story with a traditional "happy" ending. But the Hollywood version of the Rwandan genocide has its flaws. *Hotel Rwanda* leaves out important historical contexts because it is the story of one man. The genocide can only be viewed through his eyes. Director Terry George drops hints along the way about the magnitude: the box of machetes that shows planning; or Rutaganda suggesting that half the Tutsi were already dead. But since this plot device is married to the conventions of a major studio film many avenues of Rwandan politics are left unexplored. In the end, George presents a different thesis for *Hotel Rwanda* than Peck's *Lumumba*. He strives to create a universal human story not an African one. *Lumumba* chooses to go big—it is the birth of the Congo and African nationalism rolled up into one. *Hotel Rwanda* is the struggle of one ordinary man, in one hotel doing the best he could.

Hotel Rwanda provides students a human face to a tragedy. Putting aside the criticisms of the film there is something to be said for humanizing Rwanda to students. I would argue that *Hotel Rwanda* provides a powerful and accessible way to open up the dialogue in the classroom about the construction of ethnicity and how modern politicians manipulate identity for short-term material gains.

The new face of African conflicts in *Blood Diamond*

For the final film, I have chosen *Blood Diamond* (2006, dir. Edward Zwick), a major Hollywood production anchored by Leonardo Di Caprio. While the film is set during the real Sierra Leonean Civil War of the 1990s, the main character is a fictitious mercenary, and White Zimbabwean named Danny Archer. Problematically, Archer had also fought in the apartheid era South African Defense Forces. The film raises an interesting question for the classroom: can a movie with an American actor playing a White Rhodesian mercenary still be considered an appropriate film for a course on African conflicts and politics Afro-centric film? But even if we posit that the Hollywood version of the Sierra Leonean Civil War does not square with reality it can still hook students into a deeper look at the causes of low-intensity Civil Wars and the importance of natural resources in fueling conflict on the continent.

In the film, we are introduced to the fictional fisherman, Solomon Vandy who is kidnapped along with his son by the Revolutionary United Front (RUF). Forced into slave labor, Vandy finds a rare pink diamond and hides it from RUF commander Captain Poison (discussed below). Eventually Danny Archer meets Vandy in a Freetown prison and arranges for Vandy's release and promises to get his son back for the diamond.

Already the educator should start to see the problems with using a film like this in the classroom. Manohla Dargis of the *New York Times* states, the movie "plays like an exotically situated action flick . . ." She adds that "theirs might be a match made in movie-genre heaven if the filmmakers didn't insist on wagging their fingers in our faces and delivering dire statistics by the ream . . ." about the conflict diamond trade.[32] While Dargis is justified in her criticisms it is important to remember that American students only have a cursory understanding of Sierra Leone, and conflict diamonds. What needs to be stressed in the classroom is how this film becomes an important lesson on the changing face of global economics and violence.

The film is partly rooted in historical accuracy. The roots of the Sierra Leonean war trace back to 1991 when President Joseph Momoh finally planned to hold elections after many years of corrupt rule. Momoh, like Mobutu Sese Seko and Juvenal Habyarimana, used foreign aid to develop elaborate patronage networks.[33] A group calling themselves the RUF crossed into Sierra Leone from Liberia with the goal of ending the President's reign. This group included former Sierra Leonean Army officer, Foday Sankoh a Libyan-trained and Liberian backed leader. The war ended in 2001 when a UN (UNAMSIL) peacekeeping mission, led by India, was able to decisively defeat the RUF as a viable military force.

For all the criticism of the film Zwick does an excellent job showing what the RUF stood for politically. That is why Captain Poison is such a perfect name. The group initially played themselves off as a movement for a better Sierra Leone, but in reality they were no more than common thugs who killed, raped, and looted the countryside. They conducted military operations with names like: "Operation Pay Yourself" or "Operation No Living Thing."[34] According to Ibrahim Abdullah and Patrick Muana:

> The RUF . . . is neither a separatist uprising rooted in a specific demand . . . or a reformist movement with a radical agenda superior to the regime it sought to overthrow. The RUF has made history; it is a

peculiar guerilla movement without any significant national following or ethnic support.[35]

Because this is truly a Hollywood action film one needs to work closely with students in integrating the course text. Captain Poison and the RUF are the embodiment of a real warlord economy.[36] *Lumumba* depicts how African politics was impacted by Cold War intrigue. *Blood Diamond* shows the changing nature of African violence. African governments and rival groups can now turn to the private sector to fund conflict. The teaching goal is to have students understand that modern violence is fueled by a global shadow network of "extra state" activities between local elites, transnational corporations, and governments.[37] Foreign capital floods into Africa and fuels a cycle of violence in the quest for illicit (or semi-illicit) commodities, which in turn creates a new and sometimes bigger industry—war.[38] Georges Nzongola-Ntalaja calls it the "logic of plunder in the new era of globalization." He argues that it is a process where states, ". . . [m]afia groups, offshore banks, transnational mining companies enrich themselves from conflict."[39]

One way to get students to think about the deeper theoretical issues of African resource wars is to have them do independent research before the screening on the diamond industry. Get them to trace the journey of a diamond as it makes its way to the jewelry store. This exercise will help them understand Africa's place in global economics and the power of monopolistic mining companies like De Beers. Be sure to ask your students the difference between legal and conflict diamonds. According to the United Nations, conflict diamonds are those that originate in war zones and are illegally sold to fund the continuance of wars. Archer was part of a transnational smuggling operation. You can continue the discussion after the screening by having students think about other natural resources that fuel African conflicts: oil in Angola; or coltan in the Congo, a mineral used in the production of cell phones. At the end of the screening we want students to understand that the opening up of Africa to the global economy has privatized profits but socialized the violence.

But if I could identify another major flaw in using this film for an African politics class it is the unlovable Danny Archer himself. The main characters of these films: Archer, Patrice Lumumba, and Paul Rusesabagina open up the discussion of how these films can (and cannot) help American students empathize with disparate identities across the continent. A part of film enjoyment is based on the need for audiences to identify with main characters. How do students identify with Lumumba? How do they see him? The key difference in *Blood Diamond* is that Archer is White, and not only is he a smuggler but he also participated in one of the most brutal South African battalions of the apartheid era. Thus his nationality and occupation, and how students identify with him, is worth a brief discussion.

Zwick chooses Archer to be Rhodesian, a former British colony and apartheid state known today as Zimbabwe. But the simple choice of making him Rhodesian ignores or glosses over the complexity of race relations in Rhodesia (Zimbabwe), South Africa, and the rest of the continent. When Archer describes the murder of his parents at the hands of rebels the historical context is sorely missing. His parents "may" have died by the hand of Robert Mugabe's Zimbabwe African National Union, who fought a war of liberation against White minority rule. While this does not justify the fictional deaths of Archer's parents, the Zimbabwean struggle for majority self-determination against an apartheid police state is lost to some White American students who might subconsciously side with Archer—after all he is an internationally recognizable actor, the main character, and the hero of the film. So it is important to deal with Archer's identity front and center in the classroom.

Out of the three films discussed, *Blood Diamond* is the most Hollywood and subsequently the most popular with students. It can be seen as a controversial choice for an African politics class. Dargis claims that the film, "betrays an almost quasi-touristic fascination with images of black Africans." [40] In typical Hollywood fashion the conflict diamond industry is exposed, and Solomon Vandy is reunited with his family because a White Rhodesian and a White American journalist made it so. This is not what we want to teach. The strength of the film lies with the fact that while *Blood Diamond* may be fictional it is an accurate portrayal of why people fight over natural resources across the continent.

Conclusions

This chapter is an attempt to map out the pedagogical uses of the films *Lumumba, Hotel Rwanda*, and *Blood Diamond* to teach the complexity of African politics in an American classroom. These films can help students understand the modern components of African conflicts and challenge stereotypes of ancient tribal hatreds. Thus, if properly presented with pre-screening information and postviewing discussion, the selected films can help demystify African conflicts overall and enhance student understanding of the subject. It is also the hope that students can recognize the works of political scientists: Jean Francois Bayart, Rene Lemarchand, Gerard Prunier, William Reno, Donald Rothchild, and Georges Nzongola-Ntalaja to name but a few in the films screened.

However, there are some critics who will argue that the conflicts chosen here are outliers in the African experience, and that these films reinforce the negative images of Africa. To a point I agree, but with an important caveat; politics is conflictual by definition. It would be difficult (if not impossible) to teach decolonization, corruption, and the impact of global economics without discussing some level of conflict, let alone discuss the complex human emergencies and war that has marked the African Great Lakes region over the past 20 years. Furthermore, Hollywood does not make films about the regular ebb and flow of normal politics. I routinely point out to students that there are plenty of African films that are comedies, romances, and stories of personal discovery. But these films are often outside the purview of a political science course.

Students today are visual learners. But while they may be comfortable with the film medium in the classroom they are not media savvy. It is important to realize that they may never again be asked about the Hollywood gaze, and how it shapes our perceptions of the world. Furthermore, most students will never continue their studies of political science outside of college, let alone African politics but they will continue to be consumers of mainstream films. So the hope is to not only teach African conflicts but how to be critical consumers of Hollywood.

Hopefully some of the pedagogical approaches outlined in this chapter can appeal to a variety of academics teaching American students about the politics of the developing world. Films can be a powerful tool to illuminate the broader theories, concepts, and issues. Furthermore, they do not have to simply reinforce Eurocentric "conventional images" but can be used as course texts to humanize and visualize the material, while getting students to engage, confront, and question stereotypes.

Notes

1 This chapter was originally presented as a paper to the *American Political Science Association Teaching and Learning Conference*, February 2011, in Albuquerque, New Mexico. The author would like to thank the students who participated in this class, Mark Davidheiser, Mark Sachleben, Robert W. Glover, and Daniel Tagliarina for their insightful comments.
2 Robert W. Gregg, *International Relations on Film* (Boulder, CO: Lynne Rienner, 1998); Patrick Haney, "Learning about Foreign Policy at the Movies," in *The New International Studies Classroom: Active Teaching, Active Learning*, ed. Jeffrey S. Lantis et al. (Boulder, CO: Lynne Rienner, 2000); Lynn Kuzma and Patrick Haney "And . . . Action! Using Film to Learn About Foreign Policy," *International Studies Perspectives* 2 (2000): 33–50.
3 Kenneth M. Cameron, *Africa on Film: Beyond Black and White* (Continuum: New York, 1994): 13.
4 Paul Beckett, "Rubrics and Hubris: On the Teaching of African Politics," *Canadian Journal of African Studies/Revue Canadienne des Études Africaines* 15(3) (1981): 571–3.
5 Andrew Breslau, "Demonizing Quaddafy," *Africa Report* 32 (1987): 46–7.
6 J. J. Ayoade, "Teaching African Politics: Problems and Prospects," *Teaching Political Science* 7(4) (1980): 389.

7   Robert L. Ostergard, "An Introduction to African Politics (review)," *Africa Today* 53 (2007): 123–5; Alex Thomson, *An Introduction to African Politics* (New York: Routledge, 2004); William Tordoff, *Government and Politics in Africa* (Bloomington, IN: Indiana Press, 2002).

8   Stacy Ulbig, "Voice is Not Enough: The Importance of Influence in Political Trust and Policy Assessments," *Public Opinion Quarterly* 72 (2008): 523–39.

9   John Lovell, ed., *Insights from Film into Violence and Oppression: Shattered Dreams of the Good Life* (Westport, CT: Praeger, 1998).

10 Kuzma and Haney, "And . . . Action! Using Film to Learn About Foreign Policy;" Janet G. Donald, "Knowledge and the University Curriculum," *Higher Education* 15 (1986): 267–82.

11 Beverly Kelly, *Reelpolitik: Political Ideologies in '30s and '40s Films* (Westport, CT: Praeger, 1998): xv.

12 Michael Ryan and Donald Kellner, *Camera Obscura: The Political Ideology of Contemporary Hollywood Film* (Bloomington, IN: Indiana Press, 1990); Steven Mintz and Randy Roberts, *Hollywood's America: United States History through its Films* (Malden, MA: Wiley Blackwell, 2001).

13 Kellner and Ryan, *Camera Obscura*, 13.

14 Georges Nzongola-Ntalaja, "Patrice Lumumba: The Most Important Assassination of the Twentieth Century," *The Guardian* (January 17, 2011). Accessed January 26, 2011, from www.guardian.co.uk/global-development/poverty matters/2011/jan/17/patrice-lumumba-50th-anniversary-assassination.

15 The figures come from Henry Gilroy "Lumumba Assails Colonialism as Congo Is Freed," *New York Times* (July 1, 1960). However, for similar statistics see Georges Nzongola-Ntalaja, *The Congo: From Leopold to Kabila: A People's History* (London: Zed Books, 2002).

16 Gilroy, "Lumumba Assails Colonialism."

17 Kwame Nkrumah, *Neo-Colonialism: The Last Stage of Imperialism* (London: Panaf, 1965): ix.

18 Donald Rothchild, "State-Ethnic Relations in Middle Africa," in *African Independence: The First Twenty-five Years*, ed. G. M. Carter and P. O. Meara (Bloomington, IN: Indiana University Press, 1985); Jean Francois Bayart, *The State in Africa: The Politics of the Belly* (New York: Longman 1993).

19 Rothchild, "State-Ethnic relations in Middle Africa."

20 See David Moore, "Raoul Peck's Lumumba: History or Hagiography?" in *Black and White in Colour*, ed. V. Bickford-Smith and R. Mendelsohn (London: Ohio University, 2007), 223–39.

21 Moore, "Raoul Peck's Lumumba: history or hagiography?," 229.

22 Tim Shorrock, "Company Man," *The Nation* (March 14, 2002). Accessed January 26, 2011, from www.thenation.com/article/company-man.

23 Samuel Totten, "Introduction," in *Teaching about Genocide: Issues, Approaches, and Resources*, ed. Samuel Totten (Charlotte, NC: Information Age Publishing, 2004), vii.

24 Mohamed Adhikari, "Hotel Rwanda: Too Much Heroism, Too Little History—Or Horror?" in *Black and White in Colour*, ed. V. Bickford-Smith and R. Mendelsohn (London: Ohio University Press, 2007): 281.

25 Thomson, *An Introduction to African Politics*, 65.

26 Rene Lemarchand, *The Dynamics of Violence in Central Africa* (Philadelphia, PA: University of Pennsylvania Press, 2009): 34.

27 Mahmood Mandami, *When Victims become Killers: Colonialism, Nativism, and the Genocide in Rwanda* (Princeton, NJ: Princeton University Press, 2001).

28 Gerard Prunier, *The Rwanda Crisis: History of a Genocide* (London: Hurst, 1995).

29 Mohamed Adhikari, "Hotel Rwanda: Too much Heroism, Too Little History," 283.

30 Gerard Prunier, *African World War* (Oxford: Oxford Press, 2009).

31 Alex Hannaford et al., "Why the Hero of Hotel Rwanda Fears for His People," *The Telegraph* (August 8, 2010). Accessed February 3, 2012, from www.telegraph.co.uk/news/worldnews/africaandindianocean/rwanda/7931897/Why-the-hero-of-Hotel-Rwanda-fears-for-his-people.html.

32 Manhola Dargis, "Blood Diamond (2006): Diamonds and the Devil, Amid the Anguish of Africa," *New York Times* (December 8, 2006). Accessed January 26, 2011, from http://movies.nytimes.com/2006/12/08/movies /08diam.html.

33 Jean Francois Bayart, *The State in Africa: The Politics of the Belly*; see also Christopher Clapham, *Third World Politics: An Introduction* (Madison, WI: Wisconsin University Press, 1985).

34 Caroline Hawley, "A Country Torn by Conflict," *BBC Online* (January 12, 2004). Accessed March 25, 2004, from http://news.bbc.co.uk/1/hi/special_report/1999/01/99/sierra_leone/251377.stm.

35 Ibrahim Abdullah and Patrick Muana, "The Revolutionary United Front of Sierra Leone," in *African Guerrillas*, ed. C. Clapham (Indianapolis: Indiana University Press, 1998): 172–93.

36 William Reno, *Warlord Politics and African States* (Boulder, CO: Rienner, 1998).

37 William Reno, "The Privatization of Africa's International Relations," in *Africa in World Politics: Reforming Political Order*, ed. Donald Rothchild and J. Harbeson (Boulder, CO: Westview Press, 2009): 207.

38 Carolyn Nordstrom, *Shadows of War: Violence, Power, and International Profiteering in the Twenty-First Century* (Berkeley, CA: University of California Press, 2004).

39 Georges Nzongola-Ntalaja, *The Congo: From Leopold to Kabila* (London: Zed, 2003): 227.

40 Dargis, "Blood Diamond," 2006.

CHAPTER THIRTEEN

War and peace on film

Jeffrey S. Lantis[1]

I learned early on that war forms its own culture. The rush of battle is a potent and often lethal addiction, for war is a drug . . . The enduring attraction of war is this: Even with its destructiveness and carnage it can give us what we long for in life. It can give us purpose, meaning, a reason for living.[2]

Some of America's chief exports to the world are . . . war and entertainment.[3]

"War" and "Peace" are critical topics in the study of international relations. They represent powerful forms of the human condition, and they constitute the building blocks of theoretical and descriptive coverage in some international relations classes. At a deeper level, many believe these conditions are inextricably linked—that we truly cannot understand one without the other.

This chapter describes an advanced class on international peace and security taught in the Department of Political Science at The College of Wooster and designed to explore issues through the media of film, literature, and scholarly works. Key sections of the class analyze the origins of war, international terrorism, definitions of heroism, peace studies and nonviolence, wartime experiences for soldiers and civilians, national identity and patriotism, and conceptions of the "enemy other." For example, the class surveys scholarly works on peace and nonviolence as a foundation to explore the life of Mohandas Gandhi in the biopic *Gandhi* (1982). We also debate contending perspectives on the meaning of bravery in Stephen Crane's *The Red Badge of Courage* (1895) and Kathryn Bigelow's *The Hurt Locker* (2008). Together, film and literature provide enhanced opportunities for critical engagement with key themes in global politics.

This chapter addresses two important dimensions of this class experience. First, it discusses the foundations for the class in the broader literature on active teaching and learning in the classroom, as well as specific studies of film teaching in international studies. This section also provides a survey of the topics and assignments in the class and film selections employed to address educational objectives.[4] The second section of the chapter provides a preliminary assessment of the class experience based on a recent pre- and post-test experimental design. By comparing achievement of educational objectives in this class with those of a more traditional International Security class taught in a different semester, I explore whether students demonstrated increased knowledge and empathy about select issues. The project yields some very interesting results, both affirming and surprising, that are discussed in the conclusion of the chapter.

Why film?

Film is not a passive medium. To the contrary, an engaged audience does much more than simply watch a film—they examine it in relation to its primary structure, messages, and design. Like other forms of art, film is a vehicle for expression of profound themes, concerns, or emotions. And, like other forms of contemporary media, the power of the filmic image has a special lure. Films can be viewed, re-viewed, discussed, and analyzed. Modern technologies—such as hardware for viewing films, software for editing clips, and websites about films—all help to make the filmic experience more interactive today. Indeed, the publication of this edited volume coincides with a new digital age, where a generation of young people raised on media can also draw important educational lessons from it.

The emerging literature on teaching with films in political science highlights the utility of the approach for achieving educational objectives and promoting student engagement with the material. Studies of film teaching highlight the conscious selection of goals for the classroom and methods for teaching that create a sense of purpose in the educational process.[5] Scholars argue that techniques that engage students in collaborative learning practices can help achieve educational objectives, including: (1) promoting a deeper understanding of the concepts being taught; (2) allowing students to make conceptual linkages between theory and real-world examples; and (3) increasing retention of knowledge.[6] As Lee Shulman argues, active teaching promotes critical thinking because the approaches probe the "never-never land between theory and practice, between ideas and experience, between the normative ideal and the achievable real."[7] Technology also has allowed more immediate links to global politics for both instructors and students and has become a more important dimension of the educational environment at many institutions. Studies from higher education also have shown that engagement of students in the learning enterprise, and excitement about the subject, increases comprehension dramatically.[8]

Film provides a wonderful medium for student engagement in learning, eliciting discovery and the construction of knowledge. Teaching through film provides students with a deeper understanding of world politics, a visual expression of important themes for a new generation of students, and even a common bond or "language" for discussion of issues within a visual (and often emotional) context.[9] Powerful experiences on film can become common points of reference across the course of classroom discussion. Moreover, through film, students are confronted by new realities and different perspectives on international relations. As Daniel Lieberfeld argues, "the more concrete and experiential perspectives offered in films and literature may help ground the abstract generalizations typical of scholarly perspectives on war."[10]

Teaching with films also helps the instructor to think critically about pedagogy and assessment. That is, instructors must carefully consider how films or film clips will be used in any class, and why they are to be used, including reflection on the educational objectives to be achieved and how film or literature can enhance student learning. Instructors must also create integrated assignments and that can be completed through film viewing, reading related literature, linking theory foundations, and engaging in critical analysis.[11] Finally, instructors must design opportunities for discussion and reflection on films and literature in the class. These kinds of exercises help students engage with the material—moving from passive viewership to active deconstruction of the messages, themes, and theories that may apply to analyze film content.[12]

Finally, like many forms of expression, films provide a ready platform for critical analysis. Some viewers will enjoy a film about battlefield glory, for example, while others find the subject dark or nihilistic. Some will prefer zany debates about deterrence in Stanley Kubrik's *Dr. Strangelove* (1964) to the ham-fisted dialogues about mutual assured destruction in *Crimson Tide* (1995). Students will discuss the primary messages of the film or pivotal scenes, but instructors can encourage a deeper level of consideration of the film-making process itself as a creative enterprise. For example, expert James Combs warns about bias in films, and advises that students learn movies are "thoroughly political artifacts bound up with political rhetoric, ideology, agendas, and policies" in order to be savvy consumers.[13] There were reasons that Frank Capra directed the documentary/propaganda series *Why We Fight* in 1943; there were very different political motivations behind Eugene Jarecki's documentary, *Why We Fight* (2005), a bitter deconstruction of the military-industrial complex. These issues can (and should) be addressed openly from the start of a class, and instructors may encourage students to learn more about both the subject of film and the context within which films have been made along the way. Indeed, students tend to enjoy and appreciate such critical thinking exercises based on film and literature.

Educational objectives:
Exploration of war and antiwar

The goal of this course is to encourage students to think critically about dimensions of the war experience in the broader context of international relations. Throughout the course I focus on powerful juxtapositions: of the violence and chaos of battle and the stillness of a scene apart from war; of the bravery and heroism of some on the frontlines versus the motivations of the conscientious objector; of visions of peace in home-life portrayed in so many films versus the challenges of the "real world." These juxtapositions are not only powerful, they also provide great foundation for understanding the origins of political decisions behind government behaviors.

It should also be stressed that this class is as much about peace (or antiwar) as it is about the inherent contradictions of warfare. Many, if not all, of the films examined in this class have antiwar messages. If war films are a genre concerned with warfare or preparations or the aftermath of conflict, antiwar films explore many similar themes from different angles. Films like *Platoon* (1986), *Saving Private Ryan* (1998), or *In the Valley of Elah* (2007) suggest there is greater virtue in the absence of conflict, that peace is the preferred state of being. Indeed, if one thinks critically about war films, few of them set out to glorify violence for violence's sake. Rather, so many films, even those that might qualify as fitting in the war film genre, are antiwar films that convey the horror and pain of warfare and often integrate an ideological perspective into their message.

This course was explicitly designed to capture key dimensions of the politics behind war and peace, including decisions that lead to war and critical reflection on the meaning of conflict resolution and peace. The criteria that I employed in assigning readings and films included whether they would address key themes in international relations related to conflict and whether they would illuminate or engage critically students in understanding the themes at hand. At the same time, it is important to recognize that teaching with films can be problematic. I typically hold multiple discussions with students about the potential problems with using films as texts. Students recognize that films can be misinterpreted as passive media and viewers can become complacent both about the messages and production of films. They are aware that acceptance of filmic portrayals of events as "true" carries a special burden of proof.

Finally, it is very important to teach film responsibly. That is, many films that could be employed for this class present challenging, disturbing, or even inappropriate conduct that can create problems. Too many contemporary feature films contain a great deal of graphic violence, profanity, and sexual content. On the advice of other experienced film teachers, my policy is to warn students at the beginning of the course about content and offer the opportunity to discuss concerns. In addition, I provide warnings before film showings of any potentially objectionable material, and students may freely choose not to view these films or clips due to their convictions. Finally, I try to be judicious in my own selection of film material or readings; I try to weigh any potential negatives against the overall educational value of the film experience.

War and peace on film: Course design

This class was designed to present students with opportunities for critical analysis of international security through exploration of juxtapositions— between war and peace, theories of realism versus idealism, good versus evil, positive versus negative characterizations of war, and courage and fear. The number of themes that could be addressed in a class on war and peace on film is nearly limitless, but what follows is a description of some of the themes I have employed successfully in this class.

Critical analysis of US foreign policy

The class typically begins with critical reflection on war and peace in the context of US foreign policy, a common touchstone for many students. We start the class with a "bang," viewing opening scenes from *Three Kings* (1999), David O. Russell's acclaimed film set in the immediate aftermath of the first Persian Gulf War in 1991. Students view the scenes several times, taking notes on what they see and their interpretations of filmic images. I encourage discussion and student reflection on themes such as contrasts between United States and enemy soldiers, violence and celebration of victory, masculinity and identity, and music and setting. We also reflect on the film techniques employed by the director. For example, Russell created a special look for this film by using a processing technique designed to strip out color, and he employed Iraqi citizens who were once displaced by Saddam Hussein's security forces as extras in the film.

Building on scenes from *Three Kings* (and the interesting discussions that ensue), the class then investigates critical perspectives on US foreign policy. Following a brief historical overview of US foreign policy, students are asked to compare and contrast arguments and readings by Robert Kagan and Charles William Maynes regarding whether the United States can really be a "benevolent empire." I also encourage students to reflect on contemporary dilemmas of US engagement in the world. The first section of the class ends with a viewing of the opening monologue from *Patton* (1969), one of the great biographies on film. The film includes a classic 6-minute monologue about Americans and their fighting spirit. It includes powerful statements culled from Patton's speeches, with bold statements like:

> Americans traditionally love to fight. All real Americans love the sting of battle. When you were kids, you all admired the champion marble shooter, the fastest runner, the big league ball player, the toughest boxer. Americans love a winner and will not tolerate a loser. Americans play to win all the time . . . the very thought of losing is hateful to Americans.[14]

These filmic experiences provide an engaging foundation for discussion and for further critical inquiry in the class.

The causes of war

This class also investigates theories of the conditions and actors that can lead to war. For this section of the class, I pair classic and contemporary readings on theories of the causes of war with filmic illustrations. For example, I assign selections from John Stoessinger's *Why Nations Go to War* (2008), and journal articles.[15] We discuss theories of the causes of war using the levels of analysis construct, paired with their respective filmic illustrations. Levels of analysis are a theoretical framework that groups possible causes of phenomena at the level of the international system (or global politics), state system (domestic politics), and individual actors. For example, I employ clips from Frank Capra's *Why We Fight* (1943) series to illustrate traditional systemic interpretations of war causation. We discuss Capra's career as an award-winning director of films like *Mr. Smith Goes to Washington* (1939) and *It's a Wonderful Life* (1946), as well as his work for the US Army Signal Corps on the documentary project during World War II.

At the state level of analysis, we examine a range of factors that are associated with war. One of the more interesting themes is the potential link between civic nationalism and war. We raise the question that perhaps intense patriotic nationalism leads countries to do things they normally would not. Nationalism as civic pride, whipped up into a frenzy of nationalist zeal and energy due to circumstances (or by manipulative leaders), can fuel the fire of conflict. To illustrate the power of nationalism to rally the troops, we view several film clips, including the classic "St. Crispin's Day speech" from Kenneth Branagh's *Henry V* (1989). We also view excerpts from the documentary *Why We Fight* (2005), an avowedly ideological film about how the military-industrial complex, or a collaboration between defense contractors and government agencies, might encourage arms sales and perhaps even conflicts around the world to maximize their profits. Finally, these selections can be compared with Mark Twain's powerful *The War Prayer* (1904), one of his more controversial short stories that warns of the potential distortions of nationalism to fuel violence.

At the individual level of analysis, we make links including theories of innate aggression (biological and psychological/cognitive predispositions) to conflict. Here we reference arguments of Margaret Mead and Sigmund Freud, as well as diversionary theory that suggests that leaders might rally a country for war to divert public attention from a serious problem at home. I also have assigned a scholarly piece by Tom Pyszczynski, Zachary Rothschild, and Abdolhossein Abdollahi on "terror management theory," a thesis from social psychology that individuals may be more prone to violent responses to terrorist attacks and more willing to form "in-group, out-group" conceptions of the other.[16] These readings can be paired with important clips from *The Fog of War* (2003), *Road Warrior* (1982), documentaries of the US war on terrorism (such as Charles Ferguson's *No End in Sight* 2007), and other films.

The war experience

Several sections of the course deal with the actual experiences of war. For example, I assign a provocative reading selection from Chris Hedges' *War is the Force that Gives Us Meaning* (2002), which discusses the potential "appeal" of war. Hedges, a journalist and antiwar activist, strives to provide meaning to the war experience in a powerful way. Early arguments in the book include: "I learned early on that war forms its own culture. The rush of battle is a potent and often lethal addiction, for war is a drug." He goes on, "The enduring attraction of war is this: Even with its destructiveness and carnage it can give us what we long for in life. It can give us purpose, meaning, a reason for living . . . It gives us resolve, a cause." Not only does Hedges focus on the lure and "excitement" of war, but he also explores popular fascination with what war can unleash. He argues, "War exposes the capacity for evil that lurks not far below the surface within all of us. And this is why for many war is so hard to discuss once it is over."[17] This material can be nicely juxtaposed with readings selections from Karl Marlantes' book, *What It is Like to Go to War* (2011) or film clips from Stanley Kubrick's *Full Metal Jacket* (1987).

Thus, some contend war helps to order one's life and that there are profoundly different life experiences in conditions of war and peace. There is no better juxtaposition of these themes in film than *Waltz with Bashir* (2008). This is an amazing animated "documentary" film that explores the memories of its director, Ari Folman, and his compatriots who fought for

Israel in the 1982 invasion of Lebanon. Folman seeks through this film to explore the meaning of that war experience. The film is unique—indeed, an animated documentary is a rare genre (though the French–Iranian film, *Persepolis* (2007), certainly fits the mold)—but these qualities also make it uniquely powerful. It both presents stark reality and allows the potential for metaphor. The film opens with a powerful scene of rushing dogs and does not stop moving as Folman explores the vagaries of memory. In one scene, a friend recalls hiding from a firefight as his mind is filled with memories of a peaceful time at home with his mother. This film is clearly about war, but it is also about the power of memory and historical narratives. Only through a series of meetings with fellow veterans of the Lebanon invasion does the main player come to reckon with the horrors he witnessed in the Sabra and Shatila refugee camps in 1982.

The World War II experience also presents audiences with evocative scenes and raises interesting questions about historical narratives. After all, World War II was considered a "good war" in that the United States was fighting against the evil of totalitarian regimes. Most films and literature on the war experience celebrate the heroism and glory of soldiers. The movie *Saving Private Ryan* (1998) has a special place in US film canon, but so, too, does the documentary, *The Great Battle on the Volga* (1962) for Russian filmic memory. More recent narratives take interpretations of the war experience to a deeper level. The HBO series *Band of Brothers* (2001–2) presented a powerful true story of a company from the 101st Airborne Division. Their bravery and heroism in the war was profound, including parachute jumps into battle behind the front lines on D-Day. But the series also featured true stories of privation and ethical dilemmas. German soldiers who surrendered were gunned down; some allied soldiers took advantage of their status and power in occupation.

The US experience in the Vietnam War offers a powerful case to critically examine juxtapositions of war and antiwar. I begin this section of the class by examining a trend that surprises students: for much of the 1960s, many Americans supported engagement in the Vietnam War as a just cause. John Wayne's *Green Berets* (1968) makes a strong case for the war, and provides a direct response to growing debate and uncertainty on the Left and among independents about America's involvement in Vietnam. Wayne (students must be taught) was one of the most famous figures in the United States at that time. He was also a conservative, patriot, and cowboy, who personally lobbied President Johnson to make the film with the cooperation of the US Army. The story of the film focuses a skeptical reporter's journey from questioning the war to first-hand observation of the struggle for control of Indochina. Viewed by today's students, though, the film seems both quaint and surprising in its treatment of the war.

Filmic interpretations of the Vietnam War also changed significantly over time. By the 1970s, films like *Coming Home* (1978) and *The Deer*

Hunter (1978) were critical of the war experience and explored the devastating effects of the war on the American psyche. The late 1980s saw a slew of film releases even more critical of US engagement in Vietnam, including *Platoon* (1986), *Born on the Fourth of July* (1989), and *Casualties of War* (1989). The Vietnam War also spawned a number of outstanding documentaries. Certainly the best known of these is Errol Morris's *The Fog of War* (2003), which mainly consists of interviews with the Robert McNamara, the Secretary of Defense who orchestrated US engagement in the war in the 1960s. Other excellent Vietnam War-related documentaries include *Hearts and Minds* (1974) and the PBS series *Vietnam: A Television History* (1983).

Vietnam War films can be compared and contrasted with literature from (and about) the era that explores all of the critical dimensions of war and peace. Tim O'Brien's *The Things They Carried* (1990) remains a classic. While based on his own experiences, this is a work of fiction that deftly delivers on the author's thesis: "A true war story is never moral." More recently, David Maraniss' book *They Marched into Sunlight* (2003) juxtaposes the experience of soldiers in Vietnam with antiwar protestors in the United States in 1967. And the 2010 best-seller *Matterhorn* is a novel that reads like a true story of the futility and sacrifice of the war. Selected readings from these and other works can be used to compare filmic portrayals and historic memories. They raise important questions about the lessons of Vietnam—or any war—for individual morality and US foreign policy.

Nuclear weapons: Deterrence and proliferation

Beyond war itself lies the existential threat of war. In this section of the class, nuclear weapons are portrayed as the ultimate weapon of mass destruction—and their use, a potential harbinger of Armageddon. This section also provides an opportunity to explore issues of nuclear weapons proliferation, or the rapid spread of these weapons around the world. We begin with a review of classical deterrence literature that suggests the "rational" course in nuclear weapons standoffs. Deterrence theory is a popular theme in studies of arms races, and it derives insights from game theory about the incentives for building up nuclear arsenals. We then survey the history of nuclear weapons strategy (i.e. damage limitation versus assured destruction strategies, where some experts suggested missile defense and fallout shelters while others advocated a more open acceptance that nuclear war risked global annihilation). We pair these discussions with film clips that illustrate the principles and problems of deterrence, including the classic *Dr. Strangelove, or How I Learned to Stop Worrying and Love the Bomb* (1963), and Tony Scott's *Crimson Tide* (1995). *Fail Safe* (1963) is another excellent option. The section then explores how nuclear weapons have been addressed in popular culture over time, especially through US government propaganda and documentary films that downplayed the threat. We watch excerpts from the surprising *Atomic Café* (1982), which features many clips from documentaries of the past. We then juxtapose government efforts to manage threat perception with a growing antinuclear movement and critical exploration of nuclear weapons and their implications.

Beyond the Cold War threat of nuclear war between the superpowers, we also examine the potential for nuclear proliferation. While there are examples of threats of nuclear theft and even nuclear terrorism in dramatic feature films—from *The Peacemaker* (1998) to *True Lies* (1994) and *Sum of All Fears* (2001)—I have found that documentaries and academic works tend to foster more serious consideration of the topic. I typically assign chapters from Joseph Cirincione's *Bomb Scare: The History and Future of Nuclear Weapons* (2007), to pair with the documentary *Countdown to Zero* (2010) as powerful ways to understand dimensions of the threat of proliferation of weapons of mass destruction. We also compare filmic and narrative treatments of potential solutions, such as global disarmament or interdiction of illicit arms shipments.

International terrorism

Finally, terrorism and responses to terrorism represent compelling themes for critical analysis. Some truly engaging films and narratives have emerged on the subject over the past decade. In some ways, the US experience with the global war on terror was a primary motivation for me to create this course. I was intrigued by the contradictions and challenges associated with fighting wars against terrorists, tyrants, and insurgents in distant lands. I also was compelled to try to tell the story of the price of these wars, both abroad and at home.

International terrorism can be examined through an important combination of themes. I frame class discussions on terrorism about both historical and modern examples. I assign *The 9/11 Commission Report* as required reading (or the illustrated edition of this work by Sid Jacobson and Ernie Colon, 2006)[18] because it provides a powerful, first-hand account of the origins and consequences of terrorism. Using September 11th as a focal point creates opportunities to engage a variety of documentary films as well, including *9/11* (2002), a personal journey recorded by two brothers who happened to be at the scene of the attacks in New York City to film a different story, and Paul Greengrass' *United 93* (2006), a re-creation of events on the flight that crashed on September 11th in Pennsylvania.[19] To instructors, these represent important accounts of events most of us remember well, but for students these films and readings may also help to fill in gaps in their knowledge or understanding.

It is also important to provide historical perspective. I draw important links between historical experiences of the origins and potential responses to terrorism through a showing of Gillo Pontecorvo's classic *Battle of Algiers* (1966). That film is about insurgency and violence, based on the experiences of revolutionary leader Saadi Yaacef during Algeria's drive for independence that began in 1954. This struggle led to direct clashes between Algerian nationals and French colonial authorities and soldiers. One of the more fascinating dimensions of the film is that it describes the origins and motivations of insurgency and terrorist actions from the perspective of liberation, raising powerful questions about under what conditions terrorism might ever be considered "justified."

Fortunately, there is a growing scholarly literature on the justification question and related dilemmas presented by terrorism, including critical examination of motivations. I assign books and articles, including essays on terrorism and strategic choice from Walter Reich (ed.), *Origins of Terrorism: Psychologies, Ideologies, Theologies, States of Mind* (1998). In these readings, students learn of potential links to expressions of political strategy as logical processes that can be discovered and explained. This perspective sees terrorists as more "rational" than some characterizations of their pathological or radical nature. In this sense, the resort to violence is a willful choice made by an organization for political and strategic reasons, rather than as the unintended outcome of psychological or social factors. The question of suicide terrorism adds an additional layer to the problem, with the rate of such attacks rising across the globe. Robert Pape's *Dying to Win: The Strategic Logic of Suicide Terrorism* (2005) represents the quintessential examination of the motivations behind these heinous acts, a topic that lends itself well to careful investigation and critical inquiry in the classroom.

Conflicts in the Middle East provide modern-day examples of some of these dilemmas. The standoff between Israelis and Palestinians is both age-old and very timely. As historian John Stoessinger opines, "Historical tragedies do not arise from encouragers in which right clashes with wrong. Rather, they occur when right clashes with right. This is the heart of the conflict between Israel and the Arab states in Palestine." He adds that conflicts in the region are fought with "the deepest emotion. Each side regarded its rights as self-evident and firmly based on the will of God, morality, reason, and law."[20] These issues are explored respectfully in a powerful film about suicide terrorism, *Paradise Now* (2005), which tracks the lives and experiences of Palestinians living under occupation.

Finally, the class examines contemporary responses to terrorism through powerful filmic treatment since September 11, 2001. Recognizing the sacrifices and valor of troops fighting in distant wars, we begin to critically analyze the US experience with the war on terrorism since September 11. We review timelines of US responses, including viewing George W. Bush's speech to the American people on the evening of September 11th, and excerpts from speeches in 2002 in which he articulated what became known as the Bush Doctrine of preemption. An early treatment of US responses can be found in the documentary, *PBS Frontline: Campaign Against Terror* (2002). In addition, the class viewed several films and clips related to the experience of average soldiers in the war on terrorism. For example, *Restrepo* (2010) follows a group of American soldiers at a dangerous outpost.[21] *Gunner Palace* (2004) captures a more positive mood from the earlier years of the war on terrorism, focusing on a battalion of soldiers occupying one of Saddam Hussein's former palaces in the Iraq War.

The class also draws heavily on accounts of experiences in the war on terror that force introspection. Two of these that I assign regularly in my classes are John Crawford's *The Last True Story I'll Ever Tell: An Accidental Soldier's Account of the War in Iraq* (2005) and Dexter Filkins' *The Forever War* (2008). More critical films follow, including *No End in Sight* (2007) and *The Hurt Locker* (2009) an extraordinarily tense drama that follows the experiences of an explosive ordnance disposal unit in Iraq. Finally, *The Messenger* (2009) provides a close-up view of the war on terror back on the homefront, as soldiers deliver messages about the death of loved ones to family members.

Assessment

This experimental class on "War and Peace on Film" was first taught at The College of Wooster in 2010. For purposes of assessment, I set out to compare the experimental approach in this class with traditional teaching approaches in my "International Security" class related to specific educational objectives. In 2010, I conducted an experimental research design using a paired alternatives technique—comparing traditional and alternative teaching approaches in international security and used a pre- and post-test survey technique to measure results. The goal of this project was to assess alternative pedagogies, enrich my classes on international security through active teaching and learning strategies, and make a significant contribution to the curriculum. I sought to explore whether students who participated in the experimental group demonstrated increased empathy and knowledge about these issues compared with a control group who learns the same material in a traditional classroom format. Two sections of each class were used for direct pedagogic comparison: The Origins and Evolution of War and Proliferation and Deterrence Theory.

Data collected from Part I of the surveys (focused on factual questions on material that would be presented in class lectures, readings, or films) show that students gained knowledge in both traditional and nontraditional class settings through coverage of these materials. The degree of knowledge gained was slightly higher for the nontraditional film class coverage of the topic of proliferation than for the traditional class. However, the amount of knowledge gained on the topic of war was significantly higher for the traditional class. These results provide no clear pattern on knowledge gain, but an interpretation of trends suggests that the traditional approach ensures coverage of more factual information through lectures or discussions in class.

Part II of the surveys focused on opinions and views of the issues under consideration. On the topic of war, students offered slightly higher ratings of their experience of learning and critical analysis in the nontraditional film class. For example, students reported that they gained marginally more knowledge "about the topic of war in general" in the post-test survey from the film class. Students reported that they gained marginally more knowledge of political science theories of war causation in the nontraditional class. Students also reported a small increase in their "understanding of the severity of combat" from post-test surveys in the nontraditional class. Respondents in both the traditional and nontraditional classes reported the exact same "level of personal interest in issues related to war."

On the topic of proliferation, students reported no differences in their general level of concern regarding proliferation in either the traditional or nontraditional classes. However, on specific issues they reported more significant changes. First, the degree to which students perceived a threat and the severity of nuclear attack increased dramatically in the nontraditional class versus the traditional class. Indeed, this margin of change was the highest reported student opinion shift in the study. Second, students in nontraditional film class reported a significant increase in their personal interest in the subject versus the traditional class.

Part III of the surveys asked students to comment on the teaching and learning methods employed in the classes. This section was only administered in post-test surveys, allowing students the opportunity to reflect directly on their experiences. Here the data suggest some interesting differences. For example, students in the traditional class reported a slightly higher level of contribution from the readings on both subjects than did students in the nontraditional film class. Students in the traditional class reported a higher level of contribution to their knowledge from class lectures on the proliferation topic. Students in the nontraditional class reported marginally higher contributions to their learning from exercises, discussions, and film clips on the topic of war, but surprisingly less contribution on the topic of proliferation. Students in the traditional class reported that they enjoyed the readings on both topics more than students in the nontraditional class. Students in the nontraditional class reported that they enjoyed the non-reading class materials on the topic of war much more. Finally, students in the nontraditional class reported (rather honestly, I believe) that they put less effort into both sections of the class than did their counterparts in the traditional class.

In summary, the experimental design yielded the following insights regarding traditional versus nontraditional formats:

- Both traditional and nontraditional approaches helped students gain knowledge on topics such as the origins and evolution of war, nuclear proliferation, and deterrence theory.

- Students in the traditional class gained significantly greater knowledge on the topic of war (as measured in responses to knowledge/factual questions); students in the nontraditional class gained somewhat greater knowledge on the topic of nuclear proliferation.

- Students in both traditional and nontraditional classes reported the same levels of personal interest in the topics.

- Students in the nontraditional classes self-reported that they gained more knowledge about the topics.

- The nontraditional class increased student awareness and empathy regarding the severity of combat and threats of nuclear proliferation.

- Students in the nontraditional class self-reported that the films marginally increased their interest in the topics, but that they greatly enjoyed the experience.

Conclusion

These preliminary findings suggest that films (including full-length features, documentaries, and selected clips) may sometimes enhance student interest in key topics in international security and seem to promote some empathy for diverse perspectives. These results, coupled with anecdotal evidence from teaching the class as well as student evaluations of the experience, also suggest that films can do much more. They provide a deeper understanding of the complexity of security issues as well as a common bond or "language" for discussion of issues within a visual (and often emotional) context. Films that help to achieve educational objectives serve as powerful texts to explore important issues in international relations in greater depth.

The film class generated many enthusiastic comments from the students in class evaluations. As a teacher, I shared that enthusiasm. I was inspired by the process of designing and teaching the class. I learned more about specific political events through readings, such as the history of the Algerian struggle for independence, and was able to match critical lessons from the experience with filmic illustrations. I also developed creative new assignments that incorporated film and visual images with critical links to theoretical material. For example, one paper assignment on controversial war and peace memorials generated some fascinating discussions about how we remember conflicts—and what we choose to remember about them. A new assignment on heroism and film led to intense classroom discussions about how societies define heroism and glory, as well as controversies regarding filmic interpretations.

The experience of teaching this class also yielded some valuable insights regarding class design for the future. First, I recognize significant tradeoffs between teaching international security themes in traditional versus nontraditional formats. In traditional classes on international security, I spend more time establishing theoretical foundations and leading discussions of critical readings. But students in a nontraditional format film class have different expectations, including a desire to learn more from and through films rather than theoretical or historical readings. Students of the digital age are prepared to take seriously the concept of "films as text." Notably, the tradeoffs between traditional and nontraditional formats also impact the instructor. That is, I had to devote roughly twice as much time to preparations for teaching the nontraditional format class. Not only does the instructor need to know traditional international relations theories or understand themes of war and peace, but one must also be fluent in all aspects of the nontraditional materials such as film clips or literature selections.

Finally, I have begun to reflect on ways to redesign the class for future offerings. Through my constant hunt for relevant films, I have discovered several newer titles that will certainly be incorporated into new sections of the class. The PBS documentary series *Women, War, and Peace* (2011) provides a powerful foundation to explore gender and feminist theory of international relations. One special feature of this series, *Pray the Devil Back to Hell* (2008) offers an in-depth look at the role of women and nonviolence in trying to bring an end to Liberia's Civil War. Another feature film that is sure to find its way into future versions of this class is Steven Spielberg's *War Horse* (2011), a retelling of a children's book that examines juxtapositions of war and peace.

I also expect to modify the section of the class focused on the war on terrorism and the implications of the war for civil liberties and national security in the United States and beyond. Here, recent feature films such as *Rendition* (2007), and documentaries, such as the Academy Award-winning *Taxi to the Dark Side* (2007) address dilemmas of legal status of detainees in the war on terrorism. Finally, I am also intrigued by how the experiences of September 11, 2001, have played out in the American psyche. Films like *Extremely Loud and Incredibly Close* (2011) force us to grapple with tough issues of honor, memory, and the responsibilities of the living. In addition, the Christopher Nolan feature *The Dark Knight* (2008) offers a fascinating allegory of the war on terrorism; film excerpts might be paired with readings from Tom Pollard's *Hollywood 9/11: Superheroes, Supervillains, and Super Disasters* (2011) to prompt an interesting dialogue on values and vengeance.

Why not film?!

I began this chapter by reflecting on how teaching with film exhibits a number of qualities identified in the scholarship of teaching and learning. I conclude with the observation that in the digital age, classes that employ film or video clips can be highly successful and engage students in very important (even necessary) ways. As noted earlier, film is not a passive medium. Films selected for this class provided powerful expressions of important themes in international relations. Nearly every film clip employed in this class evoked responses. Group discussions of films and readings were energized by the presence of a common language or frame of reference, and students could discuss content and theory issues related to educational objectives as much as their visceral responses. Film clips helped students reflect critically on questions like how far to go in the war on terrorism, how serious are threats of proliferation of weapons of mass destruction, and whether human nature is inherently evil or inherently good.

Finally, beyond tangible assessment data lies the special lure of the filmic image. This class reaffirms studies from higher education regarding the power of student engagement in and excitement about the learning enterprise. Teaching through film provides students with a deeper understanding of world politics, a visual expression of important themes for a new generation of students, and a common bond among viewers. For these reasons, I conclude that film and related media provide essential tools for the modern political science classroom.

[Please see the companion website for the book. Details are listed on the back cover of the book.]

Notes

1   I gratefully acknowledge support for this project from the Great Lakes Colleges Association Pathways to Learning Collegium grant program and the Roy Adams Fund for Teaching Scholarship in the Department of Political Science at the College of Wooster. I would also like to thank my students and colleagues for many useful suggestions for course design.

2   Chris Hedges, *War is the Force that Gives Us Meaning* (New York: Anchor Books, 2002): 3.

3 Marilyn J. Matelski and Nancy Lynch Street, eds, *War and Film in America: Historical and Critical Essays* (New York: McFarland and Co., 2003): 1.

4 David A. Kolb, *Experiential Learning: Experience as the Source of Learning and Development* (Englewood Cliffs, NJ: Prentice Hall, 1984); R. C. Chandler and B. Adams, "Let's Go to the Movies! Using Film to Illustrate Basic Concepts in Public Administration," *Public Voices* 8(2) (1997): 11; R. L. Fox and S. A. Ronkowski, "Learning Styles of Political Science Students," *PS: Political Science & Politics* 30(4) (1997): 732–7; Lynn M. Kuzma and Patrick Haney, "And . . . Action! Using Film to Learn About Foreign Policy," *International Studies Perspectives* 2(1) (2001): 33–50; Robert W. Gregg, *International Relations on Film* (Boulder, CO: Lynne Rienner, 1998); S. M. Kiasatpour, "The Internet and Film: Teaching Middle East Politics Interactively," *PS: Political Science & Politics* 32(1) (1999): 83–9; Dan Lindley, "What I Learned Since I Stopped Worrying and Studied the Movie: A Teaching Guide to Stanley Kubrick's *Dr. Strangelove*," *PS: Political Science & Politics* 34(3) (2001): 663–7; Cynthia Weber, "The Highs and Lows of Teaching IR Theory: Using Popular Films for Theoretical Critique," *International Studies Perspectives* 2(3) (2006): 281–7; Vincent K. Pollard, "Cognitive Leverage of Film in International Studies Classrooms," *International Studies Quarterly* 3(1) (2002): 89–92; Pollard, "Emerging Issues and Impermanent Institutions: Social Movements, Early Indicators of Social Change, and Film Pedagogy," *Journal of Political Science Education* 1(3) (2005): 397–401; Robert W. Gregg, "The Ten Best Films about International Relations," *World Policy Journal* 16(2) (1999): 129–34.

5 I have collaborated for years with Professors Kent Kille and Matthew Krain on active teaching and learning techniques. I would like to acknowledge their contributions to my own understanding of active teaching, as well as acknowledge their influence on my writing on the work.

6 D. L. Schacter, *Searching for Memory: The Brain, the Mind, and the Past* (New York: Basic Books, 1996); K. Brock and B. Cameron, "Enlivening Political Science Courses with Kolb's Learning Preference Model," *PS: Political Science & Politics* 25(3) (1999): 251–6.

7 Lee S. Shulman, "Teaching and Teacher Education among the Professions," 38th Charles W. Hunt Memorial Lecture, American Association of Colleges for Teacher Education 50th Annual Meeting, New Orleans, Louisiana (February 25, 1997), transcript.

8 Eric Jensen, *Teaching with the Brain in Mind* (Alexandria, VA: Association for Supervision and Curricular Development, 1998); Kuzma and Haney, "And . . . Action! Using Film to Learn About Foreign Policy."

9 S. M. Kiasatpour, "The Internet and Film: Teaching Middle East Politics Interactively," *PS: Political Science & Politics* 32(1) (1999): 83–89; S. Waalkes, "Using Film Clips as Cases to Teach the Rise and 'Decline' of the State," *International Studies Perspectives* 4(2) (2003): 156–74; Daniel Lieberfeld, "Teaching about War through Film and Literature," *PS: Political Science & Politics* 40(3) (2007): 571–4.

10 Lieberfeld, "Teaching about War through Film and Literature," 571; Archie W. Simpson and Bernd Kaussler, "IR Teaching Reloaded: Using Films and Simulations in the Teaching of International Relations," *International Studies*

Perspectives 10(1) (2009): 413–27; Debra Holzhauer, "Film and Foreign Policy: Examining the Impact of an Active Learning Strategy," Paper prepared for the *Annual Meeting of International Studies Association*, Montreal (March 2011); Patrick Haney, "Learning about Foreign Policy at the Movies," in *The New International Studies Classroom: Active Teaching, Active Learning*, ed. J. S. Lantis, L. M. Kuzma, and J. Boehrer (Boulder, CO: Lynne Rienner, 2000): 239–53; Weber, "The Highs and Lows of Teaching IR Theory: Using Popular Films for Theoretical Critique;" Stephen Deets, "Wizarding in the Classroom: Teaching Harry Potter and Politics," *PS: Political Science & Politics* 42(4) (2009): 741–4.

11   Archie W. Simpson and Bernd Kaussler, "IR Teaching Reloaded: Using Films and Simulations in the Teaching of International Relations," *International Studies Perspectives* 10 (2009): 413–27; Debra Holzhauer, "Film and Foreign Policy: Examining the Impact of an Active Learning Strategy," Paper prepared for the *Annual Meeting of International Studies Association*, Montreal (March 2011); Stacy Ulbig, "Engaging the Unengaged: Using Visual Images to Enhance Students' Poli Sci 101 Experience," *PS: Political Science & Politics* 42(2) (2009): 385–91.

12   Simpson and Kaussler, "IR Teaching Reloaded: Using Films and Simulations in the Teaching of International Relations;" Sheri Sunderland, Jonathan C. Rothermel, and Adam Lusk, "Making Movies Active: Lessons from Simulations," *PS: Political Science & Politics* 42(3) (2009): 543–7.

13   James E. Combs, *Movies and Politics: The Dynamic Relationship* (New York: Garland Publishers, 1993), 69–70.

14   Excerpts from *Patton* (1969: Twentieth Century Fox Studios, 1969).

15   A good example is Jack S. Levy, "The Causes of War and the Conditions of Peace," *Annual Review of Political Science* 1(1) (1998): 139–65.

16   Tom Pyszczynski, Zachary Rothschild, and Abdolhossein Abdollahi, "Terrorism, Violence, and Hope for Peace," *Current Directions in Psychological Science* 17(5) (2008): 318–22.

17   Hedges' *War is the Force that Gives Us Meaning*, 3.

18   See Kenton Worcester's contribution in this volume.

19   A promising new work on filmic portrayals of war and peace in an age of international terrorism is Tom Pollard's *Hollywood 9/11: Superheroes, Supervillains, and Super Disasters* (New York: Paradigm Publishers, 2011).

20   John Stoessinger, *Why Nations Go to War* (New York: Wadsworth Publishing, 2008): 213.

21   In an interesting postscript, one of the film-makers of *Restrepo*, Tim Hetherington, was killed while reporting on the war in Libya in 2011.

PART FIVE

Internet and social media

Introduction

In June 2006, the late Alaska Senator Ted Stevens gave an impassioned speech against an amendment to a bill governing internet providers. The bill would have prohibited large internet service providers from charging fees to offer preferential access to their networks. Laying out the issue, Stevens stated, "an Internet was sent by my staff at 10 o'clock in the morning on Friday. I got it yesterday [Tuesday]. Why? Because it got tangled up with all these things going on the Internet commercially." Continuing, and inadvertently coining a memorable phrase, Stevens stated, ". . . the Internet is not something that you just dump something on. It's not a big truck. It's a series of tubes!"

Those supporting "net neutrality" and as such, supporting the amendment's efforts to prohibit preferential treatment, pounced. The phrase "a series of tubes" became a rallying cry for technophiles and web geeks everywhere, aimed at showing how those in charge of governing our high-speed internet networks had only the crudest understanding of what the internet was, and how it worked. Steven's erroneous statement that a staffer had sent "an internet," as opposed to an email, seemed to suggest that he perhaps understood the medium about as well as our befuddled elderly relatives—the crucial difference being that our relatives are not in charge of the internet's oversight or regulation.

"A series of tubes" resonated in the global echo chamber and Stevens' speech was lampooned by countless late-night funnymen. Yet precisely what was so hilarious about Stevens' discourse was the juxtaposition of this crude understanding with the utter ubiquity of the internet in (most of) our daily lives. The internet and online forms of social media have become so omnipresent in our existence and our communications that statements such as these hearken back to an era when such technologies were hardly understood. As a result, many also found them gut-bustingly hilarious.

More seriously, there are obvious political implications to the contemporary proliferation of internet technology. It is frequently claimed that new communications technologies and social media have "democratized" communicative media, giving more individuals the power to shape discourse, ideology, and the flow of information. The monumental events of the so-called Arab Spring remind us of social media's power to circumvent authoritarian methods to control the flow of information. Online platforms such as Twitter and Facebook have loosened the grip of all but the most secretive regimes, and have exposed misdeeds and brutality that previously might have gone unnoticed. Closer to home, it has been the case for many years that the internet and social media prove vital to campaign financing and grassroots mobilization. Such technologies shape not only our present but our past, as historic archives increasingly liberate their collections from temperature-controlled warehouses, digitizing their collections and making them available online.

However, the internet and social media do not merely shape the phenomena we study. Increasingly, they provide unique and exciting opportunities that change *how* we study it. We should not find it surprising then, that so many educators teaching courses on politics have turned to these powerful new forms of media and communication in the classroom. The authors in this section provide a fascinating glimpse into how such innovative new technologies can be utilized within the classroom.

Ari Kohen discusses his experiences integrating the online social networking platform, Twitter, into a course on contemporary political theory. He charts his initial resistance as a political theorist to adopt what seemed to be an impersonal medium which limited communications to 140 characters, yet ultimately finds that it did increase student engagement with the material and with one another. In a similar vein, Chapman Rackaway follows by investigating how the use of blogging in a course on political communication fostered a sense of community and helped the students engage in experiential application of concepts and ideas from the course. Lastly, Simon Lightfoot explores the many advantages in utilizing "podcasting" to create a "blended learning environment" by which to critically assess political concepts and ideas. However, he provides a sober and honest assessment of the medium's potential drawbacks as well.

Throughout, the authors argue that while such online and social networking tools create exciting new opportunities in the classroom, they are no panacea. These technologies must be incorporated carefully and with specific pedagogical and logistical objectives in mind if we are to adequately assess their utility. As we educators struggle to understand the "series of tubes" which increasingly shapes our learning environment, the authors provide helpful ways in which these technologies can enrich and enliven our classrooms.

CHAPTER FOURTEEN

Teaching political theory with Twitter: The pedagogy of social networking

Ari Kohen[1]

I have always believed the general wisdom about teaching political theory, namely that the material tends to be rather complicated and requires some serious in-class deliberation in order for undergraduate students to be able to make sense of it. After all, teaching a subject like ethics without discussion and debate probably should not qualify as teaching ethics at all. With that in mind, I have always been very clear about why I am not one of those professors who uses a lot of technology in the classroom. There are good pedagogical reasons that keep me away from PowerPoint and that serve as the foundation for only using Blackboard to post papers and book chapters for students to read. Students need to be able to talk with the professor—and with one another—about the material and the best way to do so is face-to-face, where ideas can be tested, challenged, and ultimately figured out. To be fair, I should also note that, as a political theorist, it never really made sense to me to do anything else. The best professors, in my experience, were those who came to class with a few pages of notes and discussed ideas with their students for an hour or so. Those professors never brought anything flashy into the classroom to impress their students, except their wit.

Building on this way of looking at teaching political theory, I have often argued that the best way to determine whether students in any class understand the material is to see whether they can process it in such a way as to be able to put the ideas back out into the world in their own voice. In other words, the most important way for students to show me—and themselves—what they have learned is through class participation. This often determines how well they will perform on the essays they write in my class, as someone who can speak about complex concepts with limited preparation will generally also be able to write about those same concepts when given a few weeks to put together an argument.

And yet class participation is one of the most difficult things for students to do for several important reasons. First, our classes are generally too large for everyone to participate in meaningful ways. I only teach upper-level political theory courses—designed for junior and senior undergraduate students—but I have never taught a class with an enrollment smaller than 30 students. Gambling with difficult ideas, testing out answers to serious ethical problems, can only be done by the most confident or adventurous students, those who are willing to speak up and say things that might be unpopular or unusual. Second, sufficient time for discussion simply is not available. If everyone wanted to speak about one question or another, the entire class session would be devoted to that question alone. What is more, students often note that class discussions move quickly; by the time an individual student is called on to make a point, the topic might be quite different from what it was when the student's hand went up. Third, it is often the case that political theory needs to be explained, rather than simply read and digested by students on their own. Devoting time to lecture, of course, takes time away from discussion; in addition, it is often difficult for students to talk about a reading they are having trouble understanding. Indeed, some of my students tell me they have a much better idea of the important concepts after class than they did when they did the reading on their own; with some of the most difficult material, occasionally students have even suggested they would benefit most from reading the material after the class lectures rather than beforehand. While I am disinclined to pursue this suggestion because it likely means an end to in-class discussion entirely, I understand the sentiment. I remember stumbling through Kant or Heidegger on my own and then feeling as though it made sense only after the lecture. Without hearing from the professor, I might read for weeks without actually understanding the material. And finally, students seldom respond to one another; instead, discussion—if it can be called that—is almost always run through the professor: I will ask a question and then one student after another will respond to me. None of the students ever really respond directly to one another because they seem conditioned to expect that my questions are more important than the points raised by their classmates or, at least, that answering my questions will more clearly count toward their class participation grade.

These problems might be unique to the University of Nebraska, but I suspect they are not. With all of these things in mind, I decided to try a very different approach to class participation in the Fall '09 semester. Approximately a year earlier, I had started using Twitter—an increasingly popular communications tool, used for everything from simple status updates to the propagation of news articles, information, and ideas—and, toward the end of the Spring '09 semester, I had the idea of using Twitter in conjunction with a new class I was developing. As I finished putting together the syllabus for the 35-student contemporary political theory class, I became convinced that using contemporary technologies would be fitting and also that Twitter, in particular, could engage students in a manner that is very different from other contemporary technologies. Looking back on the experiment, I am convinced that employing an emerging technology like Twitter would make a useful pedagogical contribution to any class where the discussion of ideas is a requirement. In what follows, I describe in detail the experiment I conducted—making Twitter usage a central component of an upper-level course—while also considering the ways in which the experiment succeeded and the ways it could be improved in the future.

To begin, it is important to note that other social networking sites are certainly more popular with students at the moment, with Facebook usage nearly ubiquitous among American undergraduates. I settled on Twitter for several reasons: it is fairly simple to explain even to someone who has never seen it before, the ways in which it is being used are evolving far faster than other websites, and the service most obviously allows for increased interaction (with classmates and with strangers). For those reasons, one might even imagine a time when Twitter might surpass even Facebook in the future. When I began using Twitter in my class, in 2009, twitter.com was ranked as America's No. 38 website.[2] Today, Alexa.com ranks Twitter the #9 website globally.

Usage and publicity of the service exploded only recently. The service was founded in 2006, ostensibly "for friends, family, and co-workers to communicate and stay connected through the exchange of quick, frequent messages . . . often called 'tweets' of 140 characters or fewer."[3] In April 2007, Twitter had around 94,000 users;[4] in March 2009, the site received 9.3 million visitors.[5] In March 2011, Twitter announced that the average number of new accounts created each day over the preceding month was 460,000.[6] Undoubtedly, the vast majority of people make use of Twitter as a series of status updates and this has prompted the most frequent critique of the service, namely that it is not clear why anyone should care about the minutia of anyone else's daily existence. But, as Facebook (among other Web 2.0 applications) ably demonstrates, people seem to be very much concerned with their friends' status updates, as they are being read and now—with changes to the service—commented upon with great frequency.

While many people will continue to use Twitter to keep their friends apprised of their activities, or to chat with them asynchronously, it is clear that usage of the service has expanded considerably since its inception. One reason for the change is that posting on Twitter is analogous to carrying on a private conversation in public. Every post, even a reply to another user, can be viewed by third parties who visit the user's profile page or who search for terms contained in those posts. If one Twitter user is interested, entertained, provoked, or in any other way engaged by something written by another, the former may reply to the specific post or may "follow" all of the updates by the latter. While there is no right or wrong way to use the service, it is apparent that many users are actively seeking to engage with new people around similar interests.

At present, users are sharing photos, recommending books and music, commenting on breaking news, connecting with professional actors and athletes, linking to blog posts, and even making news themselves. One of the best examples that I used with my students in 2009—combining several of these uses for Twitter—comes from the emergency landing of US Airways 1546 in the Hudson River, as the first photos came from a user on board a ferry used to rescue passengers.[7] Today, it is clear that the Arab Spring can provide students and professors with plenty of fodder for discussion about the various uses for Twitter as a means of connecting people, organizing events, and making news. Indeed, what distinguishes this service from so many others is that it connects strangers and fosters friendships, rather than simply maintaining connections between friends, co-workers, and former classmates. Those connections—built as they are on common interests, like sports or politics, rather than on people or common experiences, like high school attendance—provide a solid framework for associating with others, as online communities form themselves around the various interests. What Twitter provides, then, is a larger community with increasing interactivity: each user can easily connect with a great many new people who have similar interests and engage in more conversation than he or she ordinarily might.

With all of this in mind, I created a class account on Twitter. I decided to require my students to set up accounts of their own and to "follow" the class account, and—before the semester began—I also advertised the class to those users who "follow" my account. Before the beginning of the semester, about 20 users from around the world were following the class account. By the end of the semester, more than 70 users (including the 30 enrolled students) were following the class account. The idea was that, I would post questions through the class account a few times a week, generally before and after each class meeting. Students could then choose to answer the questions, ask one another questions, and generally discuss the readings with one another and with me. No one was required to participate, as there was no cost to ignoring the conversation that is carried out online; in fact, after setting up their accounts in the first week, students need not ever use Twitter again if they so chose. That said, I encouraged them to participate by noting in the syllabus that participation on Twitter could benefit their class participation grade. The reason I allowed Twitter to help them—but not to hurt them—is that I thought there would be some very real benefits to doing so. However, having never done such an experiment before, I did not have any proof to back up what was just an assumption on my part.

My thinking, or the pedagogical theory behind my decision to use Twitter, was relatively straightforward. Twitter can break down barriers between people who are generally perceived to be far away from us in some way, like professors might seem to students, by allowing students some access to the thoughts, ideas, or even day-to-day activities of professors. In this way, I thought I might become even more accessible to my students. Additionally, I believe that using Twitter allows quieter students to participate in ways that might seem less daunting to them. It also might encourage them to speak up by showing them at least one thing that they ought to be looking for in the assigned reading, by allowing them to start the discussion on the material before coming to class, and by giving them additional insight into the opinions of their classmates with regard to controversial or particularly difficult topics.

It is important to note that I was not the only professor intent on integrating Twitter into the higher education scene. Indeed, while I was attempting to drum up interest in the class among those who follow my personal account, I came across a short post on the blog of the *Chronicle of Higher Education*.[8] During the semester, a longer treatment came out in the *Chronicle* that examined a couple of experiments in using Twitter in the classroom.[9] In both cases, my sense was that these professors—none of whom were political scientists—were not making the most effective use of the technology.

In the first case, a professor encouraged his students to use Twitter, and he used it himself, but he did not specifically use it as a pedagogical element in the class. Thus, "The posts from students also mixed the mundane with the useful. One student twittered that she just bought a pet rabbit. Another noted that a topic from the class was being discussed on a TV-news report."[10] Though it was a bit haphazard, and though students likely were not sure what they ought to take away from many of the posts, the professor noted an improvement in classroom community and claimed, "It was the single thing that changed the classroom dynamics more than anything I've ever done teaching."[11] The full *Chronicle* article, written while my experiment was ongoing, put forward a couple of examples that seemed more like cautionary tales (and seemed like they were intended to seem that way). In the first case, a personal finance class at Purdue University, hundreds of students were encouraged to conduct what amounts to a back-channel conversation via Twitter during the lecture. The professor would occasionally look at the screen to see what was being written and would occasionally address the questions and comments there. If this sounds like a complete disaster to you, then you are not alone. Indeed, one student used the service as a way to cheat, by asking his classmates for help during a quiz. One online discussion distracted even a teaching assistant, causing him to laugh out loud during the lecture. Online conversation frequently wandered away from the topic of the lecture. All of these problems were acknowledged by both the professor and the students, but everyone still thought that—on balance—"It does more good than it does hurt."[12]

The second case, which was also featured in an earlier article, seemed to be endorsing the use of Twitter even less enthusiastically.[13] In a smaller class at the University of Texas–Dallas, a professor required students to post comments during one of three weekly class meetings. Since some students either did not have access to a computer or because text messaging services were not free, students could even write down their comments and give them to a teaching assistant to post online during the class discussion. Perhaps the most unusual aspect of this particular experiment is that the professor divided the students into small groups and gave them discussion topics. "Depending on the topic, they would tweet for ten minutes or so and then I would suggest a change of topic. Students would have mini-discussions in their small groups and each student could tweet the most relevant comments being circulated in the group."[14] Unfortunately, the professor does not spend a great deal of time explaining the benefits to using Twitter in this case, rather than simply asking one student to report back to the class about the discussions of the various groups. Nor does she go into detail about why having a so-called back-channel was useful or pedagogically helpful, especially when some students' comments turned out to be decidedly "nonproductive and nonacademic," resulting in a "flame war" on the topic of abortion.[15] Rankin only notes that she thinks "the twitter experiment was successful primarily because it encouraged students to engage who otherwise would not."[16]

Even though I had the same general feeling at the beginning of my Twitter experiment, it is not at all clear why she believes this to have been the case, especially since she also notes that the students did not seem to continue their use of Twitter outside of the time allotted for it: "I had hoped that students would continue the 'discussions' outside of class time and they would tweet interesting ideas throughout the week. Some students did post . . . class-related comments outside of class time, but this was the exception."[17]

In an effort to get around the problem of mixing up my own expectations with what actually happened when the experiment took place, I worked to quantify the use of Twitter in my class. I did so by creating a common hashtag for our class that would make our comments searchable and that would distinguish posts that were relevant to the class from posts that students wrote on other subjects. I then created an ongoing search for the hashtag and collected all of the comments on my personal computer using a feed reader—an application that downloads news articles or blog posts from websites that a user selects—to keep track of the comments over the course of the semester. From the beginning of the semester at the end of August 2009 to the semester's end in the middle of December 2009, the students and I wrote and sent more than 500 hashtagged posts via Twitter. All of these posts were written outside of our designated class meeting times and many students elected to engage one another on things they were writing, rather than simply responding one after another to the questions posed by the professor. Thus, the Twitter posts sometimes resembled a more standard back-and-forth with the professor that you might expect in a classroom, but also sometimes resembled an actual conversation among people who were reading and thinking about some philosophical topic. Consider the following quoted posts to provide some insight into exactly what we saw over the course of the semester. Here is one day's discussion about Allan Bloom's critique of John Rawls:

> **POLS386** (9/23/09, 7:40pm) Is Bloom right about the problem of greatness in a Rawlsian society? Should we, in fact, worry about the tyranny of mediocrity? #pols386
>
> **And_Matt** (9/23/09, 8:35pm) @POLS386 Yes. The mediocre majority will stifle progressive agents and cause society as a whole to never reach it's potential. #POLS386
>
> **ssafari** (9/23/09, 10:49pm) R does not take into consideration the nature of mans purpose. R discounts the fact that nature of man is to preserve oneself. #pols386
>
> **And_Matt** (9/23/09, 11:02pm) @ssafari I agree, R also changes societies goal from preserving citizens to providing happiness . . . should this be societies purpose? #POLS386
>
> **AlexaShasteen** (9/24/09, 12:01am) Is Bloom arguing for theory based on state of nature, **or** just using it as an idea to compare with original position? #pols386
>
> **AlexaShasteen** (9/24/09, 12:02am) Would Bloom, like Nozick, argue for the minimal state? His critiques of Rawls make sense, but doesn't offer much alternative. #pols386
>
> **faith9025** (9/24/09, 12:07am) @AlexaShasteen I thought he was saying R needed to explain men in state of nature as basis 4 why men come together in a community? #pols386
>
> **AlexaShasteen** (9/24/09 12:11am) In S of N they fear death so come together as community for protection. But for B this isn't a motivation in orig position? why? #pols386
>
> **jrcleveland** (9/24/09 8:18am) @AlexaShasteen Is it that O.P. still has a floor that could be implied as preventing the death feared in S of N? #pols386
>
> **tiaepeterson** (9/24/09 8:29am) @And_Matt I don't think happiness can be society's purpose as there are many definitions of it. What if one violates another? #pols386
>
> **And_Matt** (9/24/09 8:41am) @AlexaShasteen Because Rawls focuses on society creating happiness for its citizens, not protection. #POLS386

And_Matt (9/24/09 8:44am) @jrcleveland No, the OP does not consider why men enter society, namely S-P. Societies purpose is our S-P, not our happiness. #POLS386

ErazmusBDragon (9/24/09 12:29pm) @pols386 Bloom is my new hero. I also think that his observation about how the greats in society won't take Rawls is very important. #pols386

And here is another discussion, this time on Hannah Arendt's *The Human Condition*, which took place over the course of several days:

POLS386 (10/2/09 8:23am) Do you agree with Arendt about the collapse of the public/private distinction in our lives? What's right/wrong with this analysis? #pols386

And_Matt (10/2/09 9:29am) @POLS386 The cynic in me wants to shout out we're all slaves to necessity! FREEDOM!!! But, she does make you think . . . #POLS386

tiaepeterson (10/2/09 10:20am) @POLS386 I agree with her. I think the collapse shows a shift in values more than anything, but I don't think the values are that great.

a_b_debrie (10/2/09 11:19am) maybe the public sphere has expanded because we're not slaves to necessity to the same degree as in the past. #pols386

a_b_debrie (10/2/09 11:19am) what percent of our societal production goes to actual necessities compared to feudal times? Greek times? #pols386

BrianShreck (10/2/09 12:36pm) @POLS386 She got the story right, but I disagree on its consequences. Id rather be a slave to necessity than a slave to another man. #pols386

ErazmusBDragon (10/2/09 4:38pm) I think Arendt is judging modern society against ancient greek standards. We've managed to join profession and necessity . . . (cont) #pols386

ErazmusBDragon (10/2/09 4:40pm) . . . don't forget that her private lifestyle only served minority. Our lifestyle allows far more people to take part in public life. #pols386

faith9025 (10/2/09 8:14pm) @POLS386 I see what she means by the "collapse," but it's not a bad thing. People SHOULD learn to support themselves. #pols386

faith9025 (10/2/09 8:14pm) @POLS386 Nowadays supporting oneself = independence and freedom in a sense. #pols386

kohenari (10/3/09 4:51pm) @faith9025 @erazmusbdragon Is it really freedom if "supporting oneself" (even if I choose how) entails responding to necessity? #pols386

ErazmusBDragon (10/4/09 12:32pm) @kohenari People are always responding to necessity, psychologically if not physically. Humans are creatures of necessity. #pols386

ErazmusBDragon (10/4/09 12:33pm) @kohenari The entire reason we form societies is because humans instinctively crave fellowship. Food's just a more visible need. #pols386

Co_burn (10/4/09 2:08pm) @BrianShreck Well said. The basic assumption that we must master others to master necessity though is over simplified. #pols386

Co_burn (10/4/09 2:10pm) @POLS386 The goal should not b to master anything, but to control it such that the most freedom is attained without damaging others'. #pols386

faith9025 (10/5/09 4:22pm) @kohenari It is not freedom from necessity, but depending on others to work for you isn't either—just others working for you. #pols386

kohenari (10/5/09 4:28pm) @faith9025 @erazmusbdragon @co_burn @brianshreck Is having others work for me the only way to be publicly free from necessity? #pols386

This discussion continued for another full day, with an additional 23 posts on the topic. While the quality of posts certainly varied, it is clear that students were actively engaging with the material and with one another over the course of the semester. In particular, it is useful to note the way that students were able to discuss complex philosophical concepts via Twitter, disputing the claim put forward by a number of people that Twitter's 140-character limit necessarily hinders its utility as a teaching tool.[18]

While all of this amounts to a clear success story to my mind, I also believe there are good lessons to learn from this experiment. First, asking open-ended questions is incredibly important to fostering a discussion. While this is not particularly surprising, as the same is true of an in-class discussion, I believe that some of my questions were overly specific. In order to have a discussion, a balance needs to be achieved between the specifics of the readings from class and the kind of generalizing that allows people to test out ideas related to the topics covered in the reading. Looking at the conversations that I quote above highlights the difference between a question about whether or not we ought to worry about the tyranny of the majority and a question about a specific point raised by Arendt in a reading assignment. Over the course of the semester, the more specific questions tended to narrow the range of those who responded. Very few at-large Twitter users ventured a comment, though this is likely also related to the fact that the vast majority of our followers from the world outside of the university were not doing the reading along with the students. Of course, the more people from the "outside world" are following along, the more likely it is that some of them will add their comments alongside those of the students. In part, then, one of my challenges involves additional advertising to encourage others to follow and to participate, but also offering more information about how people can keep up with the reading assignment if they are inclined to do so. In addition, it is clearly important to ask questions early in the semester about which people will have strong opinions; in the case of this class, I chose to begin with the debate between John Rawls and Robert Nozick on the subject of distributive justice, which clearly got a number of people invested in the experiment and kept them participating from the beginning until the end of the class.

Second, it is clear that Twitter is not yet a part of most students' daily lives in the same way that Facebook clearly is. The vast majority of students did not check their Twitter accounts on a regular basis, which meant that a broad conversation—involving many students—only occurred by fits and starts, and sometimes the conversation only involved the small group of students who became enthusiastic Twitter users. On a related note, because students were not checking their Twitter accounts on a regular basis, they occasionally complained that they were unable to keep up with the conversation. While there were likely between 20 and 30 hashtagged messages each week, students felt overwhelmed by that volume and by the speed of the discussion; this must be attributed to the fact that they only checked Twitter once a week (or less often), as the volume of posts that most Twitter users read each day is undoubtedly more than 100.

Another important point stems directly from this observation, namely that the conversation is always about the latest tweet from the professor. Some classroom dynamics die hard and this one is no exception; it is difficult to sustain a conversation on a single topic and so they tend to die out after a day or two. Or, rather, they shift from one to the next with as much frequency as occurs in a typical discussion-based class. Indeed, the way that the class account is set up seems to discourage the continuation of a conversation about Question A once Question B has been asked. My sense is that this is not because Question A—and its related answers—stopped being interesting to students, but because attention from the regular Twitter users shifts to the newer Question B and the occasional users do not bother posting about something old. If they are going to contribute, it will be to comment on the most recent question put forward by the professor because they generally are not scrolling back through a week of hashtagged discussion.

Finally, and happily, there was a fairly noticeable change about halfway through the semester: students began posting their own content rather than simply answering questions that I put forward. Often, this took the form of links to articles or YouTube content that relates to something we discussed in class or on Twitter. Occasionally it even took the form of testing out an idea for a paper and getting suggestions from classmates about the direction of an argument. My sense is that a good deal of the change can be accounted for by an increase in students' overall comfort with one another as the semester progressed, but it is also the case that this sharing increased markedly once students were tasked with writing the first paper and studying for the midterm examination.

While some students chose not to participate, others chose to participate unevenly, and—as outlined above—a good deal of improvement can certainly be made. My sense is that this first experiment should be considered a success. In the future, I plan to implement the changes mentioned above with the goals of involving more students in the online discussion and keeping interesting discussions moving forward, even as new questions come up. These changes will be considerably easier to make as Twitter comes to be seen as fun or useful in the way that students regard Facebook or, at least, as less frustrating or bizarre than it is currently regarded by many students. In the end, a professor's ability to employ this sort of technology hinges on whether this generation will be able to think of Web 2.0 applications as educational rather than simply an amusing diversion.

Notes

1 I would like to thank the undergraduate students in my POLS 386 course, Miguel Centellas, Michael Tofias, and—of course—the editors for their helpful comments and suggestions.

2 Paul Boutin, "All You Need to Know to Twitter," *New York Times* (May 6, 2009). Accessed at www.nytimes.com/2009/05/07/technology/*personaltech*/07basics.html.

3 "Frequently Asked Questions," Twitter.com (November 4, 2008). Accessed March 26, 2012, from http://help.twitter.com/forums/10711/entries/13920.

4 Akshay Java, Xiaodan Song, Tim Finin, and Belle Tseng, "Why We Twitter: Understanding Microblogging Usage and Communities," Paper presented at the *Joint* 9th *WEBKDD and* 1st *SNA-KDD Workshop '07* (2007).

5 Sarah Radwanick, "ComScore Media Metrix Ranks Top 50 U.S. Web Properties for March 2009," ComScore Online (April 22, 2009). Accessed at http://www.comscore.com/Press_Events/Press_Releases/2009/4/Twitter_Traffic_More_than_Doubles/(language)/eng-US.

6 Twitter, "#numbers," Twitter Blog (March 14, 2011). Accessed at http://blog.twitter.com/2011/03/numbers.html

7 Helena Deards, "Twitter First Off the Mark with Hudson Plane Crash Coverage," World Editors Forum (January 19, 2009). Accessed at www.editorsweblog.org/multimedia/2009/01/twitter_first_off_the_mark_with_hudson_p.php.

8 Jeffrey R. Young, "A Professor's Tips for Using Twitter in the Classroom," Wired Campus. *The Chronicle of Higher Education* (January 28, 2008). Accessed at http://chronicle.com/blogPost/A-Professor-s-Tips-for-Using/3643.

9 Jeffrey R. Young, "Teaching With Twitter: Not for the Faint of Heart," *The Chronicle of Higher Education* (November 22, 2009). Accessed at http://chronicle.com/article/Teaching-With-Twitter-Not-for/49230/.

10 Young, "A Professor's Tips," 2008.

11 Ibid.

12 Young, "Teaching With Twitter," 2009.

13   Zach Miners, "Twitter Goes to College," *U.S. News & World Report* (June 2, 2009). Accessed at www.usnews.com/articles/education/2009/06/02/twitter-goes-to-college.html.

14   Monica Rankin, "Some General Comments on the 'Twitter Experiment' " (2009). Accessed at www.utdallas.edu/~mrankin/usweb/twitterconclusions.htm.

15   Young "Teaching With Twitter."

16   Rankin, "Some General Comments."

17   Ibid.

18   Rankin,, "Some General Comments;" Young, "Teaching With Twitter."

CHAPTER FIFTEEN

The medium is the messenger: Web 2.0 tools in the political science classroom

Chapman Rackaway[1]

Introduction

Teachers have engaged in "stand and deliver" at the front of a classroom for centuries, but that method has been shown to be less effective than active learning. Just as broadcast media has been changed by the technological advances of online media, teaching is being revolutionized by tools that empower students and encourage active learning. Commonly called "Web 2.0," the content-production tools available online are changing teaching and provide an opportunity to achieve the twin goals of putting learning in students' hands and building community among them. When students move beyond simply repeating material gleaned from a textbook and move into a new realm where they build a community around producing content under guidance from a mentoring instructor, those students embrace a twenty-first century educational method.

How can a faculty member best engage his or her students in course material and build that active learning community? Having students co-create their own supplemental text through a blog is a method this author has found to be highly effective. Using a sophomore-junior level Political Communication course at a mid-sized state comprehensive university, I introduce a community-building, active learning outcomes-focused blog assignment for students. I have since made adjustments to the tool and expanded its use into other courses.

As an assignment, blogging has evolved out of a media journal I assigned to students in Political Communication. Media journals allowed students to achieve multiple learning outcomes: regular reading and news consumption, media literacy, written communication skills, and critical thinking. Blogging allows students to use technology to achieve those learning objectives as well as community-building and social capital goals.

Academic fields use a variety of texts to teach. Considered broadly, texts can be traditional books, pieces of art, videos, or other media. Texts are important because they provide a source beyond the professor's in-class instruction to immerse students in material outside the classroom. Taking the idea of a text even more broadly, technology that allows students to create content gives us another type, one that is an evolving document. Such active learning, defined by Prince, is "any instructional method that engages students in the learning process. In short, active learning requires students to do meaningful learning activities and think about what they are doing."[2]

Online tools in the classroom

Technology is significantly impacting teaching inside and outside the classroom. Almost any element of traditional classroom teaching can be adapted to, changed by, or replaced by, technological tools. A variety of different tools exist, and it is important to match the tool to desired learning outcomes. Gradebooks have been replaced by spreadsheets, testing has moved from Blue Books to Blackboard, and educational institutions now deliver programs online. Each change has brought pushback from those who do not want to change, but change inevitably happens and educators respond to the change, finding ways to integrate technology into their work. More specifically, some have started to use Web 2.0 tools to achieve specific pedagogical goals. For instance, the open-sourced web encyclopedia known as Wikipedia has been used in lieu of textbooks in some classes. One professor has students submit papers to an internal class-only wiki within his course management system for peer review prior to submitting final drafts.[3]

Ari Kohen shares his classroom use of Twitter in this volume. Kohen began by posting questions to allow students who missed class to keep up. Over time Kohen used Twitter as a mechanism for students to briefly summarize important points within the site's 140-character limit. Far from limiting students, Kohen found that Twitter became a vital teaching tool for political theory classes. The use of Twitter transformed in-class discussions to continuing discussions outside of the classroom, let students develop the ability to concisely share their opinions, and built community among the students and interested outsiders who participated in the Twitter threads.[4]

As digital natives, college students are accustomed to using computer-based tools. From texting to time on social media, students live immersed in a sea of technology. Technology-free education may disengage students, as can randomly or inappropriately used tools. Technology is merely an apparatus, neither beneficial nor destructive in nature. Benefits of technology can include enhanced learning, community-building, and increased student engagement in learning materials. Technology can be destructive by distracting students from learning goals or by interfering with learning through usage problems. The benefit or detriment of technology is in its use. Literature on successful technological instruction integration displays a common thread: strategic goals guided the application of technology to teaching.

Yuen and Hung reinforce the point about intentional application of technology. Surveying students about social networking in the classroom, their results suggested most students' attitudes toward the use of class social networks were positive. Social networking in the observed classrooms was helpful for promoting communities of practice among students. Information sharing, both class-relevant and not, reinforced a shared experience that built social capital.[5]

For a variety of reasons, blogging presents a great promise for college teaching. Blogging weaves numerous important skills into a single activity set. Reading and consuming information as a base source, analyzing the source material, composing and writing the post, and maintaining the conversation in replies to build community all satisfy pedagogical goals. Critical thinking, collaboration, media literacy, and writing skills are all put to the test with blogging.[6]

Web 2.0

The internet, taken as a communication medium, is completely different from any other media developed since the printing press. Just as the printing press was a revolutionary development in information dissemination, the internet has provided a knowledge distribution revolution. What separates the internet from twentieth-century broadcast media such as radio and television is the ability of the end-user to produce content in addition to consume subject matter. Blogging is a flexible and useful Web 2.0 teaching method.

The barriers to entry of broadcast radio and television such as cost of equipment and licensure are obviated by the internet's low cost of content dissemination. The effect of putting content creation in the hands of the general public has been revolutionary in the realm of broadcast media. Web 2.0, as the phenomenon has been termed, has resulted in drastic changes to newspapers and television, as well as changing the culture in subtle yet significant ways.[7]

The list of Web 2.0 tools is vast and includes text, graphical, social, audio, and video content. Text tools are the most common element of the Web 2.0 milieu, such as blogs. Comments on news websites, blogs and their comments features, and collaboration sites all allow the individual consumer to interact with the writer and material and create their own material to share. As keyboards have been the main input source for computers from the beginning, it makes sense that text tools were the first and are the longest-lasting web 2.0 tools. They require no more equipment other than those needed to operate the computer.

Graphical tools are different, with free software available online to combine photos into video slideshow presentations and websites that allow the manipulation and captioning of photos. While graphical tools can be powerful pedagogical instruments, they are generally for more advanced users. Social Web 2.0 tools are well-familiar to most today: Facebook, Twitter, Google Plus, LinkedIn, and other online communities where individuals and groups post profiles and share links, personal content, and interact are examples of the social Web 2.0 world. The stable profiles of such sites give the social network a life beyond discussion boards and comments. Having a profile, where one's content and personal information are shared, is an important part of the Web 2.0 phenomenon.

Consider a newspaper's comments section. If any individual can post and not leave any identifying information, it not only allows them the freedom to make up falsehoods, attack other posters on a personal basis, and generally disrupt the conversation, it also prevents them from developing an identity on the site. By having profiles, people become known for their posts and content. The posters develop reputations and a community of sorts can be built. Local communities can emerge from such comments sections, whether it is a newspaper and its city or a class and its students.

The new Web 2.0 environment allows for the creation of living texts that can expand, contract, and change over time. The dynamic nature of Web 2.0 also allows for a communal construction of content. The ability to build community is another of the great strengths of Web 2.0.

Social capital

The internet has allowed for citizens to be more empowered in their media consumption and the political process generally. Political candidates connect directly to voters through social media, and organizations like AmericansElect.com seek to move the nominating process online. The Web 2.0 phenomenon similarly allows teachers to put more power in the hands of students to create and disseminate knowledge, expanding the toolkit of skill-building strategies available. Further, Web 2.0 tools may provide an answer to one of the great challenges of political science educa-tion in the last two decades: building a reinforcing social community.

Robert Putnam pointed out in the seminal *Bowling Alone* that social capital, a sense of connectedness between individuals and the larger com-munity, had been on the wane for 40 years and was especially acute among the youngest citizens. Declining social capital had implications for politi-cal science faculty, as citizen engagement in the political process is part of the core of the material we teach. A society less connected is one that, by definition, is less participatory.[8] Reacting to Putnam's work, many colleges entered into co-curricular arrangements such as the American Association of State Colleges and Universities' *American Democracy Project* with the express purpose of building social capital among college students.[9] Engaging students with curricular and co-curricular empowerment became high pri-orities in the classroom, conveniently at the same time Web 2.0 tools were beginning to develop.

Putnam provides a number of types of social capital in *Bowling Alone* but the two most important elements are bonding and bridging social capital. Bridging social capital involves bringing people from disparate and distant communities together, while bonding social capital refers to strengthening connections within a geographically concentrated commu-nity. Putnam's work was developed prior to the internet's rise and ubiquity, so the concept of geography as an element (and challenge) for social capi-tal is important. Distant communities were much harder to mobilize and develop social capital among preinternet, but now the geographic distance between communities is lessened if not entirely eliminated. Web 2.0 tools, especially the social media sites, allow a sustained and direct connection between people and provide the opportunity to build that social capital. Social capital is important for pedagogy because group learning has been shown to be highly effective. To foster authentic group learning, some form of community-building is necessary.[10]

A vibrant debate in the academic literature on social capital has emerged in regards to whether the internet and Web 2.0 tools boost in-person social capital, are a threat to it, or have created a unique form of social capital. Wasko and Faraj claim that without existing strong connections and commitment to a network, online participation does not build social capital.[11]

Mozorov's work is also critical of online participation. In his work, *The Net Delusion*, Mozorov posits that the internet actually boosts the individual over the community and as a result threatens the community-building nature of online participation advocated by others. Opposing internet evangelists like Andrew Sullivan, Mozorov points to unrest in Iran that Sullivan claimed was the beginning of regime change in Tehran. Mozorov shows how those protestors did not accomplish their goals of overturning their government, and in fact their use of social media allowed them to subsequently be terrorized by the government. Mozorov concluded the promise of the internet is not as limitless as its supporters claim.[12]

Wellman, Witte, and Hampton saw online participation as building community however, as a rejoinder to critics such as Wasko et al. and Mozorov.[13] Pfeil and colleagues present a more nuanced view of social networking's benefits.[14] Significantly, Pfeil et al. find that social capital gains are strongest among the young. Community-building, whether in person or online, makes for an improved learning environment.[15]

Steinfeld and colleagues investigated the value of Web 2.0 tools as a way of building social capital, especially among college-aged students. Social capital is an important element not just for community-building but for learning in general. Engagement by students, whether with communities or class material, increases student commitment and as a byproduct should improve learning outcomes through group reinforcement. Steinfeld et al. find that Web 2.0 media are used to maintain offline relationships and maintain connections that can be translated into classroom-relevant material.[16] Blogging is an accessible Web 2.0 tool for the classroom, and it has the added advantage of being similar to an assignment that many instructors have used before: the media journal.

From media journals to blogs

In some ways, the core work a student engages in while blogging is no different than a low-technology tactic used for years in many classes that stressed media literacy: the news journal. While first teaching political communication, I required students to collect stories from newspapers and magazines, make copies, and submit them in a folder with a notebook where they would summarize and analyze each article. The news journal was designed to make sure students kept abreast of current events as well as knew how to write clearly and concisely.

With the intent of having students periodically consume and analyze news, I required students to keep their media journal in a spiral-bound notebook. The students had to select news sources from a list including the *New York Times*, *Washington Post*, and the local newspaper as well as news magazines such as *The Economist*, *Newsweek*, and *U.S. News and World Report*. Students could include other sources if they cleared them with the instructor to be sure that opinion sources like *The Nation* or *National Review*, or trade publications like local alternative entertainment papers were not used in the students' journals. Each student had to make a copy of two articles every week and include them with story summaries in their notebooks.

I provided students with a guideline for each media journal entry including a copy of a news story, a summary I wrote, and my analysis of the story. Instructions provided the students a minimum length, component requirements, deadlines, and course points possible for each assignment. The assignment, usually worth an equivalent in points of 20 percent of the total course grade, would ensure that students read news content and thought critically about it.

Students responded to the news journal with mixed reviews. At first, students looked at the search for news stories that were appropriate to the course's topic as tedious, but eventually grew to be more routinely informed as they built a habit of regular news consumption. Student evaluations of the course focused on the tedium of picking out news articles on a consistent basis when they already had a textbook. But when students would display a particular area of interest the journals provided an excellent opportunity.

For students who were interested in the ways politics is communicated through mass media, it provided an opportunity to go beyond the regular sources and seek out media-specific journals like *Adweek*. When I could identify interest, I had the opportunity to steer students in a specific direction. Fort Hays State University provides five concentrations within its political science degree: legal studies, political management, public administration, international studies, and global public policy. Students enrolled in each concentration provided the instructor an opportunity to steer them toward particular media: political management students interested in a practical politics career, for instance, could take content from *Campaigns and Elections* magazine. International studies students could focus on *Foreign Affairs*, the *Economist*, or other global-focused entities. Legal studies majors had the option to focus just on legal reporting, and any major could tailor their reading to the specific area relevant to political science they chose. The educator must balance out the specific interest of students with the necessary breadth of content to encourage students to connect a significant amount of news with course content. Students must have a variety of news sources and topics to ensure the blogging assignment meshes with the course content.

From 2004 to 2006, the first years I taught political communication, I had students maintain their journals in the spiral notebook as described above. Blogging was becoming more common, though. The best blogs at the time seemed to be much like an online version of the media journals I had assigned my students: starting with a piece of journalistic source material, authors would link to the material, summarize it quickly, and then provide analysis. The similarities to the paper media journals were direct. After introducing the idea of moving the journal to a blog in 2006, students responded with concern and I maintained the paper journal.

Integrating blogging into coursework

When I returned to teaching Political Communication in 2009, the online blogging tools had reached a point of ubiquity and student familiarity was such that I believed it was possible and reasonable to move the media journal online into a blogging environment. Concerned that students would bristle at publicly available blogs on free tools like Blogger.com or Wordpress. com, I wanted to be sure students had a controlled environment where their content would not be available to the general public. The university was part of a pilot program with the Epsilen global learning system during that semester, which included a built-in blogging system. Epsilen was designed to be an improvement over other online course management systems such as Blackboard. Epsilen included a stable student profile that would connect classes throughout a college career and assessment mechanisms beyond that of other online course managers. The built-in blog (along with a dedicated private wiki) was a significant advantage for Epsilen.

Some students reacted with trepidation when we first discussed the idea about blogging instead of a media journal. Two students mentioned they did not want to have spam posted in the comments section of blogs or have strangers critiquing their writing. The idea of comments that could be seen by more people than just the professor was a shock to students used to receiving only feedback from their instructor. The concern on the part of the students was the primary reason to delay any implementation of a blog. Controlling the environment in which the students interacted was an important consideration. Simply requiring students to create publicly accessible Blogger or Wordpress accounts would be too distracting to advance the pedagogical goals of blogging. Reading regular news content and writing about the content allows achievement of the written communication and reading skills that have been explicit in the assignment from the very beginning.

Some students could come into the class with an interest in blogging, and therefore might already have a blog or want theirs to survive past the class' end. Since learning-management systems operate on a class-by-class basis, when a class semester ends the blog is erased. A student who wanted to blog beyond and after the class would then want a stable blog outside the course sandbox blog. There was no need to restrict them to the Epsilen environment if they should want to create a blog that they would extend posting in after the semester ended. I allowed students to establish their own blog on an external site if they desired and post links to their external blog within the course blog.

Epsilen provided an opportunity to keep the student blogs within a "sandbox," web slang for a controlled and private environment. As such it provided the best location to begin the student blog project. Every student had a unique login and the course was only accessible to participants enrolled in the class or allowed by the educator. The Epsilen system further offered a grading interface that allowed learning outcome-specific feedback to be given to students. Finally, students would not have to make photocopies of articles for their media journals as they could simply include links to the news stories they sourced in the blog. Assessing the technology interest and capacity of students is an important activity because students forced into unfamiliar and difficult technology runs the risk of disengaging students and undermining learning goals for the class.

Development of the course blog

The 2009 academic year began three consecutive semesters of blogging in political communication courses. Initial implementation had some challenges. Showing students how to set up their own blog accounts took time, even for tech-savvy students. Some were concerned with using existing email addresses to sign up for external blog sites as well. Initially, some mistakenly thought they had to contribute to existing blogs, such as academic blog "The Monkey Cage." Clarification of expectations and a significant set of examples of desired blog content was important.

Students desired specific directions regarding the news stories that the educator considered legitimate to include. Despite having instructions on the types of sources to use, they also wanted to use sources outside the realm described. Students looked to use blog entries from opinion or personal sites, even though instructions were given guiding students to *New York Times* articles since Epsilen integrated content from the New York Times Knowledge Network into the learning management system.

Beyond the initial technical and logistical issues, the transition to a blog for the media journal was relatively smooth. The most significant change to the administration of the media journal was in mandating periodic deadlines for the blogs. When I assigned students a media journal previously, I had those students turn the journals in one week before the end of the course and graded the entirety of the journals at that time. Written comments on student evaluations from the pre-2006 era complained about the single opportunity to turn in journals so students did not have the opportunity to get early feedback and improve their performance on later submissions.

Taking the feedback into account I distributed the journal due dates out over six 3-week periods. By creating multiple grading points for the blog, I allowed for three vital issues to be resolved: (1) students would have to stay connected to events throughout the course of the semester instead of waiting until close to the deadline and only reviewing articles from a few days or weeks prior to the submission deadlines, (2) students would get more feedback early to provide opportunities to improve throughout the semester, and (3) to allow students to use the value-added features of blogging: comments.

The value of user-created content is not solely embodied by the idea that students can produce their own original or derivative content. Online social capital theories point to the freedom to interact between users as one of the elements of Web 2.0 that allows online citizens to overcome the social capital barriers postulated by Putnam. The atomization of society that Putnam postulates can, according to online social capital theorists, finds its solution in online community-building. In fact, social media theorists believe that the interactive elements of Web 2.0 technology actually build social capital.[17]

Blogging as a means towards learning ends

An apt analogy for comments on a course blog is that of the connection between textbook learning and class discussion. Almost any class will require some form of textbook learning, with the educator assigning regular readings to the students. Student learning requires not just reading but doing something active with that learning. The professor can engage with the students during class meetings, but when students take communal charge of their readings and engage with each other in class discussion, active learning occurs and students receive the best learning outcomes.[18]

When faculty members integrate new technology into their classrooms, they must be cognizant of the pedagogical goals they wish to achieve. Blogging is not a panacea, and has its limitations. Blogs will not replace textbooks, exams, or discussions, but can integrate conversation and community better in course materials. Technology is a tool, and the intent behind its use is as important as the things the tool allows one to accomplish. Use of a technological tool without a sense of what the tool's use will achieve is a poor use of that technology. Simply using technology for technology's sake is worthless and will do nothing other than add more work to a faculty member's load and frustrate students who cannot see the value in the technology's use. Kentaro Toyama advises faculty to not simply add technology. Instead, Tomaya suggests proactively developing a plan to merge class goals and technology. Toyama notes that adding technology for its own sake confuses students, slows down the pace of teaching, disengages students, and cloud the educator's decision-making by encouraging unproductive false shortcuts to education.[19]

Discussing current events is not simply something that educators do to kill time during a class meeting. Critically thinking about newsworthy political events and discussing those topics with fellow students helps build a sense of community both in the sense of social capital and a reinforcing relationship among students that encourages active learning. Discussion is a vital tool in the political science classroom, even when students are blogging outside of class time.

The ability to make comments on blog posts takes the in-class current events discussion and expands it to the out-of-classroom assignment. Students may engage with one another during a class meeting, but their learning tends to be very solitary when not in the classroom. By introducing blogging with a comments section, we see the opportunity to not only encourage students to learn how to develop content, but to incentivize them to interact with each other in and out of the classroom.

Students do respond to incentives. Simply providing an opportunity to comment is not enough, as I learned the first semester of the blogging assignment. Focused mostly on building content-creation skills among the students, I graded only the blog posts. During class meetings I would encourage students to post comments on one another's blogs and placed comments on the student blogs myself. However, since I did not set a minimum number of comments requirement or allot points for posting comments, students participated very little. Comment participation was limited to one post where a student accused another student of blogging over the same article that the commenting student referenced in an earlier blog. I would be sure to add comment points and evaluation in later iterations of the blog assignment.

Blogging evolves in the classroom

Starting in 2010, I began requiring not only a minimum number of blog entries per week, at two, but also at least one comment on another student's blog. Since we know that incentivizing students with course credit can promote participation, making points available for both blog posts and comments ensured students would have to participate if they wanted to succeed in the course.

Another introduction for the 2010 Spring and Fall semester courses was a complete rubric for scoring the blog and comment content. The rubric is available at this book's companion website. A maximum of 25 points is available for each graded blog section. I divided the course into separate sections, so that students would blog, receive feedback, and use the feedback to improve subsequent entries. In each section I began with the desire to have the blogging assignment make up roughly one-fifth of total available course points and the same points value as one exam. Furthermore, the six deadline points for students in the Fall 2009 class was deemed as too many by the students, with deadlines coming too frequently. Therefore I decided to reduce the number of blog grading deadlines to four for the 2010 Spring and Fall semester courses. With each grading point, students were eligible to earn up to 25 points for their blog. The 25 points were distributed among five different criteria of five points each. The five criteria were: (a) number of blog posts, (b) spelling and grammar, (c) links to articles, (d) summaries of the articles, and (e) proper analysis of the article.

Students needed to submit five blog posts and comments for each graded section, so the first criteria simply recorded the number of blog posts students contributed. Every student started with five points for spelling and grammar and lost a point for each error. Each story needed a link to verify the article, making for five points. I asked students to make each blog post at least two paragraphs in length, to ensure they fully summarized the articles they linked, which completed another five points. Finally, the student was expected to critically analyze the article, worth up to another five points.

Another change came with moving the blog to another course management system. The pilot opportunity with Epsilen ended at the end of the Fall 2009 semester and fortunately the university's Blackboard package now included a native blogging system. Students responded with dissatisfaction about Epsilen, because they had familiarity with Blackboard and did not want to learn a brand new system.

The return to Blackboard meant students only had to learn the blog. While using Epsilen, students not only had to adapt to blogging but had to learn a new course management system. The rubric provided better guidance, and as a result student response to the blog was overwhelmingly positive. Beyond the simple element of student satisfaction, an interesting cultural change occurred during the class. As students blogged more and interacted both in and out of the class meeting room, a culture began to emerge where students would enter the class discussing things they had shared on one another's blogs. Rather than discussing relationships or sports when they first arrived in class before the scheduled time of class starting, the students were discussing news they had posted and discussed on their blogs. The conversation among students was on-topic and consistent with their blog posts, taking the in-class culture and spreading it to the students' out-of-class preparation. As a byproduct, student discussions were more frequent and on-topic during the course. While a statistical test comparing test scores with previous classes was not possible due to small n problems in some sections and an evolving deadline/points system for blog submissions, students appeared more interconnected with each other when they were required to create content and interact outside of the classroom, as they would bring their blog and comments discussion into the classroom.

Blogging served as a reinforcing tool for another pedagogical goal I had for the Political Communication class: media literacy. The online news environment has created opportunities for students to create their own content. Understanding the criteria that journalists and bloggers use to determine what is newsworthy and what is not is an important part of teaching students about the news collection process. Students developed the content under the supervision and guidance of an educator who wanted them to learn best practices in journalism and communication. The blog also created a teachable opportunity where there is no extant standard to judge the integrity and quality of an online news source. The students had to read news sources and make judgements about the quality of a news story for their blog posts, making them critical consumers of the news.

Media literacy is more important than ever, and as news consumption is paramount to teaching, the blog assignment extends an opportunity to teach students about source bias, differentiation, and a new reality in media. The new reality is the difference between creating one's own online outlet and existing journalistic entities with the traditional practices and safeguards that accompany preinternet journalism that have since moved online. As every blog post needed to include analysis, there was an expectation that students would put thought into how news stories were presented, who wrote the article, any bias that emerged, and any incomplete information communicated in the article. Students became increasingly critical the more they had to think about who was presenting the information they referenced in their blog posts.

Further, at least one student decided after the class to continue posting on his or her blog. While the student began his or her blog on Blackboard, when the class ended and the blog interface disappeared the student notified me via email that he or she had continued to write regularly and had created his or her own blog on a free site. The blogging exercise thus encouraged students to write outside of class as well as in the class environment.

Expanding blogging into a general education course

The success of blogging in the Political Communication class offered a chance to reflect on pedagogical goals that I had sought to achieve with the media journal/blog. The desired learning outcomes of media literacy, writing skills, critical thinking, community-building, and intentional use of technology are all connected in the blogging assignment for students in the course. But Political Communication was not the only course in which those skills were valid ones to impart. As the Fall 2010 course was coming to a close, my rotation teaching Political Communication was ending until 2012 and my teaching responsibilities moved to other courses.

While blogging was a reasonable assignment in other courses such as Political Parties or Lobbying, the connection between a media journal and those courses was not as direct. The topics of the courses would further limit the ability of students to find enough materials to regularly and consistently blog. However, there was one course that could find a wide enough base of news articles and still achieve the learning goals set forth in the Political Communication class: Introductory American Government.

For the Spring of 2011, I piloted a course blog for a 50-student American Government course section. Because the class was larger than any Political Communication class I had ever taught, I knew the grading of a blog as well as the participation in it would require much more time than previous classes, so I was unsure if the blog would translate as well. Additionally, the students in a Political Communication class were mostly political science majors with some prior interest in current affairs and politics. General education students would come in with skills less-developed and a lower level of interest in politics and current issues. However, the class seemed like an excellent opportunity to begin building those skills.

The blog requirements were the same for the American Government class except I did not provide points for comments, only for the actual blog posts. The blog was a pilot, and as I was unsure as to student reaction about the blog I made it worth 50 points of extra credit over the course of a full semester with 800 total points available. The reaction from students was also positive, though not to the same extent seen in the Political Communication course. Student conversations were not as frequently about things shared and discussed on blogs, but student participation was strong and the level of content presented in the blogs were satisfactory enough to support integrating the blog and comments into my American Government courses beginning in Fall 2011.

Next steps

As blogging has found a place within the curriculum as a method of both building online social capital and building necessary skills for students in my political science classes, the Web 2.0 advance continues. Blogging has been effective in achieving numerous pedagogical goals but other tools are available to integrate into the classroom. Kohen's work shows the value of social network sites such as Twitter, while Towner and Munoz show Facebook has become a more popular tool to integrate into coursework.[20]

But other Web 2.0 tools still lag behind written content. Blogging and other word-based systems are effective, but only focus on written skills. Podcasting and web video are underused in curricular and co-curricular forms. The barriers to entry for blogging are minimal for any student with access to a computer, but prohibitive additional costs have kept students from making audio and video. Headset microphones and webcams have not been terribly expensive, but added expense does create a barrier to entry for students to participate in audio or video production. Now most students have smartphones and/or notebook computers with built-in cameras and microphones. Freeware for audio and video editing is also available, which provides an opportunity to allow students an option to create video blogs or podcasts instead of blogs.

Future political communication students will have the option, as a result of the omnipresent technology, to not only provide commentary on news but engage in civic journalism using smartphones, iPads, or other video technology. I will encourage students to collaborate on podcasts as well, to provide the equivalent of political commentary radio shows.

Concluding observations

Technology in the classroom is just like any tool, and it must be used accordingly. To use technology for its maximum benefit, the technology must be used with a purpose by the educator. Student learning goals are important to keep in mind while designing technological elements for the classroom. The author's personal experience with blogging has shown that students who are empowered with technology to create their own content and build community produce learning on a higher, more engaged level.

Social capital builds among students through the course blog. The class comes together as a community over the posts and comments shared among students. Student communication is more class-focused, and students engage in a dialogue about the news that reinforces the learning designed into the course. Outside of class time and even after the course's end, students may continue to discuss one another's off-site blogs and maintain connections well beyond their course work.

There are limitations to the integration of blogging into the classroom. A broad subject matter is important to ensure students can find enough sources to adequately produce enough blog posts. Specific guidelines and regularized feedback is necessary to ensure students learn the vernacular of blogging and connect their work directly to the class goals. With the proper guidance, though, students can in effect create their own supplemental text in a class through blogging.

Advice for the educator

The trial-and-error process that has marked the development of blogging assignments for my political science classes provides a number of things to bear in mind when adopting blogging in one's own courses. Any faculty member starting a blogging assignment should first think about what learning outcomes they wish to achieve and build the blog and scores around those goals. One should make sure that the subject matter is broad enough to ensure enough news content that all students can find materials of their own without overlap. Assessing the blog and comments together makes sure that students will look at one another's posts, comments, and build the online social capital that makes blogging a unique learning opportunity.

Faculty should not simply create a blog and expect students to participate. Assessing technological acumen and targeting the blog around that ability is vital. Educators should also be careful not to be silent, but be a regular participant in the blog. Students not only build community among themselves, but with the educator as well. Finally, the educator should take care to avoid making a single due date for the blogs, to allow for improvement over the course of the semester.

[Please see the companion website for the book. Details are listed on the back cover of the book.]

Notes

1 I would like to thank my wife Andrea, whose love, patience, and devotion are limitless. Thanks also to the mentors and friends at FHSU who have inspired and motivated me: Chris Crawford, Rob Scott, Mark Bannister, and Larry Gould.

2 Michael Prince, "Does Active Learning Work? A Review of the Research," *Journal of Engineering Education*, 93 (2007): 223–31.

3 Heather Havenstein, "Wiki becomes Textbook in Boston College Classroom." Accessed October 2, 2011, from www.computerworld.com/s/article/9030802/ Wiki_becomes_textbook_in_Boston_College_classroom?taxonomyId=16&ints rc=hm_topic.

4 Ari Kohen, "Teaching Political Theory with Twitter: The Pedagogy of Social Networking" in *Teaching Politics beyond the Book: Film, Texts, and New Media in the Classroom*, ed. Robert Glover and Daniel Tagliarina, this volume (New York, NY: Continuum, 2012).

5 Steve Yuen and Hsiu-Ting Hung, "Exploring the Use of Social Networking in the College Classroom," Paper presented at the Society for Information Technology & Teacher Education (2010).

6 Suanna Davis, *Teaching College English*. Accessed September 20, 2011, from www.teachingcollegeenglish.com/2011/02/25/what-web-2-0-looks-like-in-my-classroom/.

7 Roger Burrows and David Beer, "Sociology and, of and in Web 2.0: Some Initial Considerations," *Sociological Research Online* (2007). Accesssed March 2, 2012, from www.socresonline.org.uk/12/5/17.html.

8 Robert Putnam, *Bowling Alone: The Collapse and Revival of American Community* (New York: Simon & Schuster, 2000).

9 Cecilia Orphan, "The American Democracy Project," *American Association of State Colleges and Universities* (2003). Retrieved September 19, 2011, from www.aascu.org/programs/ADP/.

10 Leonard Springer, Mary Stanne, and Samuel S. Donovan, "Effects of Small-Group Learning on Undergraduates in Science, Mathematics, Engineering, and Technology: A Meta-Analysis," *Review of Educational Research* 69 (1999): 21–51.

11 Molly Wasko and Samer Faraj, "Why should I Share? Examining Social Capital and Knowledge Contribution in Electronic Networks of Practice," *MIS Quarterly: Management Information Systems* 29 (2005): 35–57.

12 Evgeny Mozorov, *The Net Delusion* (New York: Public Affairs, 2011).

13 Barry Wellman, Anabel Haase, James Witte, and Keith Hampton, "Does the Internet Increase, Decrease, or Supplement Social Capital?: Social Networks, Participation, and Community Commitment," *American Behavioral Scientist* 45 (2001): 436–55.

14 Ulrike R. A. Pfeil and Panayiotis Zaphiris, "Age Differences in Online Social Networking—A Study of User Profiles and the Social Capital Divide among Teenagers and Older Users in MySpace," *Computers in Human Behavior* 25 (2009): 643–54.

15 Gert Jan Hofstede, Leon de Caluwe, and Vincent Peters, "Why Simulation Games Work-In Search of the Active Substance: A Synthesis," *Simulation and Gaming* 41 (2010): 824–43.

16 Charles Steinfield, Joan M. DiMicco, Nicole B. Ellison, and Cliff Lampe, "The Benefits of Facebook 'Friends': Social capital and College Students' Use of Online Social Network Sites," *Journal of Computer-Mediated Communication* 12 (2007): 1.

17 Charles Steinfield, Joan M. DiMicco, Nicole B. Ellison, and Cliff Lampe, "Bowling Online: Social Networking and Social Capital within the Organization," Paper presented at the Communication and Technology, University Park, PA (2009).

18 J. Patrick McCarthy and Liam Anderson, "Active Learning Techniques versus Traditional Teaching Styles: Two Experiments from History and Political Science," *Innovative Higher Education* 24 (2000): 279–94; Beverly Cameron, *Active Learning: Green Guide No. 2* (Halifax, NS: Society for Teaching and Learning in Higher Education, 2009).

19 Kentaro Toyama, "There Are No Technology Shortcuts to Good Education." Retrieved January 10, 2012, from https://edutechdebate.org/ict-in-schools/ther e-are-no-technology-shortcuts-to-good-education/.

20 Terri Towner and Caroline Munoz, "Opening Facebook: How to Use Facebook in the College Classroom," Paper presented at the *Society for Information Technology & Teacher Education International Conference*, Charleston, SC, USA (2009); Ari Kohen, "Teaching Political Theory with Twitter: The Pedagogy of Social Networking," in *Teaching Politics beyond the Book: Film, Texts, and New Media in the Classroom*, ed. Robert Glover and Daniel Tagliarina, this volume (New York: Continuum, 2012).

CHAPTER SIXTEEN

Podcasting and the teaching of politics and international relations

Simon Lightfoot[1]

This chapter explores the use of podcasts in the learning and teaching of Politics and International Relations (IR). Podcasts and other types of new media are said to appeal to the current generation of students (often described as "digital natives" or the "Google generation"). They are also said to help students engage with the ever-changing nature of politics as a discipline of study. This chapter highlights two main types of podcasts: those produced by faculty/students within an institution and those available externally through the internet. The chapter first explores the pedagogical issues associated with the use of all podcasts in the teaching of politics including student learning styles, access to technology, and ease of usage.

The second section highlights examples of good practice for using podcast material in lectures/seminars. These range from allowing students to engage with contemporary debates by listening to the different views around key contemporary arguments (the impact of the Arab Spring on EU politics) to engaging with the views of key thinkers direct via recordings. Podcasts and related new media such as using YouTube videos, therefore allow students to hear the authentic voice of the speaker and get a sense of the excitement and passion of politics (downloading Meet the Press or Face the Nation for example or accessing lectures from other universities via iTunesU).

Finally, and perhaps most importantly, the chapter outlines staff and student attitudes to the use of podcasts within learning and teaching based upon a small pilot research project carried out at the University of Leeds.[2]

Do students want university material on their iPods or their iPhones? Are staff using the material for pedagogical purposes or because it is the newish thing? Do students know how to engage with this type of material in their politics courses?

Digital natives and podcasting

Blended learning in its simplest form means combining classroom and virtual learning opportunities together for the same course.[3] This type of approach encourages staff to experiment with educational technology to augment existing classroom-based practice. One such technology that is said to have a positive impact upon the learning experience of students in Higher Education (HE) is podcasting.[4] The pedagogical research that exists outlines a number of key benefits of using podcasts in HE. The first is that they are said to appeal to the "iPod generation" or "digital natives."[5] The current generation of students have grown up with mobile technologies to access the internet and are extremely competent in using technology in their social lives. Crucially for those of us working in universities, this generation of students expect technology to be used in the university classroom as they have grown up with it in grade school and high school.

The main appeal of podcasts is that they are said to give students control over when and where they access learning materials and to crucially, "re-attend" class if necessary. The use of podcasts to facilitate "re-attending" fits with the strong pedagogical evidence that the traditional 50-minute lecture is not consistent with good learning practice.[6] Therefore podcasts are particularly valuable for those who may have struggled to pick up everything the first time around, thereby enhancing the learning experience and any subsequent reading. While we may have been able to record lectures in the past, the big difference now is that the technology makes doing it relatively easy and simple. The types of technology available are also so portable that they could be used to allow students to listen to the discussions in another seminar group. A strong argument in favor of this use of podcasts is that students can make use of those moments of "deadtime" (for instance the commute into college, the workout at the gym) to catch up on class/engage with key arguments via podcast, thereby allowing class time to be used to discuss, debate, and critique. Some colleagues have found that students questioned the showing of videos in class arguing that they took up valuable class time and that they could watch them outside the classroom, with new research suggesting that utilizing podcasts in this way can actually improve student performance.[7] Another argument in favor of using podcasts is that, given the increasing diversity of the student body, podcasts appeal to students with different learning styles, some of which may not be favored by traditional teaching methods in HE.

A major pedagogical issue associated with podcasting is that listening to podcasts could be a passive learning activity.[8] We also have to consider whether students can access the material as there are clearly access issues for students with some disabilities. Some writing on podcasting depicts undergraduate students as having access to technologically sophisticated kit (laptops, iPhones, or iPads, etc.) coupled with a willingness to use this kit in an academic environment. This chapter is not the place to engage in a full debate about whether or not current students are digital natives. However, it is clear that being familiar with certain aspects of technology such as video games, mobile phones, or Facebook does not always equate to familiarity with the types of technology used in universities. It is often assumed that because the current generation of students have grown up with Information Technology (IT) and are familiar with Web 2.0 tools in their social lives, they would be clear on how to use these tools in HE. However, evidence suggests that the use of Web 2.0 tools needs to be properly explained to students, as should all aspects of HE.[9] In particular, as Thornton[10] argues, we need to work with the Google generation to ensure they use the web in an efficient and critical way, while also ensuring they feel comfortable in a library with real books (the laboratory for social scientists). The extent to which podcasts can be used in the teaching of politics and IR (P&IR) is the question to which this chapter now turns.

Podcasting pedagogy and teaching P&IR

As the above section has shown, there are many perceived advantages of using podcasts in teaching and learning. This section looks at the discipline of P&IR to identify any subject-specific issues associated with the use of podcasts. For a teacher of P&IR, podcasts have an additional benefit in that as a medium for the conduct of politics, podcasting is particularly pronounced. This is especially true in the United States where podcasts are produced by major American universities, think-tanks, and other research institutes, alongside the media and commercial organizations.[11]

A common complaint from some staff is that in P&IR students need to "read" for their degrees and that innovation such as podcasts undermine a core skill of obtaining a degree. A major pedagogical argument against the use of podcasts and other Web 2.0 tools is that it is reinforcing a fixation with the internet by students. Stokes and Martin argue that "electronic access (to materials) often leads exclusively to the Internet,"[12] thereby reinforcing the "bad" habits increasingly identified in the literature.[13] It does appear that there is a general concern that Web 2.0 technologies and in particular search engines such as Google promote the "lowest common denominator" information available, which damages the undergraduate research processes.[14] Evidence from recent P&IR essays I have moderated suggests that for some current students a Google search is all they consider "researching" an essay to involve. Reference lists of websites, working papers, all accessed via the internet and engaged with in an uncritical manner are not uncommon.

Providing podcasts, especially via an RSS feed where the student needs to do nothing more than to sign up to the feed to get podcasts sent to them, can exacerbate the problem. An additional problem with podcasts is that they may contribute to a false sense that students can do well in a module without doing the necessary reading. It is clear that the lowest common denominator effect is visible even without Web 2.0 technologies. For example, Stokes and Martin argue that provision of reading lists may obviate the need for students to search for materials, therefore failing to acquire key research skills.[15] While it is a cliché to focus on student use of Wikipedia as a major information source, the recent article by Brown[16] highlights the issues in using Wikipedia—he found that Wikipedia has extremely frequent errors, especially for less prominent or up-to-date topics.

Ensuring critical engagement with Web 2.0 technologies is a crucial skill to develop, obviously for HE but also the world of work. Therefore, the emphasis should be on *how* the teacher uses this kind of technology to promote deeper engagement with the literature.[17] Thornton goes on to argue that academic staff need to counter this with strategies to enhance the information literacy skills of students to ensure they are able to make the most of the information opportunities open to them.[18] It is also clear that, used well, e-learning can foster critical thinking skills in P&IR students.[19]

In Politics and IR, podcasts can provide an additional role in allowing students to keep abreast of contemporary developments/cutting edge research. Podcasts in P&IR can help students and teachers overcome one of the challenges associated with studying P&IR; that of currency. As a discipline we are forced to confront the problem that our subject changes more quickly than many other subjects.[20] An obvious example for teachers of British politics can be found on May 7, 2010, when the "the UK has one party governments" PowerPoint slide was no longer valid! A great example from my own area of teaching/research comes from early March 2011 when a group of postgraduate students giving a presentation about migration into the EU and the EU's policy responses, highlighted the role played by Libya in "policing" the EU's external border. In this context and given the Arab Spring one student then said, "Gaddafi isn't going anywhere fast as no one wants to get rid of him." In the class next week she had to admit that the UN-sanctioned military action made her statement very dated! Utilizing blogs, podcasts, and news articles produced by the EU itself, think-tanks, and journalists, the students were able to get a handle on events in Libya and other countries and how the EU was responding to them. This material mix of primary material, journalistic, and academic analysis was crucial, as the nature of academic publishing meant that this change in political circumstances was not reflected in articles published in journals at the time. Accessing these materials outside the classroom allowed more time for the group to critique events and analyse them using theoretical lens from European Studies in class.

This specific illustration provides an example of how technology such as podcasts can help students in P&IR. A wide range of material is produced as podcasts that students and teachers alike can utilize. A brief look at the range of material on the iTunes U site shows that, as a discipline, we have an amazing amount of material to tap into. Many of the podcasts available allow students excellent insights into debates in a foreign country. For example, non-US students might better understand the passions raised by, and the political context around, debates about US Foreign Policy under Obama by downloading and listening to Meet the Press or Face the Nation rather than reading reports or newspaper articles on the same topic. Despite these potential benefits, the use of podcasts in undergraduate courses is a relatively new phenomenon.[21] This next section identifies ways in which podcasts can be integrated into student courses in P&IR relatively easily.

Example of practice from the discipline and student views

The podcasting of lectures and seminars is the most common way to integrate podcasting into a relatively traditional approach to the use of podcasts on a P&IR course.[22] At the University of Leeds we have also experimented with what we termed "podule" or a seminar summary. In a review of the P&IR literature on podcasting, it is clear that podcasts were generally welcomed by students when staff employed them in their courses, as students appreciated the additional flexibility they provided, with the crucial aspect being the ability to go over the points and issues raised again. When pressed though, student surveys suggest that students prefer shorter, additional materials of between 5 and 15 minutes long. The study I was involved in produced "podules" that were of 5–10 minutes listening duration and produced by the lecturer to summarize the key point of the lecture, highlight a particular issue, or act as a guide to further reading or listening. The podules acted as a means for the lecturer to do several things such as relate the lecture to the reading material, relate the student-produced podcasts which summarized the classroom discussion back to the lecture, and, where necessary, correct the students on points of fact. He could also link topics together, including topics to be discussed in forthcoming lectures, which aimed to enhance the sense of continuity across the courses.

Seminars in HE encourage students to examine the issues surrounding a topic in more depth. However, students only get to hear the views of students in their own seminar group. Asking students to summarize seminars can be seen as them participating in their own learning or active learning. As one student noted in our study at Leeds, podcasts allowed for "a deepening and widening of debate and discussion beyond confines of seminar." Another noted that the student podcast would be "something different, to see what other opinions are in other seminar groups." Our study asked students to produce their own podcast summaries of the seminar discussion. This was advertised in the course guide and asked students to summarize their discussions in seminars, which enabled students to gain an insight into the seminar discussions in other groups. This chapter argues that the student act of producing podcasts can concentrate student minds on refining presentation and broader academic skills as well as enhancing their general learning experience at university.

However, student feedback also welcomes the availability of whole lectures. The sense is that students would prefer easier to digest summaries or guides but welcome the provision of additional material, so are therefore satisfied with the whole lecture. Furthermore systematic research needs to be conducted into this area but like many things in HE, the preference is likely to rest with the individual student. The other issue was that students value the traditional contact time with academic staff. Once concerns regarding podcasts and contact time were assuaged, students saw the benefits of well-structured materials, supporting the blended learning approach adopted by many universities.

Obstacles and challenges from the student perspective

There are other pedagogical issues associated with podcasting, involving access to resources and attendance. Not all students have laptops or iPhones and are therefore reliant upon the technology available on campus, on cluster opening times, etc., while other students may have the resources to buy the latest technology and therefore obtain an advantage over fellow students. Students have found the technology easy to use but we need to be aware that not all students have access to laptops or mobile phones, so there is an issue of access here. However, evidence suggests that the majority of students listened to podcasts on either their own personal computers or the ones on campus. One said that "I set up an RSS feed, and then listened on my laptop. I don't own an MP3 player, and I think it's important to remember that not all students do, though I appreciate the majority probably do!" The fact that most students do listen to podcasts on campus allows us to make a tentative conclusion that podcasting does not appear to privilege certain groups of students over others.

There is also the fear that utilizing technologies, such as podcasts, to provide a full lecture for example, may result in declining student attendance. Supporters of podcasts argue that students are more likely to go to class because they are not worried about writing everything down and this position is supported by a variety of sources.[23] In our study, there was also no discernible dip in attendance associated with the use of the podcasts. In relation to attendance, we found some interesting comments. Students like going to lectures and therefore do not want them to be replaced by podcasts. "Leeds is not a virtual university" as one said. Another said that "I quite like going to lectures. I like listening to people. I like going to seminars as well. I like talking to people and interacting with people. Actually, I like getting a broad range of resources. It makes it more interesting if you've got a range of stuff to go to."

Pedagogical advantages

One of the perceived advantages of podcasts is that they appeal to students with different learning styles, in particular auditory learners, those who learn best through hearing things. There is considerable research that highlights that students have different learning styles and that some of these learning styles are not normally favored by traditional teaching methods in HE. Fox and Ronkowski[24] have demonstrated that students in political science courses use a variety of learning styles and they suggested that instructors expand their teaching methods to address a broader number of learning styles.

An issue here is whether podcasting would change the balance between auditory learning and reading. In the traditional P&IR course the emphasis tends be on the latter and there is perhaps a danger that the use of podcasting may raise the false expectation that a student can do well in a course without doing the necessary reading. However, in terms of delivery as was shown earlier, there is considerable evidence to suggest that the traditional 50-minute lecture is far from the most effective way of making use of the average student's attention span. Yet despite this evidence lectures remain probably the most common way to deliver material in the HE sector around the world. Lecturers support these findings with anecdotal evidence of "losing" the students in the second half of the lecture.

As this chapter has shown, providing podcasts allows students with a means of "re-attending" the lecture in their own time, repeating the material as many times as they wish to revise those points that may have been delivered at a point beyond their attention span. In P&IR we can be dealing with theoretical debates over the role of the state or describing in detail the powers of the Supreme Court. Subsequent lectures may then build on this knowledge. If a student does not "get it" they might be at a considerable disadvantage vis-à-vis their peers. If we look at the idea of threshold concepts as applied to EU Politics, we can see that teaching a complex and constantly evolving polity as the European Union is a challenge. One author has adopted a threshold concept approach, which is "essentially a 'less is more' approach that chooses to work with a few 'founding' concepts, and identifies a 'road map' for independent learning of broader but essentially inter-connected issues of the discipline."[25] Podcasts are not as deep as this approach but still enable students to keep listening until they "get" the particular concept. One student in our study said that she would like podcasts because "sometimes if the lecture goes too fast you can't actually take down the main point, so if you can pause it and play it whenever you want to then you can kind of note down the points at your own pace." Another student said that he found the week 8 podcast "so helpful for recapping and filling in which bits I missed in the lecture." It also appeared to stimulate discussion outside the classroom, with students telling us that they "found that because of the ease of access to the audio files on the blog many more students had been through a large percent of the material which led to discussions in the bar and outside of classes."

Podcasting lectures or seminars gives these students a choice about where and when to access digital material and how many times they wish to repeat it. Our findings support this literature. Student opinion was summarized by these statements: "I think I would listen to it for example on the way into uni or into town . . . so I can kill two birds with one stone;" or "there is plenty of time to kill on the bus . . . time's not an excuse not to listen particularly to a 5 minute summary." One interesting comment was that producing podcasts helped one student consider how the spoken word can differ from written text in putting across meaning appropriate for academia—you have to think very carefully about which words you use or if you use your voice intonation to imply, say irony.

Therefore podcasting is an excellent way for students to engage with the views of key activists/thinkers direct via recordings. Listening to where the emphasis is placed in a sentence can really bring a point to life. A key example is the "I have a dream" speech by Martin Luther King. Reading a text of this seminal speech has very little of the power of hearing the recording. Asking students to listen to a talk by John Kenneth Galbraith on the Great Depression can be used to encourage them to compare events then to events in 2012. Of course this can be done via reading, but podcasts, recordings and vodcasts (podcasts which add the medium of video) just give an alternative way to engage students in our subject. In a level one introductory course on globalization I teach we use podcasts and videos as part of the "compulsory reading" section. Therefore I might mention the views of Jospeh Stiglitz in the lecture and then direct the students to his writings on globalization plus his podcasts and videos of his speeches (many available on YouTube[26]). Another example would be the work of Manuel Castells and his arguments about the network society and identity. This topic can be challenging for students, yet by offering access to both his written work and podcasts of interviews he has given I expand the opportunities for students "to get it."

Podcasts can also bring other academics to different groups of students. Hearing Bertrand Russell outline his political philosophy via the BBC archive brings a great thinker into the orbit of students. The technology also potentially opens up academia. It is impractical for me to take my students to Oxford to hear Ngaire Woods talk to her researchers about the economic crisis, yet they can download podcast interviews from the Oxford website to gain her views. This point is crucial when it comes to academics in different countries. Ensuring all students have access to the views and debates taking place at say Harvard or Yale or Stanford is good for the academy. Podcasts, as a means of asynchronous communication, allow access without the problems associated with time zones, etc. In P&IR podcasts can also provide students with access to the voices of different people. A colleague in environment used podcasts to allow his students to hear the life stories of croft farmers in Northern Scotland, while it would be easy to see how podcasts based on interviews with a researcher could allow students to hear the experiences of both farmers and factory workers in, say, Ghana. This would not only provide students with access to the authentic voice of an individual experiencing what the students are studying, it would also expose students to the research carried out by their lecturers.

Here the chapter provides an example of how podcasts could be used. In week 2 of the course Prof. Ralph created a podule on the US Constitution and Foreign Policy, with a particular focus on the role of Congress and the Courts. Four students then summarized the discussions that took place in their respective seminar groups, which examined the following questions:

- Why were the founding fathers so keen on the "separation of powers doctrine?" How does the constitution separate foreign policy powers?

- What structural problems prevent Congress from taking the lead in foreign affairs?

- How has the "Israel lobby managed to divert US foreign policy . . . from what the American national interest would otherwise suggest?"[27]

Prof. Ralph then responded to their comments, developing some of them and guiding the students to further reading. As such this podule provides not only a revision function but also a way of expanding upon debates raised in the lecture and linking this course to previous courses.

In our study, some students found podules useful. One student stated that "listening to the Podcasts was useful as a kind of consolidation of some of the more complex issues which arose in the course." Another argued that directing students to a "wide variety of sources help[ed] us to deepen our understanding of the discourses surrounding American foreign policy." Of particular interest is the student-produced podcasts as they provide an innovative and interesting way for students to demonstrate achievement of the courses aims, especially develop a reasoned argument, synthesize relevant information, exercise critical judgement, and communicate effectively and fluently. The pedagogical benefit is that students are encouraged to critically assess digital media in the same way we encourage students to assess printed material and it reaffirms what the students heard from the lecturer and read in the literature, but it does so through a different media, thereby enhancing the teaching and learning experience for the student.

According to one student these podcasts "made learning the subject more of a proactive and engaging process, rather than simply absorbing designated information for analysis, by forcing us to discuss and decide what was worth focusing on, what wasn't and what else we could find that had been overlooked etc." Another argued that the process "not only deepened my understanding of American foreign policy but bolstered my ability to articulate the arguments involved." Students thought podcasts could be made part of a structured learning process. Some asked for podules to be available prior to the lecture ". . . it's the habit you could get into, just listening to the summary before you walk into the seminar or walking on your way to the lecture. If you listen to the summary first you know what he is going to talk about and then you could maybe take it in a bit better."

In our study, there was a small core of students who were very enthusiastic about the use of student-produced podcasts. However, the majority seemed rather apathetic and did not (despite the reminders) really engage with the project, except in relation to lecturer-produced material. This suggests that unless the course is totally restructured around the use of podcasting there will be little uptake of the additional material provided.[28] Making this compulsory and assessing it would obviously increase student engagement with this practice but it does raise pedagogical issues if we use assessment to encourage engagement with tasks. We used podcasts in our study as a means of providing "extra" material and material in a different way to students. Links to podcasts were integrated into the course by embedding the links within the reading lists and lecture slides. There was some evidence of student uptake of this resource in student essays, particularly on the subject of the "Israel Lobby" and US foreign policy—a debate that was in part conducted through audio programs that were podcasted.

Staff views

Supporters of podcasting and other Web 2.0 technologies stress the peda-gogical benefits of using such technologies. However, it is also important to consider the impact on staff who engage with these types of technologies. The first issue is that of time. A common fear of some academic staff is that using new technologies will take too long to master or that preparing the content will take too long, all of which means that they are reluctant to utilize the tools.[29] There is also a sense that materials produced needed high production standards, although student feedback is that they quite like the authentic recording (as long as they can hear it, the recording does not need to be that polished). Newton also highlights that developments are often led by the enthusiasm of individuals with little extrinsic reward struc-ture to encourage these innovations. Therefore, we need to consider how much time does it take to podcast a lecture summary or provide 10-minute feedback via podcast on an assessment? It was clear that for a 10-minute podule to be of value to the students it had to be carefully thought out and scripted meaning extra staff work. Having said that, it is hard to formally record time savings as our pilots suggests that, for example, time employed in providing extra materials such as podcasts may be subsequently "saved" in terms of a lower number of student emails/face-to-face meetings. This is supported by other research, such as Taylor,[30] who argues that he saw a fall in the number of clarification emails and student queries in office hours after he started podcasting his lectures.

The next issue is about access to the technology and how technologically competent should you be as a P&IR academic? The examples provided in this chapter are those attempted by academic staff and not learning tech-nologists. Having used it myself I can testify that the technology is simple and easy to use. However, there is a serious point about access to technol-ogy. Audio recordings can be possible via an iPhone, but should it be part of my job to buy such equipment? At Leeds, we had to buy a digital recorder for £100 to record the podules and lectures. Laptops are not provided by the school for staff to utilize in recording and editing material, although the university has licenses for the major packages utilized in these pilots, such as Audacity and Articulate. The big question of how easy it would be to go beyond the enthusiasm of individuals and encourage all staff to engage in the use of such technologies is more complex. This is crucial as one interest-ing finding was that the use of technology in one course leads to demands from students for its use in other courses. These demands might not be compatible with staff expertise or even the course's aim and objectives, therefore student expectations have to be managed carefully.

Linked to the question of technology is the issue of infrastructure. It is vital that the university has a sufficiently robust IT infrastructure and also that it can cope with the podcasts. We found that storage was the main issue. In the early stages of the project the university had an upload limit of 1 MB which prevented staff from uploading even just PowerPoint slides with photos. Even today I cannot upload a podcast of a 50-minute lecture because it is over 70 MB. To ensure it is available to students via the Virtual Learning Environment we need to stream it via Windows media player. The podules had some technical advantages due to their small size. The need for training and support at an institutional level is therefore crucial if you wish to develop real blended learning.

What effect does the use of podcasting in any form have on the staff–student relationship? Undoubtedly the most popular innovations were those that involved staff communicating to students either in the form of feedback or lectures/summaries. These innovations were also clearly linked to a specific module so the student could identify the benefits of engaging with the technology. In contrast, students were not clear about the benefits of listening to student summaries of seminar discussions or listening to the research seminars. In part this may not be an issue connected to the use of technology per se; it may be more that students are not trained to see the benefits of peer learning or to appreciate the wider connections between research seminars and their modules. Students also argued that their efforts in terms of making podcasts needed to be recognized in terms of marks on the module. Other Web 2.0 case studies in politics highlight how marks can be attributed. Trudeau outlines how marks could be attributed to discussion board posts based on the quality of the posts.[31] These types of posts have clear academic merit as the student is writing their opinion, which can then be assessed.[32]

Getting students to follow the US health care debate or presidential primaries could be aided by using Web 2.0 technologies to support the use of podcasts produced by the various interested parties. One group of students could be asked to listen to, say, the podcasts about Newt Gingrich and one group Mitt Romney. They could then report back to class every week thereby kick-starting a debate. The educator could then use these to bring out the themes of the course, which might be around negative campaigning, the ideological base(s) of the Republican Party, the functioning of the primary system. They also allow students to hear the authentic voice of the speaker and get a sense of the excitement and passion of politics.

Another option would be to share access to guest lectures from other universities via iTunesU. The issue of being able to re-attend is again crucial here. Students who for whatever reason cannot attend the guest lecture or missed crucial points can re-attend via a podcast. Providing access via iTunesU also allows academic work to be made available to informed members of the public. Providing access to extra material via podcasts (if used properly) can enrich the students' educational experience. Technology therefore does little to change the relationship between educator and student and does not depersonalize learning, if used well.[33] Indeed, it can be argued that podcasting is an excellent way of getting deeper access to the educator. With the podules, the "extra" information provided by the educator encouraged a deeper level of interaction with the educator in office hours, etc.[34]

Conclusions

The benefits of using podcasts for P&IR staff are to some extent the same as those in other disciplines. However, in P&IR we can use them in a whole variety of ways that not all disciplines can. We can use them to allow students to re-visit lectures and even listen to the discussions in another seminar group. We can use them to introduce students to a wider range of subject relevant materials which students can then listen to in their own time (at the gym, on the bus) allowing class time to be used to discuss, debate, and critique. Podcasts are clearly not a panacea for the time-starved research academic but they can help to increase the engagement of students in your subject and in particular with your research area. Podcasts can be a quick and easy way for P&IR students to access material that is not available in books and journals, helping them stay abreast of current developments. Podcasting can also convey to students the exciting nature of our subject areas (and by definition our research) and be used to open up research to students. However, podcasts have to be used carefully. They can encourage and reinforce bad habits in students by encouraging a fixation on the internet and technology. If providing extra material we need to educate students how to engage with this material in a critical way, just like we do when it comes to reading. Students have to see the link between the podcasts and their studies—just using technology for the sake of using technology is not worth the time or effort it involves for faculty.[35]

Podcasting on its own will not alter the tension between teaching and research excellence. But there is evidence that a new generation of academics that are both more technologically talented and more interested in the scholarship of teaching and learning are taking positions of responsibility within the profession.[36] There are obvious issues with the use of any technology and it should not be used uncritically (although it strikes me that we use a whole variety of so-called traditional teaching methods in a relatively uncritical way, especially in light of the pedagogical evidence). Therefore, the view taken in this chapter is not to shoot the messenger: "podcasting is merely a means of delivering teaching material, it does not dictate the nature of that material or its educational value."[37]

Notes

1 This chapter builds upon work previously published as Simon Lightfoot, Jason Ralph, and Naomi Head, "Engaging Students beyond the Classroom: The Experience of a Podcasting Project," in *Enhancing Learning in the Social Sciences* 1(3) (2009) from www.heacademy.ac.uk/assets/documents/subjects/csap/eliss/1–3-Lightfoot.pdf. This material is used with both the editors' and my co-authors' permission. It also draws on Simon Lightfoot, "Recent Innovations in Learning and Teaching in Politics and IR: Can Podcasts Enhance the Student Experience?" in *IT in Action. Stimulating Quality Learning at Social Science Students*, ed. Gabriela Pleschova (Leverkusen: Barbara Budrich Publishers, 2010): 17–27. I would like to thank the editors Rob Glover and Daniel Tagliarina for their extremely helpful comments on an earlier draft.

2 This project involved engaging P&IR students at the Universities of Leeds on an American Foreign Policy course. We produced podcasts of whole lectures, "podules" which were brief lecturer-produced lecture summaries and student-produced seminar summaries.

3 Randy Garrison and Norman Vaughan, *Blended Learning in Higher Education: Framework, Principles and Guidelines* (San Francisco, CA: Jossey-Bass, 2008).

4 Gilly Salmon and Palitha Edirisingha, *Podcasting for Learning in Universities* (Milton Keynes: Open University Press, 2008); Andrew Middleton, "Beyond Podcasting: Creative Approaches to Designing Educational Audio," *ALT-J* 17 (2009): 143–55; David Middleton, "Putting the Learning into E-learning," *European Political Science* 9 (2010): 5–12; Steven Lonn and Stephanie Teasley, "Podcasting in Higher Education: What are the Implications for Teaching and Learning?" *The Internet and Higher Education* 12 (2009): 88–92; Steven Draper and Joe Maguire, "Exploring Podcasting as Part of Campus-Based Teaching," *Practice and Evidence of the Scholarship of Teaching and Learning in Higher Education* 12 (2007): 43–65.

5 Marc Prensky, "Digital Natives, Digital Immigrants," *On the Horizon* 9 (2001): 1–6; Marc Prensky, "Listen to the Natives," *Educational Leadership* 63 (2005/6): 8–13.

6 Rob Phillips, "Challenging the Primacy of Lectures: The Dissonance between Theory and Practice in University Teaching," *Journal of University Teaching & Learning Practice* 2 (2005): 1–12.

7 Dani McKinney, Jennifer Dyck, and Elise Luber, "iTunes University and the Classroom: Can Podcasts Replace Professors?" *Computers & Education* 52 (2009): 617–23.

8 Salmon and Edirisingha, *Podcasting for Learning in Universities*.

9 Stephen Walls, John V. Kucsera, Joshua Walker, Taylor Acee, Nate McVaugh, and Daniel Robinson, "Podcasting in Education: Are Students as Ready and Eager as we Think they Are?" *Computers & Education* 54 (2010): 371–8.

10 Stephen Thornton, "Lessons from America: Teaching Politics with the Google Generation," *EliSS* 1 (2009) from www.heacademy.ac.uk/assets/documents/subjects/csap/eliss/1–3-Thornton.pdf.

11 Carie Windham, "Confessions of a Podcast Junkie," *EDUCAUSE Review* 42 (2007): 50–65.

12 Peter Stokes and Lindsey Martin, "Reading Lists: A Study of Tutor and Student Perceptions, Expectations and Realities," *Studies in Higher Education* 33 (2008): 113–25, 114.

13 See Richard Barberio, "The One-Armed Bandit Syndrome: Overuse of the Internet in Student Research Projects," *PS: Political Science & Politics* 37 (2004): 307–11; Andrew Robinson and Karen Schlegl, "Student Use of the Internet for Research Projects: A Problem? Our Problem? What can we Do about it?" *PS: Political Science & Politics* 38 (2005): 311–15; Wayne Selcher, "Use of Internet Sources in International Studies Teaching and Research," *International Studies Perspectives* 6 (2005): 174–89.

14 David Dolowitz, "The Big E: How Electronic Information can be Fitted into the Academic Process," *Journal of Political Science Education* 3 (2007): 177–90; Stephen Thornton, "From 'Scuba Diving' to 'Jet Skiing'? Information Behavior, Political Science, and the Google Generation," *Journal of Political Science Education* 6 (2010): 353–68.

15 Stokes and Martin, "Reading Lists," 114.

16 Adam Brown, "Wikipedia as a Data Source for Political Scientists: Accuracy and Completeness of Coverage," *PS: Political Science & Politics* 44 (2011): 339–43.

17 Jason Ralph, Naomi Head, and Simon Lightfoot, "Pol-Casting: The Use of Podcasting in the Teaching and Learning of Politics and International Relations," *European Political Science* 9 (2010): 13–24.

18 Thornton, "Scuba Diving."

19 Cristina Leston-Bandeira, "Using E-Learning to Promote Critical Thinking in Politics," *Enhancing Learning in the Social Sciences* 1 (2009), from http://www.heacademy.ac.uk/assets/documents/subjects/csap/eliss/1-3-Leston-Bandeira.pdf

20 John Craig, "What is Different (if Anything) about Teaching Politics?" in *Teaching Politics and IR,* ed. Cathy Gormley Heenan and Simon Lightfoot (Basingstoke: Palgrave, 2012): 22–37.

21 Charli Carpenter and Daniel Drezner, "International Relations 2.0: The Implications of New Media for an Old Profession," *International Studies Perspectives* 11 (2010): 255–72.

22 Mark Roberts, "Adventures in Podcasting," *PS: Political Science & Politics* 41 (2008): 585–93; Zach Taylor, "Podcast Lectures as a Primary Teaching Technology: Results of a One-Year Trial," *Journal of Political Science Education* 5 (2009): 135–53.

23 See Roberts, "Adventures in Podcasting;" Taylor, "Podcast Lectures."

24 Richard Fox and Shirley Ronkowski, "*Learning Styles of Political Students,*" *PS: Political Science & Politics* 30 (1997): 732– 7.

25 Elena Korosteleva, "Threshold Concepts through Enactive Learning: How Effective Are they in the Study of European Politics?" *International Studies Perspectives* 11 (2010): 37–50.

26 It is important to note here that copyright issues are crucial. Some of the videos or podcasts I would like my students to listen to are subject to copyright and can disappear from vehicles such as YouTube, causing problems for the students.

27 John Mearsheimer and Stephen Walt, *The Israel Lobby and U.S. Foreign Policy* (New York: Farrar, Straus, and Giroux, 2007).

28 New research is questioning the benefits of podcasting, see Alanah Kazlauskas and Kathy Robinson, "Podcasts are Not for Everyone," *British Journal of Educational Technology* 43 (2012): 321–30.

29 Robert Newton, "Staff Attitudes to the Development and Delivery of E-learning," *New Library World* 104 (2003): 412–25.

30 Taylor, "Podcast Lectures."

31 Robert Trudeau, "Get them to Read, Get them to Talk: Using Discussion Forums to Enhance Student Learning," *Journal of Political Science Education* 1 (2005): 289–322.

32 Rosalee Clawson, Rebecca Deen, and Zoe M. Oxley, "Online Discussions across Three Universities: Student Participation and Pedagogy," *PS: Political Science & Politics* 35 (2002): 713–18.

33 Chik Collins, Brian Slocock, and Lucy Hughes, "The Role of a VLE in the Teaching of Political Concepts and Reasoning," *European Political Science* 5 (2006): 209–19.

34 This supports Taylor's (2009) findings.

35 See Middleton, "Put Learning into E-Learning."

36 Kerstin Hamann, Philip Pollock, and Bruce Wilson, "Who SoTLs Where? Publishing the Scholarship of Teaching and Learning in Political Science," *PS: Political Science & Politics* 42 (2009): 729–35.

37 Ralph, Head, and Lightfoot, "Polcasting," 16.

CONCLUSION

"Decontextualizing and Recontextualizing Alternative Texts in Teaching Politics"

Daniel Tagliarina

Much of the power from using alternative texts in the classroom comes from the ways in which these alternative texts can be employed to explore some political concept or phenomenon through decontextualizing the class material. That is, alternative texts provide examples of concepts as well as a different source for applying the concept being taught. Using alternative texts in this way requires students to transfer class learning to a new context—from class text to alternative text. Here, as is the case throughout this volume, alternative texts or nontraditional texts refer to a range of material that go beyond standard textbooks and academic articles. For example, when teaching Marx's labor theory of value and his theory of class conflict, I wrapped up a short lecture on the material by playing "A Little Priest" from *Sweeney Todd: The Demon Barber of Fleet Street*. Marx argues that labor produces all value in society, but that the property owners drain this value out of the workers through a process of exploitation. Marx also argues that this process of one class effectively feeding off of the work product of another class is indicative of the history of class conflict in all forms of society. In "A Little Priest," Sweeney Todd and Mrs. Lovett sing about cooking various individuals into pies and consuming them. In the song, these characters hypothesize about what various individuals would taste like based on their careers or social status. The song also describes social relations as man eating man. In a play on words, the characters also make reference to history being about those below serving those above, but now those above will serve those below. While Marx never explicitly used the metaphor of cannibalism to discuss his labor theory of value and class conflict, "A Little Priest" nevertheless resonates strongly with his critique of capitalist society.

What began with quizzical looks from the students soon turned into a thoughtful, prolonged discussion of the ways in which the song captures (and fails to capture) the nuances of Marx's argument. Not only did students engage fully in this discussion, including students who did not normally participate, but they also came up with connections beyond the ones that originally prompted the use of this material. Students discussed how the capitalist system (and the shortage of meat that was also referenced in the song) was driving people to destructive, dehumanizing practices. These students posited that, as the characters suggest, cannibalism is a new manifestation of extant class warfare produced by capitalistic exploitation. These students even ventured that the song is inherently antithetical to Marx's arguments that humans are much more than their jobs because the song argues that what a person would taste like is determined by the person's job. I was amazed at just how much the students pulled out of one song. A number of the student evaluations that semester mentioned how use of this clip helped them to better understand ideas that are difficult and which they were not previously inclined to consider thoroughly. While this is but one passing example, the chapters within this volume are full of similar stories. These moments, potentially fleeting, open up the potential for meaningful, lasting learning that students can carry forward beyond the classroom. Such rare moments are the intrinsic rewards for the dedicated educator. If not for the changed classroom dynamic that came through the introduction of part of *Sweeney Todd*, I doubt the discussion of Marx would have been so robust. The embrace of a nontraditional text allowed for students to think differently about a class text and evaluate what Marx's arguments really mean. This brief example, and the pedagogically beneficial class discussion it produced, is indicative of the spirit that animates the volume before you.

This volume, in many ways, is the story of gaps and curiosity. While looking for ways to anchor our own teaching with concrete examples, my co-editor and I noticed that there was a stunning lack of resources available to educators looking to use nontraditional resources. While there are an increasing number of academic outlets for discussing teaching and pedagogy, many of these provide limited space for reflection and pedagogical justification for various teaching experiments. The gaps we address with this volume emanate from this embryonic literature on the what, why, and how of nontraditional texts as a resource for teaching about politics. It was this search for a discussion of using nontraditional materials in teaching political subjects that spawned the idea that eventually matured into this volume. This curiosity, of how to integrate nontraditional texts and media within our classes, as well as the perplexing nature of why there was little evidence of a broader pedagogical conversation, led to the creation of the book before you. What we have presented is an attempt to both fill these gaps and to address educators' curiosity surrounding the use of nontraditional texts in the classroom.

In collecting the chapters contained here, it is our sincere hope to advance what we see as an emergent conversation. This conversation is an open and honest reflection on trying to reach students in an age increasingly marked by students' connections to technology and general disengagement from the "standard" learning experience. Moreover, the traditional model of PhD training focuses on research, while devoting inadequate (if any) time to instruction about *how* to teach. This model of preparing graduate students for careers as academics is further evidence of the missing conversation—another gap in reflections on pedagogy. The previous chapters offer an opening salvo in what is hopefully an ongoing discussion about teaching politics "beyond the book." What these chapters present are the authors' reflections on their own experiences trying to reach students through nontraditional means. These authors offer justifications for why they tried what they did, what worked, what did not, and how these ideas can be applied to courses across a variety of political subjects. These are not definitive statements on the entirety of pedagogical possibilities. These are conversation pieces meant to open a discourse, not to stultify thought. Consequently, the intent of this volume and its contributors is both modest and hopeful. This volume exists within the context of a developing discourse and a growing backlash against turning a blind eye to pedagogy within higher education.

Ideally, the proposals within these chapters have closed some gaps, encouraged reflection on pedagogy, and perhaps offered some useful suggestions for embracing curiosity within the classroom. If nothing else, maybe the chapters have encouraged you to try out an innovative idea you have had, or maybe sparked a new one while reading. Yet, we must stress, all of these changes and innovations must be done with a sense of exploration, but more importantly with a strong pedagogical justification. Using nontraditional texts and media is not about being the "hip" teacher, it is about reaching out to students in ways that will engage them while bettering the educational process. This volume presents a twofold offering. First, this volume is a guide for instructional use. Second, it functions as an impetus for pedagogical reflection about how to synthesize the new-and-different into the old-and-traditional in a way that allows us to do our jobs better as educators.

In many ways, teaching is an art, a craft to be practiced, altered, and perfected. Like the masters of old, we must constantly work on our art or risk becoming stilted in what we do. We live in a dynamic world—both regarding socio-cultural change and political change. Perhaps we should aim to have our pedagogy and curricula reflect this dynamism, not to pander to our students, but to reach out to them where they are and try to get them to engage in critical reflection. The power of nontraditional texts and media is notable for its ability to create destabilizing disequilibria all in an effort to advance critical thought and reflection. No longer allowed to be mere passive observers of the world around them, students will hopefully start to see how politics is involved in most aspects of their lives. This realm of critical reflection, through its destabilizing effects, allows students to evaluate their preconceived notions and the world around them. This reflection and critical evaluation is held up by most institutions of higher learning as the apex of academic learning.

One common model of thinking about the learning process is Bloom's Taxonomy. Originally created by Benjamin Bloom and other educational psychologists, his taxonomy has been updated by a new wave of educational psychologists to embrace the realities of the twenty-first century.[1] This revised taxonomy traces levels of learning and intellectual behavior from lower levels—remembering, understanding, and applying—of academic thought to higher levels—analyzing, evaluating, and creating. If we are to take Bloom's taxonomy as a guide for higher-ordered thinking, then getting students to move beyond merely understanding or explaining concepts toward thoughtful analysis of material is key to having these students embrace their full academic potential.

The integration of nontraditional materials is not just about promoting students' critical thinking, but also about how educators think about the teaching process. Asking, "what novels can help me explain this concept better," forces educators to think more closely about what a specific concept means and how it can be taught effectively. Reflecting on the craft of teaching can lead to deeper understanding for both the educator and the students.

I conclude here with one final example of using a nontraditional text to advance student comprehension of a political concept and also the justification used in picking effective examples. Machiavelli (in)famously counsels princes that there might come a time when they need to use cruelty, and to use it "well." Machiavelli's advice is that if a situation demands cruelty, princes should not shy away from it, but they should be careful to use cruelty sparingly. To this end, he suggests engaging in swift, brutal acts of violence to eliminate all threats at once, and then cease the use of cruelty while turning this use to the people's advantage. Moreover, he suggests that if a prince can maintain the appearance of a benevolent ruler who has the people's best interests in mind, he will have great success at maintaining power. While this advice is fairly straightforward, students sometimes struggle with the reasoning behind the specifics of Machiavelli's advice. To find an example that works to explain this advice, the educator must first fully comprehend Machiavelli's reasoning, what it is about the advice that becomes confusing for students, and what example can present the "why" of the reasoning without the confusion students face. Enter Michael Corleone. At the end of *The Godfather*, Michael embodies Machiavelli's advice. Newly installed as the head of the Corleone crime family, Michael gets his revenge when he orchestrates simultaneous hits on the heads of the other crime families, all while he maintains a benevolent appearance in church becoming the actual godfather to his nephew (whose father he also has killed in this purge). Michael, in truly Machiavellian fashion, swiftly takes revenge. He ends the threats to his "family's" business, and secures the safety of those loyal to him. He does not sully his reputation by appearing guilty. He eliminates his enemies and maintains the support of his people. This is the driving force behind Machiavelli's advice, and thus this example, in my experience, has helped students to understand the *why* of Machiavelli's advice. Again, an understanding of what students are supposed to get out of course material, and a willingness to use an alternative text to emphasis this point, allows for better student comprehension and broader class discussion. This example, and the volume as a whole, opens a pedagogical discussion that has far too often been missing in higher education. We feel that embracing alternative texts, when pedagogically relevant, can help improve teaching and learning in ways that textbooks and lectures simply cannot.

Note

1 David R. Krathwohl, "A Revision of Bloom's Taxonomy: An Overview," *Theory into Practice* 41 (2002): 212–18.

BIBLIOGRAPHY

50 Cent and Robert Greene, *The 50th Law*, 1st edn. New York: HarperStudio, 2009.

Abdullah, Ibrahim and Patrick Muana, "The Revolutionary United Front of Sierra Leone," in *African Guerrillas*, ed. C. Clapham, 172–93. Indianapolis: Indiana University Press, 1998.

Adhikari, Mohammed, "*Hotel Rwanda*: Too Much Heroism, Too Little History—Or Horror?" in *Black and White in Colour*, ed. V. Bickford-Smith and R. Mendelsohn, 279–99. London: Ohio University Press, 2007.

Adler, John and Draper Hill, *Doomed by Cartoon: How Cartoonist Thomas Nast and the New York Times Brought Down Boss Tweed and His Ring of Thieves*. Garden City, NY: Morgan James Publishing, 2008.

Adoni, Hanna, "The Functions of Mass Media in the Political Socialization of Adolescents," *Communication Research* 6 (1979): 84–106.

Ahn, Byongji, "The *West Wing* as an Inspiring Teacher," Paper presented at the *Annual Meeting of the American Political Science Association*. Boston, MA, 2002.

Ahrens, Jörn and Arno Meteling, *Comics and the City: Urban Space in Print, Picture and Sequence*. New York: Continuum, 2010.

Albanese, M. and S. Mitchell, "Problem Based Learning – A Review of Literature on its Outcomes and Implementation Issues," *Academic Medicine* 68 (1993): 52–81.

Alim, H. Samy, *Roc the Mic Right: The Language of Hip Hop Culture* [in English]. New York; London: Routledge, 2006.

Allen, Meg and Paul R. Brewer, "*Saturday Night Live* Goes to High School: Conducting and Advising a Political Science Fair Project," *PS: Political Science & Politics* 43 (2010): 767–71.

American Bible Society, *The Holy Bible, Contemporary English Version*. New York, NY: The American Bible Society, 1995.

American FactFinder, United States Census Bureau Publication. *Clarkston, Georgia* (2010).

Anderson, Ho Che, *King: A Comics Biography of Martin Luther King, Jr.* Seattle: Fantagraphics, 2005.

Anker, Elisabeth, "Subversion and Satire in the 'Manchurian Candidate': Aligning Political Context and Historical Reception," Paper presented at the *Annual Meeting of the American Political Science Association*, Philadelphia, PA, 2003.

Apple, Michael, "Whose Markets, Whose Knowledge," in *Sociology of Education: A Critical Reader*, ed. Alan R. Sadovnik, 177–94. New York: Routledge, 2007.

Asal, Victor and Elizabeth L. Blake, "Creating Simulations for Political Science Education," *Journal of Political Science Education* 2 (2006): 1–18.

Ashcroft, Bill, Gareth Griffiths, and Helen Tiffin, eds, *The Post-Colonial Studies Reader*. New York: Routledge Publishers, 1997.

Astin, Alexander W, *Achieving Educational Excellence*. San Francisco, CA: Jossey-Bass, 1985.

Axe, David and Matt Bors, *War is Boring: Bored Stiff, Scared to Death in the World's Worst War Zones*. New York: New American Library, 2010.

Ayoade, J. A. A, "Teaching African Politics: Problems and Prospects," *Teaching Political Science* 7 (1980): 389–406.

Bagdikian, Ben, *The New Media Monopoly*. Boston: Beacon Press, 2004.

Baker, Houston A., *Black Studies Rap, and the Academy. Black Literature and Culture*. Chicago, IL: University of Chicago Press, 1993.

Baker, Kyle, Reginald Hudlin, and Aaron McGruder. *Birth of a Nation: A Comic Novel*. New York: Crown, 2004.

Baker, Nancy, "The Trials of Teaching the Supreme Court," *PS: Political Science & Politics* 27 (1994): 253–5.

Baloche, Lynda A., *The Cooperative Classroom: Empowering Learning*. Upper Saddle River, NJ: Prentice Hall, 1998.

Banas, John, Norah Dunar, Dariela Rodriguez, and Shr-Jie Liu, "A Review of Humor in Educational Settings: Four Decades of Research," *Communication Education* 60 (2011): 115–44.

Barberio, Richard, "The One-Armed Bandit Syndrome: Overuse of the Internet in Student Research Projects," *PS: Political Science & Politics* 37 (2004): 307–11.

Barkley, Elizabeth F., *Student Engagement Techniques: A Handbook for College Faculty*. San Francisco, CA: Jossey-Bass, 2009.

Baum, Matthew A., "Soft News and Political Knowledge: Evidence of Absence or Absence of Evidence?" *Political Communication* 20 (2003): 173–90.

Baumgartner, Jody and Jonathan S. Morris, "The *Daily Show* Effect: Candidate Evaluations, Efficacy and American Youth," *American Political Research* 34 (2006): 341–67.

— "Jon Stewart Comes to Class: The Learning Effects of *America (The Book)* in Introduction to American Government Courses," *The Journal of Political Science Education* 4 (2008): 169–86.

Barakat, Halim, *Days of Dust*. Boulder, CO: Lynne Rienner Publishers, 1997.

Baranowski, Michael and Kimberly Weir, "Power and Politics in the Classroom: The Effect of Student Roles in Simulations," *Journal of Political Science Education* 6 (2010): 217–26.

Bayart, Jean Francois, *The State in Africa: The Politics of the Belly*. New York: Longman, 1993.

Bean, John C., *Engaging Ideas*. San Francisco, CA: Jossey-Bass, 2001.

Beavers, Staci, "*The West Wing* as a Pedagogical Tool," *PS: Political Science & Politics* 35 (2002): 213–16.

— "Getting Political Science in on the Joke: Using *The Daily Show* and Other Comedy to Teach Politics," *PS: Political Science & Politics* 44 (2011): 415–19.

Bechdel, Alison, *Fun Home: A Family Tragicomic*. New York: Mariner Books, 2007.

— *The Essential Dykes to Watch Out For*. New York: Houghton Mifflin, 2008.

Beckett, Paul, "Rubrics and Hubris: On the Teaching of African Politics," *Canadian Journal of African Studies/Revue Canadienne des Études Africaines* 15 (1981): 571–3.

Beighey, Catherine, and N. Prabha Unnitham, "Political Rap: The Music of Oppositional Resistance," *Sociological Focus* 39 (2006): 133–43.

Bellamy, Edward, *Looking Backward 2000–1887.* Oxford, UK: Oxford World Classics, 2009.

Bennett, W. Lance, *News: The Politics of Illusion*, 9th edn. New York: Longman, 2012.

Berk, Ronald A, "Multimedia Teaching with Video Clips: TV, Movies, YouTube, and MTVU in the College Classroom," *International Journal of Technology in Teaching and Learning* 5 (2009): 1–21.

Berlin, Isaiah, "Does Political Theory Still Exist?" in *Philosophy, Politics, and Society,* 2nd Series, ed. Peter Laslett and W. G. Runciman, 1–33. Oxford: Blackwell, 1962.

Bevevino, Mary M., Joan Dengel, and Kenneth Adams, "Constructivist Theory in the Classroom: Internalizing Concepts through Inquiry Learning," *The Clearing House* 72 (1999): 275–8.

Bihrle, Amy, Hiram H. Brownell, John A. Powelson, and Howard Gardner, "Comprehension of Humorous and Nonhumorous Materials by Left- and Right-Brain Damaged Patients," *Brain and Cognition* 5 (1986): 399–411.

Blount, Alma G., "Critical Reflection for Public Life: How Reflective Practice Helps Students become Politically Engaged," *Journal of Political Science Education* 2 (2006): 271–83.

Boak, Josh, "Enter the Era of the Super PACs," *Campaigns and Elections Magazine* (September 8, 2011).

Bonwell, Charles C. and James A. Eison, *Active Learning: Creating Excitement in the Classroom.* Washington, DC: George Washington University, 1991.

Bormann, Ernest G., Jolene Koester, and Janet Bennett, "Political Cartoons and Salient Rhetorical Fantasies: An Empirical Analysis of the '76 Presidential Campaign," *Communication Monographs* 45 (1978): 317–29.

Bourdieu, Pierre, *Outline of a Theory of Practice* [in Translation with revisions of *Esquisse d'une thÈorie de la pratique*]. Cambridge, UK; New York: Cambridge University Press, 1977.

Boutin, Paul, "All You Need to Know to Twitter," *New York Times* (May 6, 2009). Accessed March 24, 2012, from www.nytimes.com/2009/05/07/technology/ personaltech/07basics.html.

Bradley, Adam and Andrew DuBois, *The Anthology of Rap.* New Haven, CT: Yale University Press, 2010.

Bravender, Robin, "Colbert Gets Love at the FEC," *Politico.com* (December 1, 2011). Accessed December 10, 2011, from www.politico.com/news/ stories/1211/69536. html#ixzz1fxbpr9P5.

Breslau, Andrew, "Demonizing Quaddafy," *Africa Report* 32 (1987): 46–7.

Brewer, Paul R. and Xiaoxia Cao, "Late Night Comedy Shows as News Sources: What the Polls Say," in *Laughing Matters: Humor and American Politics in the Media Age*, ed. Jody C. Baumgartner and Jonathan S. Morris, 263–77. New York: Routledge, 2008.

British Broadcasting Company, "Zombie Attack: Leicester City Council Overrun by Undead," *BBC News* (June 18, 2011). Accessed September 1, 2011, from www.bbc.co. uk/news/uk-england-leicestershire-13823427.

Brock, Kathy and Beverly J. Cameron, "Enlivening Political Science Courses with Kolb's Learning Preference Model," *PS: Political Science & Politics* 32 (1999): 251–6.

Brown, Adam, "Wikipedia as a Data Source for Political Scientists: Accuracy and Completeness of Coverage," *PS: Political Science & Politics* 44 (2011): 339–43.

Brozek, Jason, "Boom! Thwak! Teaching War with Comics," Paper presented at the *Annual Meeting of the Midwest Political Science Association*, Chicago, IL, March 30–April 3, 2011.

Bryant, Jennings and Dolf Zillmann, "Using Humor to Promote Learning in the Classroom," *Journal of Children in Contemporary Society* 20 (1988): 49–78.

Bryant, Jennings, Paul W. Comisky, Jon S. Crane, and Dolf Zillmann, "Relationship between College Instructors' Use of Humor in the Classroom and Students' Evaluations of Their Instructors," *Journal of Educational Psychology* 72 (1980): 511–19.

Buckingham, David, "News Media, Political Socialization and Popular Citizenship: Towards a New Agenda," *Critical Studies in Mass Communication* 14 (1997): 344–66.

Buell, Jr., Emmett H., and Mike Maus, "Is the Pen Mightier than the Word? Editorial Cartoons and 1988 Presidential Nominating Politics," *PS: Political Science & Politics* 21 (1988): 847–58.

Buhle, Paul, Gary Dumm, and Harvey Pekar, *Students for a Democratic Society: A Graphic History*. New York: Hill and Wang, 2009.

Buhle, Paul, Mike Konopacki, and Howard Zinn, *A People's History of American Empire*. New York: Metropolitan Books, 2008.

Burden, Robert L., "Psychology in Education and Instruction," in *International Handbook of Psychology*, ed. K. Pawlik and M. R. Rosenweig, 466–78. London: Sage, 2000.

Burgess, Susan, "See Jane Rock: Using Popular Music in Political Science and Women's Studies Classes," Paper presented at the *Annual Meeting of the Western Political Science Association*, San Francisco, CA, April 21–24, 2010.

Burrows, Roger and David Beer, "Sociology and, of, and in Web 2.0: Some Initial Considerations," *Sociological Research Online* (2007). Accesssed March 2, 2012, from www.socresonline.org.uk/12/5/17.html.

California Democratic Party, "History of the Democratic Donkey" (2005). Accessed January 20, 2012, from www.kintera.org/site/pp.asp?c=fvLRK7O3E&b=33708.

Cameron, Beverly, *Active Learning: Green Guide No. 2*. Halifax, NS: Society for Teaching and Learning in Higher Education, 1999.

Cameron, Kenneth, *Africa on Film: Beyond Black and White*. New York: Continuum, 1994.

Cao, Xiaoxia, "Political Comedy Shows and Knowledge about Campaigns: The Moderating Effects of Age and Education," *Mass Communication and Society* 11 (2008): 43–61.

— "Hearing it from Jon Stewart: The Impact of *The Daily Show* on Public Attentiveness to Politics," *International Journal of Public Opinion Research* 22 (2010): 26–46.

Carpenter, Charli and Daniel Drezner, "International Relations 2.0: The Implications of New Media for an Old Profession," *International Studies Perspectives* 11 (2010): 255–72.

Carter, James Bucky, ed., *Building Literacy Connections with Graphic Novels: Page by Page, Panel by Panel*. Urbana, IL: National Council of Teachers of English, 2007.

Centellas, Miguel, "Pop Culture in the Classroom: *American Idol*, Karl Marx and Alexis de Tocqueville," *PS: Political Science & Politics* 43 (2010): 561–5.

Centers for Disease Control, "Zombie Preparedness." Accessed September 1, 2011, from www.cdc.gov/phpr/zombies.htm.

Chaffee, Steven H., Clifford I. Nass, and Seung-Mock Yang, "The Bridging Role of Television in Immigrant Political Socialization," *Human Communication Research* 17 (1990): 266–88.

Chandler, Ralph Clark and Barbara A. K. Adams, "Let's Go to the Movies! Using Film to Illustrate Basic Concepts in Public Administration," *Public Voices* 8 (1997): 9–26.

Chang, Jeff, *Can't Stop, Won't Stop: A History of the Hip-Hop Generation*, 1st edn. New York: St. Martin's Press, 2005.

Ciccariello-Maher, George, "Brechtian Hip Hop: Didactics and Self-Production in Post-Gangsta Political Mixtapes," *Journal of Black Studies* 36 (2005): 129–60.

Ciliotta-Rubery, Andrea, "A Crisis of Legitimacy: Shakespeare's *Richard II* and the Problems of Modern Executive Leadership," *The Journal of Political Science Education* 4 (2008): 131–48.

Clapham, Christopher. *Third World Politics: An Introduction*. Madison, WI: Wisconsin, 1985.

Clark, J. P. *All for the Oil*. Lagos, Nigeria: Malthouse Press, 2000.

Clawson, Rosalee, Rebecca Deen, and Zoe M. Oxley, "Online Discussions Across Three Universities: Student Participation and Pedagogy," *PS: Political Science & Politics* 35 (2002): 713–18.

Cochran, David Caroll, "Using *The Godfather* to Teach *The Prince*," Paper presented at the *Annual Meeting of the American Political Science Association*, Boston, MA, 2002.

Coffey, Daniel J., William J. Miller, and Derek Feuerstein, "Classroom as Reality: Demonstrating Campaign Effects through Live Simulation," *Journal of Political Science Education* 7 (2011): 14–33.

Collins, Chik, Brian Slocock, and Lucy Hughes, "The Role of a VLE in the Teaching of Political Concepts and Reasoning," *European Political Science* 5 (2006): 209–19.

Combs, James E., *Movies and Politics: The Dynamic Relationship*. New York: Garland Publishers, 1993.

Connell, Robert W., *The Child's Construction of Politics*. Melbourne: Melbourne University Press, 1971.

Conners, Joan L, "Visual Representations of the 2004 Presidential Campaign: Political Cartoons and Popular Culture References," *American Behavioral Scientist* 49 (2005): 479–87.

— "Popular Culture in Political Cartoons: Analyzing Cartoonist Approaches," *PS: Political Science & Politics* 40 (2007): 261–5.

— "Barack versus Hillary: Race, Gender, and Political Cartoon Imagery of the 2008 Presidential Primaries," *American Behavioral Scientist* 54 (2010): 298–312.

Conway, M. Margaret, Mikel L. Wyckoff, Eleanor Feldbaum, and David Ahern, "The News Media in Children's Political Socialization," *Public Opinion Quarterly* 45 (1981): 164–78.

Cook, Timothy, *Governing with the News: The News Media as a Political Institution*. Chicago, IL: University of Chicago Press, 1998.

Costello, Matthew J., *Secret Identity Crisis: Comic Books and the Unmasking of Cold War America*. New York: Continuum, 2009.

Coulson, Seana, *Semantic Leaps: Frame-Shifting and Conceptual Blending in Meaning Construction*. New York and Cambridge: Cambridge University Press, 2001.

Coulson, Seana and Christopher Lovett, "Handedness, Hemispheric Asymmetries, and Joke Comprehension," *Cognitive Brain Research* 19 (2004): 275–88.

Coulson, Seana and Marta Kutas, "Getting it: Human Event-Related Brain Response to Jokes in Good and Poor Comprehenders," *Neuroscience Letters* 316 (2001): 71–4.

Coulson, Seana and Robert Williams, "Hemispheric Asymmetries and Joke Comprehension," *Neuropsychologia* 43 (2005): 128–41.

Cowell-Meyers, Kimberly, "Teaching Politics Using *Antigone*," *PS: Political Science & Politics* 39 (2006): 347–9.

Craig, John, "What (if Anything) is Different about Teaching Politics?" in *Teaching Politics and IR*, ed. Cathy Gormley Heenan and Simon Lightfoot. Palgrave: Basingstoke, 2012.

Cranton, Patricia, *Understanding and Promoting Transformative Learning: A Guide for Educators of Adults*. San Francisco, CA: Jossey-Bass, 2006.

Cruse, Howard. *Stuck Rubber Baby: A Novel*. New York: Paradox Press, 1995.

Cunion, William, "Learn This," Paper presented at the *Annual APSA Teaching and Learning Conference*, Baltimore, MD, February 6–8, 2009.

Damrosch, David, ed., *The Longman Anthology of World Literature: The Twentieth Century*. New York: Pearson-Longman, 2004.

Dargis, Manhola, "*Blood Diamond* (2006): Diamonds and the Devil, Amid the Anguish of Africa," *New York Times* (December 8, 2006). Accessed January 26, 2011, from http://movies.nytimes.com/2006/12/08/movies/08diam.html.

Davis, Suanna, "Teaching College English." Accessed September 20, 2011, from www.teachingcollegeenglish.com/2011/02/25/what-web-2-0-looks-like-in-my-classroom/.

Deards, Helena, "Twitter First Off the Mark with Hudson Plane Crash Coverage," *World Editors Forum* (January 19, 2009). Accessed March 24, 2012, from www.editorsweblog.org/multimedia/2009/01/twitter_first_off_the_mark_with_hudson_p.php.

Deets, Stephen, "Wizarding in the Classroom: Teaching Harry Potters and Politics," *PS: Political Science & Politics* 42 (2009): 741–4.

Deibel, Terri L., "Teaching Foreign Policy with Memoirs," *International Studies Perspectives* 3 (2002): 128–38.

Delisle, Guy. *Pyongyang: A Journey in North Korea*. Montreal: Drawn and Quarterly, 2005.

— *Burma Chronicles*. Montreal: Drawn and Quarterly, 2010.

DeSousa, Michael A. and Martin J. Medhurst, M. J, "Political Cartoons and American Culture: Significant Symbols of Campaign 1980," *Studies in Visual Communication* 8 (1982): 84–97.

Detterman, Douglas K., "The von Restorff Effect and Induced Amnesia: Production by Manipulation of Sound Intensity," *Journal of Experimental Psychology: Human Learning and Memory* 104 (1975): 614–28.

Detterman, Douglas K. and Norman Ellis, "Determinants of Induced Amnesia in Short Term Memory," *Journal of Experimental Psychology* 95 (1972): 308–16.

Dolowitz, David, "The Big E: How Electronic Information can be Fitted into the Academic Process," *Journal of Political Science Education* 3 (2008): 177–90.

Donald, J. G, "Knowledge and the University Curriculum," *Higher Education* 15 (1986): 267–82.

Draper, Steven and Joe Maguire, "Exploring Podcasting as Part of Campus-Based Teaching," *Practice and Evidence of the Scholarship of Teaching and Learning in Higher Education* 12 (2007): 43–65.

Dreyer, David R., "Learning from Popular Culture: The 'Politics' of Competitive Reality Television Programs," *PS: Political Science & Politics* 44 (2011): 409–13.

Duncan, Randy and Matthew J. Smith, *The Power of Comics: History, Form and Culture*. New York: Continuum, 2009.

Durkheim, Emile, "What is Social Fact?" in *The Rules of Sociological Method*, ed. Steven Lukes, 50–9. New York: The Free Press, 1982 [1895].

Dyson, Michael Eric. *Know What I Mean?: Reflections on Hip-Hop*. New York: Basic Civitas Books, 2007.

Easton, David and Jack Dennis, *Children in the Political System*. Chicago, IL: University of Chicago Press, 1969.

Edwards, Janis L., *Political Cartoons in the 1988 Presidential Campaign: Image, Metaphor, and Narrative*. New York: Garland Publishing, 1997.

— "Running in the Shadows in Campaign 2000: Candidate Metaphors in Editorial Cartoons," *American Behavioral Scientist* 44 (2001): 2140–51.

— "Presidential Campaign Cartoons and Political Authenticity: Visual Reflections in 2008," in *The 2008 Presidential Campaign: A Communication Perspective*, ed. Robert E. Denton, Jr., 191–208. Lanham, NJ: Rowman & Littlefield Publishers, Inc., 2009.

Eisner, Will, *Comics and Sequential Art*. New York: Norton, 2008.

Erikson, Robert S. and Kent L. Tedin, *American Public Opinion*. New York: Pearson, 2005.

Feldman, Lauren and Dannagal G. Young, "Late-Night Comedy as a Gateway to Traditional News: An Analysis of Time Trends in News Attention among Late-Night Comedy Viewers during the 2004 Presidential Primaries," *Political Communication* 25 (2008): 401–22.

Feldman, Lauren, Anthony Leiserowitz, and Edward Maibach, "The Science of Satire: *The Daily Show* and *The Colbert Report* as Sources of Public Attention to Science and the Environment," in *The Stewart/Colbert Effect: Essays on the*

Real Impact of Fake News, ed. Amarnath Amarasingam, 25–46. Jefferson, NC: McFarland and Company, 2011.

Fido, directed by Andrew Currie. Vancouver, BC: Anagram Pictures, 2006.

Fisgón, El, *How to Succeed at Globalization: A Primer for Roadside Vendors*. New York: Metropolitan Books, 2004.

Fiske, Susan T., "Social Cognition and Social Perception," *Annual Review of Psychology* 44 (1993): 155–94.

Fleming, N., *VARK: A Guide to Learning Styles* (2001). Accessed March 24, 2012, from www.vark-learn.com/english/index.asp.

Fliter, John, "Incorporating a Sophisticated Supreme Court Simulation into an Undergraduate Constitutional Law Class," *Journal of Political Science Education* 5 (2009): 12–26.

Forman, Murray and Mark Anthony Neal. *That's the Joint!: The Hip-Hop Studies Reader*. New York: Routledge, 2004.

Fox, Richard L. and Shirley A. Ronkowski, "Learning Styles of Political Science Students," *PS: Political Science & Politics* 30 (1997): 732–7.

Frederking, Brian, "Simulations and Student Learning," *Journal of Political Science Education* 1 (2005): 385–93.

Freire, Paulo, *Pedagogy of the Oppressed*. New York: Continuum Publishing, 1970.

"Frequently Asked Questions," Twitter.com (November 4, 2008). Accessed March 26, 2012, from http://help.twitter.com/forums/10711/entries/13920.

Frewen, Paul, Elspeth M. Evans, Nicholas Maraj, David J. Dozois, and Kate Partridge, "Letting Go: Mindfulness and Negative Automatic Thinking," *Cognitive Therapy and Research* 32 (2008): 758–74.

Frey, Nancy and Douglas B. Fisher, *Teaching Visual Literacy: Using Comic Books, Graphic Novels, Anime, Cartoons, and More to Develop Comprehension and Thinking Skills*. Thousand Oaks, CA: Corwin Press, 2008.

Fukuyama, Francis, *The End of History and the Last Man*. New York: Free Press, 2006.

Gallagher, David F., "For the Mix Tape, a Digital Upgrade and Notoriety," *The New York Times* (January 30, 2003).

Gardner, Howard, *Frames of Mind: The Theory of Multiple Intelligences*. New York: Basic Books, 1983.

Garner, Randall L., "Humor in Pedagogy: How Ha-Ha Can Lead to Aha!" *College Teaching* 54 (2006): 177–9.

Garrison, Randy and Norman Vaughan, *Blended Learning in Higher Education: Framework, Principles and Guidelines*. San Francisco, CA: Jossey-Bass, 2008.

Gatrell, Vic., *City of Laughter: Sex and Satire in Eighteenth-Century London*. New York: Walker and Company, 2006.

Gershkoff, Amy R., "Multiple Methods, More Success: How to Help Students of All Learning Styles Succeed in Quantitative Political Analysis Courses," *PS: Political Science & Politics* 38 (2005): 299–304.

Gilroy, Henry, "Lumumba Assails Colonialism as Congo Is Freed," *New York Times* (July 1, 1960).

Glaser, Robert, "Education and Thinking: The Role of Knowledge," *American Psychologist* 39 (1984): 93–104.

Glazier, Rebecca, "Using Current Events to Design Classroom Simulations," Paper presented at the *APSA Teaching and Learning Conference*, San Jose, CA, February 22, 2008.

Goel, Vinod, and Raymond Dolan, "The Functional Anatomy of Humor: Segregating Cognitive and Affective Components," *Nature Neuroscience* 4 (2001): 237–8.

Gonick, Larry, *A Cartoon History of the United States*. New York: Collins Reference, 1991.

Goodman, Martha K., "Using Middle Eastern Literature and Allusions in Class," *VCCA Journal* 7 (1992): 14–25.

Gordon, April A. and Donald L. Gordon, eds, *Understanding Contemporary Africa*, 4th edn. Boulder, CO: Lynne Rienner Publishers, 2007.

Greenstein, Fred, *Children and Politics*. New Haven, CT: Yale University Press, 1965.

Gregg, Robert W., *International Relations on Film*. Boulder, CO: Lynne Reinner, 1998.

— "The Ten Best Films about International Relations," *World Policy Journal* 16 (1999): 129–34.

Griffin, Dustin, *Satire: A Critical Reintroduction*. Lexington: The University Press of Kentucky, 1994.

Groensteen, Thierry, *The System of Comics*. Jackson, MS: University Press of Mississippi, 2007.

Gurin, Patricia, "Expert Report of Patricia Gurin – Gratz Et Al V. Bollinger Et Al. No. 97–75321 (E.D. Mich.), Grutter Et Al. V. Bollinger Et Al., No. 97–75928 (E.D. Mich.)." Accessed December 9, 2009, from www.vpcomm.umich.edu/admissions/legal/expert/gurintoc.html.

Gurin, Patricia, Biren A. Nagda, and Gretchen A. Lopez, "The Benefits of Diversity in Education for Democratic Citizenship," *The Journal of Social Issues* 60 (2003): 17–34.

Gurin, Patricia, Eric L. Dey, Sylvia Hurtado, and Gerald Gurin, "The Benefits of Diversity in Higher Education: Theory and Impact on Educational Outcomes," *Harvard Educational Review* 72 (2002): 330–66.

Hamann, Kerstin, Philip Pollock, and Bruce Wilson, "Who SoTLs Where? Publishing the Scholarship of Teaching and Learning in Political Science," *PS: Political Science & Politics* 42 (2009): 729–35.

Haney, Patrick, "Learning about Foreign Policy at the Movies," in *The New International Studies Classroom: Active Teaching, Active Learning*, ed. J. S. Lantis, L. M. Kuzma, and J. Boehrer, 239–53. Boulder, CO: Lynne Reinner, 2000.

Hanndaford, Alex, Mike Pflanz, Hereward Holland, and Colin Freeman, "Why the Hero of *Hotel Rwanda* Fears for His People," *The Telegraph* (August 8, 2010). Accessed October 26, 2011, from www.telegraph.co.uk/news/world-news/africaandindianocean/rwanda/7931897/Why-the-hero-of-Hotel-Rwanda-fears-for-his-people.html.

Harkness, S. Suzan J., Mohamed Magid, Jameka Roberts, and Michael Richardson, "Crossing the Line? Freedom of Speech and Religious Sensibilities," *PS: Political Science & Politics* 40 (2007): 275–8.

Harrison, Anthony Kwame, *Hip Hop Underground: The Integrity and Ethics of Racial Identification* [in English]. Philadelphia, PA: Temple University Press, 2009.

Harsell, Dana Michael, "Wikis in the Classroom: Faculty and Student Perspectives," *Journal of Political Science Education* 6 (2010): 310–14.

Hastie, Reid, "Causes and Effects of Causal Attribution," *Journal of Personality and Social Psychology* 46 (1984): 44–56.

Hatfield, Charles, *Alternative Comics: An Emerging Literature*. Jackson, MS: University Press of Mississippi, 2005.

Havenstein, Heather, "Wiki becomes Textbook in Boston College Classroom" (August 15, 2007). Accessed October 2, 2011, from www.computerworld. com/s/article/9030802/Wiki_becomes_textbook_in_Boston_College_classroo m?taxonomyId=16&intsrc=hm_topic.

Hawley, Caroline, "A Country Torn by Conflict," *BBC Online* (January 12, 2004). Accessed March 25, 2004, from http://news.bbc.co.uk/1/hi/special_ report/1999/01/99/sierra_leone/251377.stm.

Hay, Margaret Jean, ed., *African Novels in the Classroom*. Boulder, CO: Lynne Rienner Publishers, 2000.

Head, Bessie. *When Rainclouds Gather*. Oxford: Heinemann, 1986.

Hedges, Chris. *War Is the Force that Gives Us Meaning*. New York: Anchor Books, 2002.

Heer, Jeet and Kent Worcester, eds, "Introduction," in *Arguing Comics: Literary Masters on a Popular Medium*, vii–xxiii. Jackson, MS: University Press of Mississippi, 2004.

— eds, *A Comics Studies Reader*. Jackson, MS: University Press of Mississippi, 2009.

Hennessey, Jonathan and Aaron McConnell, *The United States Constitution: A Graphic Adaptation*. New York: FSG, 2008.

Hertel, John Paul and Barbara Millis, *Using Simulations to Promote Learning in Higher Education*. Sterling: Stylus Publishing, 2002.

Hess, Robert D. and Judith V. Torney, *The Development of Political Attitudes in Children*. Chicago, IL: Aldine, 1967.

Hill, Alette, "The Carter Campaign in Retrospect: Decoding the Cartoons," in *Rhetorical Dimensions in Media: A Critical Casebook*, ed. Martin J. Medhurst and Thomas W. Benson, 182–203. Dubuque, IA: Kendall/Hunt, 1984.

Hill, Marc Lamont, *Beats, Rhymes, and Classroom Life: Hip-Hop Pedagogy and the Politics of Identity*. New York: Teachers College Press, 2009.

Hillman, Richard S., ed., *Understanding Contemporary Latin America*, 3rd edn. Boulder: Lynne Rienner Publishers, 2005.

Hillman, Richard S. and Thomas J. D'Agostino, eds, *Understanding the Contemporary Caribbean*. Boulder, CO: Lynne Rienner Publishing, 2003.

Hilton, James L. and Willam von Hippel, "Stereotypes," *Annual Review of Psychology* 47 (1996): 237–71.

Hobbes, Thomas, *Leviathan*. New York: Oxford University Press, 1998.

Hoffman, Lindsay H. and Dannagal G. Young, "Satire, Punch Lines, and the Nightly News: Untangling Media Effects on Political Participation," *Communication Research Reports* 28 (2011): 1–10.

Hofstede, Gert Jan, Leon de Caluwe, and Vincent Peters, "Why Simulation Games Work-In Search of the Active Substance: A Synthesis," *Simulation and Gaming* 41 (2010): 824–43.

Holzhauer, Debra, "Film and Foreign Policy: Examining the Impact of an Active Learning Strategy," Paper prepared for the *Annual Meeting of International Studies Association*, Montreal (March 2011).

Horton, John and Andrea T. Baumeister, *Literature and the Political Imagination*. London: Routledge, 1996.

Iommi, Lucrecia Garcia, "Let's Watch a Movie! Using Film and Film Theory to Teach Theories of International Politics from a Critical Perspective," Paper presented at the *Annual Meeting of the Midwest Political Science Association*, Chicago, IL, March 30–April 3, 2011.

Jacobson, Sid and Ernie Colón, *The 9/11 Report: A Graphic Adaptation*. New York: Hill and Wang, 2006.

— *After 9/11: America's War on Terror*. New York: Hill and Wang, 2008.

Jansen, Bas, "Tape Cassettes and Former Selves: How Mix Tapes Mediate Memories," in *Sound Souvenirs: Audio Technologies, Memory and Cultural Practices*, ed. Karin Bijsterveld and Jose van Dijck, 43–54. Amsterdam: Amsterdam University Press, 2009.

Java, Akshay, Xiaodan Song, Tim Finin, and Belle Tseng, "Why we Twitter: Understanding Microblogging Usage and Communities," Paper presented at the *Joint 9th WEBKDD and 1st SNA-KDD Workshop '07*, San Jose, CA, 2007.

Jay-Z, *Decoded*. New York: Spiegel & Grau, 2010.

Jennings, M. Kent and Richard G. Niemi, *The Political Character of Adolescence*. Princeton, NJ: Princeton University Press, 1974.

Jensen, Eric, *Teaching with the Brain in Mind*. Alexandria, VA: Association for Supervision and Curricular Development, 1998.

Joanette, Yves, Pierre Goulet, and Didier Hannequin, *Right Hemisphere and Verbal Communication*. New York: Springer Verlag, 1990.

Johnson, Isabel Simeral, "Cartoons," *The Public Opinion Quarterly* 1 (1937): 21–44.

Jones, Jeffrey P., *Entertaining Politics: Satire Television and Political Engagement*. Lahman, MD: Rowman & Littlefield, 2009.

Justice, Donald, *New and Selected Poems*. New York: Alfred A. Knopf, 2003.

Kaplan, Robert M. and Gregory C. Pascoe, "Humorous Lectures and Humorous Examples: Some Effects upon Comprehension Retention," *Journal of Educational Psychology* 69 (1977): 61–5.

Katin, Miriam, *We Are on our Own*. Montreal: Drawn and Quarterly, 2006.

Kaufman, D. M., "Problem Based Learning – Time to Step Back?" *Medical Education* 34 (2000): 504–11.

Kaup, Katherine Palmer, ed., *Understanding Contemporary Asia Pacific*. Boulder, CO: Lynne Rienner Publishers, 2007.

Kazlauskas, Alanah and Kathy Robinson, "Podcasts are Not for Everyone," *British Journal of Educational Technology* 43 (2012): 321–30.

Kellaris, James and Vincent Kline, "Humor and Ad Memorability: On the Contributions of Humor Expectancy, Relevancy, and Need for Humor," *Psychology and Marketing* 24 (2007): 497–509.

Kelly, Beverly M., *Reelpolitik: Political Ideologies in '30s and '40s Films*. Westport, CT: Praeger 1998.

— *Reelpolitik II: Political Ideologies in '50s and '60s Films*. Lanham, MD: Rowman & Littlefield, 2004.

Kennedy, Robert C., "On this Day: Nov. 17, 1874," *New York Times* (November 17, 2001). Accessed January 4, 2012, www.nytimes.com/learning/general/onthisday/harp/1107.html.

Kernell, Samuel, Gary C. Jacobson, and Thad Kousser, *The Logic of American Politics*, 5th edn. Washington, DC: C.Q. Press, 2012.

Kiasatpour, S. M., "The Internet and Film: Teaching Middle East Politics Interactively," *PS: Political Science & Politics* 32 (1999): 83–9.

Kitwana, Bakari, *The Hip Hop Generation: Young Blacks and the Crisis in African American Culture*, 1st edn. New York: Basic Civitas Books, 2002.

— *Why White Kids Love Hip-Hop: Wankstas, Wiggers, Wannabes, and the New Reality of Race in America*. New York: Basic Civitas Books, 2005.

Klein, Naomi, *Shock Doctrine: The Rise of Disaster Capitalism*. New York: Picador, 2007.

Kluender, Robert and Marta Kutas, "Subjacency as a Processing Phenomenon," *Language and Cognitive Processes* 8 (1993): 573–633.

Knight, Marisa and Mara Mather, "Reconciling Findings of Emotion-Induced Memory Enhancement and Impairment of Preceding Items," *Emotion* 9 (2011): 763–81.

Koeppel, Dan, *Banana: The Fate of the Fruit that Changed the World*. New York: The Penguin Group, 2009.

Koestler, Arthur, *The Act of Creation*. London: Hutchinson and Co., 1964.

Koetzle, W. M. and Thomas L. Brunell, "Lip-Reading, Draft-Dodging, and Perot-noia: Presidential Campaigns in Editorial Cartoons," *Harvard International Journal of Press/Politics* 1 (1996): 94–115.

Kolb, Alice Y. and David A. Kolb, "Learning Styles and Learning Spaces: Enhancing Experiential Learning in Higher Education," *Academy of Management Learning and Education* 4 (2005): 193–212.

Kolb, David A., *Experiential Learning: Experience as the Source of Learning and Development*. Upper Saddle River, NJ: Prentice-Hall, 1984.

Korobkin, Debra, "Humor in the Classroom: Considerations and Strategies," *College Teaching* 36 (1988): 154–8.

Korosteleva, Elena, "Threshold Concepts through Enactive Learning: How Effective Are they in the Study of European Politics?" *International Studies Perspectives* 11 (2010): 37–50.

Kortab, Joseph A. and Phillip Vannini, *Understanding Society through Popular Music*. Boca Raton, FL: Taylor & Francis, 2009.

Krathwohl, David R., "A Revision of Bloom's Taxonomy: An Overview," *Theory into Practice* 41 (2002): 212–18.

Kunzle, David, *The Early Comic Strip: Narrative Strips and Picture Stories in the European Broadsheet from c. 1450 to 1825*. Berkeley, CA: University of California Press, 1973.

Kuzma, Lynn M., and Patrick Haney, "And . . . Action! Using Film to Learn about Foreign Policy," *International Studies Perspectives* 2 (2001): 33–50.

La Fave, Lawrence, "Humor Judgments as a Function of Reference Groups and Identification Classes," in *The Psychology of Humor*, ed. Jeffrey H. Goldstein and Paul E. McGhee, 195–210. New York: Academic Press, 1972.

Lahiri, Jhumpa, *Interpreter of Maladies*. New York: Houghton Mifflin, 1999.

Lamb, Chris and Joseph E. Burns, "What's Wrong with this Picture? The Anti-Incumbent Bias of Cartoons During the '92 Campaign," Paper presented at the *Association for Education in Journalism and Mass Communication Southeast Colloquium*, Roanoke, VA, 1996.

Land of the Dead, directed by George A. Romero. Universal City, CA: Universal Pictures, 2005.

Landreville, Kristen, R., Lance Holbert, and Heather LaMarre, "The Influence of Late-Night TV Comedy Viewing on Political Talk: A Moderated-Mediation Model," *International Journal of Press/Politics* 15 (2010): 482–98.

Lang, Anthony F. and James M. Lang, "Between Theory and History: *The Remains of the Day* in the International Relations Classroom," *PS: Political Science & Politics* 31 (1998): 209–15.

Langer, Ellen J., "Rethinking the Role of Thought in Social Interaction," in Vol. 2 of *New Directions in Attribution Research*, ed. J. H. Harvey, W. Ickes, and R.F. Kidd, 36–58. Hillsdale, NJ: Lawrence Erlbaum Associates, 1978.

Langton, Kenneth P., *Political Socialization*. New York: Oxford University Press, 1969.

Lantis, Jeffrey S., Lynn M. Kuzma, and John Boehrer, eds, *The New International Studies Classroom: Active Teaching, Active Learning*. Boulder, CO: Lynne Reiner, 2000.

Lantis, Jeffrey S., Kent J. Kille, and Matthew Krain, "Active Learning across Borders: Lessons from an Interactive Workshop in Brazil," *International Studies Perspectives* 9 (2008): 411–29.

Lantis, Jeffrey S., Matthew Krain, and Kent J. Kille, "The State of Active Teaching and Learning Literature," in *The International Studies Compendium Project*, Volume X, edited by R. A. Denemark. Accessed March 26, 2012, from www.isacompendium.com/fragr_image/media/ISA_43

Larsson, L. Margareta, *Tips for Teaching Non-Native English Speaking Students*. Atlanta: Center for Teaching and Learning, Georgia State University, 2011.

Laz, Cheryl, "Science Fiction and Introductory Sociology: The *Handmaid* in the Classroom," *Teaching Sociology* 24 (1996): 54–63.

Leckrone, J. Wesley, "Hippies, Feminists and NeoCons: Learning about Politics through the Big Lebowski," Paper presented at the *Annual Meeting of the Midwest Political Science Association*, Chicago, IL, March 30–April 3, 2011.

Leira, Halvard, "Anarchy in the IR!" *International Studies Perspectives* 8 (2007): vi–vii.

Lemarchand, Rene, *The Dynamics of Violence in Central Africa*. Philadelphia, PA: Penn, 2009.

Lepler, Jessica, "Pictures of Panic: Constructing Hard Times in Words and Images," *Common-Place*, April 2010. Accessed January 20, 2012, from www.common-place.org/vol-10/no-03/lepler/.

Leston-Bandeira, Cristina, "Using E-Learning to Promote Critical Thinking in Politics," *Enhancing Learning in the Social Sciences* 1 (2009). Accessed March 24, 2012, from www.heacademy.ac.uk/assets/documents/subjects/csap/eliss/1-3-Leston-Bandeira.pdf.

Levy, Jack S., "The Causes of War and the Conditions of Peace," *Annual Review of Political Science* 1 (1998): 139–65.

Lieberfeld, Daniel, "Teaching about War through Film and Literature," *PS: Political Science & Politics* 40 (2007): 571–4.

Lightfoot, Simon, "Recent Innovations in Learning and Teaching in Politics and IR: Can Podcasts Enhance the Student Experience?" in *IT in Action: Stimulating Quality Learning at Undergraduate Students*, ed. Gabriela Pleschová, 17–27. Leverkusen: Bundrich UniPress, 2010.

Liles, Kevin and Samantha Marshall, *Make it Happen: The Hip Hop Generation Guide to Success*. New York: Atria Books, 2005.

Lindley, Dan, "What I Learned Since I Stopped Worrying and Studied the Movie: A Teaching Guide to Stanley Kubrick's *Dr. Strangelove*," *PS: Political Science & Politics* 34 (2001): 663–7.

Liptak, Adam, "Justices, 5–4 Reject Corporate Spending Limit," *New York Times* (January 21, 2010): A1.

Locke, John, *Second Treatise of Government*. Indianapolis, IN: Hackett Publishing Company, 1980.

Lonn, Steven and Stephanie Teasley, "Podcasting in Higher Education: What are the Implications for Teaching and Learning?" *The Internet and Higher Education* 12 (2009): 88–92.

Lovell, John, ed., *Insights from Film into Violence and Oppression: Shattered Dreams of the Good Life*. Westport, CT: Praeger, 1998.

Machiavelli, Nicolo, *The Prince*, trans. David Wooton. Indianapolis, IN: Hackett, 1995.

Mandami, Mahmood, *When Victims become Killers: Colonialism, Nativism, and the Genocide in Rwanda*. Princeton, NJ: Princeton University Press, 2001.

Manuel, Frank E. and Fritzie P. Manuel, *Utopian Thought in the Western World*. Cambridge, MA: Belknap/Harvard University Press, 1979.

Matelski, Marilyn J. and Nancy Lynch Street, eds, *War and Film in America: Historical and Critical Essays*. New York: McFarland and Co., 2003.

Mather, Mara, "Emotional Arousal and Memory Binding: An Object-Based Framework," *Perspectives on Psychological Science* 2 (2007): 33–52.

McAllister, Matthew P., Ian Gordon, and Edward H. Sewell, *Comics and Ideology*. New York: Peter Lang, 2001.

McCarthy, J. Patrick. and Liam Anderson ,"Active Learning Techniques versus Traditional Teaching Styles: Two Experiments from History and Political Science," *Innovative Higher Education* 24 (2000): 279–94.

McChesney, Robert, *Rich Media, Poor Democracy: Communication Politics in Dubious Times*. Paperback edition, with a new preface by the author. New York: The New Press, 2000.

McCloud, Scott, *Understanding Comics: The Invisible Art*. Northampton, MA: Tundra, 1993.

McKeachie, Wilbert James and Barabara K. Hofer, *Teaching Tips: Strategies, Research and Theory for College and University Teachers*. Lexington: Houghton Mifflin, 2001.

McKinney, Dani, Jennifer Dyck, and Elise Luber, "iTunes University and the Classroom: Can Podcasts Replace Professors?" *Computers & Education* 52 (2009): 617–23.

Mearsheimer, John and Stephen Walt, *The Israel Lobby and U.S. Foreign Policy*. New York: Farrar, Straus, and Giroux, 2007.

Medhurst, Martin. J. and Michael A. DeSousa, "Political Cartoons as Rhetorical Form: A Taxonomy of Graphic Discourse," *Communication Monographs* 48 (1981): 197–236.

Middleton, Andrew, "Beyond Podcasting: Creative Approaches to Designing Educational Audio," *ALT-J* 17 (2009): 143–55.

Middleton, David, "Putting the Learning into E-learning," *European Political Science* 9 (2009): 5–12.

Millar, Mark, *Superman: Red Son*. New York: DC Comics, 2004.

Min, Anchee, *Becoming Madam Mao*. New York: Houghton Mifflin, 2000.

Mindich, David. *Just the Facts: How "Objectivity" Came to Define American Journalism*. New York: NYU Press, 1998.

Miners, Zach, "Twitter Goes to College," *U.S. News & World Report* (June 2, 2009). Accessed March 24, 2012, from www.usnews.com/articles/education/2009/06/02/twitter-goes-to-college.html.

Mintz, Steven and Randy Roberts. *Hollywood's America: United States History Through Its Films*. Malden, MA: Wiley Blackwell, 2001.

Moore, Alan and Gibbons, Dave. *Watchmen*. New York: DC Comics, 1987.

Moore, David, "Raoul Peck's *Lumumba*: History or Hagiography?" in *Black and White in Colour*, ed. V. Bickford-Smith and R. Mendelsohn, 223–39. London: Ohio University Press, 2007.

Morgan, April, "*The Poisonwood Bible:* An Antidote for What Ails International Relations?" *International Political Science Review* 27 (2006): 379–403.

Mozorov, Evgeny, *The Net Delusion*. New York, NY: Public Affairs, 2011.

Morrone, Anastasia S. and Terri A. Tarr, "Theoretical Eclecticism in the College Classroom," *Innovative Higher Education* 30 (2005): 7–21.

Myers, Chet and Thomas B. Jones, *Promoting Active Learning: Strategies for the College Classroom*. San Francisco, CA: Jossey-Bass, 1993.

Nabi, Robin L., Emily Moyer-Guse, and Sahara Byrne, "All Joking Aside: A Serious Investigation into the Persuasive Effect of Funny Social Issue Messages," *Communication Monographs* 74 (2007): 29–54.

Neal, Mark Anthony. *Soul Babies: Black Popular Culture and the Post-Soul Aesthetic*. New York: Routledge, 2002.

Negash, Girma, "Art Invoked: A Mode of Understanding and Shaping the Political," *International Political Science Review* 25 (2004): 185–201.

New American Media, "California Dreamers: A Public Opinion Portrait of the Most Diverse Generation the Nation Has Known," last modified March 1, 2011. Accessed March 9, 2012, from http://news.newamericamedia.org/news/view_article.html?article_id=a4449ee6c67f1191537a19781c2293fd.

Newton, Robert, "Staff Attitudes to the Development and Delivery of E-learning," *New Library World* 104 (2003): 412–25.

Neufeld, Josh, *A.D.: New Orleans After the Deluge*. New York: Pantheon, 2010.

Nietzsche, Friedrich, *The Will to Power*. New York: Vintage, 1967.

Nkrumah, Kwame, *Neo-Colonialism: The Last Stage of Imperialism*. London: Panaf, 1965.

Nordstrom, Carolyn, *Shadows of War: Violence, Power, and International Profiteering in the Twenty-First Century*. Los Angeles, CA: California Press, 2004.

Nzongola-Ntalaja, Georges, *The Congo: From Leopold to Kabila*. London: Zed, 2002.

— "Patrice Lumumba: The Most Important Assassination of the Twentieth Century," *The Guardian* (January 17, 2011). Accessed January 26, 2011, from www.guardian.co.uk/global-development/poverty-matters/2011/jan/17/patrice-lumumba-50th-anniversary-assassination.

North, Adrian C., David J. Hargreaves, and Susan A. O'Neill, "The Importance of Music to Adolescents," *British Journal of Educational Psychology* 70 (2000): 255–72.

Orphan, Cecilia, "The American Democracy Project," *American Association of State Colleges and Universities*. Accessed March, 24, 2012, from www.aascu.org/programs/ADP/.

Ostergard, Robert L., "An Introduction to African Politics (review)," *Africa Today* 53 (2007): 123–5.

Pfeil, Ulrike R. A. and Panayiotis Zaphiris, "Age Differences in Online Social Networking – A Study of User Profiles and the Social Capital Divide Among Teenagers and Older Users in MySpace," *Computers in Human Behavior* 25 (2009): 643–54.

Ogbar, Jeffrey Ogbonna Green. *Hip-Hop Revolution: The Culture and Politics of Rap. Cultureamerica*. Lawrence: University Press of Kansas, 2007.

Ohio State University Libraries, "Thomas Nast Portfolio," 2002. Accessed January 4, 2012, from http://cartoons.osu.edu/nast/kicking_lion.htm.

Olson, Lester C, "Benjamin Franklin's Pictorial Representations of the British Colonies in America: A Study in Rhetorical Iconology," *Quarterly Journal of Speech* 73 (1987): 18–42.

Pappas, Christine, " 'You Hafta Push': Using Sapphire's Novel to Teach Introduction to American Government," *The Journal of Political Science Education* 3 (2007): 39–50.

Pate, Alexs D., *In the Heart of the Beat: The Poetry of Rap. African American Cultural Theory*. Lanham, MD: Scarecrow Press, 2009.

Patton, Twentieth Century Fox Studios, 1969.

Paul, James, "Last Night a Mix Tape Saved My Life," *The Guardian* (September 25, 2003).

Perry, Imani, *Prophets of the Hood: Politics and Poetics in Hip Hop*. Durham: Duke University Press, 2004.

Phillips, Rob, "Challenging the Primacy of Lectures: The Dissonance Between Theory and Practice in University Teaching," *Journal of University Teaching & Learning Practice* 2 (2005). Accessed March 24, 2012, from http://jutlp.uow.edu.au/2005_v02_i01/pdf/phillips_003.pdf.

Piaget, Jean, *The Equilibration of Cognitive Structures: The Central Problem of Intellectual Development*. Chicago, IL: University of Chicago Press, 1985.

— "Problems of Equilibration," in *The Essential Piaget*, ed. Howard E. Gruber and J. Jacques Voneche, 838–41. Northvale, NJ: Jason Aaronson, 1995 [1975].

Piaget, Jean and Bärbel Inhelder, "Intellectual Operations and their Development," in *The Essential Piaget*, ed. Howard E. Gruber and J. Jacques Voneche, 342–58. Northvale, NJ: Jason Aaronson, 1995 [1963].

Pollard, Tom, *Hollywood 9/11: Superheroes, Supervillains, and Super Disasters*. New York: Paradigm Publishers, 2011.

Pollard, Vincent K., "Cognitive Leverage of Film in International Studies Classrooms," *International Studies Quarterly* 3 (2002): 89–92.

— "Emerging Issues and Impermanent Institutions: Social Movements, Early Indicators of Social Change, and Film Pedagogy," *Journal of Political Science Education* 1 (2005): 397–401.

Postman, Neil, *Amusing Ourselves to Death*. New York: Penguin, 1985.

Prensky, Marc, "Digital Natives, Digital Immigrants," *On the Horizon* 9 (2001): 1–6.

— "Listen to the Natives," *Educational Leadership* 63 (2005/6): 8–13.

Preves, Sharon and Denise Stephenson, "The Classroom as Stage: Impression Management in Collaborative Teaching," *Teaching Sociology* 37 (2009): 245–56.

Prince, Michael, "Does Active Learning Work? A Review of the Research," *Journal of Engineering Education* 93 (2007): 223–31.

Prodigy and Laura Checkoway, *My Infamous Life: The Autobiography of Mobb Deep's Prodigy*. New York: Simon & Schuster, 2011.

Prunier, Gerard, *The Rwanda Crisis: History of a Genocide*. London: Hurst, 1995.

— *African World War*. Oxford: Oxford Press, 2009.

Psaltis, Charis, Gerard Duveen, and Anne-Nelly Perret-Clermont, "The Social and the Psychological: Structure and Context in Intellectual Development," *Human Development* 52 (2009): 291–312.

Pyszczynski, Tom, Zachary Rothschild, and Abdolhossein Abdollahi, "Terrorism, Violence, and Hope for Peace," *Current Directions in Psychological Science* 17 (2008): 318–22.

Putnam, Robert, *Bowling Alone: The Collapse and Revival of American Community*. New York, NY: Simon & Schuster, 2000.

Radwanick, Sarah, "ComScore Media Metrix Ranks Top 50 U.S. Web Properties for March 2009," *ComScore Online* (April 22, 2009). Accessed March 24, 2012, from www.comscore.com/Press_Events/Press_Releases/2009/4/Twitter_Traffic_More_than_Doubles/(language)/eng-US.

Rage against the Machine, "Guerilla Radio," *The Battle of Los Angeles*, © 1999 by Sony Music, B00002MZ2C, compact disc.

Ralph, Jason, Naomi Head, and Simon Lightfoot, "Engaging Students Beyond the Classroom: The Experience of a Podcasting Project," *Enhancing Learning in the Social Sciences* 1 (2009). Accessed March 24, 2012, from www.heacademy.ac.uk/assets/documents/subjects/csap/eliss/1–3-Lightfoot.pdf.

— "Pol-Casting: The Use of Podcasting in the Teaching and Learning of Politics and International Relations," *European Political Science* 9 (2010): 13–24.

Ramsden, Paul, *Learning to Teach in Higher Education*. New York: Routledge, 2003.

Rankin, Monica, "Some General Comments on the 'Twitter Experiment,' " 2009. Accessed March 3, 2009, from www.utdallas.edu/~mrankin/usweb/ twitter-conclusions.htm.

Raymond, Chad, "Do Role-Playing Simulations Generate Measurable and Meaningful Outcomes? A Simulation's Effect on Exam Scores and Teaching Evaluations," *International Studies Perspectives* 11 (2010): 51–60.

Reno, William, *Warlord Politics and African States*. Boulder, CO: Lynne Rienner, 1998.

— "The Privatization of Africa's International Relations," in *Africa in World Politics: Reforming Political Order*, ed. D. Rothchild and J. Harbeson. Boulder, CO: Westview Press, 2009.

Resnick, Michael, "Burnlists: The Digital 'Mix Tape' Comes of Age," last modified March 1, 2012. Accessed March 9, 2012, from www.events-in-music.com/burnlist-mix-tapes.html.

Rivera, Sharon Werning and Janet Thomas Simons, "Engaging Students Through Extended Simulations," *Journal of Political Science Education* 4 (2008): 298–316.

Roberts, Mark, "Adventures in Podcasting," *PS: Political Science & Politics* 41 (2008): 585–93.

Robinson, Andrew and Karen Schlegl, "Student Use of the Internet for Research Projects: A Problem? Our Problem? What Can We Do About It?" *PS: Political Science & Politics* 38 (2005): 311–15.

Rose, Tricia, *Black Noise: Rap Music and Black Culture in Contemporary America*. Hanover: Wesleyan University Press, 1994.

— "Keynote Address," Paper presented at the *Born in the Bronx conference*, Cornell University, Ithaca, NY, 2008.

Rothchild, Donald, "State-Ethnic Relations in Middle Africa," in *African Independence: The First Twenty-Five Years*, ed. G. M. Carter and P. O. Meara. Bloomington, IN: Indiana University Press, 1985.

Ruble, Diane, Ronda Eisenburg, and E. Tory Higgins, "Developmental Changes in Achievement Evaluation: Motivational Implications of Self-Other Differences," *Child Development* 65 (1994): 1095–110.

Rushdie, Salman, *East, West*. New York: Vintage International Books, 1994.

Ryan, Michael and Donald Kellner, *Camera Obscura: The Political Ideology of Contemporary Hollywood Film*. Bloomington, IN: Indiana Press, 1988.

RZA, *The Tao of Wu*. New York: Riverhead Books, 2009.

Sacco, Joe. *Palestine*. Seattle: Fantagraphics, 2002.

— *Footnotes in Gaza*. New York: Metropolitan Books, 2009.

Salmon, Gilly and Parithia Edirisingha, *Podcasting for Learning in Universities*. Milton Keynes: Open University Press, 2008.

Salomon, Gavriel, *Interaction of Media, Cognition, and Learning*. Hillsdale, NJ: Lawrence Erlbaum Associates, 1994.

Sante, Luc, "Disco Dreams," *The New York Review of Books* (May 13, 2004).

Sargisson, Lucy, "Contemporary Feminist Utopianism: Practicing Utopia on Utopia," in *Literature and the Political Imagination*, ed. Andrea Baumeister and John Horton, 238–60. New York: Routledge Publishing, 1996.

Sartori, Giovanni, *The Theory of Democracy Revisited*. Chatam, NJ: Chatam House, 1987.

Satrapi, Marjane, *The Complete Persepolis*. New York: Pantheon, 2004.

Schacter, Daniel L., *Searching for Memory: The Brain, the Mind, and the Past*. New York: Basic Books, 1996.

Schacter, Sarah, "The Barracuda Lacuna: Music, Political Campaigns and the First Amendment," *The Georgetown Law Journal* 99 (2011): 571–604.

Schantz, Meredith, "Mixed Signals: How Mixtapes Have Blurred the Changing Legal Landscape in the Music Industry," *The University of Miami Business Law Review* 17 (2009): 293–324.

Schmidt, H. D., "Problem Based Learning: Rationale and Description," *Medical Education* 17 (1983): 11–16.

Schmidt, Stephen R., "Can We Have a Distinctive Theory of Memory?" *Memory and Cognition* 19 (1991): 523–42.

— "Effects of Humor on Sentence Memory," *Journal of Experimental Psychology: Learning, Memory, and Cognition* 20 (1994): 953–67.

— "The Humour Effect: Differential Processing and Privileged Retrieval," *Memory* 10 (2002): 127–38.

Schraeder, Peter, *African Politics and Society: A Mosaic in Transformation*, 2nd edn. Belmont, CA: Thomson/Wadsworth, 2004.

Schwedler, Jillian and Deborah Gerner, eds, *Understanding the Contemporary Middle East*. Boulder, CO: Lynne Rienner Publishers, 2008.

Selcher, Wayne, "Use of Internet Sources in International Studies Teaching and Research," *International Studies Perspectives* 6 (2005): 174–89.

Self, D. J., D. C. Baldwin, and M. Olivarez, "Teaching Medical Ethics to First-Year Students by Using Film Discussion to Develop their Moral Reasoning," *Academic Medicine: Journal of the Association of American Medical Colleges* 68 (1993): 383–5.

Sewell, Edward H. Jr., " 'Torture-by-Tedium' or Editorial Cartoons during the 1996 Presidential Campaign," in *The 1996 Presidential Campaign: A Communication Perspective*, ed. Robert E. Denton, Jr., 161–77. Westport, CT: Praeger, 1998.

Sexton, Adam. *Rap on Rap: Straight-up Talk on Hip-Hop Culture*. New York: Delta, 1995.

Shammi, Prathba and Donald Stuss, "Humour Appreciation: A Role of the Right Frontal Lobe," *Brain* 122 (1999): 657–66.

Shaun of the Dead, directed by Edgar Wright. Universal City, CA: Rogue Pictures, 2004.

Sheeran, Paul, *Literature and International Relations*. Aldershot: Ashgate, 2007.

Shelby, Tommie, *We Who Are Dark: The Philosophical Foundations of Black Solidarity*. Cambridge, MA: Belknap Press of Harvard University Press, 2005.

Sherman, Daniel J. and Israel Waismel-Manor, "Get it in Writing: Using Politics to Teach Writing and Writing to Teach Politics," *PS: Political Science & Politics* 36 (2003): 755–7.

Shinkle, Krik, "Damage Report 2008: U.S. Household Wealth Down $10 Trillion," *U.S. News and World Report*, December 12, 2008.

Shklar, Judith, *Men & Citizens: A Study of Rousseau's Social Theory*. Cambridge, UK: Cambridge University Press, 1969.

Shorrock, Tim, "Company Man," *The Nation* (March 14, 2002). Accessed January 26, 2011, from www.thenation.com/article/company-man.

Shulman, Lee S., "Teaching and Teacher Education among the Professions," 38th Charles W. Hunt Memorial Lecture, American Association of Colleges for Teacher Education 50th Annual Meeting, New Orleans, Louisiana, February 25, 1997, transcript.

Sigel, Roberta S., *Learning about Politics*. New York: Random House, 1970.

Simpson, Archie W. and Bernd Kaussler, "IR Teaching Reloaded: Using Films and Simulations in the Teaching of International Relations," *International Studies Perspectives* 10 (2009): 413–27.

Sinnerbrink, Robert, "Goodbye Lenin? Žižek on Neo-Liberal Ideology and Post-Marxist Politics," *International Journal of Žižek Studies* 4 (2010): 1–24.

Smith, Elizabeth T. and Mark A. Boyer, "Designing In-Class Simulations," *PS: Political Science & Politics* 29 (1996): 690–4.

Smith, Robbin, "Simulations, American Government, and Student Learning Styles," Paper presented at the APSA Teaching and Learning Conference, Baltimore, MD, February 6–8, 2009.

Snow, Lois Wheeler, *China on Stage*. New York: Vantage Press, 1973.

Soper, Christopher, "Rock and Roll Will Never Die: Using Music to Engage Students in the Study of Political Science," *PS: Political Science & Politics* 43 (2010): 363–7.

Sorauf, Frank J. and Paul Allen Beck, *Party Politics in America*. New York: Harper Collins, 1988.

Spiegelman, Art, *The Complete Maus: A Survivor's Tale*. New York: Pantheon, 1996.

Springer, Leonard, Mary Stanne, and Samuel S. Donovan, "Effects of Small-Group Learning on Undergraduates in Science, Mathematics, Engineering, and Technology: A Meta-Analysis," *Review of Educational Research* 69 (1999): 21–51.

Sriram, Shyam K., "Review of Karline McLain's 'India's Immortal Comic Books: Gods, Kings and Other Heroes.' " Reviewed in *Pop Matters*, August 28, 2009. Accessed March 9, 2012, from www.popmatters.com/pm/review/110238-indias-immortal-comic-books-gods-kings-and-other-heroes-by-karline-m.

St. John, Warren, "The World Comes to Georgia, and an Old Church Adapts," *The New York Times*, September 22, 2007. Accessed March 9, 2012, from www.nytimes.com/2007/09/22/us/22church.html?pagewanted=all.

Stoessinger, John, *Why Nations Go to War*. New York: Wadsworth Publishing, 2008.

Stein, Robert, "Seeing White through Rap: A Classroom Exercise for Examining Race Using a Hip-Hop Video," *Journal of Political Science Education* 7 (2011): 312–28.

Steinbeck, John, "Like Captured Fireflies," *California Teachers Association Journal* 51 (1955): 6–9.

Steinfield, Charles, Joan M. DiMicco, Nicole B. Ellison, and Cliff Lampe, "The Benefits of Facebook 'Friends:' Social Capital and College Students' Use of Online Social Network Sites," *Journal of Computer-Mediated Communication* 12 (2007): 1143–68.

— "Bowling Online: Social Networking and Social Capital within the Organization," Paper presented at the *Communication and Technology*, University Park, PA, 2009.

Stice, James E., "Using Kolb's Learning Cycle to Improve Student Learning," *Engineering Education* 77 (1987): 291–6.

Stokes, Peter and Lindsey Martin, "Reading Lists: A Study of Tutor and Student Perceptions, Expectations and Realities," *Studies in Higher Education* 33 (2008): 113–25.

Street, John, *Rebel Rock: The Politics of Popular Music*. Malden, MA: Blackwell, 1986.

— "Breaking the Silence: The Role of Music and Musicians in Political Participation," *Critical Review of International Social and Political Philosophy* 10 (2007): 321–37.

— *Politics and Popular Culture*. Philadelphia, PA: Temple University Press, 2007.

Street, John, Seth Hague, and Heather Savigny, "Playing to the Crowd: The Role of Music and Musicians in Political Participation," *British Journal of Politics and International Relations* 10 (2008): 269–85.

Strick, Madelign, Robert W. Holland, Rick Van Baaren, and Ad Van Knippenberg, "Humor in the Eye Tracker: Attention Capture and Distraction from Context Cues," *Journal of General Psychology* 137 (2010): 37–48.

Stover, William James, "Teaching and Learning Empathy: An Interactive, Online Diplomatic Simulation of Middle East Conflict," *Journal of Political Science Education* 1 (2005): 207–19.

Suls, Jerry M, "A Two-Stage Model for the Appreciation of Jokes and Cartoons: An Information-Processing Analysis," in *The Psychology of Humor*, ed. Jeffrey Goldstein and Paul McGhee, 81–100. New York: Academic Press, 1972.

Sunderland, Sheri, Jonathan C. Rothermel, and Adam Lusk, "Making Movies Active: Lessons from Simulations," *PS: Political Science & Politics* 42 (2009): 543–7.

Tabachnick, Stephen E., ed., *Teaching the Graphic Novel*. New York: The Modern Language Association, 2009.

Taylor, Mark Zachary, "Podcast Lectures as a Primary Teaching Technology: Results of a One-Year Trial," *Journal of Political Science Education* 5 (2009): 135–53.

Thomson, Alex, *An Introduction to African Politics*. New York: Routledge, 2004.

Thornton, Stephen, "Lessons from America: Teaching Politics with the Google Generation," *Enhancing Learning in the Social Sciences* 1 (2009). Accessed March 24, 2012, from www.heacademy.ac.uk/assets/documents/subjects/csap/eliss/1–3-Thornton.pdf.

— "From 'Scuba Diving' to 'Jet Skiing'? Information Behavior, Political Science, and the Google Generation," *Journal of Political Science Education* 6 (2010): 353–68.

Tilly, Charles, *Democracy*. New York: Cambridge University Press, 2007.

Tobocman, Seth, *War in the Neighborhood*. New York: Autonomedia, 2000.

Tordoff, William, *Government and Politics in Africa*. Bloomington, IN: Indiana Press, 2002.

Torok, Sarah E., Robert F. McMorris, and Wen-Chi Lin, "Is Humor an Appropriate Teaching Tool?: Perceptions of Professors' Teaching Styles and Use of Humor," *College Teaching* 52 (2004): 14–20.

Towner, Terri and Caroline Munoz, "Opening Facebook: How to Use Facebook in the College Classroom," Paper presented at the *Society for Information Technology & Teacher Education International Conference*, Charleston, SC, 2009.

Toyama, Kentaro, "There Are No Technology Shortcuts to Good Education." Accessed January 10, 2012, from https://edutechdebate.org/ict-in-schools/there-are-no-technology-shortcuts-to-good-education/.

Trudeau, Robert, "Get Them to Read, Get Them to Talk: Using Discussion Forums to Enhance Student Learning," *Journal of Political Science Education* 1 (2005): 289–322.

Turner, Charles C., "The Motivating Text: Assigning Hanna Arendt's *Eichmann in Jerusalem*," *PS: Political Science & Politics* 28 (2005): 67–9.

Twitter, "#numbers," *Twitter Blog*, March 14, 2011. Accessed March 24, 2012, from http://blog.twitter.com/2011/03/numbers.html.

Ulbig, Stacy, "Engaging the Unengaged: Using Visual Images to Enhance Students' Poli Sci 101 Experience," *Political Science & Politics* 42 (2009): 385–91.

Van Assendelft, Laura, " 'It's the Supreme Court, Stupid': A Simulation Approach to Feminist Thinking," *Feminist Teacher* 16 (2006): 216–24.

Van Belle, Douglas A. and Kenneth M. Mash, *A Novel Approach to Politics: Introducing Political Science through Books, Movies, and Popular Culture*, 2nd edn. Washington, DC: CQ Press, 2010.

Van Zoonen, Liesbet, *Entertaining the Citizen: When Politics and Popular Culture Converge*. Boulder, CO: Rowman and Littlefield, 2005.

Waalkes, S., "Using Film Clips as Cases to Teach the Rise and 'Decline' of the State," *International Studies Perspectives* 4 (2003): 156–74.

Walls, Stephen, John Kucsera, Joshua Walker, Taylor Acee, Nate McVaugh, and Daniel Robinson, "Podcasting in Education: Are Students as Ready and Eager as We Think They Are?" *Computers & Education* 54 (2010): 371–8.

Wanzer, Melissa B. and Ann Bainbridge Frymier, "The Relationship between Student Perceptions of Instructor Humor and Students' Reports of 'Earning'," *Communication Education* 48 (1999): 48–61.

Wanzer, Melissa, Ann Bainbridge Frymier, and Jeffrey Irwin, "An Explanation of the Relationship between Instructor Humor and Student Learning: Instructional Humor Processing Theory," *Communication Education* 59 (2010): 1–18.

Wasko, Molly and Samer Faraj, "Why Should I Share? Examining Social Capital and Knowledge Contribution in Electronic Networks of Practice," *MIS Quarterly: Management Information Systems* 29 (2005): 35–57.

Watkins, S. Craig, *Hip Hop Matters: Politics, Pop Culture, and the Struggle for the Soul of a Movement*. Boston: Beacon Press, 2005.

— "The Hip Hop Lifestyle: Exploring the Perils and Possibilities of Black Youth's Media Environment," Paper presented at the *Getting Real: The Future of Hip Hop Scholarship*, University of Wisconsin-Madison, 2009.

Watson, Karli K., Benjamin Matthews, and John Allman, "Brain Activation during Sight Gags and Language-Dependent Humor," *Cerebral Cortex* 17 (2007): 314–24.

Weber, Cynthia, "The Highs and Lows of Teaching IR Theory: Using Popular Films for Theoretical Critique," *International Studies Perspectives* 2 (2001): 281–7.

Weber, Max, *Politics as a Vocation*. Philadelphia, PA: Fortress Press, 1968.

Weinberger, Marc G. and Charles S. Gulas, "The Impact of Humor in Advertising: A Review," *Journal of Advertising* 21 (1992): 35–59.

Wellman, Barry, Anabel Haase, James Witte, and Keith Hampton, "Does the Internet Increase, Decrease, or Supplement Social Capital?: Social Networks, Participation, and Community Commitment," *American Behavioral Scientist* 45 (2001): 436–55.

Wheeler, Sarah M., "Role-Playing Games and Simulations for International Issues Courses," *Journal of Political Science Education* 2 (2006): 331–47.

Wilkerson, Luann and Wim H Gijselaers, *Bringing Problem-Based Learning to Higher Education: Theory and Practice: New Directions for Teaching and Learning, no. 68*. Hoboken, NJ: Jossey-Bass Inc, 1996.

Windham, Carie, "Confessions of a Podcast Junkie," *EDUCAUSE Review* 42 (2007): 50–65.

Windschitl, Mark, "Framing Constructivism in Practice as the Negotiation of Dilemmas: An Analysis of Conceptual, Pedagogical, Cultural, and Political Challenges Facing Teachers," *Review of Educational Research* 72 (2002): 131–75.

Wright, Barbara D., "More Art than Science: The Postsecondary Assessment Movement Today," American Political Science Association (APSA). Accessed August 23, 2011, from www.apsanet.org/imgtest/MoreArtThanScience.doc.

Wright, Bradford W., *Comic Book Nation: The Transformation of Youth Culture in America*. Baltimore, MD: The Johns Hopkins University Press, 2001.

Wudel, Darcy, "Shakespeare's *Coriolanus* in the Political Science Classroom," *PS: Political Science & Politics* 35 (2002): 217–22.

Wyer, Robert S. and James Collins, "A Theory of Humour Elicitation," *Psychological Review* 99 (1992): 663–88.

Xenos, Michael A. and Amy B. Becker, "Moments of Zen: Effects of *The Daily Show* on Information Seeking and Political Learning," *Political Communication* 26 (2009): 317–32.

Young, Dannagal G., "The Privileged Role of the Late-Night Joke: Exploring Humor's Role in Disrupting Argument Scrutiny," *Media Psychology* 11 (2008): 119–42.

Young, Dannagal G. and Sarah Esralew, "Jon Stewart a Heretic? Surely you Jest: Political Participation and Discussion among Viewers of Late-night Comedy Programming," in *The Stewart/Colbert Effect: Essays on the Real Impact of Fake News*, ed. Armarnath Amarasinga, 99–116. Jefferson, NC: McFarland and Co. Publishers, 2011.

Young, Jeffrey R., "A Professor's Tips for Using Twitter in the Classroom," Wired Campus, *The Chronicle of Higher Education*, January 28, 2008. Accessed March 24, 2012, http://chronicle.com/blogPost/A-Professor-s-Tips-for-Using/3643.

— "Teaching with Twitter: Not for the Faint of Heart," *The Chronicle of Higher Education*, November 22, 2009. Accessed March 24, 2012, from http://chronicle.com/article/Teaching-With-Twitter-Not-for/49230/.

Yuen, Steve and Hsiu-Ting Hung, "Exploring the Use of Social Networking in the College Classroom," Paper presented at the *Society for Information Technology & Teacher Education*, 2010.

Ziv, Avner, *L'humor en Education: Approche Psychologique*. Paris: Editions Social Francaises, 1979.

— "Teaching and Learning with Humor: Experiment and Replication," *Journal of Experimental Education* 57 (1988): 5–15.

Zombieland, directed by Ruben Fleischer. Culver City, CA: Sony Pictures, 2009.

Zurbriggen, Eileen L. and Aurora M. Sherman, "Race and Gender in the 2008 U.S. Presidential Election: A Content Analysis of Editorial Cartoons," *Analyses of Social Issues and Public Policy* 10 (2010): 223–47.

INDEX